Long Sunset

To my wife, family and dogs, without
whose loving attentions this book would
have been written much more quickly,
but much less happily

Long Sunset

MEMOIRS OF
WINSTON CHURCHILL'S
LAST PRIVATE SECRETARY

ANTHONY MONTAGUE BROWNE

WITH A FOREWORD BY
THE LADY SOAMES D.B.E.

CASSELL

First published 1995 by
Cassell Publishers Ltd
Wellington House
125 Strand
London WC2R OBB

British Library Cataloguing-in-Publication Data
A catalogue record for this book is available from the British Library

ISBN 0–304–34478–8

Typeset by August Filmsetting, Haydock, St Helens

Printed and bound in Great Britain by
Butler & Tanner Ltd, Frome and London

All photographs in this book are taken from the author's collection, with the exception of
that of Winston Churchill's funeral, reproduced by permission of The Press Association.

Contents

Foreword

———— ❧ ————

BY MARY SOAMES

I AM touched and honoured that Anthony Montague Browne should have asked me to write a Foreword to his book. Some years ago he was kind enough to ask if I would mind him writing about the years he spent so close to my father; I told him then that not only did I not *mind* – I thought that he *should* do so.

AMB's witty, whimsical and self-deprecatory pen recounts his own earlier life: University; the Air Force, where, after sundry and widespread postings he spent long, dangerous hours in Beaufighters over-flying the jungles of Burma. He was awarded the Distinguished Flying Cross in 1945. Home again, it was to pick up the threads at Oxford, and soon to enter the Foreign Office. His account of the life and functions of the Resident Clerk on duty is most engaging, and his sketches of his colleagues and superiors illuminating. It was from his posting at the British Embassy, Paris, in 1952 that he was seconded at the age of twenty-nine to join Winston Churchill's prime ministerial Private Office team at Number Ten, an appointment that started a connection which in the event was to last the rest of my father's life.

In recalling his early days as Private Secretary, AMB describes very well Winston's perennial reluctance to accept a new face in his close entourage; but also – once accepted – the unquestioning trust and naturalness of the relationship which ensued. And it is his story of these years from 1952 until 1965 which will certainly be regarded as invaluable material for historians, or indeed anyone interested in Winston Churchill's life and personality.

Anthony Montague Browne's account of the last three years of Churchill's second prime ministership makes a rich contribution to the picture other witnesses have also drawn of his methods of work; his relationship with his ministerial colleagues; and their various views (often reflected through their own Private Offices) as to the desirability for personal or party reasons of Churchill, now approaching eighty, to resign and allow the long-agreed succession of his political heir, Sir Anthony Eden.

After Winston Churchill's resignation as Prime Minister in April 1955, AMB returned to the Foreign Office. He continued to be in touch with his former chief, and in the late summer of that year he was seconded indefinitely as Private Secretary to Churchill: as the new Foreign Secretary, Harold Macmillan, put it: 'Winston needs you.' Indeed he did.

And it is from this point in time that Anthony Montague Browne's account becomes unique: I think I can say without exaggeration that, Clementine apart, AMB saw my father more continuously, both in what remained for him of public life and in private, than any other person.

Clementine and members of the family had already taken to Anthony in the last lap at Number Ten, but over the ensuing ten years our liking and appreciation of a clever and amusing personality grew to an affection, and a feeling of gratitude, which the passage of time has only served to increase.

In the earlier years of his retirement Winston Churchill's life was still quite a busy one. He would stand for his Woodford seat in two more General Elections (1955 and 1959); and these years saw also the finalising and publication of his four-volume *History of the English-Speaking Peoples*. Both at home and when he travelled abroad, he received and would be received by the important, the great and the famous, and his views were sought on numerous events and topics of political importance requiring carefully conceived letters or statements. Churchill was still a world figure, and AMB's appointment as his Private Secretary was officially and generally thought to be in the national interest. (The taxpayer, incidentally, was not burdened with the expense, as WSC reimbursed the Treasury for his salary.)

In all these activities AMB was constantly involved. His Foreign Office and Number Ten experience, combined with his own intense interest in public affairs, his savoir-faire, charm and – above all – his integrity made him the ideal and indispensable right-hand man he became.

AMB was also great fun, and no account of my father's character should neglect his own sense of humour and love of divertissements. AMB's account of convivial conversations and agreeable outings revives most vividly for me the joy and fun of my father's company when he was in good form with close friends or in the bosom of his family.

But slowly and inevitably the pace slackened; a series of spasms (minor strokes) took their toll; and in 1958 a bout of pneumonia in the south of France marked a milestone in Winston's slow decline. He ceased painting around 1960; and in 1962 a severe jolt was given to his physical and mental health when he fell in his hotel room in Monte Carlo and broke his hip. AMB's presence was quite as necessary in these twilight times as before – but his role was now a more protective one, and he guarded Winston's interests with a vigilant eye. And as a companion he was perfect: patient, seeking to stimulate and divert, or playing cards for long hours. Clementine had come more and more to rely on his judgement and tact, which could avoid or defuse difficult situations.

One of the many aspects of this account of my father's latter years, however, is that AMB has faithfully recorded the shafts of late sunshine which quite often illuminated the fading landscape. Sometimes a motivated question called forth considered judgements, or even sharp reactions; sometimes AMB would record spontaneous recollections or reflections. For someone who holds very strong political opinions I think he admirably distinguishes between what is WSC and what is AMB – and moreover he marks the difference between what was an off-the-cuff remark and what was a considered judgement.

Anthony's sense of honour, his fidelity and, I believe, his true devotion to my father ensured that he bore it all out to the end of the long day, and it was fit indeed that he was there with us that cold Sunday morning when Winston Churchill quietly yielded up his great spirit.

In the years since, Anthony's close friendship with our family has remained. And from the inception on the morrow of my father's death of the Winston Churchill Memorial Trust, Anthony has devoted many hours of time and thought to establishing and developing this living memorial. The Trust sends abroad one hundred Fellows every year: men and women from all walks of life, and covering an age span from sixteen to the seventies, to study subjects selected yearly from a wide spectrum, encompassing scientific projects; social and environmental questions; the arts; sport and adventure. AMB is currently Chairman of the Trust Council.

Anthony Montague Browne's long years of service to my father undoubtedly cost him a continuing and predictably brilliant career in the Foreign Office. His perhaps good judgement made him decline a role at Buckingham Palace; and his integrity made his career afterwards in business and the City less well rewarded, because he would never accept any offer (and there must have been many) that included writing for money about his years with Winston Churchill. It must have been a temptation – and one that only a very few others have felt able to resist.

Now I am glad with all my heart that after this long passage of years Anthony's scruples are overcome, and I know that in overcoming them he has rendered a great service to my father's memory and to history.

Acknowledgements

———— ❧ ————

L ADY SOAMES has been of enormous help to me, not only in writing a kind and graceful Foreword, but also in meticulously reading my manuscript, correcting my errors and allowing me to quote from her biography *Clementine Churchill* and her letters.

I am much indebted to Lady Sargant (Nonie) for her unselfish assistance with her recollections and diaries, particularly relating to the *Christina* cruises, and to my daughter Jane (Mrs Piers Hoare-Temple) for the use of photographs from her diary.

I express my warm thanks to those who have unstintingly allowed me to quote from letters and published works. Winston Churchill, Lady Margaret Colville and Martin Gilbert have been particularly generous.

I am also indebted to the Countess of Avon, the Rt. Hon. Sir Edward Heath, Viscount Montgomery, the Earl of Rosebery and Lady Gage for the use of quotations.

The Rt. Hon. Sir Robert Fellowes has most kindly allowed me to publish my exchange of letters with Sir Michael Adeane on my resignation from the Palace and the Diplomatic Service, and Mr Richard Bone of the Foreign and Commonwealth Office gave clearance to my manuscript with exemplary speed and courtesy.

Mr Sean Magee, Senior Commissioning Editor of Cassell, has been an indulgent, wise and sprightly adviser and Miss Gillian Bromley a patient, sympathetic and erudite copy-editor. Mr Mark Le Fanu of the Society of Authors has been unstinting and painstaking with friendly and significant counsel. Mrs Mary Pitt has patiently and indefatigably typed out my manuscript from a writing described by Sir Winston Churchill as 'the one unbreakable cypher'.

Finally, my wife Shelagh has ably assisted me with her recollections of Lady Churchill, to whom she was Private Secretary, and with comments, not always favourable, on text and style.

AMB

Preface

———— ✤ ————

I A M cursed with a totally capricious memory. Events, conversations and fragments of poetry from the distant and close past jumble and clutter my mind, sometimes falling into coherent sequence but more often isolated patches of light in growing darkness. Doubtless a diary would have helped, but I never kept one. However, over the years I took elliptical notes of a multitude of incidents that captured attention in their time. They are sometimes illegible; Winston Churchill once wearily commented: 'Really, my dear, your handwriting is a disgrace. It is like three spiders arm in arm . . . the one unbreakable cypher.' Moreover, my jottings were frequently divorced from any reasonable framework of time or history; but I have been to some extent helped by the letters I received over those years, my correspondents varying from President Eisenhower to Jean Cocteau, from Lord Beaverbrook to Maria Callas, from Harold Macmillan to Somerset Maugham. They were mostly addressed to me, of course, as a post office for Winston Churchill (henceforth usually WSC) but they are to an extent revealing of their authors and are landmarks of dates and places, even if only concerned with social trivia.

I am now attempting to make something of this pot-pourri, fortified by two letters, one from Lady Churchill (henceforth usually CSC) giving her blessing to a book of reminiscence and one from Randolph Churchill indicating his active approval. Whether they would have approved the outcome is uncertain. My original intention was to write solely about Winston Churchill from the time of my joining him in 1952 until a sufficiently advanced point in his progressive withdrawal of interest from public affairs, which was a good deal later than most people think. A more logical time-frame then seemed to be 1945 to 1965. I joined the Foreign Office in 1946, and was fortunate enough in those short-staffed days to be pitchforked at the age of twenty-three into the midst of great events, first as Assistant Private Secretary to the Permanent Under-Secretary of State, then as a Resident Clerk, the Foreign Office's political night duty officer, and simultaneously as a member of the small Western Union Secretariat concerned with the regeneration of Western European cooperation, initially with the Brussels Treaty and then with the drafting and infrastructure of the North Atlantic Treaty, both of them key to Western survival and the avoidance of open war between the Great Powers. The emphasis at that time was of course predominantly on defence.

These twenty years saw in the first place the re-arousing of our national will to resist the growing and appalling threat of Stalinist aggression and subversion. This was no easy task in the immediate post-war years when the country was weary, bored, poor and hungry and the adrenalin of patriotic exhortation had lost its appeal. On a wider historical plane these years witnessed the vertiginous acceleration of Britain's hitherto gentle decline as a first-class power. This phenomenon certainly deserves analysis, not least in terms of the 'great man' theory of history. WSC agreed with Emerson: 'There is properly no history, only biography.'

But all this is a much-ploughed field, on which professional historians have kicked up their heels, and sometimes each other, for many years. What then was left? Perhaps an anecdotal glimpse of the ways of life and especially the conversational hindsight of some of those who had played leading parts. WSC is obviously central to this theme. Some months after his resignation from his second prime ministership in the spring of 1955 he 'borrowed' me from the Foreign Office to which I had returned after three years' service at Number Ten. I was later formally seconded to him and remained with him until his death in 1965. During this time I accompanied him on his journeys and saw him daily, lunching and dining, often à deux, more times than I can count. It was here that the richest historical vein lay, for even in WSC's old age his conversation was a joy, a flow of wit, reminiscence and comment, quite often self-critical. As time went on the larger luncheons and dinners became fewer and fewer. It was publicly suggested that WSC was senile long before his mind had dimmed. His deafness, especially in a hum of voices, prevented him from following the conversation and he became increasingly withdrawn and unwilling to subject himself to strangers. But paradoxically his own conversation, though lapidary, was sometimes more revealing and more philosophical, especially if prompted by friendly questions. I once asked him if he did not fear indiscretion from his listeners, indeed from me. 'No,' he replied, 'it don't much matter any more.' Then, with a grin: 'Well, it all depends on what you say.'

I had thought of calling this book *Anecdotage*, both parts of the word relating to myself, because I have endeavoured to give a personal biographical preface and framework to these years and this has swollen grossly with the prolixity of old age. It is almost impossible to bring my central theme, WSC's obiter dicta, into a reasonable narrative as they frequently had no relevance to the moment at which they were spoken. Others will have heard the same remarks before, because WSC, like most of us, liked to repeat something he felt had been well said. I have deliberately refrained from correcting or filling in blanks in WCS's quotations. That was the way they were spoken.

Anecdotes may be a somewhat flimsy and even trivial material but they form a mosaic from which a picture can emerge, fragmentary, incomplete but a powerful supplement. History should be new and true. With all the provisos of my opening sentence, I have at least tried to meet the second of these requirements. Those of us who can claim close acquaintance, indeed close friendship, with Winston Churchill are now very few, and it is perhaps right to record what one can before this endangered species is extinct.

AMB, 1991–1994

Prologue

————— ✣ —————

O N A Friday in September 1952, I was late for the morning meeting at the Embassy in Paris where I was a Second Secretary. I had tried to be punctual, breakfast in plenty of time, bidding my wife and our stray cat, Min, goodbye; but Min had then climbed a Gobelin tapestry in the salon and sat at the top lashing his tail and pulling out Gobelin stitches one by one with malice and deliberation. The flat was in the Latin Quarter and was reputed to be haunted. Neither it nor the Gobelin belonged to me and the latter cost 4,000 (old, thank God) francs a stitch to repair. The situation demanded attention. My subsequent journey to the Embassy was not unusual in the Paris rush hour. A taxi driver scraped my car and called me a *cochon distingué*, presumably a reference to my CD plate. I replied with old-world Parisian street courtesy that he was a *con illustre*. When I reached the Embassy the meeting, with inevitable British hilarity styled 'morning prayers', was long over and a message was on my desk to call forthwith on the Ambassador, Sir Oliver Harvey.

Oliver Harvey was a thoroughly decent old stick (as viewed by a twenty-six-year-old) in his late fifties. He had a good First World War record, loved the French and his political views leaned to the left. He had been a strong anti-Munichois and as Anthony Eden's Private Secretary had been a steadying and sober influence on that volatile figure. Harvey had replaced the glittering, witty but somewhat raffish entertainment style of his predecessors in Paris, Duff and Diana Cooper, with his own lower key. Invitations to the Embassy went to those who had helped us in the War, then recently ended, and to politicians, civil servants and newspaper editors – in fact, to people who were useful or worthy. The *monde* was not excluded but it no longer sufficed to be entertaining or socially prominent to win a place on the Embassy guest list. Any hint of former social association with the Germans, and you were out.

Contrary to accepted custom, the Duff Coopers ran a sort of Embassy in exile close to Paris in a pretty chateau at Chantilly. This set-up was entertainingly parodied by Nancy Mitford in her book *Don't Tell Alfred* which was not far from the truth. It was fun to go there and the hospitality was lavish, but I stopped when Diana Cooper said to a colleague: 'You can't work for the Harveys; they're squalid.' She made the same remark to other members of the Embassy and I think we all had the same reaction. The Harveys were very far from squalid and Maudie (Lady Harvey) was enchanting, highly intelligent and of great kindness. I married when I had been at the

I

Embassy a year. My wife Nonie was young, beautiful and shy, and her luggage was lost on the way from London. As was the custom for a new Embassy wife, we were invited to a grand lunch and Nonie was seated on the Ambassador's right. In those days hats were de rigueur and she did not have one. She apologised to her hostess, who replied: 'Nonie, with hair as lovely as yours, you should never wear a hat,' transforming embarrassment into happiness.

I nevertheless went to the Ambassador's office on that Friday morning expecting a rebuke. He silently handed me a blue sheet of Foreign Office writing paper and pointed enigmatically at the ceiling. Following his gaze I could see only gilded cherubs. (His office, changed later, was like an expensive Belgian chocolate box.) The letter indicated that the Prime Minister wanted a new Private Secretary and had picked me from a short list supplied by the Treasury. The Foreign Office had no doubt that I would do them credit, the writer added dubiously. I was to report to Number Ten in forty-eight hours.

Being both vain and inquisitive I later set out to discover why I had been chosen. Apart from the influence of Jock Colville,* the Prime Minister's Joint Principal Private Secretary, whom WSC much liked and trusted, there were, it seems, the following reasons. The Prime Minister had wanted a Foreign Office man on the totally mistaken grounds that he would be less likely to embarrass him at the dinner table. By 'embarrass' I think he probably meant 'bore'. WSC had a great affection for and trust in my first Foreign Office boss, Sir Orme 'Moley' Sárgent (of whom more later). Moley was a splendid and sardonic old eagle and he gave me an unduly favourable reference, probably shaking with mirth, because he had suffered at my inadvertent hands and thought that Winston Churchill would soon sort me out. WSC insisted that the candidate should have fought in the War and he had a penchant for the Royal Air Force at that time. Finally, with their usual two years out of date records, the Foreign Office had indicated that I was a bachelor. There were other candidates who were stronger and moreover endowed with 'gravitas' (weight? wisdom? impressive exterior?), but they had been doing important civilian jobs in the War whereas I had flown aeroplanes. Apparently that did it.

*Sir John Colville, diplomat and Private Secretary to Neville Chamberlain and then Winston Churchill during the War. He returned to Number Ten in 1951 and was close to the Prime Minister and his family. Later he wrote a number of elegant and significant books on the period. With the Prime Minister's encouragement he had absented himself for a time during the War to train as a pilot and flew fighter aircraft courageously in spite of bad eyesight.

BOOK ONE

———— ✤ ————

Frivolity and Flying
1941–1945

Chapter 1

AND WHY had I flown aeroplanes? Because on a hot afternoon in 1940 I was crawling about with a rifle in the long grass at my school, Stowe. I was a staunch Munichois and I had confidently prophesied that there would be no war and refused to join the Officers' Training Corps until the beastly thing broke out. Now I was stalking an imaginary machine-gun post, my puttees hanging round my ankles, and sneezing miserably with a frequency and muzzle velocity that would have put the gun to shame.

Hay-fever. I've suffered from it all my life and this time it altered events for the better. A single Fairey Battle* pottered over high in a blue sky. That, I said, is the way to go to war if you must. (Well, perhaps not precisely in a Fairey Battle.) No hay-fever, sitting down, coming home to glory and super food and drink in a well-appointed Mess (Ha!); and then the girls . . . I was just seventeen at the time and the die was cast.

My family was less than enthusiastic. My father, a retired regular army officer who had sacrificed a great deal to educate me, pointed out that I would never pass the pilot's medical tests. We had lived in Switzerland, ironically because in those days at 21 Swiss francs to the pound it was a cheap place to bring up your children, and I had gone to a mountain school because of an alleged patch on the lung – actually I suspected a device by the doctor, who was a shareholder in the exceedingly expensive institution (no, not Le Rosey). My uncle, a Rifle Brigade Colonel, said that I should join his regiment: 'Only garage mechanics and eccentrics join the Air Force.' I insisted, and my mother looked sad: 'Would I please go up to the University first, just for a term or two?' Having loftily agreed to this, in 1941 I fluked a scholarship to Magdalen College, Oxford, on the strength of my fluent but very Swiss French and a minor talent for improvisation in essays when knowledge ran out. As soon as I reached Oxford I joined the University Air Squadron, then still a rather jolly sort of club. I had loathed Stowe, in spite of the beauty of the place (Capability Brown had been Head Gardener there for seventeen years) and the influence of a very great headmaster and educationalist J.F. Roxburgh, a man of enormous charm, wit, erudition and kind understanding of the young. But my little friends and I were barbarians and we tended to dislike each other. The food was horrible. The beds were hard and cold. The recreation was rugger and I saw no fun in being crushed into freezing mud by North Country oafs (Stowe recruited rather a lot from beyond the Watford

---

* An obsolete light bomber that was massacred by German fighters in the early days of the War.

5

Gap). In short, I was a prig and rather a snob, but awfully homesick too. I avoided rugger, went pike fishing, and played golf.

But Oxford ... The night I arrived at Magdalen there was a Feast for the Demies* and the scholars and the dons of Magdalen. Oysters, venison from Magdalen's own herd (they lived in the Grove where C.S. Lewis† supposed Merlin to be buried and were allegedly culled to maintain equilibrium with the dons), *mandarines givrées*, a savoury, Chablis, first-class claret from Magdalen's amazing cellar, vintage port. All this in wartime and without contravening rationing regulations. And one's companions were fun, friendly and frivolous – at least some of the time. The War beckoned and was in its most disastrous phase. Most of us were going into that sausage-machine; so we enjoyed ourselves. The most expensive wine in the cellar was fifteen shillings and sixpence, a 1919 Château d'Yquem, after that a 1928 Pol Roger champagne at fifteen shillings. One's education progressed, if not academically. Occasionally I graced a lecture with my presence, but seldom on my own subjects. Looking for something unusual, I fastened on 'Lycanthropy'. It did indeed turn out to be unusual. It was about werewolves, and the lecturer looked like one with a nice grey pelt, long canine teeth, and the third finger longer than the second.

By the end of the Spring term (all right: Hilary) my tutor was muttering, 'I can't understand why you produce essays of this deplorable quality. You're supposed to be a scholar.' The subject was, God help us, mediaeval French. I went down from Oxford without taking any examination at all. I was to repeat this performance five years later and it stood me in good stead.

On an average day I rose just in time for an unshaven breakfast in Hall, then to the Junior Common Room to read the newspapers until eleven when it was time for a cup of coffee and a gossip at the Copper Kettle Tea Shoppe. Thence to Boot's Book Lovers' Library to pick up a trashy novel. The celebrated Dr Onions, Librarian of Magdalen, once intercepted me and asked what I was doing. The reply sent him into revulsive shock. 'And with my magnificent library at your door-step,' he muttered and never addressed me again. Lunch with my friends in Hall, a short walk or on special occasions an even shorter game of squash. Then it was time for the cinema. At about six Bond's Room opened. Bond was the Steward, a man with a proper sense of old-fashioned social values, but a warm heart. You were admitted by invitation to drink sherry, madeira, port or claret and to smoke cigars or cheroots. The prices, even for those days, were unbelievably low. A glass of Taylor's 1912 port cost one shilling and ninepence (just under ten new pence). All one's friends were there and we waxed awfully witty at the world's and each other's expense. It was after one of these sessions that I inadvertently punched the Dean, an eminent dietitian, in the tummy and the blackout. He outran me and fined me ten shillings.

Oxford was where one made one's lifelong friends, if indeed there is such an animal. The company was excellent and diverse. An enjoyable episode

---

* The traditional Magdalen name for older established scholarships.
† English Literature don at Magdalen; religious philosopher and novelist.

was an acquaintance, fleeting alas, with Auberon Herbert, a gifted linguist and eccentric. His father was Aubrey Herbert, who had been offered the Crown of Albania and wisely refused it. Late one night Auberon and I climbed into Christ Church, the doors having been locked at ten o'clock, to have a nightcap with one of his mates. As far as I recall we slithered over the cathedral roof in the blackout, Auberon singing in Flemish. His friend was out, but a welcoming fire blazed and a bottle of hock stood on a table. 'He won't mind,' said Auberon, pouring us each out a tumbler. It was curiously colourless and smelt like a hospital. What . . . ? Too late. Auberon took a swig of surgical spirit (pure alcohol), which his friend used to pep up his cocktails. He spat it out and threw the remains into the fire, glass and all. There was a deep 'woof' and we were both enveloped in blue and orange flames. No great harm was suffered except to eyebrows. I never met the occupant of the rooms but must assume he was vexed. Amazingly, Auberon told me that it was the second time that it had happened.

This privileged and happy existence ended abruptly in the spring of 1942 when I joined the Royal Air Force. My parents pointed out that I could stay at Oxford for another term and take a 'War Time Degree'. I knew what the intellectually disastrous outcome of that would be and, out of vanity, went down then and there. My friends were nearly all going into the Army, mostly the Scots Guards and the Rifle Brigade, and I did not see any of those who survived until after the War.

Shortly before my nineteenth birthday in May 1942, I reported to Abbey House, Regents Park, with fellow members of the Oxford University Air Squadron. Our greeting was less than cordial. Having a degree of elementary training, drilling, navigational theory, Morse Code, etc., we were designated Leading Aircraftsmen (the equivalent of a Lance Corporal) and the old rankers who ran these reception establishments reasonably enough thought little of us. A delicately nurtured colleague who had read Classics at Oxford was told to get a move on or the speaker would give him a meat injection in the right ear. He looked pained at this curious threat. His name was John Pinsent and he later intended to inscribe his aircraft *Numquam me pinsent* ('They'll never cop me'). I hope he was right.

The Oxford, Cambridge and St Andrews University Air Squadron members lived in a block of gutted flats in St John's Wood while we digested our many prophylactic jabs and our cardboard-like uniforms. Harmony reigned in the chilly discomfort, but in an adjoining flat a northern University Air Squadron was housed. They appeared to resent our voices, the fact that we had friends in London, wore pyjamas and showed other manifestations of effete and snobbish complacency. I was rather pleased to learn later that we did a good deal better than they did in completing our courses as pilots or navigators. There is not much worthy of recollection of those weeks, except that an aspirant air crew member among us was arrested, tried and hanged for murdering prostitutes. As we left to our different destinations for pre-training dispersal, in a last attempt at friendliness I asked one of our critics how he had passed his last night in London. 'Droonk and fook,' he replied morosely.

Our lot were sent to Brighton where we roosted on the sixth floor of the Metropole Hotel in a tiny maids' room, then housing six. The view was superb, but we had doubts when one day two ME 109s swept in from the sea and enthusiastically shot up the hotel. We were out and didn't see a thing and there was remarkably little loss of life.

Our days were spent doing PT on the beach and shooting clay pigeons, an exercise supposed to improve prowess at aerial gunnery. Bored by this, an Oxford mate, John Davidson, and I used to place ourselves at the end of the crocodile heading for the beach and peel off at the first corner, heading for the ice-skating rink and a bar presided over by an improbably 1920ish but amiable barmaid named Primrose with whom we exchanged badinage until lunchtime. A rather degenerate exercise, we both concluded.

One morning six of us were sent without explanation in a truck to the railway station. There we were told to pick up a coffin. In it lay the body of a sergeant air-gunner, who had been killed over Cologne; we were to take him home to his parents. It was a small, desperately clean little house in a long row. We were ill-assorted as to height, and to get the coffin through the narrow front door and into the front parlour was difficult. The father helped us. Then we stood awkwardly trying to say something to the dry-eyed, silent parents, who offered us tea. We took our leave. The mother gave us a long searching look and said: 'Thank you for bringing him home. I hope you have better luck than he did.' Looking back through the window I saw her in her husband's arms. They were both weeping uncontrollably.

From Brighton to Anstey, a grass airfield near Coventry. The food was controlled by a mad Sergeant Cook. At mealtimes he would raise a shutter on a dispensing bar and chant: 'Mind your fingers, mind your toes! Canteen open – canteen closed!' And we went hungry. Anstey sorted us out into pilots, navigators and air-gunners on the basis of an eight-hour flying course in Tiger Moths, during which you had to solo if you were to be a pilot. I did. It was a difficult airfield to find. Some wit had painted sump-oil criss-crosses over it, so it looked like the usual checkerboard of fields and hedges. The Germans were not at all interested in it, and the air raid and fire signals were given by bugle call. A gremlin had got into the Adjutant's typewriter. 'The bulger will sound the fire alarm . . .', 'The buger will sound the all clear . . .' and even 'The bungler will sound reveille.'

I don't think anyone forgets their maiden solo flight. My apprehensions lay not in crashing the aircraft, but in being eliminated as a pilot for doing so. In the event nothing dramatic happened. After a series of kangaroo hops across the field on landing, the Tiger Moth finally came to rest. My instructor strolled over, lifted the flap of my helmet and shouted over the engine noise: 'You didn't land, you arrived. But these are hard times, so go off and do a little flying on your own.'

Thereafter we were sent to Heaton Park in Manchester to await a ship to the United States. Early flying training was done in Canada, the US, South Africa and Rhodesia. It saved importing fuel, it kept the domestic air-space free of blundering novices, it removed sitting-duck targets from German intruders, and above all the weather was consistently better than in England.

Heaton Park was a sea of mud. We lived in tents: there were no beds and we slept on duck-boards. There were a few cold-water taps scattered about and an inadequate supply of loos. It was depressing. My immediate reaction was to withdraw to the Midland Hotel on the strength of the generous fare-well present from my parents and to get drunk on champagne cider, not nearly so nasty as it sounds. My room, I think, cost ten shillings. Alas, I was rounded up and the Heaton Park Commanding Officer quite kindly told me that we had to be on call in case a ship was to become available unexpectedly. He went on, rather surprisingly, to ask if I spoke French. I forgot the oldest military axiom and agreed that I did. 'Aha,' he said, 'you're the man we need. We've got half a dozen Mauritians. They're black and they speak only French. You will share their tent and keep them informed.'

They were in fact café au lait and charming. Being used to monsoons, they surrounded the tents with drainage ditches and devised ingenious hooks to keep our clothes dry. The only time I resented them was when there was an early morning raid by Junkers 88s on the nearby Avro factory, and they trampled me underfoot to see the fireworks. During the day some of us chatted up the WAAFs* on an adjacent barrage-balloon site. They were a fairly earthy lot and on my first visit I found them using the balloon's rubber-solution repair kit and a broom handle to make articles that had little to do with intercepting low-flying aircraft. Later, as a result of another sortie to the Midland Hotel, I was sentenced to flatten tin cans for salvage on a Manchester municipal dump. My companion was an understandably melancholy black Jamaican named Jordan. Clad in dripping rain-capes, our caps clinging to our heads like diseased mushrooms, we exchanged Godot-like philosophies on our lot, enveloped in miasmic Mancunian fumes.

Considering the squalor and boredom, which lasted eight weeks, we were a well-behaved lot. We were volunteer air crew and driven by impatience to get into the air, to finish our training and to engage in operational flying against the enemy. Had we known the numbers who would not see the end of the War would it have been different? I don't know. A high proportion went ultimately to Bomber Command, where the casualties exceeded in relative scale even the horrors of the First World War.

> Why haste you to the grave?
> What seek you there?
> Oh, you busy hearts and busy purposes
> All that pale expectation feigneth fair.

Or words to that effect.

---

* Women's Auxiliary Air Force.

Chapter 2

———————— ✤ ————————

AT TWO hours' notice we were told to be ready to leave and after the inevitable and inexplicable military delays, were sardined into an unlit train heading for Greenock on the Clyde. En route regular airmen on their way to Canada for ground-crew duties regaled us with stories of their (probably phantom) exploits that would have set Dr Kinsey's teeth on edge. We were glad to leave that foetid atmosphere and bob out on a tug to a small grey vessel in mid-Clyde flying the Stars and Stripes. 'It looks awfully small,' someone said doubtfully. It was in fact 8,000 tons and said to have been a coffee ship. Several hundred of us were herded down a metal ladder into the holds filled with three-tier bunks. It stank of coffee. Not the cheerful, aromatic, breakfast-time coffee, but decayed, acrid, dead coffee.

This was at the height of the U-Boat war and many of us resolved not to fight for that single narrow ladder if we were torpedoed. I wonder whether we would have kept to that resolution? We were not put to the test. The weather was perfect and our convoy of four troop-carriers was escorted by the obsolete US battleship *Arkansas*, the heavy cruiser *Brooklyn* and nine destroyers. We felt very important. It was a pleasant enough nine-day journey to New York. We ate standing up as benches were considered to risk delay in getting away. We sat in the sun all day and in the evening watched with horror the crew dispose of half-eaten hams, legs of lamb and beef and much else by throwing them overboard, frequently accompanied by plates. One fine afternoon as I watched the ship immediately ahead of us, the former liner *Manhattan*, a trickle of smoke came from her, no bigger than a small camp fire. She turned out of line, and before she had gone astern she was on fire from end to end. Not the enemy; just someone's carelessness and the forced ventilation. In those calm seas casualties were few. *Manhattan* burnt out and was towed into Boston.

Clichés are usually true, which of course is why they are clichés. One of the truest is that memories of youth are the most vividly retained. It is an agreeable temptation to maunder on. The perils of a cut-throat razor on the American steam trains, with their almost orgasmic starts, the bleakness of the transit camp at Monckton, New Brunswick, the astonishment at the bright lights and the abundance of food and drink have all left a rather happy impression. However, we fetched up at last at a US Navy Reserve Air Base on Grosse Isle, some sixteen miles from Detroit. The base was a curious mixture of large numbers of paunchy reservists, who lived in and around Detroit and came daily to the base in their cars, and a dedicated and highly skilled flying staff. America had only entered the war (or been kicked into it, as some unkindly put it) a few months earlier.

Many years later I asked WSC if he thought that the Americans would have come in without Pearl Harbor. 'Almost certainly,' he replied, 'but God knows when.' I recalled that before December 1941 the US was already effectively escorting some of our convoys in the Western borders of the Atlantic, and that a US destroyer had been torpedoed by a U-Boat. 'Very helpful symptoms for us,' he said, 'but not necessarily a casus belli. If Britain had obviously been losing the war, the US could have been presented with the dilemma of either attempting to salvage a near corpse or fighting a war without a European base and with Japan at her back. They might well have opted for an accommodation.'

Be that as it may, in mid-1942 the US Navy flying instructors were the crème de la crème, anxious to join the Fleet in the Pacific but meanwhile determined to turn out pilots as near their own high standards as the raw material allowed. What the British raw material allowed was very mixed. We flew Stearmans, sturdy single-engine biplanes with two open cockpits. Some survive to this day and are used for crop-spraying. Aerobatics were an essential part of the curriculum and I was scared of them. In those days US military aircraft had only a single lap-strap, like a modern airliner, and one felt perpetually on the verge of flying out of the inverted aircraft. My vertigo and fear were made no better when a dashing young instructor introduced me to more advanced manoeuvres with an inverted spin. This involves stalling the aircraft on its back and letting it spin in that position, with the pilot underneath and on the outside of the spin. The sensation is singularly disagreeable. On landing the instructor restored my morale by telling me to go up and do three consecutive inverted spins while he watched. Later I was comforted to read that Richard Hillary, the celebrated fighter pilot and author of *The Last Enemy*, considered that aerobatics served little purpose in aerial combat. Perhaps not, but they did accustom you to dealing with unusual attitudes of the aircraft, and later on this once saved my life. In 1945 I was flying alone in a Mosquito, monitoring four new crews carrying out a simulated low-level attack. I clumsily hit their combined slipstream while turning tightly, and flipped on my back. The handling qualities of the Mosquito, this early aerobatic training and above all luck saved me from going in.

My main instructor, later to die in the Pacific, had a picturesque flow of language. Stung by a particularly glaring piece of ineptitude, he addressed me thus:

'Take your hands and feet off the controls.'

I complied.

'Grasp your left wrist with your right hand.'

'?'

'Brace your feet on the instrument panel.'

'??'

'Now, with a short, sharp grunt, pull your blank blank finger out! You Goddam Limey bastard, you sit there on your Goddam ass, fat, dumb and happy and you don't do a Goddam thing! Now do me a snap-roll to the left.'

It worked.

'Well, I'll kiss my hairy ass!'

His methods were surprisingly effective and in the evening, when I was pining to join my jolly and unprincipled Polish friends in the Detroit suburbs of Wyandotte and River Rouge, and he was presumably equally pining to join his pretty wife and young family, he would for an hour or more take me through my mistakes, with a blackboard and a model aircraft. And all this over a Coca-Cola. His valedictory to me was melancholy. 'You'd better shape up if you want to live. Just now, you're nothing but a razzle-dazzle dive and zoom boy.'

Detroit is on the Canadian border and the Great Lakes. When winter comes it makes itself noticed. In peacetime in the North no-one trained in open-cockpit aircraft in winter, but this was different. The ground temperature was well below zero and the propwash (American for slipstream) and the aircraft's speed brought the chill factor to something daunting. We dressed in long-johns, sweaters, thick blue battle dress, a leather US Navy flying jacket. On top of this went a quilted full-length zipped inner suit and a false-fur-collared outer suit. On our hands we wore silk gloves, then woollen ones and finally elbow-length gauntlets. Our heads were protected by a leather helmet, goggles and a face mask. We waddled to our aircraft, drenched in sweat, like so many Michelin men. In the air the heat withdrew within minutes and cold such as I have never experienced paralysed one. An extremely tough and go-go colleague, Tony Ellwood, took me aside and said: 'Anthony, I'm breaking up. There's something radically wrong with me. When I fly solo, all I do is clasp the stick between my knees, crouch down in the cockpit and weep.' I was greatly relieved to hear this from such a robust figure as I was doing exactly the same. My bacon was saved, except for a minor frostbite, by a sympathetic instructor, Lt. (jg) Al Pisani, who hustled me through my last flying checks, which I should have failed, and despatched me to Pensacola, a main US Navy training base in Florida.

America being still a recent combatant, the British and especially the RAF were a popular novelty. The train taking us south put Air Force roundels on its menu cards and when we stopped for six hours in Cincinnati a queue of hospitable people were waiting to take us individually out to dinner and to see the town. It was heart-warming.

Pensacola was the last stage of our basic training before getting our wings. We flew single-engined Vultee Valiants in increasingly complex and tight formations. This was a trial to me. I've never been able to march in step, to dance or to fly in formation. One of these has been a handicap in life. Later we went on to Harvards (an excellent single-engined fighter trainer) and then, with a strange leap, to Catalinas. The Cat was a ponderous flying boat, with a cruising speed of not much more than 100 knots, a large crew and an enormous range. It was used for anti-submarine patrols and reconnaissance. It was a Cat that found the *Bismarck* in the middle stages of that epic hunt. A fine aircraft but, to me at least, dead boring. On getting my wings I asked not to be posted to a Catalina squadron on the grounds that I was tired of the seagulls sneering as they overtook me.

I was very proud to get US Navy wings as well as those of the RAF (it did not in fact indicate any additional merit, but it looked good), but I marred the award ceremony which was conducted with characteristic razzmatazz. Large US and UK flags were planted in the lawn in front of the American Admiral who handed out the insignia. The flags hung idle, but as I approached the table a vagrant gust unfurled the Stars and Stripes and I became entangled in it. No-one laughed.

During all this time I had dutifully written once a week to my parents. The young are insensitive to the worries of the old, but even we realised that there must be sad anxieties at home. There was a sort of shorthand system of numbered telegraphic messages. You merely sent, for instance, '53, love Anthony', which would be delivered as: 'I am well and expect to be moving soon. Best regards to all at home,' or '15', which said: 'Happy Christmas,' etc., etc. So far so good; but it sometimes went wrong. My message on this occasion should have read: 'I have got my wings and commission and hope to see you soon.' Another number was transmitted which arrived as: 'May the sound of the shofar awake you to a happy New Year.' It was not New Year, so my puzzled parents looked up 'shofar' in the encyclopaedia; it turned out to be a Jewish ram's horn trumpet. They deduced that I was going to Palestine in seven months' time. In fact they were wrong by five months.

On leaving Florida the tempo quickened. We spent a few weeks on Prince Edward Island in the Gulf of St Lawrence, doing a navigational and ship recognition course. Astro-navigation became deeply interesting. I never used it operationally (you couldn't on fighter-bombers anyway) and the elaborate and presumably expensive training was wasted, but I was left with a lasting fascination for the stars and to this day I find solace in gazing, ignorantly alas, into their depths. It is a powerful analgesic to failure. But beware of looking through binoculars, for then the sparkling icy outposts lose their lonely splendour, and merge into a densely crowded and rather uninspiring background.

In 1943 we left for Britain on the *Queen Mary*. She carried nearly 15,000 troops and sailed unescorted at her maximum speed of some 30 knots. The gamble the Admiralty took on her and the *Queen Elizabeth* was amply justified, for neither of these 80,000 ton liners was even damaged by U-Boats for whom they would have been the juiciest of prizes – a whole division gone in minutes. It is fair to say that they were a bit crowded. 'Hot bedding' was the order of the day: the troops slept for six hours, then gave their bunks up to another relay. Food queues went right round the ship. I was privileged, for officers who had done the Prince Edward Island course were given watches on the bridge with a sixty-degree angle of horizon to scrutinise, and were allotted better accommodation. The weather was abominable and the ship, with her speed, her zig-zagging under full helm and the weight of the many guns on her upper decks, rolled with frightening violence. At times on the wings of the bridge you felt that you could put out a hand and touch the wall of black water. We were allowed to use the ship's cinema. One afternoon, watching an agreeably insouciant social comedy, the ship gave an almighty roll and a row of seats broke loose, carrying their unfortunate occupants, who were black, like passengers riding side-saddle on a bobsleigh. The seats, still linked, came briefly to rest, then, before the occupants could disembark, hurtled back with growing speed. They went through the gap they had vacated with uncanny accuracy and, to the accompaniment of Southern cries of dismay, crashed resoundingly into the far bulkhead. The occupants were carried off with concussion, contusions and broken limbs. An American officer sitting next to me was helpless with laughter.

'Why', I said, 'are you laughing so heartlessly?'

'You don't understand,' he replied, 'Those are the 780th Sanitary Corps. They dig latrines and so forth. They've been wiped out to a man. When people read the casualty lists they will assume that the Sanitary Corps is a suicide squad.'

Britain in 1943 wasn't particularly alluring. Cold, blacked-out, overcrowded with soldiers. A request for anything at all out of the ordinary was met with 'Don't you know there's a war on?', usually from people who had no intention whatsoever of engaging in it. We went from one bleak airfield to another, converting to twin-engined aircraft, and flying extensively by night and in weather that we had never experienced in America. We were quite evidently destined for that devouring Moloch, Bomber Command. Most of us viewed the prospect with a mixture of excitement, trepidation and fatalism. There were few entertaining episodes, and crashes were frequent and often macabre. At Little Rissington, in the Cotswolds, I was awoken one foggy night by the roar of engines just overhead followed by a resounding 'crump' and then silence. I went out to help but was told to go away as the emergency services had the matter in hand. Next morning on the hangar roof were the remains of an aircraft and on the ground a large pool of blood with a flying boot in it. The most spectacular accident I ever witnessed was at Chipping Warden where we were doing a blind approach beam course. A Mosquito, then a rare bird, overtook my aircraft on the final approach as though we were standing still. It made a low-level pass over the airfield, climbed vertically and came back for a second run, travelling faster than I had ever seen. There was an explosion of turf as the Mosquito's propeller blades touched the airfield. It flicked on its back and went through the flight hut, where pilots were waiting to fly. The hut vanished in a cloud of dust. Such is the unpredictability, or selfishness, of human instinct that my first thought was for the safety of my new greatcoat. The Mosquito then went through the roof of the main hangar, leaving its tail embedded in it like a dart, and finally did a series of involuntary vertical flick rolls, trailing smoke and debris, before nosing over and diving into the main road. Miraculously, the Mosquito's crew apart, there were few fatalities.

It is strange that scenes like this, and more personal losses in a closely knit squadron, had little lasting effect on most people. It wasn't callousness; we mourned our friends deeply and bitterly. It was more the reaction of rabbits when a stoat hunts one of their number. Other than the intended victim, they go on grazing obliviously. The Psalmist has something to say about this phenomenon: 'A thousand shall die on thy right hand, but it shall not come nigh thee.' Equally, of course, one did reflect that in Flecker's words, 'Death was a difficult trade,' and one had better learn from the experienced.

Chipping Warden was a Bomber Command Operational Training Unit and the atmosphere in the Mess was not particularly cheerful, sometimes swinging from silence to the frenetic for no apparent reason. There was a good deal of singing, not all of it bawdy. The chorus of 'Vive l'amour – vive la compagnie' was rendered, with English accent, into the macabrely appropriate 'Vive la mort . . . ' In pre-Christmas carols 'We will rock you, rock you, rock you' was enthusiastically recognised as having acquired quite a new meaning with the arrival of the super blockbuster bombs.

Shortly after the Chipping Warden incident I was much relieved to learn that I was to be posted to Beaufighters and not heavy bombers. I said good-bye to my family, whom I was not to see again until the end of the War, and was sent somewhat anticlimactically to Blackpool, to await a ship for the Middle East. I have happy memories of the little private hotel on the front in which I was billeted. Lancashire folk were, no doubt are, warm-hearted and Blackpool didn't particularly believe in rationing anything. Blackpool was also the site of one of the only two firearms accidents that befell me in the War, which was peppered with these in all three services. I shared a room with an agreeable chum, Mike Hawkey, from St Andrew's University, and we were packing our tropical kit for the morrow's embarkation. We had been issued with Smith & Wesson .38 revolvers. I was cleaning the grease off my gun, and put a round in a chamber, spinning the cylinder so that the round stopped in the one o'clock position.

'Achtung,' said Mike mildly, 'that's in the firing position.'

'No it's not,' I said, bristling with expertise, 'Smith & Wessons go clock-wise. I'd have to pull the trigger five times to fire it.'

A heated argument ensued. To establish my point, I drew a bead on my foot, propped up on a chair. Well, no, I thought, perhaps not, and shifted my aim to a beer bottle on the dressing table before clicking the trigger. But it was not a click. The bottle exploded, covering us both in beer, and the bullet ricocheted under the bed. After that I always believed tall defence stories told at inquiries, for who would have believed me, with a self-inflicted wound in a foot just before leaving for the theatre of war?

We travelled to Egypt in the *Orion*, an unmemorable passage except for an incident that partially deafened me for a long time. I was napping in the sun in a nest of net rafts when a 3.7 anti-aircraft gun rotated its muzzle just over my head and fired. I felt the heat and a filling fell out of my teeth. Characteristically, the gun was firing at one of our own aircraft.

I celebrated, if that is the mot juste, my twenty-first birthday in Port Said, or to be exact in a tent in a coal-yard in Port Fouad on the opposite bank of the Suez Canal. That night I took an Egytian girl to dinner and to a night club. She was pretty and vivacious and smelt strongly of cloves – a not unpleasant odour, but it reminded me of the dentist. She also drank cider. A curious combination. The mysterious East. We were bound from Egypt to Cyprus where I believed our interminable saga of training, much of it never to be used operationally, would come to an end. It was not to be. I picked up a ferocious attack of dysentery in Jerusalem and was sent to an RAF hospital at Tel Etwinsky near Tel Aviv until various sulfa drugs effected a partial cure. The ambulance ride 2,000 feet down the hills was disagreeable. The ambulance driver either had a hot date or suicidal tendencies, and as we skidded round the corners I was frequently thrown off the stretcher to crash on to the floor. Dizzy with fever, I finally banged on the partition with the butt of my revolver and made the driver's mate sit beside me to hold me in.

I was alone in a ward with a lunatic (later certified); his bizarre conversation, gestures at the moon, and my temperature of 104 caused me to wonder if my mind was permanently unhinged. Gossip in the hospital was lurid. A New Zealand air-gunner had a stomach wound, slashed open by a 20 mm shell fragment. His wound was not healing as it should and he became a guinea pig for a visiting surgeon who had come out to demonstrate an early model of a gastroscope, known in the Middle East, of course, as a shuftiscope.* The New Zealander, lying in a good light by the window, had his dressings stripped off and dutifully swallowed the shuftiscope.

'Look in this and tell me the state of the stomach wall,' said the visiting surgeon to his resident opposite number. There was a long silence. 'Well??'

'I see a field and some trees,' muttered the resident doubtfully.

'I haven't come all this way for silly jokes,' snapped the visitor. 'Let me look.' He staggered back in amazement. 'So do I – and what's more, I see an Arab on a donkey.'

They gazed at each other with wild surmise. The patient pointed out that the end of the shuftiscope had emerged from the gaping wound and was looking out of the window. (He recovered.)

I wanted to visit the Holy Places while in Palestine, and the hospital padre lent me a jeep while I was recuperating. It was a mixed experience. In the Church of the Holy Sepulchre a pimp tried to sell me a Polish girl. A visit to the Sea of Galilee was more pleasant, indeed moving. I was sitting eating my sandwiches near the Roman ruins at Capernaum when a stout bespectacled little figure with long khaki shorts accosted me politely. Could I spare him a sandwich, his own having been mislaid? We ate together and he launched into an enchanting and erudite exposition of the events that had taken place where we were sitting. Time passed all too quickly and as we left I asked him his name. 'Tubby Clayton,'† he said. I was next to meet him at the British Petroleum Fiftieth Anniversary dinner in 1959, where I represented Churchill. I sat between Tubby, who was chaplain to the BP tanker fleet, and Nubar Gulbenkian of the blue beard and private London taxi, of which he is

---

* From 'shufti': Arabic, to have a look.
† The Reverend 'Tubby' Clayton was a famous figure from the First World War, when he spent his time in the worst areas of the trenches bringing comfort to frightened, wounded and worn-out men. He founded a series of clubs to cater for the troops, known as Tock H.

alleged to have said: 'Most manoeuvrable. It turns on a sixpence – whatever that may be.'

The name of Armageddon rang like a distant bugle. I drove a long way to visit it. A quiet, grassy place with not much happening – yet.

I emerged from the hospital weighing seven and a half stone (twelve and a half now, alas) and the doctors proposed to send me back to England. I resisted. It seemed absurd to have come all this way and done all the training for nothing. All dressed up and nowhere to go. The examining panel relented, put me on a beer diet and sent me on leave. Jerusalem was no fun at all. Alexandria was, for a whole number of reasons. Travel was very difficult, so I hitch-hiked. All went well until I reached Asluj, the last petrol point on the northern edge of the Sinai Desert, from which a desultory tarred road, often drifted over with sand, led to Ismalia on the Suez Canal. Here I stuck, with abundant flies for company. Finally the local transport officer, bored by my presence, put me in the back of a three-ton truck, with a Greek para-trooper who spoke French and classical Arabic (and, one must suppose, Greek) and an elderly Warrant Officer from the Arab Legion. He spoke classical Arabic, wore medal ribbons of the First World War and informed me that he had served with El Loran (Lawrence of Arabia). In this triangular conversation with the Greek as interpreter, he added that he was a Bedou. His family wandered the desert beyond the Great Wadi (the continuation of the Jordan and Dead Sea Valleys in the desert, and geologically the beginning of the Great Rift Valley in Kenya). I had flown over the desert in that area and had noticed the outline of a large building showing in the sand and gravel. 'Naught beside remained, beyond the lone and level sands stretched far away,' except that it was hilly on the whole. I asked the venerable Bedou, who had charming and courtly manners and some rather vulgar proverbs, mostly about the Egyptians, if he could identify the site. 'Yes,' he said. He thought it was where his tribe took their animals on the very rare occasions when there was some pasture. But in his father's father's father's father's day (it went on as long as the begats in the Old Testament) there had been water there and a palace. The palace was built of mud bricks. The bricks of the rooms that looked on the west were mixed with rose water and the rooms smelt of roses. The bricks of the rooms that looked on the north were mixed with violet water and the rooms smelt of violets. The bricks of the rooms that looked on the south were mixed with saffron water and the rooms smelt of saffron. But the bricks of the rooms that looked on the east were mixed with fresh water, and they looked on the desert and they smelt of the desert. This was delivered in measured cadences, which lasted many a dusty and bumpy mile, and I was romantically impressed. Later I told the tale to Stuart Per-owne, a great Arabist. He smiled: 'They say that of many of their ruins.'

At last I arrived in Cyprus, escorted in an excursion-style little steamer from Haifa, where there was a bubonic plague outbreak, by an Italian light cruiser. Italy was now termed a 'co-belligerent' after their collapse in Sicily and the fall of Mussolini, but it looked odd. I had wanted to see my maternal grandfather's house on Mount Carmel, above Haifa (now, I believe, the

Israeli Navy's headquarters), but the plague forbade it. My grandfather was a strange figure, taking three medical degrees in his youth but never practising medicine. He researched the effect of light on bacteria and on one occasion allegedly persuaded a Member of Parliament, before he spoke in the House, to gargle with a culture that caused a pink mould on raw potatoes but was otherwise harmless (he hoped), and other Members to smuggle in saucers of raw sliced potatoes to see if they were infected (they were). He left a large tract of land to Haifa City for a park, and named it after his brother-in-law, General Allenby, who had driven the Turks out of Palestine in 1917. A rum thing to do because he was neither Jewish nor a Zionist, but there were then many more Arabs than Jews in Haifa; and in any case I reflected on his blood relationship with Jack Mytton, the strangest of the many strange eccentrics of the 1820s. Mytton had shot his cuckoo-clock as a punishment for striking two hundred at midnight, and had set fire to his own shirt-tail to frighten away the hiccups, so I suppose giving a park away was a minor matter in the family.

Cyprus was serious flying and a garish night life in Nicosia. A great many cabaret owners and 'artistes' had fled from Central Europe before the Nazi tide and had found refuge there. The island was also out-of-bounds for troops from the mainland, so it was not unduly crowded. I remember the tremendous thrill on first flying a real operational aircraft, the Beaufighter. The Beau was an ugly great bruiser, originally employed most successfully as a night fighter and then as a 'strike' aircraft, primarily against shipping. It had two huge radial engines and a crew of a pilot and navigator. The latter sat behind armour plate at the rear of the aircraft with a small window and a single Browning machine gun. (It had little purpose, but was loaded with very bright 'headlight' tracer ammunition and was supposed to act as a deterrent to an enemy on your tail. I don't think it did.) Although rather slow and unmanoeuvrable the Beau had a formidable forward armament of four 20 mm cannon, each firing 600 shells a minute. Under the wings were eight large rockets and alternatively it could carry a torpedo. It was a singularly quiet aircraft and this was a great advantage when operating low-level over land. The enemy could not hear you coming and you were under the radar. The Japanese dubbed it 'Whispering Death'. In some ways the Beau was an awkward sort of beast, swinging viciously on take-off if you were careless and easy enough to induce a high-speed stall in, if handled clumsily. A Free French pilot described it as 'Un avion qui ne pardonne pas',* but nevertheless it was a wonderfully sturdy machine and a very good friend when you knew it. A first flight in it was just that, as there was no question of dual control.

The risk of blacking out in a prolonged steep turn or in the pull-out from a dive was slight in Beaufighters, but real enough later in Mosquitos. The term was applied to the effect of centrifugal force on a pilot, and it simply meant that the blood was forced away from your head. Your face felt as

---

* An aircraft that does not forgive you.

though it was falling into bloodhound folds, which indeed it was. Your arms and legs became as heavy as lead, as indeed they were, and your vision blurred, became grey and ultimately black without total loss of consciousness. The word inevitably came to be journalistically vulgarised. In a London court a pick-pocket on the Underground railway explained that he had stolen because he had suffered a black-out. One had a vision of arse-splitting high-speed turns by the train and vertiginous pull-outs by the escalator.

In Cyprus, living in metal Nissen huts in that boiling summer of 1944, we were introduced to legal low-flying, down to heights where the slipstream left a wake on the sea. The totally illegal low-flying I had done over the winter fields of flat Michigan, sometimes going under power-lines, here paid off. Others were not so fortunate, and many years later, when on a banking trip to Beirut, I visited the military cemetery at Nicosia, beautifully kept as all the Commonwealth graves are, and saw the resting places of some of my friends. One was a Canadian, Les Corney of Summerside, Prince Edward Island, who had falsified his age and joined the Royal Canadian Air Force at the age of fifteen. He had collided at low level and flown into the sea.

We were presided over by a most gallant old rooster, Air Commodore Knocker, who was celebrated for flying recalcitrant aircraft that younger men avoided. He was in the Mess one night when I was deep in conversation with a Canadian, who had a gramophone and a collection of Beethoven, Bach and Mozart records. 'Yes,' I concluded, 'I have a lot of time for these Germans.' A Squadron Leader advanced on me. 'You've got a lot of time for the Germans? They've been trying to kill me for four years!' Incautiously I suggested that it was a pity that they had not made a better job of it, and he punched me on the nose. Knocker intervened magisterially (thank goodness) and banished us both.

A rocket firing course, and aerial combat with camera guns in the desert at Shallufa near Suez, and we were finally on our way. We flew in a rickety old Dakota from Cairo West to Karachi, with numerous sandy stops en route. There were no seats and we lay on our kit on the metal floor. We were joined by an Army Major, immaculate in a gabardine uniform. The non-combatant staff in Cairo were known as the gabardine swine, and this one was not a very attractive specimen. His soldier-servant inflated an air mattress for him and he went rather inelegantly to sleep. We then encountered a minor sand-storm and climbed to go over it. The aircraft was, of course, unpressurised and the air mattress grew and grew until it was totally rigid. Still the Major slept on like a Canova figure on its marble cushion. At about 15,000 feet the mattress exploded with a roar, to our enormous satisfaction, marred by the fact that the Major took it totally in his stride, looked at us contemptuously and went back to sleep in his ruins.

India was a series of brief halts, delightful train journeys and inexplicable delays on our way to what, in the First World War, would have been called the front, except that in Burma there was no front, only a complicated topography of high mountains, dense rain forests, large areas of scrub, paddy fields, vast rivers, swamps and even a desert with cacti. In this strange and intensely difficult terrain, large British (and Indian) and Japanese armies clashed and recoiled wherever communications allowed, and quite often in areas where they apparently didn't.

One totally essential pause for us was at Ranchi in Bihar, where pilots with recent operational experience taught us the tricks and wrinkles of true low attack. Here one realised the enormous gap between a reasonably competent mastery of an aircraft and flying it in action against the enemy. All sorts of factors came into the equation in low-level attack: attention to the position of the sun, intervening trees and power-lines, cover from flak behind the dust-clouds stirred up, and so on. All distanced the experienced assassin from the tyro. The unit was called SLAIS (Special Low Attack and Interception School) and here I lost a very dear friend, Eric von Bock, from that old and distinguished German military family, but for several generations British. He was a vivid figure, with blazing red hair, blue eyes and a total commitment to flying. He also loved girls and they loved him. He died in a high-speed stall at the end of a rocket-firing exercise. Alas, alas. The news of his death was given to us in the flight-hut, somewhat callously. The School Commander, who had predicted that one of the seven of us would perish, put his head through the window and said 'I told you so.'

And then, at last, all training was over.

Chapter 3

———— ❧ ————

AND SO in the autumn of 1944 I joined 211 Squadron at Chiringa in the Arakan. The airfield, or rather strip, lay close to the Burma-Bengal border where the mountains of the Arakan Yoma reached the sea. Around it lay a few paddy (rice) fields, a muddy river leading to the mangrove swamps and the sea, and to the east unending forests and razor mountain ridges culminating in Mount Victoria, nearly 11,000 feet high. Access from the land was down the grandly named Arakan Highway, a track so appallingly dusty that locals were employed to throw water on it at fifty-yard intervals. To drive down it was to arrive looking like a snowman. We lived in bamboo-thatched bashas – long huts subdivided by bamboo partitions to give an illusion of privacy. There was no electric power and obviously no piped water or anything at all that could give a pretence of comfort. The food was dreadful; it was said, with some truth, that the sources of Air Force recruitment were not of the kind that carried a background of knowledge or appreciation of cooking. Drink was exiguous. We got a monthly ration of four bottles of Australian beer and one bottle of spirits each. When this was exhausted we drank a horrible concoction of local palm toddy arak (which could take the enamel off a mug), concentrated lime juice, chlorinated water and enough Angostura bitters to take away the taste and turn it bright red. It was known as Rum, Bum and Broken Glass and the effect on one's interior must have been dire. Nevertheless, the Squadron was a friendly place and newcomers were made welcome in an unpatronising way. No doubt compared with the Army we were living in luxury.

Security was intense and with reason. At one point a force of some 300 Japanese had erupted from the supposedly impenetrable mountains and briefly occupied an airfield. The pilots had just time to fly out their aircraft and the Japs wandered about in a desultory way, burning odd bits and pieces and contemptuously defecating on the (absent) Station Commander's desk before departing again into the mountains. We were told that not one of them ever reached home, but for this the ferocious terrain rather than our counter-measures was responsible.

At every point on the airfield there were Bofors guns and sentries, and one day this caused me much grief. Our role was that of long-range intruders and we usually operated singly, attacking trains, road and especially river transport, shipping, and, on rare and rash occasions, enemy airfields. These were all styled 'targets of opportunity'. It was rather like a huge, muddled and deeply unfriendly rough shoot, where we were the pheasants as well as the guns. To avoid trouble, we tried to arrive over our targets, deep inside Burma, at dawn or dusk. One morning I reached my aircraft at four o'clock, expecting to find it polished, welcoming and ready to go. It was at a remote dispersal with no field telephone and it sat shrouded in tarpaulins, with the ground crew dispiritedly crouching some fifty yards away.

'What are you unmentionable asterisk layabouts up to?' I yelled.

They pointed to a Gurkha standing at ease with his rifle by the aircraft. 'That Johnny won't let us near it, sir, and we can't find his officer.'

'Don't be bloody fools, I'll sort him out.'

I advanced towards the aircraft. The Gurkha raised his rifle, cocked it with an ominous click and said all in one word 'Haltorifire.' It was his only English and he meant it. Impasse. Time passed and the Gurkha began to stand out silhouetted against the first dawn light while still the Flight Sergeant searched in vain for his officer. Having no ambition to be a clay pigeon I did not wish to arrive in broad daylight and alone over a heavily defended area hundreds of miles from home. I danced up and down with frustration and even contemplated shooting the sentry, which would have been easy, but too like shooting a faithful but obstinate guard dog to be contemplated. (There is no racial prejudice here; I would have had the same emotions if he had been Norwegian. Such was the spirit of the times.) Like most dramas it ended in anti-climax, but it later made me reflect on Graham Greene's description of war as a landscape of savage and irrational events.

After a few days of local flying we were given our first operational task. I should explain who 'we' were. As I have said, a Beaufighter had a crew of two, pilot and navigator. At our Operational Training Unit we had all been put together and asked to pair off à choix. As there were equal numbers this had to work out, unless violent and instant antipathy was manifested. In this haphazard mating I drew a winner, George Price, a cherubic and highly intelligent Sergeant who had been an engineering apprentice in Birmingham. He became a friend as well as my involuntary companion on our long and usually solitary flights. And long they were. My logbook tells me that one lasted seven hours and twenty minutes, something of an endurance test seated immovably on a steel plate and weaving the aircraft about at 50 to 100 feet. (The distance covered, even at the speeds of those days, was greater than from Britain to Prague and back.) In the aircraft we could not see each other, the navigator being tucked away behind armour plate in the rear, and communication was entirely by intercom unless he undertook an arduous and cramped crawl up the fuselage over the ammunition tanks. Navigating at low level was never easy, and George was further hindered by facing backwards, so that, like a prawn, he could not see where he was going but only where he had been. On the whole this worked quite well if the pilot had studied the route with great care and recognised landmarks, but on one occasion at least it went wrong. When returning west from enemy-held central Burma, one had to allow a considerable distance to climb over the mountains. At this point you were highly vulnerable, and you chose a remote place, usually on the Irrawaddy, to leave the relative safety of low-level. As we chugged laboriously upwards from the chosen point, at only 600 feet to my consternation what passed in Burma for a major town began to unfurl beneath us. It had a railway station, active road traffic and lots of people gazing at us in the noon sun. In the distance dust was rising from an airfield from which presumably aircraft were taking off.

'Christ, George,' I yelped, 'We're over Prome.'

There was a puzzled silence, then: 'Shhh, they'll hear us.' Nobody molested us and not a gun fired.

The night before my first operational flight I slept badly with butterflies in my stomach. I drank no alcohol at dinner, an error I did not repeat. I don't think any of us got plastered before an operation, but a drink did help one to sleep, and a good night's sleep did leave one with the necessary sharpness to fly acceptably. Weighed down with pistols, water-bottles, medical kit, K rations (American packs of food for the field), maps, a money belt containing 200 silver rupees and another two pounds of salt in a waterproof bag (currency in Upper Burma), water-purifying tablets, a Commando dagger, a kukri, a 'blood chit' printed on stout canvas in several languages and claiming that we were the reader's friends (!) and other bits and pieces we climbed into the aircraft with, for the first time, murderous intentions. All these gee-gaws were, I think, more to promote the belief that someone cared for our welfare than to serve any practical purpose, but on notable occasions they did just that, though not for me, thank God. In this first instance we were to follow an experienced pilot to attack craft on the Irrawaddy. This gigantic river was a main thoroughfare for supplies and ammunition for the Japanese armies in the north. All went well initially as we climbed into the cool upper air, weaving between sunlit cloud towers over the Arakan Yoma, to pass over Mount Victoria and descend at high speed into central Burma. Then I lost my leader in the clouds and we were on our own, an ordinary enough occurrence. Suddenly the clouds parted and before and below us lay the vast Burma plain and the shining Irrawaddy. I had the sensation of crossing the threshold of a savage and hostile place, with scant protection. It was a lonely feeling and I pushed the nose down to get out of sight and out of radar contact as soon as possible.

We banged and bumped in the violent thermal currents for which the area was notorious, and which in the frequent thunderstorms could be, quite literally, lethal. Still no sign of my leader, but it was easy to pinpoint one's position and we weren't far off our patrol area and time. A plump motorised sampan* was heading up the river, heavily laden. This was our characteristic quarry. Its destruction should have been swift and easy. It wasn't. The Beaufighter's gunsight was a reflected red ring on glass, with a blade and a dot in the middle. You could keep both eyes open when you fired, with the conventional gun-button on the stick. The blade sight was for rockets, the dot for the guns. I chose the wrong one. I had never fired all four 20 mm cannon together before; in training you used one to save ammunition, gun

---

* Typical Burmese river and coastal craft.

wear and armourer's labour. A truly appalling racket broke out. Sitting a few feet over the muzzles of the guns, each firing 600 shells a minute, the vibration was enough to blur one's vision and the sound deafening, like heavy silk being ripped, multiplied a thousand times. For an instant, the flight of shells caught the sunlight, shimmering like a swarm of silver bees. But then, as in 'The Jackdaw of Rheims', 'in spite of this terrible curse, nobody seemed one penny the worse', until I saw, about a mile beyond the sampan, the river erupt in a curtain of heavy spray. Happily my error gave the boat's crew a chance to abandon ship before it was rectified and the sampan, fuel-carrying, went up in thirty-foot flames. One could not take the chance of humanely buzzing a vessel before attack; not infrequently they were heavily armed.

On returning to base I found that the flight leader had reported me missing and had read the remains of the burning sampan as being those of my aircraft. Conventionally after an operation one was debriefed by the Intelligence Officer, and the photographs, automatically taken when you fired the guns, were developed to justify or belie your tales of derring-do.

Life settled into a fairly predictable pattern, with operational flying every second or third day unless there was a flap. Losses were steady, but not heavy, and individual and discreet. They were usually unwitnessed, and only the lost crew would ever know, and that momentarily, whether their end had been caused by flak, fighters, the sometimes terrible weather, the mountains, mechanical failure (rare) or a simple error of judgement at low level. Very few indeed survived as prisoners. To fall into Japanese hands as air-crew was a fate to be avoided.

At one time I had the fancy that I could tell if an aircraft would fail to return. The beat of its engine seemed to have a dwindling, plaintive, final note as it climbed away into the east, and I used to look at the black tyre marks on the runway threshold, wondering which was the footprint of its last landing.

The Japanese gunners had become accustomed to being under constant attack, mostly by the same sort of aircraft travelling at the same sort of speeds. Their sights were set and they were dangerously accurate. I adopted my own style of attack, coming in much more slowly and, contrary to the accepted RAF doctrine of close engagement, opening fire at a much greater distance. The 20 mm cannon had an effective range of well over a mile, so why not use it? I held the glowing dot of the sight about 20 feet over the target and opened fire at 2,000 yards. The shells were alternately high-explosive, armour-piercing and incendiary and the dust cloud they raised on the target was far more blinding to the gunners than obstructive to the aircraft. Anyway the theory seemed to work and I received fewer flak hits than most of my colleagues.

During the full moon we operated at night. People speak of the brilliant tropical moon: true enough, but attacking at low-level had its own quirks, and a shadow could only too easily turn out to be a large tree. Japanese rail traffic had increased in this period, and one night I spotted a large train halted in a station at Okkan. Trains in the theatre of operations were all military and I had no qualms. Unfortunately this one had a particularly spiteful defensive force, and I had to go round on six cannon runs before it was satisfactorily zapped. Each time the flak was heavier, the gunners hose-piping tracer at me and in my path so that I had to turn more and more tightly at ground level as I broke off each attack, with condensation trails coming off the wingtips, the prelude to a high-speed stall.

So when I got home, I was tired and jumpy. I took a sleeping pill after my debriefing and hoped for an amnesiac eight hours. I was shaken awake two hours later by a military figure, a Gunner Major attached to the Wing for unknown purposes. 'I've read your debriefing,' he said. 'Was the flak alternately green and white tracer, or did the colours come from different guns?' I very nearly ended the conversation with a perfectly ordinary revolver bullet.

211 Squadron's past history had been dramatic. It had, quite literally, been annihilated in Greece in that disastrous but politically necessary foray. (A book, *Signed with their Honour*, had been written about its destruction.) Then the reformed squadron had been sent to Sumatra where the same thing happened in 1942. A squadron is not like a regiment, where a soldier may spend his entire career. Individuals come, complete their tour of operations if they are lucky, and depart. Only some of the ground crew might be semi-permanent, and no-one serving in my time had been present at these two catastrophes.

Social life was scant. For a start there was nothing outside the airfield, except for a few rice-farming villages whose inhabitants kept themselves to themselves. They suffered from endemic malaria, were Christian in many cases, and were persecuted by Burmese Buddhists and Bengali Moslems alike: a sad lot, and accident-prone. Some of them once stole a small store of high-octane aviation fuel. We feared that they would use it for their paraffin lamps, and drove round the villages in jeeps, imploring the inhabitants through inadequate interpreters not to do it. That night the sky was red with burning huts and pathetic little queues formed outside the medical units for treatment.

From our selfish point of view a more serious form of theft was the cutting of the telephone land-line that meandered back towards Group Headquarters. Literally hundreds of yards of it disappeared, and we were on occasion reduced to taking an aircraft up to communicate urgently by VHF radio.

The Chiringa Wing consisted of two other squadrons besides our own. One, 27 Squadron, was commanded by the only Battle of Britain fighter VC, Nicholson, by then a Wing Commander. In spite of his gallantry 27 was not an outstandingly successful squadron, losing too many aircraft by swinging on take-off. As someone unfortunately toasted at one of our rare get-togethers, 'To 27 Squadron – in which we swerve.' Nicholson's personal luck was tragically bad. He completed his tour of operations and on his way back to India was tempted to accept a trip in a B-24 bomber. It was lost with no survivors. Recently his widow was forced by the inadequacy of her pension to sell his Victoria Cross.

The third was probably the best squadron of all: No. 177, commanded by George Nottage. A large, imperturbable and charismatic figure, he was universally liked and respected. Eventually he was shot down, but he and his navigator managed to belly-land in a remote area, burn their aircraft and by an extraordinary mixture of luck and intelligence join up with one of the few British guerrilla groups operating, Force 136. With them they spent a hair-raising period of being hunted by the Japanese. I later met one of the guerrillas, who told me that the enemy once surrounded them in scrub, and beat it through as though they were shooting partridges. The guerrillas lay stone still and the beaters walked over them. They lay with the muzzles of their pistols in their mouths, for they knew what their fate would be if they were captured. George Nottage survived. He claimed that the worst part of the experience was not being able to clean his teeth.

Our own lot were rather rum. The acting Squadron Commander when I arrived had been a ballet instructor in civilian life. He had a gramophone and he revved himself up for battle by playing 'Les Sylphides'. He was brave and efficient, and no, he wasn't homosexual. I met very few air-crew who were.

The air-crew were a mixture of Canadians, Australians, New Zealanders, two Poles (very briefly) and a predominance of Brits. In the evenings, by the light of lanterns, we drank, ate the filthy food, played poker, talked interminably and went to bed early. It was very difficult to take exercise as there were no recreational facilities and it was inadvisable to walk in the neighbouring forest or swamp. The mail service was, however, excellent. A Dakota flew daily over the strip, very low and slow, and dropped sacks of letters and papers. I got the airmail edition of *The Times* only five days late and our morale was undoubtedly raised by this illusory proximity to England. It sometimes needed raising. We were all bright yellow from the anti-malarial drug mepacrine and forms of dysentery were commonplace.

And yet we were not melancholy and I only knew one case of proven cowardice – LMF (lacking in moral fibre) as the RAF euphemistically called it. Operational flying is intensely exhilarating, especially low-level, and one saw all sorts of strange sights, as from a fast-moving train. I remember coming on a water-borne wedding (as I later found it out to be) in the innumerable creeks and canals of the Irrawaddy delta. All were dressed in the gayest colours and they passed just below me like a dream of exotic butterflies. Sadly, they read my passing as a threat and one and all jumped into the canal. What a way to start a marriage. Then there was the Inle Lake, in the uplands, where the fishermen propelled their boats with their feet, sitting in the bows. They were said to be web-footed. One memorable but fleeting gift was the sight of a wild elephant with its calf crossing a road in Thailand. So peaceful and dignified.

On return to Chiringa, usually tired beyond reason, I used to sit in the cockpit, listening to the dying whine of the gyros after the engines had been shut down. It was marvellously relaxing, but the ground-crew wondered why I did not get out. After debriefing, a bath in a tub like a coal-miner of long ago, with hot water poured from jerry cans.

Theoretically we were not allowed bearers (personal servants) in the forward areas, but we all got them as was the age-old custom in the East, not only for the British. I had a splendid man, like an older Mowgli. He came from the northern hills, and when a tornado blew all our huts away he wove me a banana-leaf shelter like a Cameroon gorilla's, which kept me dry and comfortable when my brother officers were not. He somewhat disconcertingly spoke English with a strong American Middle West accent which he had acquired from Baptist missionaries. When we left the forward area I asked him what he most wanted to take back to his village. The answer: blankets, and a favourable reference. Money was of no use.

So all in all I was very far from unhappy. I enjoyed the low-level flying in a way that, with hindsight and old age, was barbaric. But it wasn't bloodlust. Just a wild, tearing excitement, and the occasional prize, such as a military train or a vessel at sea. And on return a huge drink, and seeing the shrill flights of brilliant green parakeets against a gentle evening sky, as they headed over the palm trees to their roosts in the mountain forests.

In due course a new CO arrived, Wing Commander Colin Lovelock DFC. Colin was a distinctly unusual character, even for the RAF. He had served in the Navy and the Merchant Navy and had recently finished an operational tour on Sunderlands (four-engined flying boats). He was of an intellectual and somewhat ascetic turn of mind and was at first viewed with a degree of suspicion by the old hands. In fact, you became an old hand with great rapidity on an operating squadron. Experience was a most precious commodity and only a fool disregarded the advice of those with up-to-date knowledge of conditions and enemy tactics. Colin was a stricter disciplinarian than we were used to, though when I reflect on it I think that the only parades I ever attended were for funerals. However, we increasingly came to like and respect him. He was unflinching, and he made up his own mind, but he did listen, and was totally fair. Unlike so many pilots he took his ground responsibilities with full attention and care and the squadron was the better for it.

On one of Colin's early operations, I was bidden to fly number two to him. He was unused to low-level flight. Formation flying, even the loose variety we adopted, was not my forte. On return he asked me what his leadership had been like. With more truth than tact I said that it was like trying to fly formation on a butterfly. (Ill-received.) More and more I came to like and admire this brisk, cool man. He was a staunch Catholic and when the RC Padre visited our Wing, he would be closeted with him in his thatched hut for lengthy periods. The only time his religion obtruded was when he crossed himself before entering the dive in a rare formation attack. The participants, who of course could see him quite clearly, begged him not to do it again. It looked doom-laden and distinctly disconcerting, they said.

Colin survived the War and our friendship did not diminish, though long intervals separated us. His individualism was inviolate in the difficult post-war days. After entering industry and finding it not to his taste nor meeting his high ethical standards, he returned to flying for eleven years. His skill and courage, recognised by the Queen's Commendation, enabled him to pull off the outstanding feat of landing a Hermes trooping aircraft, almost unflyable with two engines out, in a field near Orléans in pitch darkness, without loss of life. He also graduated with distinctions from a schoolmasters' training college at the age of fifty, navigated yachts on the Fastnet race, brought up a very successful family of children and lived with his pretty and devoted wife until a comparatively early death. A remarkable man: I do wish we had more like him. When I took the Foreign Office entrance exam in 1946 I gave Colin as one of my referees. What he wrote I know not, but a member of the Interview Board said: 'One of your referees has written the most unusual style of commendation.' I remain inquisitive.

My memory of those days is blurred and my flying logbook of little help. Prolixity in this document was never encouraged. I find this haziness strange, because I am able to recall the preceding periods of training without reference or difficulty. Perhaps fatigue was the reason. We were often very tired.

I would like to ascribe another incident to flying fatigue but in fact it was sheer carelessness, insouciance or absent-mindedness, traits which have dogged me all my life, so that I frequently seem to be laying booby-traps for myself. Six of us had set out to do something or somebody a painful mischief. We went out, as usual, low down to go under the radar. The Beaufighter had the simplest of fuel systems: two tanks in each wing, controlled by two levers just above the pilot's head. You could select 'off', 'inner tanks' or 'outer tanks'. A blind man or a drunk could manage them, but I reached up and turned both levers to 'off', instead of changing from 'inner' to 'outer'. Two unwonted little red lights started to wink – the fuel-pressure warning lights. The engines faltered and we sank towards the forest trees just below. Fortunately in those days I had quick reactions, and we were travelling fast enough for the windmilling propellers to pick up when I slammed the levers back. Never let's do that again, I said to myself, waving cheerfully to the rest of the formation who had gazed at my sudden descent with puzzlement. I reached up and did exactly the same thing again. I could almost hear my guardian angel demanding a rise for unusual and repeated exertions.

The background of our war was the slow advance of our Fourteenth Army under General Slim, first from the north down the Chindwin and Irrawaddy rivers, later by amphibious landings on the Arakan coast and finally at Rangoon in early May 1945. The conflict in Europe was virtually over by then, but the Japanese war looked as though it would drag on for years, with slow advances on the mainland of Asia and more dramatic island-hopping by the Americans in the Pacific. Slaughter was expected to be terrible. The enemy were fanatical and ingenious, and firm believers in 'Take some of them with you'. All this, of course, was abbreviated by the atomic bomb, but we were not to know that.

Our progress to the liberation of Burma was extraordinarily lengthy. We had superiority in every arm and after the early toe-to-toe slogging at Imphal, in the hills dividing northern Burma and India, the terrain progressively improved for armour and transport as our army moved south. Why were we so dilatory? Of course we lacked landing craft for amphibious leap-frogging down the coast, and the Navy, who had a well-justified apprehension of the effectiveness of Japanese air attacks, were loath to venture into the restricted and shallow waters of the Burmese coast. (I never saw a Royal Navy vessel in Burmese waters until 1945.) But even so we surely could have moved faster. I was later intrigued to find that Churchill shared this view. He had a sustained high opinion of Slim (I was to meet the latter at Number Ten, after his retirement, when he was Deputy Governor of Windsor Castle, and his personality was truly impressive) but a rapidly dwindling one of Mountbatten, the C-in-C in South-East Asia. More of this in its proper place. Mountbatten and his huge staff, with a total strength of over 6,000 men and women at his Headquarters in Ceylon, seemed to us to fall below the level of events. A fighter-bomber pilot's is not an elevated point of view. But flying over battle areas, communication lines and the sea you are in a much better position than most to test the flavour of the opposition.

The Ceylon Headquarters' failings were many. They were much too far away (over a thousand miles) to know what was happening in Burma. Ceylon had of course been chosen on the mistaken assumption that the South-East Asian war would be mainly naval. It never proved to be so, though there certainly were naval operations towards the close.

In late April 1945, an aircraft from our Wing spotted a large Japanese convoy leaving the mouth of the Rangoon river. The vessels were packed with troops and equipment and quite obviously evacuating the best they could. As our amphibious attack on Rangoon (Operation Dracula) was due to take place within a few days, a very strict 'Bomb Line' had been drawn up to ensure that we did not attack our own people. It could not be transgressed without the highest authority. Such a valuable target as the Japanese convoy was what a primarily anti-shipping Wing was waiting for. We waited in vain. When permission to attack finally arrived, darkness was about to fall and the convoy would have arrived at its destination, Moulmein at the head of the Malay peninsula. The many Japanese troops evacuated would have been a most disagreeable factor in the intended invasion of Malaya and Singapore. Fortunately the war ended before it took place.

Who was to blame for this débâcle? We believed that it was the Headquarters in Ceylon. Unkind rumour suggested that the senior staff had gone to a beach picnic, but of course those in the field have a long established habit of attacking the Staff. Our own Group Commander, Air Vice Marshal the Earl of Bandon, was a highly decorated light-bomber pilot of aggressive military disposition. He was known as the Abandoned Earl, but he was an excellent commander and he made us aware of his frustration at the missed chance.

We had other grievances, major and minor, against the back area people. Promotions, when given in the field, often took months to come through. When they did it was sometimes too late for the recipient to spend his back pay. An excellent compact flying ration had been developed, with sour fruit juice, boiled sweets and other items that could easily be unpacked with one hand and were entirely suitable for flying in a hot climate. The Maintenance Units back in India seemed to have plenty of them, but they never reached our Squadron. More seriously, a new type of simple and drag-efficient attachment for rockets was in plentiful supply in Europe as the war there approached its end, but we were unable to get them for our aircraft right up to the end of our own war in September 1945.

I find it hard to analyse what 'we' – ground and air crew in the forward areas – thought of Mountbatten. The young are endemically cynical, or wish to seem so, and we were not of course privy to strategic planning. But little incidents rankled. We were very sensibly forbidden to wear shorts, because of malarial mosquitoes, but the Commander-in-Chief allegedly visited a forward area airfield in chic little white ones. He had asked for 'a soap-box and an audience of any men who were not working'. This he got, but on an operational strip the noise and dust are considerable and drowned out his punchy address. He therefore ordered the shutting down of engines on the aircraft being run-up for ground testing. Not disastrous but unhelpful.

Enough of these discontents. They are perhaps magnified by old age and I think we accepted them philosophically at the time, reflecting that the Japanese had good reason to be a great deal ruder about their Nation's commanders. As I have said, the Squadron was a happy enough place and so was the Wing. For every man who actually fired at the enemy in the Second World War there were said to be forty in uniform supporting him. Combatants were sometimes apt to resent non-combatants, who in turn counterresented their arrogance. This was not so at Chiringa. The ground-crews were devoted and thorough, working always in the open, in withering heat or pelting rain, and delivering our aircraft in as near mechanical perfection as one could get.

Very occasionally something did go wrong. Taking off one day on an operation my Beaufighter started to swing gently but uncontrollably to the left. The strip was narrow and fringed with parked aircraft, motor transport and trees. I was going too fast to stop and too slowly to fly, and heading straight for the parked aircraft. I pulled the reluctant Beaufighter bodily off the ground, where it hung crab-like about twenty feet up. To avoid disaster I had to turn, thereby raising the stalling speed and reducing the chances of staying in the air. The Beaufighter was lurching and sinking under me, the controls soft and unresponsive. I felt as though I was holding something vastly precious and fragile in my sweating hands, and it was starting to disintegrate. Then the propellers at maximum power began to bite and we lurched round. I could see the startled faces of men working on the aircraft, and my own starboard wing tip raising dust eddies on the ground. After that it was over, except for uncontrollably shaking hands and legs and a uniform soaked in sweat. George Price was eloquently silent until it was time to alter course half an hour later, when he said gently: 'If you do that again I'll resign my non-commission.' I returned after the operation to vituperation from one and all and was vastly relieved when two days later Pete Smith, a very experienced pilot and ex-instructor, flew the same aircraft and suffered the same fate; but Pete had the good sense to abort his take-off early enough to escape with nothing worse than a collapsed tail wheel. A jamming wheel-brake was found to be the cause.

On another occasion I went down the coast to Tavoy to attack shipping. There was none, so I followed the road north to pick off motor transport. In the hills I saw a cloud of red laterite dust on the twisting road. It was a petrol-tanker and definitely worth having. There was slight opposition from the ground, and as we turned tightly to dive on the target, something must have cut my hydraulic lines: no flaps, no undercarriage. For the time being this did not matter, but on nearing Chiringa in the dark, Flying Control told me uncharitably that we must belly-land on rough ground and not on the runway, for fear of burning and blocking it. We were offered the alternative of jumping over the base. I reflected that not long before a crew had abandoned their aircraft at night and the parachutes had drifted off into the mountain rain forest. They were never seen again, and I suppose that their skeletons hung from the 150 foot trees for many a year. I therefore chose the belly landing. Without flaps the ten-ton Beaufighter hit fast and hard. It sounded like all the tin cans in Asia falling downstairs. The aircraft seemed to take forever to come to a halt, finally standing on its nose and collapsing with a huge thump that did long-lasting things to my vertebrae. The safety harness had snapped, leaving a bright red St Andrew's Cross branded on my chest, and I had banged my front teeth permanently crooked. These things seemed of slight account compared with the fact that the Beaufighter did not burn. At the age of twenty-one, bones are resilient.

As the Japanese were gradually driven out of the north of Burma, their flak became more concentrated and more effective. We had probably become over-confident in our ability to avoid it in the huge operational area, which took us into Thailand and to the Chinese border in the north and east, and to the Malay Peninsula in the south. A large flak-map which hung in the Operations Room gradually came to look like an attack of exotically virulent measles, as the symbols for different types of anti-aircraft installations were marked on it. One day I saw a new one, a small black triangle amid the red, yellow, blue and green dots. I looked down to the legend for enlightenment. It said 'Men with sticks'. (Well, we did fly very low.)

It was perhaps this over-confidence that led me to near disaster. As usual leaving the Irrawaddy plain to climb over the mountains, we passed a road junction. Looking down from 500 feet I was puzzled by four gently turning foreshortened objects. Suddenly the ground lit up like summer lightning. It was a heavy flak battery with attendant light stuff. Fortunately I was too low for effective heavy (time-fused) flak, and too fleeting a target for the light (contact-detonated). But if I had been a hen it would have put me off the lay.

A very much lesser manifestation of hostility came close to putting an end to me. We were patrolling a railway line, looking for customers. Nothing unusual was in view and we appeared to be in empty scrub-land. There was a vicious crack, as though someone had thrown a stone at one's car windscreen.

Nothing more, and I paid no further attention. On reaching home I found that a single heavy armour-piercing bullet had come up through the floor, passed under my raised arm and exited through the back of my seat.

With the approach of the little brother of the great monsoon, known as the Chota Monsoon, the weather deteriorated. Two Chinese officers appeared on the Wing. They were sleek and immaculate in well-cut gabardine uniforms with many medal ribbons. Their polished spectacles gleamed menacingly. They had come, it seemed, to enlist our help. The Japanese were apparently preparing to build a highway through the mountains of northern Thailand into China, to attack the Chinese in their soft under-belly. This was explained with a wealth of maps and chinagraph (appropriately) arrows, and references to Chinese Route Armies. (What is a Route Army?) We were said to be the only aircraft with the range and capability of putting a stop to these threatening procedures by shooting up the Japanese road-building machinery in the mountains.

Somewhat dubiously a number of aircraft were despatched, mine amongst them. I flew across Burma and into Thailand, avoiding all defended areas, and in due course followed a dirt road north up a valley and into the mountains. Nothing was to be seen as we followed the roaring, muddy river into ever-deteriorating visibility. The valley narrowed abruptly and it started to rain. With the clouds only some 400 feet above the valley floor, we appeared to be flying into a tunnel.

'How high are the mountains, George?' I asked with feigned nonchalance.

'The near ones are about six thousand feet, but the high ones don't appear to have been surveyed,' was the somewhat disconcerting answer.

The valley was now too narrow to attempt a conventional turn, however tight. To go on could only end in one way and to climb invited the high chance of flying into what the RAF called a stuffed cloud. My mind was furiously stimulated. The shortest way to reverse course is a stall turn, but a Beaufighter couldn't attempt this at that altitude. What about a wing-over? We had been taught these ad nauseam by the Americans. They consisted of flying the aircraft steeply upward in a tight turn until the point of stall was reached but not passed and then diving out of the turn.

Well, it was, as they say, shit or bust. At the top of the wing-over we were in cloud. In those days gyros toppled at the vertical point, so one could only rely on the primitive turn and bank indicator and the altimeter. Through the murk something solid loomed and I had a split-second glimpse of a streaming black wall of rock, horribly close. Then we dived out of the turn, into clear air and facing down the valley. I was speechless with relief. George hadn't turned a hair; his head had been in the office, looking at maps, and he hadn't particularly noticed the manoeuvre.

I always wondered what the Chinese were really up to, for no-one found anything in the mountains. Perhaps attempting to prove to us that they really were actively fighting the Japanese? Anyway, hunting for steam-rollers in the high mountains of South-East Asia would have been an agreeably surrealist way to end one's life.

During all this time, leave was quite plentiful. We were given two weeks in every eight and were told we had to be off the base. The imperative amused us. Usually the Calcutta-bound crew took a Beaufighter, which the returning one brought back. We landed at Alipore, the former Calcutta racecourse. Sometimes the returning crew would lunch at Firpo's, the best restaurant in Calcutta, fill zinc tubs with ice and every sort of precious edible and beer and hurry to Alipore to take off and climb to cold altitude before it melted. On these occasions we all had an excellent but ephemeral buffet on arrival. I once hit a vulture on my way back. There was an ugly clunk and a hole appeared in my starboard wing. Vultures are very heavy birds and had caused a good many fatalities, not to mention their own. My mates at Chiringa were far more concerned about the safe arrival of the Firpo provisions, but the Beaufighter was a total write-off.

I was rather puzzled when dining in Firpo's by the reaction to my request for beckty, a delicious Indian Ocean fish. It was as though I had ordered a cobra, and the atmosphere registered total dismay when my companion wanted a second helping. It appeared that the previous year an officer had ordered a second helping of beckty, followed by a third. The waiter explained that there was none left, whereupon the diner is alleged to have shot him dead. I don't really believe it, but something must have occurred to convert an order for beckty into the Indian equivalent of the pirate's Black Spot.

From Calcutta we usually went to Darjeeling. It was a tin-roofed shanty town, but the air at 7,000 feet was a powerful remedy to the Arakan. The view, looking straight on to Kangchenjunga's summit at 28,000 feet, was unforgettable, and when the clouds lifted you could see Everest some sixty miles away. I used to hire a pony and go on short treks, accompanied by a charming Scots girl. She had been a friend of two successive pilots, both of whom had been killed, and had gained, in the rather ugly Air Force parlance, the title of a 'Chop Girl'. (To be killed was to 'get the chop'.) Superstition isolated her from those who knew, and it saddened her.

The Turf Club in Calcutta had most hospitably made over their little annexe in Russell Street to air-crew on leave. Arriving one evening, hot and dirty, with the mountains in prospect for the morrow, I spotted a dusty bottle of absinthe in the bar. Its production had been banned in France and, having read my Rimbaud, I thought it romantically illicit. The barman obligingly poured out all there was, making five swirling greeny-white drinks, and had them sent up to my bath. I put them on the rim and sank back luxuriating. Something very heavy rumbled by in the street. The room vibrated. Before my horrified eyes the five drinks, undoubtedly the last French absinthe in Asia, dived into my bath one by one like penguins off an ice-floe.

After dinner a brother officer and I considered what mischief we could get up to. We knew nobody – indeed, during my entire time in India I was never invited to a private house – and bar girls were rare, risky, expensive and unappealing. 'I know,' said my friend, 'let's go to an opium den.' We hired a ghari (light carriage) and loftily instructed the driver to take us to the nearest opium den. We didn't even know if there were such things, but the driver accepted the instruction as calmly as a fare to the railway station. We arrived in a grim and sinister street. Those who have read Kipling's account of Calcutta, 'The City of Awful Night', will realise its full nastiness. It is always gratifying if real events live up to their fictional counterparts. We were greeted by the conventional villainous Chinaman. The interior of the single large room into which we were ushered looked like the forecastle of a clipper ship (yes, I have seen one), with bare wooden bunks, hollowed out wooden head-rests, and by each one a little table with a spirit lamp. At least, that is what it looked like when we eventually got accustomed to the dark and the suffocating atmosphere through whose folds it appeared that we had physically to cut our way.

'We want to smoke opium,' we proclaimed importantly.

'You've come to the right place,' said the Chinaman in very pure English. 'How many pipes do you want to smoke?'

In the manner of a connoisseur consulting a sommelier we asked how many he suggested?

'Nine,' he asserted firmly. It sounded rather a lot. It was. But the ritual was intriguing, with a little pot of heavy treacle-like opium and a large bodkin on which a blob was wound, cooked in the spirit lamp and inserted into a long-stemmed pipe with a bowl like a thimble. A boy carried out these operations and handed you the pipe with a bow. You were supposed to inhale deeply and hold the smoke in your lungs. In my case the result was a coughing fit of tubercular violence. The smokers looked up with affront from their dreams. It was as though one had been sick in the dining room at Boodles. After that our parallel with fiction still ran true. We both had gentle, happy thoughts, half-dreams. Perhaps it was auto-suggestion. When we left we both felt clear-headed, cheerful and well. Far better than alcohol, we concluded. The following morning brought retribution. Never had either of us had a hang-over of such appalling dimensions. We were unable to catch our train to Darjeeling. We were unable to eat or drink or sleep. We hated each other, but did not have the strength to argue about it. Forty-eight hours later, pale and evil-tempered, we reached the mountains, where it was raining.

Chapter 4

———— ✾ ————

B
Y THE early spring of 1945 the Japanese were in full retreat, albeit slow and stubborn, and the Army had begun advancing not only in the north but down the Arakan coast, where Akyab was by now in our hands. Amphibious landings began to take place, presumably so enabled by the release of landing craft from Europe, and the Navy started to appear – not an unmixed blessing as they were apt to fire on any aircraft, friend or foe, with impartial but fortunate inaccuracy. I once saw them pelting a poor old Dakota as it went peaceably on its way near Chittagong harbour. How anyone, even a naval gunner, could fail to recognise a Dakota remains beyond me.

The RAF were not guiltless in this respect. I was despatched to patrol over the site of a landing well down the coast. My task was to attack Japanese gun positions when called on to do so from the ground, the targets being identified by yellow smoke when possible. The ground was silent. It later transpired that the wireless jeep and its occupants had been blown up by a mortar bomb. So I hovered up and down awaiting developments. When they came they were unpleasant. Two Spitfires dived out of the sun in a perfect beam-to-quarter attack. What to do? If I reacted in the correct defensive move, turning steeply into the attack, the idiots would be convinced that they were right in their misidentification. If I remained static, they would blow me out of the sky. Luckily George reached his own decision and fired the treble recognition colours of the day from a signal pistol. This was not supposed to be used, as the colours would be compromised, but George was nearer the receiving end of the attack than I was.

In April 1945 it was apparent that a major operation was imminent: the large-scale landing south of Rangoon. As I have related, we were well aware that the Japanese were pulling out. We had seen them departing by road, rail and sea. Our advance continued with the caution of a spider approaching a web-entangled wasp. Such prudence may be admirable, especially for those in the van of an offensive, but there is a proverb that suggests that a general seeking victory without slaughter will have slaughter without victory. In this instance events far away in the Pacific disposed of the question unanswered in Burma and Malaya.

One of the concluding operations of this phase for 211 Squadron was an attack on 1 May on the heavy gun positions at Elephant Point, at the entrance to the Rangoon River. We were supposed to fly down singly in the night to rendezvous at first light and carry out a formation rocket-attack in the dawn. The weather had been deteriorating rapidly with the oncoming monsoon. On one occasion I had flown through rain so heavy that I thought that it must stop the engines. On climbing away from the sea, invisible in daylight from only 200 feet, we encountered violent hail, which took the resilient camouflage paint off the leading edge of the wings and burnished the metal until it shone like silver.

On the night of the Elephant Point attack we encountered a solid line of thunderstorms in our path down the coast. We tried to go under them but the turbulence was so violent that we desisted. To go over them, with their crests reaching 40,000 feet, was obviously impossible, especially as we carried no oxygen. To go through them would have been suicide. The up and down draughts, with velocities of several thousand feet a minute, could and frequently did break up aircraft, and we were heavily laden with fuel, rockets and ammunition. In daylight the maxim was that if vitally necessary you could fly through a black tropical storm. A dark blue one should only be attempted in extremis, and the final degree, a bronze storm, must be avoided at all costs. Our storm was the most menacing I had ever witnessed. Having in vain flown some 180 miles out to sea to try and outflank it, I stuck my nose into it and was spat out, going every which way with the artificial horizon tumbled into a corner. Tail between legs, we all but one slunk home.

The following dawn we repeated the manoeuvre in better weather. Rangoon, normally a hornet's nest, was singularly quiet. We salvoed our rockets into the alleged gun-positions. Nothing happened, and our only peril arose from possible collision with the swarms of aircraft now over the area. I decided to investigate and after shooting up a small and probably deserted armed steamer, I buzzed central Rangoon. Not a cat stirred. Then on a roof of a concentric diagonal of buildings, I saw painted in huge letters 'JAPS GONE' and on the other side of the roof 'EXTRACT DIGIT'. It was Rangoon jail. The painters were British prisoners. Their irritated impatience is entirely understandable.

Japanese opposition to all these goings on was scant to nil. A few weeks earlier, however, an urgent appeal had come from the Navy to hunt down seven Japanese motor torpedo-boats. They were large – 80 feet long – and heavily armed with torpedoes and guns, and their role was to wreak havoc in our invasion fleet. Meanwhile they were in hiding in one of the innumerable creeks of the Bassein delta, part of the Irrawaddy complex west of Rangoon. Their position was pinpointed by the clandestine activities of Force 136 but it was extraordinarily difficult to identify from the air in the myriad of wooded chaungs (waterways). The Japanese had camouflaged the boats with great care and did not open fire on passing aircraft until molested. We finally found them, but so well hidden among tall trees that you could not see them until you were on top, with no chance to fire rockets. I had the idea of circling above the attacking aircraft and correcting the blind fire of rockets, like an artillery observation post. It worked and we learnt later that we had destroyed five of the seven vessels.

After the fall of Rangoon the monsoon broke in full strength and our low-level activities could not reap any harvest commensurate with the potential losses. 211 Squadron was withdrawn to Bangalore, in central south India. We left our aircraft behind and had a lengthy and enjoyable journey overland in our own train. There were no corridors, but on the broad-gauge lines the compartments were spacious, with comfortable bunks for two or four, a lavatory, a shower and a powerful fan. We travelled so slowly that it was often possible to walk along the running-board of the carriage to visit your friends for a drink or a game of cards. Telegrams were sent ahead to order al fresco meals at halts. I soon learned that the only safe course was to order a vegetarian meal, nearly always acceptable in India.

Awaking early one morning with the train stopped in a wood, I felt a weight on my feet. It was a small and charming grey monkey. He eyed me doubtfully and did not like what he saw. With a muttered imprecation he seized a mango, intended by my travelling companion for breakfast, together with his silver spoon, and jumped out of the window. The would be mango-eater was sound asleep, missed the incident and took some convincing that I was not responsible. He was, if I remember correctly, a navigator who in peacetime had been editor of the *Poultry News*. I imagine he must be the only editor of that publication who had been robbed of his breakfast on a train by a monkey.

Arriving at Yelahanka, just outside Bangalore, we found our new aircraft waiting for us. They were Mosquitos, a bonded-wood aircraft powered by two Rolls-Royce Merlin engines. The Mosquito had attained fame as one of the most versatile high-speed aircraft. It was for a time the fastest and highest-flying aircraft in any air force. It looked and behaved like a thoroughbred and was a delight to handle, so responsive that a very light touch on the controls was mandatory. The Mosquito came in many versions: as a bomber carrying a 4,000 pound bomb at very high altitude; a photographic reconnaissance aircraft of great range that was to an extent immune until the German jet fighters arrived on the scene; a night-fighter; and our own version, the Mark VI fighter-bomber, with four 20 mm cannon, four machine guns and either four 500 pound bombs or eight rockets, designed for low-level attack. We wasted no time in converting to our new toys, because already heavy hints were being dropped of a forthcoming invasion of Malaya and Singapore across the Indian Ocean from Madras. We were destined to go into Kuala Lumpur on D + 3, we later discovered.

My first flight in a Mosquito was nearly my last. Every aircraft has a pre-take-off checklist with a number of 'vital actions'. I have always been appallingly absent-minded. On this occasion I forgot to ensure that the aircraft's flaps were retracted. As I started to open up the engines for take-off, I saw a figure running desperately in the crushing heat, waving his arms. A lunatic, I thought, or a very enthusiastic well-wisher. Then I recognised the senior ground-crew NCO, Flight-Sergeant Haddock. Purple and exhausted, he pointed speechlessly at my wings and I saw my error. To attempt take-off with full flap was to invite certain disaster on a short runway; you would never become airborne. I hope if Flight-Sergeant Haddock ever reads this he will understand why my stammered thanks to him were totally inadequate. I fully realised that he had saved my life, but the young are often too embarrassed to express their feelings. Moreover, I was ashamed of my elementary lapse.

There was now a feeling of urgency and we worked-up as rapidly as possible, perhaps too rapidly. Apart from intensive low-level and formation flying at much higher speeds than we were accustomed to, we practised dive bombing and 'fighter affiliation' - mock aerial combat with a Spitfire Squadron. Both of these caused fatalities. A sergeant pilot miscalculated his pull-out from a dive-bombing demonstration for troops and went in, in front of all of us. Remarkably there was no explosion, but the Mosquito flew into a thousand pieces, like so many matchsticks. The pilot and navigator looked curiously intact, though the impact had stripped them of all their clothes, but their bodies were like sawdust with every bone shattered.

The second crash took place while I was supervising a pay parade. Just overhead a Mosquito was taking violent low-level evasive action from a Spitfire. He overdid it and dived into the ground close to the airfield. The usual flickering red and black clouds of smoke, flame and dust went up, and then more and more smoke and flames from around the point of impact. We jumped into jeeps, seizing first-aid kits from the parked aircraft, and headed for the crash. It had taken place with full petrol tanks in a village and the exploding aircraft had set everything on fire, villagers, huts, even chickens. It was a scene of paralysing horror. We did the best we could with the morphia in the first aid kits. It was contained in little toothpaste tubes with a protected needle protruding. We pushed it into anything living we could find. They were all horribly burned, and the able-bodied, pathetically, had fled, believing it to be a bombing attack. (Madras, not very far away, had in fact been bombed in a desultory way by the Japanese in 1942.) No other incident had made such an impression on us. The mess was very silent and no-one discussed what had happened. Thirty-eight villagers were thought to have died, along with the Mosquito's crew.

Soon after, with the Malay invasion imminent, we moved to St Thomas' Mount, just outside Madras. It wasn't very far, and we shuttled to and fro taking our belongings, which had accumulated considerably. I was asked to move the Squadron pets and had a most uncomfortable flight in the cramped cockpit with a Labrador, a mongoose with his head sticking out of my breast pocket, and a somnolent parrot on my shoulder like Long John Silver's bird. (Its name was 'Dead Loss'.) I didn't enjoy it. The Labrador howled and the mongoose's whiskers tickled my jugular.

Madras was hot and sticky in the high summer. We continued our training without further tragedy, though we came terribly close to one. Rockets and their attendant bits and pieces had been sent out from England without instructions on the correct angle of dive, speed, range and so forth at which they should be fired from a Mosquito. It was rather like a child's complicated toy arriving for Christmas without the box, so we had to find out for ourselves. We used sixty-pound concrete practice heads on the rockets, instead of the high-explosive or armour-piercing ones. It fell to me to calibrate these by trial and error, diving on an outline of a ship on the range by the sea just outside Madras. I fired several of the eight we carried and was climbing in a tight turn to fire the remainder and go home for lunch. At the top of the turn, with a roar and a hiss, a rocket fired. It headed straight for Madras and I could follow it by its trail of smoke as it disappeared into the edge of that ant's nest of a city. There was a huge puff of red brick dust, then the rocket ricocheted, going straight for the Naval Hospital by the shore. It cleared the roof by feet and struck the sea in a column of spray between two fishing boats. I was frozen with guilt and horror. Really and truly it was not my fault (a short circuit was later found to be responsible), but how many people in that swarming place had I killed? The answer was: none. The rocket had struck some abandoned buildings and the locals, at noon, were at home out of the sun. Moreover nobody, not the police, the fire brigade or the Naval Hospital, ever reported the incident.

At about this time, for no reason that was obvious to us, the excitement and urgency seemed to be slowly petering out, like the end of a brushwood fire. Everything looked as though the invasion of Malaya was to be postponed, though we could not guess the reason. In fact, it was extremely lucky for those who were to be involved that this should be so. Some of the planning errors I learnt of later were horrific – landings on mud rather than sand beaches, armour intended to advance on roads that could not take it and over bridges too weak to sustain its weight, and much else. To be charitable, perhaps this was all in a preliminary draft, to be corrected later. But I doubt it.

Then one day we heard the news of the 'Fat Man' and the 'Little Boy' – the Hiroshima and Nagasaki nuclear bombs. None of us realised the true import. Would our Squadron be equipped with something on a smaller scale, we wondered?

The end of the War caused little rejoicing. We were wound up to carry out our destructive but intensely exciting tasks and we felt like a team whose key match had been cancelled at the eleventh hour. Never have I experienced such an atmosphere of dismal anti-climax. I was lucky enough to escape it soon, being given an early release for demobilisation as I had interrupted my university course to join up, and in October 1945 I left Madras for Bombay and home.

The train journey turned out to be unexpectedly interesting. I shared a compartment with a charming and highly educated Indian Army Captain. His father was editor of a newspaper and he was eloquently in favour of immediate Indian independence. Gandhi was his hero and he begged me to realise the universality of his appeal in the whole of the subcontinent and the negligibility of Jinnah, the leader of the Moslem League and later father of independent Pakistan.

The train broke down at Raichur, a sizeable town smack in the middle of India. We were told that the delay could be eight hours. My companion knew the town and went off to make private enquiries. 'We're going to be here for at least forty-eight hours,' he informed me gloomily, 'we can't stay in this bloody carriage. Come with me. I've found somewhere for us to stay.' 'Somewhere' turned out to be an airy if dusty bungalow with no furniture, but in military India this is not a drawback as everyone carries a vast pack of camp bed, collapsible chair, wash-stand, mosquito-net and other necessities, and we were soon comfortably installed and looked after by two locals who appeared out of the earth with worn chits of reference from bygone officers whom they said they had served. The two were young, and some of the references went back to 1919.

To pass the time, we hired ponies. My companion knew the area and the language and we conversed with passers-by (I believe there are over twenty-five distinct languages in India, without counting dialects). Our exchanges were desultory, except on one point, where the universal answer surprised me and stunned my Indian friend. To my interpreted enquiry: 'What do you think of Gandhi?' we received without exception the reply: 'Who is Gandhi?' Admittedly in 1945 India was, I think over 90 per cent rural and communications very mixed. But even so . . .

Eventually we reached Bombay. My expectations of stepping immediately and stylishly on to a homebound liner were not fulfilled. Day after day passed, living a curiously apathetic life at the seaside suburb of Worli. I didn't much mind: the mainspring of the last four years had unwound and I was content to do very little, keeping company with a colourful member of the Special Operations Executive, Toto Bartroli.

Toto had been a considerable figure in our missions to the French Resistance in the Lyons area. He had witnessed more action, and more horrors (not by any means all German) than most and had been awarded the Distinguished Service Order. Together we used to visit the up-market houses of ill-fame in Grant Road, not to purchase their wares but to drink good and vastly expensive whisky with the madames. They were nearly all French and quite enjoyed talking their own language. Their conversation was a good deal more interesting than that of the Mess or the clubs to which we were admitted, and they were very up-to-date with news.

One night on returning to Worli I found a telegram from my parents congratulating me on a Distinguished Flying Cross. (They had read it, printed upside down, in the local newspaper.) This was the first I had heard of it. Later a cheerful Air Commodore turned up, primarily to stir the transport staff at Worli into some semblance of ordered activity. He sent for me and apologised for the omission, then took me to dine at the Bombay Yacht Club, which admitted only senior officers and, most foolishly, no Indians. During dinner a fat box-wallah,* bald as an egg, took it on himself to criticise the Air Force in violent terms. Much of what he said might have been right, but he was not the man to say it, and my host hit him on the head with a soup-spoon so hard that I feared the shell would crack. No-one turned a hair (and of course the box-wallah couldn't anyway).

---

* Indian for commercial gent.

It would be foolish to pretend that I was not proud to receive this showy little ribbon, with its diagonal purple and white stripes. But only the recipient knows if he has earned a military decoration, certainly in flying where one is rarely observed. I sadly reached the conclusion that I had not, when set alongside the achievements and deaths of so many friends.

The eventual November 1945 voyage home in the *Mauretania* was not agreeable. The ship was inevitably crowded and uncomfortable, and while discipline, which helps to make poor conditions tolerable, had not exactly broken down it was distinctly rocky. Quite a number of members of the women's services were on board, and couples lay about the decks under suggestively active blankets while senior officers affected not to notice.

They were perhaps uneasy. There had been at least one British mutiny in India at the end of the war. Shamefully it had occurred among non-combatant RAF men at a Maintenance Unit. It had been led by a Communist, name of Zymbalist, later sentenced to ten years' imprisonment by a court martial, which, of course, under the Socialist Government he did not serve. It was entertaining to reflect on the historical persistence of the Russians and their servants, who from Tsarist days onwards had attempted to make our tenure in India difficult. They might as well have saved themselves the trouble. As Winston Churchill said, 'I think that I can save the British Empire from anything – except the British.'

Liverpool was appropriately cold and foggy. No bands or greeting for the returning heroes, nor did we expect them. We had heard of alleged demonstrations for peace by the Liverpool Irish after initial German bombing, though the news was silenced by censorship at the time. In any case, bands were totally inappropriate both to our own mood and to that of the country in 1945. We were jammed into trains for rapid demobilisation, which was right and exactly what we wanted.

The demobilisation centre for RAF officers was at Rugely. The name rang a bell. It was the scene of the last public execution in England, during Palmerston's prime ministership. The condemned man was Palmer the Poisoner, and ghoulish sightseers frequented Rugely thereafter. The burgesses didn't like this and asked Palmerston to allow them to change the town's name. He suggested that they should re-christen it 'Palmerston' ... And there, in a dusty jumble of all those high ranks and bright ribbons, our faces still yellow with mepacrine and pinched with cold, we took our issue civilian clothes and without farewell left for our homes.

If I have written at too great length of this period, it is because it remains intermittently the clearest in my memory. Those who engaged in operational flying were, I think, illuminated or branded by the experience for the rest of their lives. Winston Churchill said: 'The air is a seductive mistress, but an affair with her does not always end in old age.' I was, I suppose, rather glad that it was over. My luck had been remarkably good but I had a feeling that it

was not far from running out. Nevertheless, nothing again was ever so poignant, so absorbing or so intoxicatingly vivid.

> Weep for all the handsome faces;
> Earth had better hiding places;
> Those who hid, not those who died
> Are now their grateful country's pride.

BOOK TWO

———— ❧ ————

Serious Foreign Affairs
1946–1952

Chapter 5

In NOVEMBER 1945 I returned to Oxford, in the words of a candid friend 'greatly aged and changed for the worse in every possible way'. Magdalen received me kindly and allowed me to change my school from modern languages to history. They even gave me rooms with running water in the bedroom, an unheard-of luxury.

My first tutor was Bruce Macfarlane, an amiable and placid mediaevalist who liked cats and could not read my writing. I asked to transfer to more modern history and was sent to A.J.P. Taylor, a controversial and ambitious historian whose left-wing views were rather advanced. We did not get on a bit, then or later. When I had joined the Foreign Office I sometimes came down to dine and spend the night at Magdalen in order to catch up with my friends. On the first of these visits I saw Alan Taylor, who rebuked me for going down without taking a degree. I replied that the Foreign Office were very short-staffed and I had been told to start work forthwith. Alan Taylor's political views put him in among the extremists of the Labour Party, then in office. 'Aha,' he said, 'the Foreign Office must have known that I was your tutor and thought that they would extract you from my influence and save a brand from the burning. Do please find out what the professional Foreign Office say about me.' I did as I was bidden. The Foreign Office was a friendly place and nobody, even very senior people, minded being asked extraneous questions. The answer to my enquiries was totally dismissive. With the tactlessness of a twenty-three-year-old I passed on this reaction when I was next at Magdalen and realised too late that I had bitterly hurt his feelings. When he was writing the official biography of Lord Beaverbrook[*] I offered him the letters I had received over the years, some of which were indiscreet and all of which were fascinating. Taylor loftily declined them, saying that he had copies of everything Beaverbrook had written. As some of the letters were manuscript, this did not seem very likely, but I did not pursue the matter.

In other ways too Oxford was melancholy, so I resolved on early escape. The President of Magdalen, Sir Henry Tizard, encouraged me to attempt the Diplomatic Service[†] entrance examination, which was indeed a high hurdle, with failures outnumbering entrants by thirty to forty to one. Tizard

---

[*] Hardly necessary to note! The genius of the press, Minister of Aircraft Production in 1940 and close friend of WSC. A quirky, sometimes mischievous but generous and gallant personality. A wonderful friend and a most formidable enemy.
[†] Then styled 'Foreign Service'.

was an erudite and effective scientist who had rendered great service in the secret scientific war (of which Professor R.V. Jones has written in fascinating and modest terms in *Most Secret War*), but he had fallen foul of the Prof. – Professor Lindemann, later Lord Cherwell, WSC's principal scientific adviser – and had not received full recognition for his remarkable work. He was an excellent President of Magdalen and took an individual interest in the undergraduates. So I took his advice.

I was indeed fortunate, first because the style of examination of the day favoured the poker player's technique – a mixture of assessing the examiners' psychology with a large proportion of bluff and luck – and secondly because I could approach with a blank Oxford examination record. If I had taken a degree I am reasonably confident that its quality would have been inadequate. The Foreign Office examinations were partly written, conducted in Burlington Gardens in London, and traditional and unsurprising in content, with essays, basic history, mathematics and economics papers and an oral in a language of your choice. I was then still almost bilingual in French, albeit with a schoolboy's vocabulary, and the amiable French examiner and I got on well. He dismissed me with 'Méfiez-vous d'un Anglais qui parle trop bien le francais.'★

The next stage was a so-called 'country house party' at Stoke D'Abernon in Surrey, where candidates spent two or three days, living with the examiners, and were assessed in a whole number of ways, including interviews with psychologists and on occasion sessions of cooperative tasks such as elementary bridge-building. I thought that it was deeply bogus, but perforce played along with it. When it came to the psychologist I kept in mind two dicta: Sam Goldwyn's 'Anyone going to a psychiatrist needs his head seeing to' and James Thurber's 'Leave your mind alone'. I maintained that Dr Rohrshach's ink-blot was just an ink-blot; I stated, truthfully, that I had loving parents and one sister, Jeanne, who is a dear and lifelong friend (which doesn't always happen). Moreover, I had a happy home and what I considered to be a normal sex life. I was fortunate enough to bore the psychologist.

One test was to be given a subject on which one had to make a ten-minute speech after ten minutes preparation. I was confronted, I suppose on the strength of my early education, with 'The cultural position of Switzerland'. (Had it got one?) I bluffed. The shops in Montreux were pressed into service: Monsieur Kammer, the grocer, became a formative sculptor in wood of the eighteenth century. Herr Zürcher, who made delicious cakes, was the earliest critic fully to understand Goethe. Monsieur Seinet, the fishmonger, was a friend and inspirer of Voltaire when he lived at Ferney.

The final stage was the most daunting; a long, searching and serious interview with a panel of swells in London. I was too nervous to remember many of them, but there featured a trade union leader, Sir David Scott, the kindest and most erudite of senior diplomats and, I think, Lady Violet Bonham

---

★ 'Beware of an Englishman who speaks French too well.'

Carter, Asquith's daughter and in consequence an old and close friend of Winston Churchill's.

Some weeks later I was genuinely surprised to hear that I had succeeded, and with unexpectedly good marks. Within three days I was summoned to the Foreign Office to be allocated to an appropriate department of the Service. The friendly casualness of the interview impressed me deeply. One might have been discussing whether to dine at a French or an Italian restaurant. The Head of Personnel Department (What a name! Why not 'Staff'?), Roddie Barclay,* greeted me warmly, looked at me thoughtfully and suggested the Cultural Relations Department. Luckily I had a certain shallow knack of quotation, and I replied that like the late Marshal Goering, 'Every time I heard the word culture I drew my pistol.' (This was actually unfair to the Marshal. He was referring to the *Kulturkampf*, or struggle between religious and lay education, which had bedevilled Bismarck. Be that as it may, the suggestion was withdrawn and I was grateful.)

The man who actually did go to that department started off badly. Harold Caccia, later Lord Caccia and our Ambassador to the US and finally Head of the Diplomatic Service, was returning to the UK from Caserta, our military and political HQ in Italy at the time. He sent a telegram about the transport of some of his possessions, in this case a grand piano. Out of error or whimsicality, it was referred to the Cultural Relations Department and landed on the desk of the newcomer, who had never heard of the great and good Harold Caccia. 'Who is this Wop,' he fulminated, 'who is trying to get His Majesty's Government to pay for his piano? A typical Italian manoeuvre.' Nobody actually minded, least of all Harold.

And so, no doubt with many inward doubts on Roddie's part, I was sent to be Assistant Private Secretary to Sir Orme Sargent, the Head of the Service. Even then I realised that this appointment was an extraordinary stroke of luck. Moley† was a remarkable figure by any standard. Extremely tall, stooped and distinguished, he was then a bachelor in his sixties and had spent almost all his career in the Foreign Office, never venturing abroad unless he had to. During the time I was with him he twice accepted an invitation to stay with our Ambassador in Brussels and twice cancelled it. He never went to any conferences abroad, and indeed avoided them studiously in London. He lived in rooms in the Conservative Club, and later in Pratt's, the dining club belonging to the Duke of Devonshire. His recreations were very few, apart from an occasional visit to the theatre with an old chum. For these he used to make the bookings personally, simply giving the switchboard the number. The ticket agency, now vanished, had rather an exotic name and I suppose it is typical that for some time I presumed he was making an appointment in an up-market bordel or talking to his bookie. His

---

* Later Sir Roderick Barclay, Ambassador to Denmark.
† Sir Orme Sargent was nicknamed 'Moley'. This derived from his sickly childhood, when his parents had to alter their whole way of life to accommodate the fashionable medical ideas of the late nineteenth century. His father exclaimed: 'Is everything to be sacrificed to this Moloch?' and the name stuck.

outlook was disillusioned and mildly sardonic, his knowledge vast, his integrity total. Even Ernest Bevin, the great trade unionist, wartime Minister of Labour and Foreign Secretary in the 1945 Labour Government, was somewhat in awe of him. I certainly was, and extremely fond of him too.*

When Neville Chamberlain was returning from Munich, Moley had watched the enthusiastic crowds in Downing Street and observed: 'You'd suppose we were celebrating a major victory, instead of the betrayal of a minor ally. I think that I can stand anything unless he calls it peace with honour.' And that was exactly what Chamberlain did. It was evident that this unswerving attitude won Moley great respect, not least from Winston Churchill as I have indicated earlier. I shared this respect, but differed totally on Munich. Of course, if we and the French had intervened years previously, when Hitler had reoccupied the demilitarised Rhineland, all might have been well. But 1938 was different, for a most material reason. Air forces, like flowers, women and wine, have a season of full blossom. The Luftwaffe in 1938 was at its apogee. Its aircraft were not only the best but also by far the most numerous and were in large-scale production. The RAF's eight-gun fighters were only just coming on stream, and in particular there were very few Spitfires. The two years' grace until the summer of 1940 were an inestimable boon. Without them we would have stood an excellent chance of final defeat.

Of course, the argument advanced was that before Munich we would have had the 'powerful Czech army' on our side and that Russia would have joined us. But a glance at the 1938 map and an elementary knowledge of military affairs indicate that Germany would have polished off Czechoslovakia as easily as she did Poland in 1939, and Soviet Russia was already considering that hangman's pact with Hitler – the Molotov–Ribbentrop treaty of August 1939. A most revealing document on this cynical union of the cannibals is *Nazi–Soviet Relations*, a book edited by Raymond Sontag and published by the State Department in about 1948. (I lent my copy to Anthony Eden many years later, though he was already well aware of its contents. He kept it. The same fate befell a spiteful book on General de Gaulle's literary efforts called *Le style du Général*, which I lent to Harold Macmillan. Doubtless in both cases the books were inadvertently absorbed, but it reminds one of Chesterfield's advice: 'Never lend books; only fools lend books.' And then, waving his hand round his vast library, he added: 'These once belonged to fools'.) The book records, without comment, the most important of the exchanges in 1938–41 between the German Ambassador in Moscow, Count Schulenberg, and the Wilhelmstrasse (the German Foreign Office), and throws a vivid light on the secret clauses of the 1939 treaty, providing for the carving-up of Poland and Eastern Europe. Thereafter the Russian Foreign Minister, Molotov, sent Ribbentrop, his German opposite number, a telegram of congratulations on the German capture of Paris in

---

* Lord Vansittart, the former Permanent Under-Secretary, described him as 'a philosopher who strayed into Whitehall. He knew all the answers; when politicians did not want to hear them he went out to lunch.'

1940. At another point he offered the Germans a submarine base on Russian soil near Murmansk, so that the U-Boats could outflank the North Sea minefields. The final whining protestations of friendship to Germany, when the Russians belatedly began to suspect the German preparations for invasion in 1941, are nauseating.

It is against this background that one views, with a sort of disgusted awe, British left-wing attacks on the Conservatives for not going to war in 1938. Of course opposition to Munich is a perfectly respectable point of view: WSC believed that Hitler would have been dissuaded from attacking if we had stood firm. But the left and the unions had opposed our rearmament, and in particular the introduction of conscription, tooth and nail. Some of them were carrying out Moscow's policy, often consciously. And later Michael Foot had the sauce to write (with others) *Guilty Men*!

This was a sort of intellectual jujitsu, of which another example is styling the Nazi and Fascist regimes right-wing movements, which of course they were not. They were radical left-wing tyrannies. 'Nazi' obviously means 'National Socialist' and Mussolini was after all a leader of the Italian Socialist Party. Attempted coups against Hitler came from the aristocracy and officer cadre, which Hitler styled 'those blue-blooded swine'. Winston Churchill best summed it up when someone suggested that Communist Russia was the antithesis of Nazi Germany. He said, 'Well, if you were blindfolded, and placed on the ice at the South Pole, you wouldn't know the difference from the North Pole, which is indeed its antithesis.'

Moley, like Winston Churchill six years later, tolerated my political heresies with good grace. The Permanent Under-Secretary's private office in those days was unusually large and duties later relegated to specialist departments fell on its members. We dealt with a number of distinctly rum activities. On one occasion we tried to arrange for a foreign miscreant's luggage to be dropped into Boulogne harbour because our own Customs were too scrupulous to confiscate the malevolent contents. The head of the Private Office was Aubrey Halford,[*] a pre-war diplomat. He had a distinguished presence, was an outstanding linguist (French, Italian, German, Arabic, Persian, I think Danish, and certainly a sufficient veneer of Gaelic) and had served a good deal of his career in the Middle East. The number two was Laurie Pumphrey,[†] who had been taken prisoner by the Germans in Crete and joined the Service a year before me. He was the most intellectually inclined of us and was also the most sympathetic towards the Labour Government. He was later appointed to be the Foreign Office Private Secretary at 10 Downing Street, working for Clement Attlee. Possibly because of his long prisoner-of-war experience, Laurie was something of an iconoclast, and later started a fine old stir when he was given misleading information which led him to conclude that there had been a leak of a change in the Bank Rate. (I have always liked the American term for misinformation: 'a bum

---

[*] Aubrey's final post was Ambassador in Iceland: thereafter he retired to a beautiful and remote spot in the Outer Hebrides.
[†] Sir Laurence Pumphrey, later High Commissioner in Pakistan.

steer'.) Laurie was wrong, but there was a formal inquiry into the allegations. I admired and liked both Laurie and Aubrey, in their own disparate ways, and counted myself fortunate to enjoy their friendship then and today.

After 1945 the Diplomatic Service was short-staffed, the Foreign Office most of all, and we worked long hours including Saturdays. The Permanent Under-Secretary's office was not itself a policy-making department, but it was the focal point for the whole of the Office and papers going to the Secretary of State, the Cabinet and many other destinations passed through it. It was the last point of call before decisions or recommendations reached ministers. Foreign envoys had an ultimate right of access to the Secretary of State, but sensibly they rarely exercised it and called on Moley instead, usually in preference to junior ministers.

As I have said, absent-mindedness has haunted my life. It soon manifested itself in ways that could easily have been final without such an amiable boss. The new Philippine Ambassador wished to call. I made the appointment and when he came informed Moley that the Panamanian envoy had arrived. After the usual courtesies, Moley, who was encyclopaedic in his knowledge, begun to discuss Panamanian matters – crops, relations with neighbours and so on. The Filipino looked more and more bewildered. Finally Moley approached the rather delicate question of the Canal. The forthright but totally uninformed answers puzzled him and he showed it. The Filipino, who spoke excellent English, exploded:

'How do you expect me to know about that damn Canal?'

'Because you are the Ambassador of Panama,' was the bewildered answer.

'No, I'm bloody well not.' Collapse of diplomatic exchanges.

Moley's reproach to me was mildness personified: 'Anthony, what sort of a coarse country joke was that?'

While in the vein of self-indictment I might as well add an even more embarrassing occasion. 'Tommy' Lascelles* telephoned to ask Moley to lunch alone with the King the following week. This was a not infrequent occurrence, as the King liked Moley and wanted to be kept informed from this personal source of the progress of affairs, although he had of course total access through distribution of Foreign Office telegrams (exchanges with Embassies, etc.), Cabinet papers, the Prime Minister's weekly audiences and meetings with the Foreign Secretary. I forgot to tell Moley of his engagement, and he went off in a worn old Burberry to lunch on whale meat, as it turned out in those days of stringent rationing, at Brooks's Club. About one-thirty, as I ate sandwiches at my desk, Lascelles telephoned. 'Where the hell is Moley? The Sovereign's in a fearful bait; there was a soufflé.' The King was known to be meticulous in his observation of rationing. I awaited Moley's return, reflecting that mine would have been one of the shortest diplomatic careers on record. All he said was: 'Another free meal gone west.' He never referred to it again.

---

* Sir Alan Lascelles, Principal Private Secretary to the King. A most admirable, albeit somewhat austere, servant of the Crown and State.

In spite of his iconoclastic attitude to ceremonial, Moley did have a keen sense of occasion and even of theatre. One afternoon he summoned me. 'Come with me. Today I think that we shall witness a decisive and tragic historical event. I want you to see it.' We went over to Lancaster House where the last hours of the conference between the wartime allies were being played out. Round the table sat Ernest Bevin for Britain, General Marshall for the USA, Georges Bidault for France and Molotov for the USSR. The Western attempts at cooperation and conciliation were collapsing one by one in the face of blank Soviet intransigence. The final minutes were approaching.

Molotov sat stone-faced as always. At that time we did not know what degree of authority he really possessed. It now appears that it was considerable, and that he urged an aggressive Soviet policy of expansion, either by indirect or, if necessary, by military means. Was this dictated by genuine fear of a resurrected Germany and a Western attack? I doubt it. Our traitors were feeding their Russian masters with every scrap of information they could lay their hands on, and every policy paper pointed the same way: the West was resolved on peace and reconstruction and had absolutely no intention of attacking the Soviet Union. Moreover, the Soviet Embassy had a massively staffed and effective reporting system. Members of their staff could and did travel at will all over the Western countries, speak to whomever they wished and see everything except the most secret establishments. Journalists and Members of Parliament, some of whom were on the Russian side anyway, were readily accessible and very chatty. Was it possible that with all this evidence at hand, and with a considerable secret knowledge of our relative military disarray, the Kremlin could believe in a forthcoming Western offensive? As Field Marshal Montgomery used to say, in a French accent as idiosyncratic as Churchill's, 'C'est possible, mais ce n'est pas probable.'

In the stale and smoky atmosphere of the large and ornate Lancaster House conference room, the delegates were strained and exhausted. Marshall, who was at that moment acting as spokesman for the West, looked desperately worried, but his words were concise, measured and crystal clear. Bidault's face reflected tragedy. Bevin was grim, his eyes never leaving Molotov's motionless figure. It may be auto-suggestion but I thought Molotov radiated evil in a way that I have never encountered before or since. Anthony Eden told me that he was the cruellest man he had ever met. In 1991 I read General Dmitri Volkoganov's biography of Stalin, described by critics as the first serious treatment of Stalin to come out of Moscow. The references to Molotov's role are chilling, and his signature appears again and again with Stalin's on documents condemning hundreds upon hundreds of men and women to death.

Marshall concluded his remarks on a note of invitation and hope. Molotov replied immediately and briefly. The translation ran: 'I neither agree nor disagree.'

As we returned to the Foreign Office, Moley said: 'Well, that's that. We are now either in for a war or wars, or at best a lengthy and arduous period of defensive vigilance and rearmament.'

Long Sunset

I did manage to do Moley one good turn. The winter weather was bitter. Fuel was short and the power stations rationed on coal – something of a miracle of disorganisation by the Ministry of Fuel and Power and the unions. It was decreed that there should be no electric fires in Government offices. Moley was painfully thin, his health frail and his resistance to cold very low. He sat huddled in an old overcoat in his huge office, working desperately hard to all hours and visibly deteriorating in stamina. We got him an illicit one-bar stove. The Foreign Office electrical union took exception, showing the ugliest face of vindictive levelling. ('Why should he have it when I haven't?' 'Because he is old and unwell and his work for the Nation is worth one hundred times more than yours.') They confiscated the stove at night. We replaced it. They took off the cover of the wall-plug and severed the connections. We got a clandestine electrician to restore it, and locked the door at night. Triumph for heat and light.

Chapter 6

FOR AN almost totally impecunious bachelor of twenty-three to find somewhere to live in London had not been easy. My parents were generous, but far from rich, and I had no intention of being a drain on them. The Government claimed that the Diplomatic/Foreign Service had been democratised and to some extent this was true: for instance there was no longer the pre-war requirement for a private income of £400 a year – a considerable sum then – but one was still expected, if not absolutely required, to dress appropriately for diplomatic life in London. Dinner jacket, tail coat, morning coat and so on were all desirable. The salary was £368 a year and you received no allowances until you were posted abroad. However, an old friend and contemporary of my mother's, Elsie Lea, came to the rescue and I boarded happily and in comfort in her flat in Chelsea for four guineas a week, including breakfast and dinner. Elsie was kindness personified. She was a widow, who mourned her sociable and charming soldier husband. I would like to say that he was 'gay', which is an excellent and descriptive term, but it has been annexed by the homosexuals who have managed to impose it on the community. This is verbal pollution. (And what about the Gordon Highlanders, known as the Gay Gordons for their high spirited approach to life and battle?)

Elsie took a benevolent interest in the lives of the two of us who boarded with her and gave little parties designed to further our social lives. In those days, and no doubt today, mothers had lists of supposedly acceptable young men to ask to the balls and dances that had come sweeping back with the end of the war. In spite of rationing, which included clothes, these parties were enjoyable and gay (I insist on using this charming adjective correctly). In retrospect we young men behaved extraordinarily badly, or at least selfishly and inconsiderately. We made a beeline for the champagne; we chatted up the prettiest girls whether they were in our party or not; we guffawed with each other in corners and sometimes condescendingly danced with our hostesses' daughters or friends. We weren't particularly kind to wallflowers. It makes my toes curl with shame and embarrassment, for it does not take much imagination to realise the unhappy time a neglected and (often only temporarily, thank goodness) plain girl must have suffered, sitting with her mother and observed by her more fortunate friends. God forgive us, for the mothers never will.

Some of the older men, usually rather more senior ex-officers, for we were nearly all ex-Service, would make a dead set at the plainest of girls, in the supposition, erroneous in most cases, that they would get more action out of sheer gratitude. After the ball, the more adventurous girls would accompany us to a night club, where one had one's own bottle of whisky or whatever, to evade the licensing laws of the time. My haunt was the Astor, where the Latin American rhythm of Edmundo Ros's band drowned out one's more risqué observations.

The dances in the country were less frequent but more fun. Hostesses imposed young men on all their local friends and one had a jolly time. Attending one of these on a foggy night in Essex, I expected to encounter one of the more sprightly Ambassadors to the Court of St James, who had befriended me. He didn't turn up. Driving down from London after a good dinner, his party had got lost in the fog. They found a tall Essex signpost, the sign itself invisible in the murk. The Ambassador, full of wine and mindful more of his athletic youth than of his white tie and tails, sashes, decorations and orders, shinned up the post. He lit his gold lighter to see the sign. It said 'Wet paint'. Understandably disconcerted, he dropped the lighter, which disappeared in the grass. One of his party suggested that as he was so coated in paint a bit more would make no difference. He should climb up again and drop something else so that they could find the lighter. He climbed, and dropped his signet ring. They lost that too. So they went home.

Junior members of the Foreign Office in London did not suffer from the exhausting and on the whole unproductive pressure of the intense official social life that pervaded diplomacy. When, later, I went to Paris it was a different story, with sometimes three foreign Embassy parties in one evening. Such supposed frivolity was self-defeating and wasteful of all things, especially time. After all, if you wanted to meet someone in an informal social atmosphere, it was usually easy enough to arrange it. The only real benefit of these gatherings was to bring in the French, who, along with most non-professionals, liked Embassy parties, and the Ambassador naturally wanted his staff to help. But many foreign Embassies appeared to entertain only each other and one got mightily sick of a huge ants' nest of *chers collègues*.

In London, however, with everything, including bread, rationed, it was quite jolly to get a square meal and some decent wine. Moley – whom, by the way, I never addressed thus – used to call from time to time on the Portuguese Ambassador, the Duke of Palmella. Portugal is of course Britain's oldest ally, and Palmella had been a staunch friend in difficult times. One morning Moley asked me to accompany him. Palmella was courtly and very much of the old school. 'Young man,' he said, 'do you like wine?' On hearing my obvious answer he gave an order to a manservant who appeared with a decanter, three glasses and three biscuits. 'This', announced our host, 'is an 1804 vintage madeira. Not a Solera, where the wine in the wood is topped up year by year by subsequent vintages until it is meaningless. You will not see it again.' We drank reverently, while Moley and Palmella discussed the military usefulness of the Azores. On the way back he asked me to describe the wine. I tried hard: 'It is like the lively ghost of a most dashing but mature eighteenth-century gallant. What did you think?'

Moley pondered: 'It tasted like fruit cake to me,' he concluded.

Moley introduced me to a number of his contemporaries, some of them émigrés from Soviet-occupied countries. One was George Constantinescu, known as Gou. Gou had been a great landowner in Roumania, and had started his diplomatic career well before the First World War, finally serving with the Roumanian government in exile in London during the Second World War under Tilea, their distinguished Foreign Minister. His anecdotes were sometimes scandalous and always entertaining. I remember only two.

A Russian Ambassador under the last Tsar had a wife noted for her great wealth and her striking ugliness. One day, returning unexpectedly from St Petersburg where he had been summoned for consultation, he found her in bed with his Military Attaché. He ignored his wife, but addressed the Attaché. 'Et vous, qui n'étiez pas obligé!'* His wife was so wounded by this nasty if understandable remark that she fell into a decline. Shortly after, the Ambassador was moved to Madrid. His wife's health continued to deteriorate and she died on the eve of an official visit by one of the Imperial Family.

This presented the Ambassador with a dilemma. To go into mourning would upset both the visit and the Imperial Visitor. To ignore his wife's death would be considered totally improper. He saw only one solution: he swore the doctor and the Embassy staff to silence and had his wife's body placed in the cellar on the ice provided to deal with the caviar and smoked sturgeon of the Visit. To enquiries about her health, he replied truthfully: 'Elle est toujours dans le même état.'†

Gou's Roumanian estates were too large for him to visit in one day, so on one occasion he stayed in an inn, which also belonged to him. The innkeeper asked if a company of strolling players might perform in the courtyard and Gou readily agreed, although the semi-Turkish dialect they spoke was unknown to him. As the play progressed, he had an increasing sense of déjà vu. 'What', he asked the innkeeper, 'is the name of this play?'

'It is called "Omlet Pasha",' was the reply.

My lasting memory of Gou was of his dignity. Although clearly badly off, he maintained an immaculate style. At the end of one dinner, he left the table briefly and returned very pale, with blood on his lips, and unwontedly silent. It was only later that we learned that he had slipped in the cloakroom and broken his jaw. He had not allowed it to spoil the evening.

Gou married a charming English girl, a good deal younger than himself, and I hope and believe lived out the rest of his life of exile in happiness.

If the impression conveyed by the preceding pages is redolent more of good company and good wine than of hard work, I should mention perhaps that the former is easier to describe than the latter. I have always been morbidly sensitive about breaches of security, and even after the publication of official documents under the thirty-year retention rule some things seem better left alone. They were not particularly interesting or discreditable, but I don't want to lose my magnificent Foreign Office pension, and officialdom

---

* 'And you, who didn't have to!'
† 'She is still in the same condition.'

can be, and often is, both petty and spiteful. Thus I find it difficult to substantiate my claim of frantic activity and long hours.

In old age I have come to the conclusion that women are more security-conscious than men, and the young more than the old. Certainly in those days I was positively tongue-tied if anyone broached anything touching on foreign policy. I used from time to time to lunch in a Westminster pub called The Two Chairmen, and there I met Denis Healey, the future Labour Chancellor of the Exchequer. Someone had told me that he had been a member of the Communist Party and my response to his perfectly reasonable observations was precisely nil. In any case I didn't like his conversational style, which seemed to veer between the treacly and the bullying. And anyone in Britain who had been a member of the Communist Party in Stalin's day and up to 1940 was either a fool or a knave.

On my way back from that lunch I suddenly realised that it was the day of Indian Independence, preceded and followed by the appalling slaughter of innocents as hapless people tried to flee from villages in which they had lived all their lives to areas which were not expecting them and where no facilities, not even adequate water, were available. And this in the main because of the vainglorious haste in which the new borders had been drawn. I bought some flowers and put them at the foot of Clive of India's statue at the bottom of King Charles Street.

While on the subject of security, I recollect dining with WSC at Number Ten when I was duty Private Secretary. The only guest was Lord Swinton, the Secretary of State for Commonwealth Relations. WSC, in an expansive mood, said: 'Over-discretion is a mistake. I have been indiscreet all my life and it has usually paid.' Neither of these last statements was in fact strictly true.

Swinton disagreed: 'That's very bad advice you are giving him, Winston. You are different. You have a canine quality and people don't like letting dogs down.' A zoological conclusion I profoundly endorse.

Working in the Permanent Under-Secretary of State's office did cause one to meet nearly all the senior British diplomats of the day and to read outside high-level official papers. Looking at recommendations for the Honours List I was astounded and dismayed to read of J.F. Roxburgh, the great headmaster of Stowe, 'Does not stand out among his contemporaries'. I wondered what malicious pen had written so gross an untruth. I tried to do something, but of course it was not Foreign Office business, and I was brusquely seen off. Compared with the buffoonish debauchery, and commercialisation (if no worse), of some later Honours Lists I suppose the system then was a model of rectitude. There is a sort of Gresham's Law in these matters and it is all too easy to bring the Honours system into disrepute. Under Napoleon the Legion of Honour was a great thing, and in their time the Croix de Guerre and the Médaille Militaire were of the highest dignity and value. They still are – but only in some cases. In Edward VII's reign, the Victorian Order was apparently awarded by the Sovereign somewhat indiscriminately. On informing a courtier that he was going to give a rather unpopular member of the Court a CVO, the King was vexed to receive the reply: 'Serves him right, Sir.'

Moley's attitude to these matters was dismissive. On being informed that the Foreign Office ration at that moment was one GCMG,* and that it was proposed to give it to him, he replied: 'Give it to X' (one of our senior ambassadors). 'It will be of more use to him and he needs the distinction.' When he retired, he declined a peerage and lived in a delightful Georgian house in Bath. Mysteriously, he kept goats. I wish I could think of him in a happy and peaceful retirement, but he lost the use of an arm, which must have been the more galling to such a dignified and self-sufficient figure.

Among my recollections of Moley in office are my desperate efforts to retrieve a manuscript letter which he had sent by King's Messenger to the Foreign Secretary, Ernest Bevin, who was in Moscow. It contained his resignation, and he had changed his mind. Trying to get through to the Embassy on the telephone was fraught as time was very short. Eventually I reached John Henniker-Major, one of the Secretary of State's Private Office, but the line was so feeble that we could not understand one another. (We later concluded that the line was so heavily tapped in East Germany, Poland and Russia that they had drained all the juice out of it. The Communists have always been obsessive buggers, in the telephonic sense if in no other.) Also I had to speak obliquely. I was about to give up in despair when John suddenly came through in a deafening boom: 'You're wasting your time. Your en clair telegram reached us an hour ago. All is well.'

I went in one morning to remind Moley that he was to attend the unveiling of a statue of George V at eleven o'clock. He looked out of the window. 'It's raining. I shan't go.'

'But', I protested, 'you must. The King [George VI] is going to be there'.

'He'll get wet then,' murmured Moley without looking up from his work. It was not disrespect, just a proper sense of priorities.

Senior appointments and disciplinary cases also came through the PUS's office (Permanent Under-Secretary of State: Harold Caccia always referred to him as 'Puss', as in 'Is Puss at home?' It had an agreeably nursery-rhyme flavour.) One case that I remember well seemed to me a shocking miscarriage of justice that deprived the country of one of its ablest servants. Bill Cavendish-Bentinck had been one of the best wartime Chairmen of the Joint Intelligence Committee. He was highly intelligent, with an unconventional flair for policy and information. Moreover he was an engaging and humorous figure. He became Ambassador to Communist Poland and his private reports, often beginning 'My dog Angus tells me . . .' were models of cogent news. (Angus was an Aberdeen terrier, who, when being walked by his master, sometimes took off into out-of-bounds areas, from which he had to be retrieved.) He was appointed Ambassador to Brazil when the blow fell. In his younger days he had a roving eye, and remained highly attractive to women. He was divorced in what should have been an unremarkable case,

---

* Knight Grand Cross of the Order of St Michael and St George. Sometimes styled 'God calls me God'.

but his former wife chose to bring out a whole list of previous liaisons galantes. The judge, a censorious old Pecksniff, commented on these in some detail, which enabled the press to write them up. Brazil is a Catholic country, and Bill had to resign. What an unnecessary waste. He made a successful career in finance and in his old age succeeded to the Dukedom of Portland. He was most happily married to a truly delightful wife, Kay. Kay told me that over the many years they had never quarrelled, and the nearest Bill had come to rebuking her was when he said reproachfully: 'Kay, you spoke to me impatiently.'

We also had to deal with retired or about-to-retire senior members of the Service. They were nearly always courteous, friendly and humorous. Possibly they had accepted the axiom that if you want a sleeper on a full train you don't bribe the station-master, you bribe the sleeping-car attendant. An ex-Ambassador, Sir Lancelot Oliphant, used to telephone me, always beginning with the words 'This is Oliphant bothering you' (what a lesson to us all in our old age). Actually he wasn't bothering at all. He once related how, when he was serving in a Middle East Embassy, Tehran or Baghdad I suppose, an en clair (not cyphered) telegram had been sent to one of our Political Agents in the Gulf saying: 'Highly confidential message is on its way to you by hand of Oliphant.' The puzzled Agent replied: 'Your telegram not understood. Camel usual means of transport here.' Another retired dignitary noticed a letter addressed to a member of the Service named Somers-Cocks. 'And some 'asn't,' he observed, 'but it's all the same to Harold Nicolson.' (Moley Sargent remarked of the left-wing MP Seymour Cocks: 'Yes. Seymnour Cocks and hear more balls.')

It would be laborious, and possibly libellous, to attempt a dissection by recollection of the Foreign Office personalities. I am only writing of a few of the many very hardworking and in general highly competent and dedicated men who were significant in the Foreign Office in this period of 1946–9. To describe their achievements, which in any case has in many instances already been done by a more serious pen, would be immensely lengthy and redundant. I am not mocking those I mention, and held many in high regard and sometimes affection. But we are all of us balloons dancing in a world of pins.

A young woman who worked in the Foreign Office had written in the immediate pre-war years a funny but satirical novel about it called *Baggage for Diplomacy*. It was a 'roman à clef' and some of those I met came into it. Oliver Warner, a Deputy Under-Secretary of State, was characterised as 'bespectacled, lean, argumentative, obstinate as a Spanish mule, pointing the moral of his interminable tale with a long, thin umbrella'; and Sir George Rendel is seen as inevitably rushing to catch a train with the words: 'A must flay to the Ale of Wate.' Not a very kind book, but senior figures took a pleasure in enlightening one on who was who in the dramatis personae.

The Foreign Office political contingent consisted of three: Ernest Bevin, the Secretary of State; Hector McNeil, the Minister of State; and Christopher Mayhew, the Parliamentary Under-Secretary. Now, when we are no longer a first-class power, there are five ministers, though to be fair this includes the Commonwealth Office. Perhaps being a little power makes it the more necessary to communicate?

Tucked away in St James's Square lay the Control Commission for Germany, of whose competence and conduct on the ground it was easy to be dubious, in spite of the devoted efforts of the best to restore a degree of order and well-being to that devastated morass of misery. It was presided over by a Labour Minister, one Hind, and of course the St James's building was called Hindquarters. The Germans knew the Allied regime as 'the rule of the mistresses and the interpreters'.

Ernest Bevin was a great man. To try to sum him up in a few lines is silly, but I can only write of the impression he made on me. I started with an innate distrust of any trade unionist. I had been brought up on the General Strike of 1926, and I knew at first hand of the strikes fomented in our most vital industries in our desperate hours of 1940–41. These included aircraft production and were easily ascribable to Moscow's orders to weaken Great Britain. One knew that the trade unions had originated with full justification to right the imbalance against hard-hearted exploitation, but they had outgrown this excellent purpose and had changed in many cases into an anachronistic tyranny, devoid of patriotism and selfishly and destructively oblivious of our disastrous economic decline. Later I will record WSC's views on this topic and on Bevin, who had stood out in the War as a most notable Minister of Labour and a trusted ally of the Prime Minister's, though he never entirely lost the taint of vindictive Socialism.

Attlee's initial intention after his 1945 electoral victory was to make Hugh Dalton Foreign Secretary. Objections to this course were vociferous and well-founded and included those of the King. So Dalton went to the Treasury and Bevin was enabled to reach his full stature as our greatest post-war Foreign Secretary. He was exceedingly popular in the Service and the stories about him were many and affectionate, and ipso facto embroidered. One concerned Guatemala's claim to the British Honduras. The Guatemalan Ambassador, General Ydigoras (I think) insisted on calling on the Secretary of State to press his claim. The latter was signing autographs and listened in silence. He then walked to a large globe, and twiddled it with a stubby hand until assistance brought his finger to a little red patch in Central America. He gazed at it with astonishment: 'But that's ours. That's British! 'Oo did you say you were?'

'I am the Ambassador of the Republic of Guatemala.'

''Oo ever heard of Gootemalia? Go away, you silly man.' And he went. He was said later to have challenged Marcus Cheke, who ran the ceremonial and protocol side of things, to a duel, blaming him for this fiasco. It wouldn't have been a very fair match for Marcus was not accustomed to firearms or swords, and they were an everyday matter to the Ambassador, later to become dictator of his country.

Bevin had blind spots and his reactions were not always far-sighted, notably in the Middle East, though there he was sorely provoked. But on the greatest issue of all, the Russian threat to Western Europe, he was indomitable and clear-eyed. It is not just Great Britain that owes him homage and gratitude.

There followed McNeil, the Minister of State, and Mayhew, the Parliamentary Under-Secretary of State. Hector McNeil's constituency was Greenock. He was an agreeable man who had worked for the Express newspapers, but was not particularly notable. Christopher Mayhew was knowledgeable and did an efficient low-key job. There must be a great deal more to be said of these two, but I do not know of it. This is not meant in any derogatory way: both men were highly regarded.

My contact with the swells was through their Private Offices. All the Private Secretaries tended to meet for tea in the Ambassadors' Waiting Room on the first floor and we exchanged news and views. To this tea room also drifted various senior figures with ten minutes to spare. In a little adjoining office had sat, before the War, the Private Secretary (Diplomatic), who was responsible for appointments, when the members of the Service of diplomatic or officer status numbered no more than 250 regulars worldwide. (In 1946–7 we were still only about 600, including the newly amalgamated Consular Service.) Over his desk hung a Victorian print. It showed a stately morning-coated gentleman with stoically clenched fists and a desperate face standing in front of the desk of a senior medical consultant, also morning-coated, who is gazing at him sternly. Its original title was 'Sentence of death'. Underneath someone had written, in faded ink, 'We want a particularly good man for Bogotá.'

The Secretary of State's Private Office consisted of Bob Dixon, assisted by Nicko Henderson and John Henniker-Major. Bob was probably the best Private Secretary I ever knew in my own fifteen years as such an animal. His influence on Bevin was always for the good and his presentation of a case fair and totally calm. It was exactly what Bevin needed. Bob ended his career as Ambassador in Paris and sadly died soon thereafter. I am lucky enough to enjoy the friendship of his children.

Nicko Henderson had a first-class brain and rapid responses. He is the only man to have held successively the three Embassies of Bonn, Paris and Washington. Nicko was what was called a 'Parlour Pink' in those days, but he was sufficiently flexible to be able to modify his convictions in the light of circumstances.

John Henniker-Major is an admirable and charming figure. He had been parachuted into Yugoslavia during the War and won a Military Cross. He was later Ambassador to Denmark and was ultimately appointed to run the British Council, a body responsible for propagating British culture and education. The Council did contain good people, but overall did not always impress. John is the most straightforward of men and the Council appeared to mug him whenever his back was turned. When I was at Number Ten I was deeply impressed by one of the Council's more egregious feats. They brought some Burmese journalists to Britain to witness, among other things, an Eisteddfod. I gave the news to the Prime Minister, who shuddered. I feel that a reasonable financial subvention would have achieved our purposes to much greater effect. Third World journalists were not expensive, and Chesterton's axiom did not apply:

> You cannot hope to bribe or twist,
> Thank God, the British journalist
> But seeing what the brute will do
> Unbribed, there's no occasion to.

(Does it still apply in Britain?)

Hector McNeil was served by Freddie Warner and Guy Burgess. Freddie had been a wartime sailor. He had a private fortune and lived in some state in Albany. When Burgess was rumbled and fled to Russia, Freddie went through a difficult period, but bounced back and finally became Ambassador in Tokyo and, after retirement, an MEP. I don't think anybody doubted his integrity, but it was felt that he might have been more perceptive as he shared an office with, and was a friend of Burgess, whose faults were glaring.

Burgess. What is left to say about that horrible man? A drunk, physically dirty, a pathological liar, a blatant homosexual, and a traitor. He was probably recruited at Cambridge by an older homosexual don in a society known as 'The Apostles', to which Anthony Blunt also belonged. During the War he had avoided combat by employment in various exempt areas, including the BBC. Our vetting procedures in those days were primitive and sloppy, and the Soviets had been our involuntary allies, which made it easier for those concerned to condone a background that later would be considered deeply suspect. Not everyone was taken in by him. Moley had written a top secret letter to Ernest Bevin that had missed the King's Messenger to Scarborough, where a Labour Party Conference was taking place. It was suggested to John Henniker-Major, who was in London, that it could be given to Burgess who was going to the Conference to join Hector McNeil. John snorted. 'I wouldn't entrust anything to that drunken homosexual.' So we didn't.

The only time that Burgess told me anything entertaining was when he claimed that he had been inadvertently poisoned at Pruniers, the excellent fish restaurant. Burgess intended to sue them. Pruniers had asked him to tell them the source of his poisoning, so that they could make sure it didn't happen again. He said that it was a piece of cauliflower. Exit Pruniers, chuckling merrily. There was no case. I later reflected that it was a great pity someone hadn't poisoned him properly.

Finally among the Private Secretaries, there was Norman Reddaway, a most competent and agreeable man who served Christopher Mayhew well. Later he became Private Secretary to Frank Pakenham (Lord Longford), who had somewhat mysteriously been given ministerial responsibility for Germany. He collided with Pakenham while they were playing squash and the latter broke his Achilles tendon. 'Well done thou good and faithful servant' – except it wasn't Norman's fault. Pakenham was, if 'was' is the correct tense, a somewhat dotty and absurd figure, but he must be a charitable and kind man, for in ex-President Richard Nixon's time of disgrace he entertained and looked after him in London, although Nixon's politics must have been anathema to him. I don't doubt his sincerity over Myra Hindley and other cases, however ill-judged his conclusions may be.

Among the senior figures with whom I came into frequent contact was William Hayter, whom I was to know much better in Paris where he was the Minister. William was an accomplished and sensible diplomat of firmly independent views. He had been educated at Winchester and New College Oxford, but had not been infected by the Wykehamist's tendency to see other countries' points of view more clearly than our own. He had (has) a first-class intellect and a charming and persuasive method of expression. Together with his delightful and kind wife Iris, who became my daughter's god-mother, he was a model of effective and well-mannered professionalism, ending his career as Ambassador in Moscow and finally as Warden of New College, which must have been a most satisfactory conclusion for a Wyke-hamist. When I knew him at the Foreign Office he was Chairman of the Joint Intelligence Committee, which, after its wartime apogee, was just getting into effective stride to face the Soviet threat. William is a good-looking man who dresses immaculately. One of my fondest memories of him is his gazing with marked distaste at our delegation as it left for Moscow in the winter of 1947. Few had the pre-war fur-lined overcoats and astrakhan hats, and they had been equipped in the most bizarre outfits of tarpaulin jackets with canvas pixie-hoods, which looked as though they had been stolen from an Arctic convoy. William muttered: 'This is deplorable. They have turned the entire delegation into figures of fun.'

Sir Edmund Hall-Patch, who had been adviser to the Bank of China, was the senior economics man. Sadly, regrettably, reprehensibly, economics and commercial affairs were not highly regarded in the upper reaches of the Service. When a junior professional member of the Service got an important position that Hall-Patch coveted, he protested vigorously but in vain to Moley, muttering as he exited: 'I am not born to the purple.' He had the improper but effective habit of telephoning directly Monsieur Guindey, his opposite number in the Quai d'Orsay, without going through the Embassy. One day, by understandable accident, he was put through to Christopher Gandy, a member of his own staff, with whom he had an increasingly confus-ing conversation in French before Christopher twigged and silently hung up. When Hall-Patch and Guindey subsequently connected, they each thought the other had lost his reason.

A most entertaining caller on Moley was Lord Inverchapel (Archie Clark-Kerr), our Ambassador in Washington. He had been a successful Ambassa-dor in wartime Moscow – at least, as successful as any Ambassador could be in the freezingly circumscribed circumstances in which Western missions were forced to operate. He had a much-trusted Russian valet, and as a parting present the Russians allowed the latter to leave when Clark-Kerr was trans-ferred. I do not think that there was ever any suggestion of another 'Cicero'.* One day while Inverchapel was on leave at his home in western Scotland, Ernest Bevin wished to consult him and we summoned him down for the next week by telegram. (He had no telephone, and telegrams actually worked then, were quick and cost very little. Progress, progress.) Back came a reply saying that he could not attend because on the day in question he was (a) getting married and (b) exorcising a witch. Moley was not amused by this lack of sérieux, but both statements turned out to be precisely true. In his sixties Inverchapel was remarrying his former wife. Moreover, an exorcist Catholic priest was coming on that day to deal with something that persistently knocked down a stone wall as fast as it was rebuilt. Human malice was ruled out and the locals all said that it was a witch, who took the shape of a hare, and resented the obstruction of her usual path to the north.

And then there was Gladwyn Jebb. Yes, indeed there was Gladwyn Jebb. It was impossible to ignore him, even if one wished to do so. A large, booming, somewhat overwhelming figure with considerable presence, a brilliant mind, an exemplary dedication to his work and a remarkable degree of historical perception. On the other side of the coin were selfish arrogance, bad manners, a penchant for bullying anyone who permitted it and a self-regard of such inflated proportions that it invited ridicule. It would however have been difficult to pull his leg because he wouldn't have noticed it. Moley, who did not go in for personal jokes, once said: 'Gladwyn can of course never serve in Moscow.'

'Why?' I enquired.

'Because "Jebb" in Russian is pronounced "Yop", a word that has more to do with sexual than with diplomatic intercourse. For similar but not identical reasons, no one called "Coote" should serve in Iran.'

In spite or because of this chiaroscuro of character Gladwyn rendered not only Britain but the whole Western world extraordinary service. If it could be said, which of course it can't, that the setting up of the North Atlantic Treaty was due to any single man, one would have to include Jebb in a very short list which Joseph Stalin obviously heads. The Treaty kept the peace among the great powers; it saved Western Europe from invasion or Moscow-inspired subversion; it held the line against barbarism, albeit in a limited area, until gentler and warmer winds blew in the Soviet Union. And it was Gladwyn who bore a great responsibility for carrying it forward, when the idea of the United States binding themselves to come to the aid of Western Europe by all means 'including the use of armed force' in the event of aggression seemed unthinkable and certainly impossible to get through Congress. His forceful personal persuasion, his lucid and eloquent memoranda, his mustering of effective and powerful supporters both inside and outside politics were amazingly effective.

Strangely, he appeared to take greater pride in his exchanges with the Soviet representatives at the United Nations. It made a television personality of him, but the Russians with their appalling record of falsehood, tyranny

---

* 'Cicero' was the code name of an Albanian agent of Nazi Germany who was valet to Knatchbull Hugessen, our Ambassador in Turkey. He managed to photograph top secret documents, but the policy they dealt with was so high-level that the Germans thought they were plants. They paid their agent mainly in counterfeit money.

and bloodshed are the most obvious straight men and Aunt Sallies in any slanging match. (I reflect on Harold Macmillan's intervention when Khrushchev took off a shoe and banged it on his desk at the General Assembly. Macmillan asked mildly: 'Translation?') And of course immediately after the War Gladwyn had played a major part in the setting up of the United Nations, which has done Britain far more harm than good. If there was one persistent slogan which could be attributed to that organisation it is: 'If it's anti-British, I'm in favour of it.'

At the UNO Headquarters at Lake Success, usually known as 'Muddle Puddle', one of our delegation declined a Latin irregular verb, thus: 'UNO, UNESCO, UNITE, UNANIMOUS, UVETO, EUNUCH'. The only time I went there, I met the stupid, boorish and pro-Russian Secretary General Trygve Lie. He was picking his nose.

After his last post as Ambassador in Paris, Gladwyn, by then Lord Gladwyn, became the Liberal Party's spokesman in the House of Lords. A very odd choice for him to make, but perhaps he had no other. I was to meet him again in the next phase of my career and to have my earlier conclusions of admiration and dislike confirmed as time went on.

Roger Makins, now Lord Sherfield, was an unforgettable part of the Foreign Office scene. He radiated humour, energy and good sense and dealt with whatever came his way with despatch, conciseness and usually success. Roger was as considerable physically as in what WSC called 'mental muscle'. Bounding about the Office from one meeting to another he seemed to many of us to be plural rather than singular, as in: 'Makins were annoyed that the Western Department were badly represented at the economic meeting. They suggest that we pull our fingers out.' He (or they) had the unusual distinction of being not only Ambassador in Washington but at one point Head of the Treasury, a unique right and left.

A charming and bright star who appeared from time to time was Sir Berkeley Gage, then serving at The Hague. Never one to pull his punches, he had his ups and downs with the Dutch, a great people whose bluff representatives are sometimes unattractively sly. One of Berkeley's major feats was achieved when he was Consul-General in Chicago, a stronghold of anti-British prejudice at that time. The arch-Anglophobe was one 'Colonel' Bertie McCormick who owned the principal Brit-baiting newspaper, the *Chicago Tribune*. Berkeley established a remarkable relationship with him based on the former's patrician ease of manner and unselfconscious geniality, plus a lavish supply of Armagnac highballs. Berkeley was a great cheerer-upper. He wrote a sparkling book of extremely frank memoirs, sadly only privately printed. One of his stories relates that in China, in the stuffier days of diplomacy, the British Ambassador and his wife were leaving for Church one Sunday morning in the grand official rickshaw. They were startled to encounter, entering the British compound, another rickshaw, known to belong to a celebrated house of ill-fame. Inside, still clad in a dinner jacket, lay the snoring figure of one of their diplomatic staff. His address had been written in lipstick on his stiff shirt front.

The few individuals I have endeavoured to describe are those who made the greatest impact on me at the time, and it would be foolish to generalise from these particulars. The pre-war Diplomatic Service had an alleged tradition of containing a disproportionate number of homosexuals and Roman Catholics (I am most certainly not equating them!). I wasn't there before the War, but I believe this to be nonsense. Certainly and observably post-war we had both, but they seemed to be in much the same proportion as in the more highly educated reaches of the British public.

There were very few members of the Service who lacked knowledge and intelligence – indeed, the entrance examination was unlikely to let obvious dolts through – but there is a yawning gap between possessing these qualities and putting them to practical use in the service of the country. I think the senior members of the Service in the immediate post-war period had a clearer idea of our national interest and a more robust approach to furthering it than those who came later. They had, after all, been confronted in the most brutal way with the perils of national weakness. Moreover, they had not yet been demoralised by witnessing our unctuously self-congratulatory retreat from Empire and the horrible consequences that ensued. In general I thought the Service extremely hard-working and dedicated, and my contemporaries agreeable, entertaining and not obtrusively personally ambitious. The grindingly long hours did seem to produce results, and the political leadership – for after all, we were Civil Servants even if in the most policy-forming Department of Government – was astonishingly good in some of the most vital sections, particularly considering that we were ruled by the Labour Party.

To attempt to summarise the whole range of British foreign policy at that time is outside my scope. There were so many areas in which we were actively involved, and involved as principals, not, as now, bit-players with a walk-on part and a couple of congratulatory lines if we are lucky. I will venture brief comment on such aspects as came my way for anyone who has the patience to pursue my story.

Chapter 7

———— 🎋 ————

I T W A S unkindly said that the pre-war Foreign Office was like the foun-
tains in Trafalgar Square: it played at the public expense between
eleven and four. I found a copy of the actual pre-war regulation on the
topic. It read something like this: 'Although the Office is open 24 hours a
day, 365 days a year, working hours, by courtesy [whose courtesy, one
wonders?] are from 10 to 5.' In the interim, at night, weekends and holidays,
there was a twenty-four-hour watch of cypherers to deal with the never-
ceasing flow of incoming telegrams, plus, of course, messengers, printing
staff, telephonists, guards and so on. The final out-of-hours tier of responsibility was the Resident Clerks – the political duty officers. These were bach-
elors, with a reasonable knowledge of Whitehall and the Office. They lived
in flats at the top of the Office, each with a sitting room and bedroom and
with a shared kitchen, dining room and bathroom. The view from the flats
was superb, looking over Horse Guards Parade on one side and St James's
Park at the other. A Resident Clerkship was a much coveted position. It gave
an impecunious bachelor free lodging, light and heat plus £52 a year. Moreover it was an excellent education in what was going on, and a most responsible post that could lead to higher things.

One of the Resident Clerks was Martin Anderson. Martin was slightly
off-beat. His mother was French and he wore a beret. He was universally
liked and respected and I became exceedingly fond of this gentle, humorous
character. (He died, tragically, when he was en poste at Delhi, in an accident
on one of the lethal Indian roads.) Martin invited me to stand in for him
when he was on leave and it suited me very well. After a while Martin was
posted abroad and, to my delight, I was offered the position on a permanent
basis. Shortly thereafter I was moved from the PUS's Private Office to the
Western Department, to be what the Americans describe as Desk Officer for
France. Moley's valediction to me ran thus: 'The Diplomatic Service is like
the London Underground system. You can either choose to be on the Inner
Circle Line, and revolve round the Foreign Office, Western Europe and
Washington or you can step on to the Bakerloo Line, and hurtle from Rio de
Janeiro to Tokyo. I advise the former. Also do remember that it is unwise to
learn an exotic language. You may be very proud of your mastery of Japanese
or Arabic but where do you think you will spend your days?' He wasn't quite
right about the languages, but I took the hint.

Life at the Resident Clerkery was lived at a brisk pace. Our regime was for
each of the three Resident Clerks to be on duty for a week, taking over when

the Office closed until working hours the next morning, while doing his ordinary work by day. His two colleagues took one night each off his shoulders.

This was an admirable system when the pace of international life was slower, but it became distinctly onerous with the post-1945 feverish series of negotiations, trade agreements and much else. The rule was that the Resident Clerk had to be awakened for any incoming telegram of top priority, then styled 'Most Immediate' and subsequently rechristened 'Emergency' to slow down the impetuosity of the despatchers. The system was well understood by Embassies and rarely misused. Not so for the odds and ends of delegations from the Board of Trade, Ministries of Food, Labour, Fuel, etc., who seemed to seek to magnify the importance of their tasks by adding a breathless urgency to their communications.

On being awoken at two in the morning by a telegram beginning 'Most Immediate. Tomato Pulp', I had had enough. I telephoned the Permanent Secretary of the Department concerned at his home (in Esher, I think). I told him that there was a 'Most Immediate' telegram for his Department. I didn't understand the urgency, but then I didn't understand the ins and outs of tomato pulp. No, I couldn't read it to him over an open line: it was headed Confidential. Had he got a scrambler telephone? No? Well, in that case someone would have to come in and read it. No more 'Most Immediates', from that source at least.

Night communications were not always trivial. One arrived about ten o'clock from General Airey, the Commander of the British and American forces in the Trieste area, where the Yugoslavs were claiming Italian Venezia Julia, having been stopped from collaring it in 1945 only by the prompt action of General Freyberg, the New Zealand VC. The telegram was brief and said that there was reason to believe that the Jugs might molest the disputed territory that night.

The Resident Clerks had a so-called 'War Book' with procedures to be carried out in many different situations. We maintained that we kept it so up to date that it opened at the right page if you showed it the newspaper headlines. The correct course in the present juncture was perfectly clear. Copies of the telegram went immediately to the Service Departments, Prime Minister, Foreign Secretary, some Embassies abroad, etc., and meanwhile I telephoned them on a truly excellent telephone system designed for just such emergency purposes. Ernest Bevin was asleep. I read the telegram to him over the scrambler. He said: 'Well, I won't 'ave it,' and hung up. I pondered my next move. A telephone call to Tito?

'Marshal Tito? This is Anthony Montague Browne. Yes, I know you don't know who I am, but Mr Bevin says he won't 'ave it.' It didn't sound a good idea, but I was relieved from any decision by Bevin, who had merely been reflecting, ringing back with cogent instructions.

Mr Attlee's reaction was different. 'This telegram from Airey. Am I expected to take any action?' One saw what he meant of course, but I did reflect that, say, Winston Churchill would have phrased it differently.

The crisis blew over: I was told, though on what authority I know not, that the hero who had prevented the incident overlipping the brink of war was a US lieutenant from a Southern State. It was said that he had been awoken, at the barber's-pole frontier barrier that he was guarding, by the rumble of tanks. He had grumpily confronted the lead tank's Commander, who spoke English, and told him to eff off or he would open fire. He had only a light machine gun and some fifteen men, but the Jugs' orders were apparently not to shed Allied blood and to push ahead only if there was no resistance. The American South had the reputation for producing the soldiers with the most guts ('I viscera in Dixie'?). I don't know if this one was very brave, very well-informed or just plain stupid. But he succeeded in forcing the Jugs to retreat.

After-duty oddities were often thrown at us in the Resident Clerkery. They varied from tragic to funny. One night an unfortunate woman was put on to me because she refused to speak to the duty consular officer. (We were supposed to be political.) She said that her daughter had eloped with a Swiss lover. They had gone to Geneva and had both committed suicide, leaving a note beseeching that they should be buried together. The mother said that I was to contact the Swiss authorities and prevent this. I proffered the Consul-General in Geneva. He was summarily rejected. I explained that I didn't think we had the power to issue such instructions to the Swiss authorities. In any case would it not be Christian to grant the pathetic lovers their last wishes? No, and would I please stop laughing. I wasn't laughing, but had a hacking cough which was misinterpreted. It was heartbreaking.

The Resident Clerks' quarters adjoined the flat roof of that part of the Foreign Office. I managed to get a very long telephone extension so that I could sit on the roof and sunbathe at weekends. One day a very grand Admiral rang from his office across Horse Guards Parade. He was friendly and expansive. 'I suppose that you, like me, are cooped up in a stuffy office on this beautiful day?' he enquired kindly. 'On the contrary,' I said, 'I am nude, I am on the Foreign Office roof and I'm covered in soot.' He hung up.

My companions in the two years I spent as a Resident Clerk were all agreeable and some became close friends. There was Donald Maitland, a very small, very able, very ambitious Scot. He subsequently became Press Secretary to Ted Heath, Permanent Representative at the United Nations and many other important things. I seem to remember that he had been bayoneted in the leg by a Japanese Imperial Guard in Burma. Given their relative sizes, it must have been a terrifying experience. Anyway, he got an MC.

Another Scot, although of a totally different kind both physically and by nature, was Gordon Campbell. He looked what he had been, a first-class Regular Army officer and a Gunner. He had fought a most gallant war, won an MC and Bar and been severely wounded, leaving him in pain a good deal of the time and partially disabled. This did not stop him from being both remarkably efficient and the most jolly and humorous of companions. When he married the attractive and intelligent Nicola Madden, who worked in the

Foreign Office, I was his best man and made a terrible botch of it. Gordon left the Diplomatic Service and went into politics, rising to be Secretary of State for Scotland before going to the Lords.

I owe Gordon various debts of gratitude. Not the least was his introducing me to Noel Arnold Wallinger, who became my first wife. Noel (Nonie: her father had been a planter in Sumatra and the word meant 'little girl') was an ace physiotherapist and was treating Gordon at Westminster Hospital. She was and is a very dear person, and although we parted in 1970 she remains a close and treasured friend and bore me a daughter who is a great happiness.

Peter Stephens was the third of us. He had wonderfully good taste and a beautiful house in Dorset. We added to the Ministry of Works furniture of our flats with bits of our own. Actually the government furniture wasn't at all bad. Peter had Pitt the Younger's desk. I had a truly enormous bed from Hampton Court, with a petit-point head. When Aliki Russell, the wife of my Western Department colleague John Russell, saw it, she exclaimed: 'Mais Anthony, ce n'est pas un lit. C'est un champ de bataille!'* I could see Piccadilly Circus while lying in it, and used to give myself an extra few minutes' rest in the morning while counting the changes of the traffic lights in Lower Regent Street.

Peter had some beautiful Chinese silk cushions. One evening he was cooking himself some exotic sausages when he was distracted by the telephone and a sequence of consequential actions. He forgot the sausages, which were in the oven with a hot gas flame and the door open. Through some strange chemical process which none of us, least of all Peter, understood, the sausages inflated like little balloons, floated out of the oven, wafted on the breeze into his sitting room, and burst on his cushions like fire-ships.

The three of us were looked after by an elderly housekeeper, employed by ourselves rather than the Foreign Office. She was, she said, a retired Gaiety Girl, which, if true, was proof of outstanding longevity. Her cooking was erratic, varying with alcohol intake. (Hers, not ours, though undoubtedly based on our beverages.) She also loved animals and looked after the official mouser named Tiger. Tiger's remuneration from the Treasury was one shilling and threepence a week. He was a long-haired Persian and careless of his appearance. One summer evening three of us, though I can't remember who else was present other than Peter Stephens, were dining together. This was unusual, and so was the food: turbot with anchovy sauce. Tiger sauntered in. One of my colleagues addressed him: 'Tiger, you are a disgrace. They say that to clean a cat you should throw dirt on it. Try this, so that your ablutions will be a pleasure as well as a duty,' with which he poured a large spoon of warm anchovy sauce over Tiger's hindquarters. With a glare of outrage, Tiger sprang out of the window. This was on the third floor, and we were aghast. We flew to the window. The first to reach it leaned out over the low sill. The rug on which he stood slipped on the polished floor and he started to topple beyond his centre of gravity. The second of us grabbed him

* 'Anthony, it isn't a bed, it is a battlefield.'

by the waist. The carpet slipped further and he started to go too. I grabbed him by the legs and we all fell back in a confused heap on to the floor. There was a long, dumbfounded silence. Tiger, who had merely jumped on to a pigeon-stalking ledge, re-entered the room and started to lick himself nonchalantly.

This was about the time that Jan Masaryk, the Czech Foreign Minister, had either been thrown or jumped to his death from a Foreign Ministry window in Prague. All sorts of macabre stories were told, and most supported the theory of assassination, for the Russians had recently organised a coup in Czechoslovakia and had supplanted the legitimate regime with a cruel and ice-cold Communist tyranny. I am personally convinced that it was suicide, for I had seen a letter from Masaryk to his beloved English mistress, in which he talked of his misery and shame, and accused himself of having been responsible for the atmosphere in which the coup could take place.

But think what an enduring mystery our ludicrous little incident could have created! Three healthy, happy young diplomats throw anchovy sauce over their cat, then bale out of the Foreign Office window like a string of sausages. The *Marie Celeste* would have been as nothing.

A previous Foreign Office cat had been less lucky. Outside my flat door on the third floor were row upon row of archives. I used to pull the more promising ones out and peruse them. One was entitled 'Cases of Morals of China Consuls 1870–1890'. The things some of those Consuls had got up to were unbelievable. Krafft-Ebing simply would not have credited them. But one's sympathy for the perpetrators was restored by the coldly contemptuous letters of dismissal they received from London, sometimes leaving them semi-destitute in the middle of China. Next to the record of the China Consuls' shenanigans was a bulky file entitled 'Lunatics, Marriages, Deportations' (were they sequentially connected?) and behind lay a mummified cat. Poor puss, what a strange place to die.

We were allowed, within the limits of security that would today seem incredibly lax, to treat our flats as our own homes, and to entertain accordingly. It was left to the individual's discretion to whom and how entertainment was offered. It was nevertheless embarrassing for lady visitors to have to run the gauntlet of the elderly messengers and guards in the main entrance. I earned my colleagues' gratitude by obtaining for us keys to the Park Door, a small entrance with a lift (and in those days no guard) at the foot of Downing Street steps.

This initiative nearly ended in tears. On a winter Saturday afternoon, I had brought in a friend for a chaste rendezvous of tea and home-made scones. There was a builder's hole in the wall into the old India Office library. It was vast, labyrinthine, musty, full of intriguing pictures, tapestries and statues, and totally deserted. We were fascinated until all the lights failed. We groped in vain in the faintly spiced darkness, bumping into things. Then sat down and waited. No-one came, because no-one knew we were there. An hour passed. My companion became uneasy. Suddenly she giggled. God, she's getting hysterics, I thought. Then she said, 'I've just remembered, I've got my cigarette lighter.' So, with the aid of spills from long unemptied waste-paper baskets, we found our way back to the hole in the wall.

An old messenger told that when Curzon was Foreign Secretary, he insisted on the Park Door lift being for his sole use. A large printed card announced 'Reserved for the Secretary of State'. T.E. Lawrence (of Arabia) came frequently to the Foreign Office at that time. He invariably carried off the card. 'They just thought it was one of Colonel Lawrence's little ways,' the old messenger said, 'but they did wonder why he wanted them.' Later someone enlightened them. Curzon had been invited to spend the weekend at an Oxford College of which Lawrence was a Fellow (All Souls?). All the lavatories in those days were built in a long line, like chicken coops. Curzon was not particularly amused to find, nailed to every door: 'Reserved for the Secretary of State'.

I have dwelt at some length on the Resident Clerkery, but it was great fun and gave one an unequalled insight into the workings of the Office. It also gave one an unhealthily arrogant illusion of power, unfitting in anybody and especially in the young. For instance, I was confronted late at night by a quite well-known figure who had lost his passport. He wanted to go immediately to Strasbourg to apply for the job as Information Officer of the Council of Europe. I thought that it was in our interest that he should do so, and gave him an improvised manuscript passport on a sheet of Office paper, stamped it, and told him he must return it immediately he got a real passport in Strasbourg. It worked, and he didn't.

I have harped on my absent-mindedness and it did indeed lead me into a truly awful situation. It was Bevin's custom to have a despatch box left with the Resident Clerk when he went away for the weekend. During Saturday and Sunday it filled up and was then taken to him at the Foreign Secretary's official residence in Carlton Gardens. The duty Resident Clerk was supposed to look through the papers, especially Foreign Office ones, and add any relevant developments.

That Sunday afternoon, I was electrified to find a file relating to the manufacturing of Britain's first atomic bomb. This was the deadliest of secrets. Although huge sums were being spent on it, at Harwell and Aldermaston, it had never been announced and would have been, so to speak, dynamite to the left wing of the Labour Party, who in any case hated Bevin for his patriotism. I read the file with fascination and enthusiasm. After all, it was Britain who had taken the first steps on practical research and development, and moralise how one may, the possession of the nuclear weapon was the key to peace or war.

The later development had of course gone to the United States, as the so-called Manhattan Project. (Our work was styled Tube Alloys.) We had given the USA all our secrets so that progress could be made without danger of bombing and with facilities of siting, electrical power and skilled technicians that wartime Britain could only with difficulty have provided. Under the Churchill–Roosevelt Quebec Agreement, we had agreed to share nuclear secrets, and not to use the weapon without the other party's assent. The Truman administration had wheedled, or bought, our Labour Government out of this contract. (I will revert to this later.)

Later that afternoon Bevin telephoned from the Isle of Wight. He had just heard that Hector McNeil (the Minister of State, Bevin's number two) had let off a speech in his Greenock constituency in which he claimed that America's aid to our economic recovery was unnecessary. Bevin was furious. 'That silly man 'Ector,' he kept repeating, 'find him and tell him from me 'e's a silly man and when you've done that, be a good boy and sort out my box and send it over to Carlton Gardens.' I located McNeil in a Greenock pub and gave him the message, with which I entirely agreed, unadulterated. He was perturbed but did not hang the messenger.

I went back to sort the contents of the despatch box. A pang like an electric shock went through me and I felt physically sick. The nuclear file had vanished. Frantically I sorted the papers again. Nothing. Nowhere in the room was it visible: not under the chairs, not on the bookshelves, not on my desk or in the drawers. Could it have blown out of the window on to Horse Guards Parade? No, it was too heavy.

I had had only two visitors, an official from the Treasury and another from the Ministry of Labour, both bringing Cabinet papers for Bevin. It could only have been one of them, and no doubt the nuclear papers were now in the Soviet Embassy. But I never left secret papers in the open . . . Dripping with sweat, I contemplated my contemptible position. I had been careless once too often. Instant and ignominious dismissal from the Diplomatic Service was the least I could expect. A prison sentence under the Official Secrets Act was not impossible. My poor parents . . .

I mixed myself a huge dry Martini and dialled the Security Service (MI5). As I did so I sank into my deep sofa. (I had distinct difficulty in standing up.) There was a crackle of paper. Under the cushions were the nuclear papers, put there to conceal them from the visitors' eyes. I managed to hang up before MI5 answered.

When the Secretary of State reached London he rang for his box. No messenger was immediately available, so I took it over myself. Bevin wanted to know how his message to McNeil had gone. I told him. He gave me a drink and said kindly: 'You don't look very well. You young men should take more exercise.' I could only weakly agree with both propositions.

Although my personal contacts with Ernest Bevin were few, I was left with a lasting impression of a steadfast, patriotic, brave, sensible and humane personality. I once asked Winston Churchill what he would have done if the Germans had secured a landing in southern England in 1940–41. He said that as a last resort he would have tried to establish a line on the River Thames, though he had little hope of it holding. What about Government, I enquired? WSC replied that he would have ruled with a triumvirate: himself, Bevin and Beaverbrook. I reflected that this would indeed have been a formidable troika, except that two of the horses hated each other.

My last memory of Bevin was, strangely, from a night club. The Resident Clerk on duty was allowed 'to dine in his club as long as it was rapidly accessible to the Foreign Office and he could be readily reached by telephone'. The atmosphere in which this had been written was clearly pre–1939, but on this occasion I interpreted it literally, and took a girl to the Astor, in Hamilton Place, a few yards from Hyde Park Corner. I left its telephone number with the ultra-reliable and friendly night telephone operators, all experienced men. I was however rather disconcerted to see a waiter unwinding to our table a long cord with a white telephone on the end. Surely this only happened in Hollywood films? The voice of the Foreign Office operator was a little strained: 'The Secretary of State is on the line, sir. I told him you would ring him back, but he wants to speak to you now and I'm putting him through.' A well-known voice came dimly through the crashing of Edmundo Ros's rumba drums. 'Oh, do turn that gramophone off. I can 'ardly 'ear myself think.' I've forgotten what his requirement was, but it was easily dealt with. I paid the bill, caught a cab, and in those days of petrol rationing and empty streets was back at the Office in under ten minutes. Sadly, sans girl.

So much for the Resident Clerkery. A happy time.

Chapter 8

———— ❧ ————

DEALING WITH France at my rank was not a particularly important task. Any policy decisions were obviously made at a much
higher level and the advice also originated there. The theoretical
mechanism of policy-making started with recommendations at the bottom,
based on Embassy reports, inter-office and inter-Whitehall consultations
and working up the ladder via the Head of Department, the supervising
Under-Secretary, to the Permanent Under-Secretary of State or his
Deputy, whence, if significant enough, they went on to Ministers or even the
Cabinet. But this mechanism was much too slow and too cumbersome, and
also rested at base on junior and inexperienced officials, so that except for
routine business it was invariably short-circuited. Thus my activities were
diminished from the lofty matters of the PUS's Office and I was no longer
able to give myself the airs and graces of one in the know and the conduit of
significant exchanges between great personalities.

On the plus side I was for the first time at the coal-face, and the despatches
and telegrams dealing with the internal situation in France did arrive on my
desk as their first destination for comment. Here arose the dangerous temptation to pontificate from a void, but I had read Cardinal Manning's dictum
on Lord Acton: 'He has all the inflation of a German professor and the
ruthless talk of an undergraduate,' and managed to restrain myself and
absolve my seniors from the humiliating necessity of pasting over my observations, consigning me and my views to oblivion in the style of the unperson
and the memory-hole of George Orwell's *1984*.

Other advantages lay in dealing with the mass of small inter-governmen-
tal matters which could blow up into a storm. An unlikely incident was the
row British pigeon fanciers got into with the French Ministry of Agricul-
ture. The former had mistranslated a pedantic letter from the latter into a
bizarre series of insults to which they had taken extreme exception and had
invoked the assistance of a semi-literate Member of Parliament, who
jumped on his xenophobic hobby-horse and rode off into confusion. I
enjoyed settling that.

A more serious case was the gun-tunnel affair. The wartime Germans had
dug out a huge slanting tunnel in the chalk of the Pas de Calais. It was
designed to house a smooth-barrelled gun of immense length which could
propel a rapid fire of eight-inch shells. The tunnel pointed at London and if
it had had time to work before we over-ran it, and if the gun itself had lived
up to expectations, it would have made life in the capital distinctly uncom-

fortable (anticipating the Iraqi 'super-gun' of 1990). Our military concluded that the tunnel and its satellite underground chambers consituted a threat, if the Russians should ever over-run France, which did not seem unlikely at that time. So we asked the French to blow it up. They declined, as it was serving a quite useful purpose for storage, or for growing mushrooms, or something. Hard words were exchanged. Our military thought that there was something sinister in the French obstinacy and that the FO were wet not to do something more effective. I disagreed with the former view as an absurdity but sympathised with the latter, and therefore sneaked to a friend in the press. His paper published photographs and the French, who really did not attach that much importance to the matter, let the tunnel cave in to avoid a public dispute.

During this period the Channel Tunnel made one of its periodical appearances on the agenda and many Government Departments were asked to comment. One of the objectors was the Home Office, which, among other points, suggested that the Tunnel would be undesirable as it would facilitate the entry of continental ladies of the night into our pure capital. I never was able to find out if this was serious or some way-out joke by that usually constipated Department of State.

These and more mundane activities took place in what was called the Third Room, where the junior diplomatists sat in a convival but untidy and uncomfortable huddle. There were about six of us and it was jolly. One of my senior companions was Neil Hogg, Quintin Hailsham's younger brother. He had an outstanding talent for light verse, often bawdy and always funny. I hope he will forgive the plagiarism of the only piece I can remember. Neil had been to a party given by a very old White Russian princess. She had inveighed against the immorality of Stalinist society and said of modern Russian girls: 'They do it for a piece of cheese.' Of course she was wildly off-beam, the contemporary Russians being of an excessive and pedantic sexual morality, but Neil made of her observation the foundation stone of a ballade, the recurring punch-line being 'They do it for a piece of cheese.' The Envoi ran:

> So shipman fill thy argosie
> With Stilton, Wensleydale and Brie,
> And haste to snowy Muscovie:
> They do it for a piece of cheese.

The deputy head of Western Department was the memorable, delightful and totally original John Russell. An eccentric ceases to be an eccentric if he believes that he is eccentric, and John was just on the safe side of that border-line. He was the son of Russell Pasha, the celebrated head of the Egyptian police. (He claimed at one point that as the son of a Pasha was a Bey, then that was the correct style in which to address him.) He was married to Aliki, a striking figure who had been elected Miss Europe in a Parisian beauty competition. She had been in the audience, and when Miss Greece failed to turn up Aliki had volunteered for the position and won by acclaim. I enjoyed their friendship for many years, and John was as effective in diplomacy as he was colourful socially.

When the early and very secret Atlantic Pact discussions were going on, Sir Stafford Cripps, the Labour Chancellor of the Exchequer, presided over a Whitehall meeting to discuss the costs of the probable infrastructure. John had served under Cripps when he was our wartime Ambassador in Moscow and was not awed by his chilly and intellectually rarefied demeanour. (WSC used to refer to him as 'Stifford Crapps' and once remarked 'There, but for the Grace of God, goes God.')

The meeting, on a hot afternoon in the old India Office, droned on and on. John and I, with a measurable gap between us, were the junior Foreign Office representatives. I was puzzled and then electrified by John's actions. He unbuttoned the left sleeve of his jacket. (Being from a good tailor it did unbutton.) He then undid his cuff-links and rolled up both sleeves. By now all eyes were on him. He then produced a plastic pig of lighter fuel, bit off the end and poured it into his mouth, provoking a startled exclamation of: 'Christ, does he drink that stuff?' Unperturbed, he held his cigarette lighter at arm's length, ignited it, and blew a ball of flame across the room. It singed the hairs of his bare forearm, and, elongating and swirling like a nuclear cloud, went up into the dome of the high room and made a black mark on the ceiling. There was a stunned silence. Stafford Cripps merely said 'Really, John,' and proceeded with the meeting. I warmed to him from that moment. What was it Hemingway said, 'Grace under pressure'?

John left a train of anecdotes in his wake, all improbable and all true. When Ambassador in Tehran he rode his horse into the dining room. When in Addis Ababa he hired a witch doctor to avert rain from a Royal picnic, and put it down on his expenses. The Foreign Office declined to pay, so John altered the item to 'Meteorological Forecast Assistance' and the Office sullenly forked out.

Our departmental boss was Moore Crosthwaite, a dessicated bachelor but agreeable and competent. Above him came Ivone Kirkpatrick, the Assistant Under-Secretary of State, who was later to become Head of the Service. One obituary described him as a 'discreet, witty man, who rode well to hounds'. He was a good deal more than that. He had rendered great service in the First World War, running agents into the Low Countries. Small, neat, bright-eyed, he radiated efficiency and contempt for those who did not come up to his own very high standards. I held him in the highest regard for his dedication and patriotism. Sadly, this was not reciprocated.

At the time I was dealing in the greatest secrecy at the lowest level with an enormous volume of new problems arising from the military and security aspects of the Brussels Treaty. Faute de mieux, matters of considerable importance landed on my desk and I was labouring from first light until the duties of the Resident Clerk took me to my flat, where work continued until late at night, interrupted by telephone calls and minor night emergencies. The stress, long hours and poor food of the strictly rationed era had given me, at the age of twenty-five, a duodenal ulcer and a temper to match it. One evening I received a billet-doux from Kirkpatrick. It ran: 'Mr Montague Browne. Unless you can increase the tempo of your work, I shall hesitate to entrust you with anything of importance.' This was too much. Incompetent I might be, but I was the fastest and most superficial worker I knew. I seized a half-dozen weighty files, marched into Kirkpatrick's room and delivered a petulant and coarsely worded harangue. Kirkpatrick listened without interruption. Then he said:

'Are you on duty in the Resident Clerkery tonight?'

'No'.

'Well, lock those files up and come and have dinner with me'. Ulcer or no, I went, and drank a good deal, and felt much better.

The hard work was leavened by side-lights of humour. Some of us kept a so-called Nonsense File, where we recorded the grosser absurdities. Mine has vanished and I can only find one or two fragments, mostly misprints or cyphering errors. One ambassadorial telegram began 'It must not appear that our policy in X is dictated by elfish reasons' (Moley noted sadly: 'It so often is'). When cypherers could not make sense of the groups of numbers in incoming telegrams they used the expression 'corrupt group', as in 'five corrupt groups'. Another telegram began 'My friends and I, one corrupt group ...' An ambassador's despatch concluded: 'The original of the Foreign Minister's letter is enclosed under flying seal' – and indeed it was, with a most lifelike winged sea-mammal in full colour on the envelope. A yellowed calling card announced that the owner was 'Nai Pridi Panomyong. Senior Statesman of Siam'. I had handed it to Moley, telling him that the gentleman in question wanted to see him urgently. Moley, deeply harrassed by events but retaining his eternal courtesy, looked up and said: 'But of course, Anthony, I'll see anyone with a fatuous title like that.'

The strategic backdrop to our more serious affairs was, as I have already indicated, our attempts to shore up ruined, demoralised, fractionalised Western Europe against Soviet aggression or subversion. A peculiar by-play at the time was an informal approach from the Netherlands and Belgium to join the British Commonwealth. It was tentative and delicate, but I think genuine enough. It was supposedly inspired by the Regent of Belgium, Prince Charles and his altogether admirable friend and counsellor André de Staercke, but it never came to anything. It is intriguing to speculate on the results if it had been otherwise.

The first of the formal steps to what was then loosely defined as Western Union was the Dunkirk Treaty, which bound Britain and France to assist each other in the event of war. Then came the Brussels Treaty, of wider scope both economically and socially, but essentially a military pact of mutual support. This was signed by ourselves, France, the Netherlands, Belgium and Luxembourg and provided inter alia for the setting up of a Permanent Commission in London to implement and further its aims. (The name caused a certain amount of argument. The French had originally suggested 'The Designated Instrument' or the 'Standing Organ of the Treaty'. Unfortunate.) It was the Dutch who provided the Commission's first Secretary-

General. He was called Starr-Bussman. Gladwyn commented that he sounded like a new variety of shrub and someone unkindly added that if he was indeed the star, what could the rest of the transport company be like? In fact he was a conscientious albeit rather dull functionary who took himself too seriously and ultimately became, I believe, a judge at the International Court. It was unlucky that one of the first documents issued by the organisation was misprinted as from 'The Brussels Treaty Permanent Omission'.

A curious episode somewhat marred my relations with the Dutch. A large reception for the Brussels Treaty powers was being given at the Secretary of State's house in Carlton Gardens. The Dutch Embassy telephoned and asked if a new Second Secretary, who was Indonesian, could be added to those already invited. The Dutch at the time were quite reasonably resentful of the efforts of the United Nations, led by the United States, to oust them from their East Indies empire. (They had been even more angry, and with ample reason, at our failure to follow up the Japanese surrender in 1945 with the removal of the Japanese-installed puppet government in Indonesia, who were still holding Dutch prisoners in foul conditions.) It was presumed that the production of an Indonesian Dutch diplomat was an effort to emphasise the continuing imperial links. Be that as it may, I readily agreed to the additional guest and informed the Government Hospitality Department. They reacted with dismay; it appeared that the Ministry of Works had informed them that the floor at Carlton Gardens was totally insecure. The safe maximum had already been substantially exceeded and not one guest more could be included. I somewhat lamely passed on this unlikely explanation to the Dutch, and with many apologies withdrew the invitation. A little later I was summoned to see Hector McNeil, the Minister of State, who told me that the Dutch had complained that I was a racist. McNeil accepted my improbable explanation with a chuckle and I heard no more.

The Western Department had spawned a new semi-independent entity to deal with Western Union and the hoped-for American alliance. It was called the Western Union Secretariat and originally consisted of John Russell and myself. Then Michael Rose took over from Russell and Evelyn Shuckburgh became the head of the Western Department. They were very different personalities. Michael was charming, able and modest. He suffered the disadvantage of looking dramatically fit and bronzed while patiently putting up with perpetual ill-health. We both had duodenal ulcers, and we both sipped milk from thermoses. I nibbled rather nasty biscuits and Michael ate slices of an equally nasty cake. The treatment did neither of us any good. (I only started to get better a couple of years later in Paris. My thermos of milk flew from the back of my car when I was rammed in the Bois de Boulogne and smashed on the back of my head. I abandoned the milk habit in disgust, ate and drank immoderately and rapidly improved. But perhaps it was the more relaxed tempo of work.)

I got on well with Michael and enjoyed working with him, but as is the nature of the young, and especially me, I took too much on myself in the way of unilateral and unadvised decisions. Michael finally said: 'Anthony, you are dragging the whole Department behind you like tin-cans on a dog's tail. It won't do.' This was as near a crushing rebuke as you got in the Diplomatic Service of those days, and at the age of twenty-five I took the hint.

Evelyn Shuckburgh was different. When I first met him, I had a sense of déjà vu. Then it dawned on me. He bore a striking resemblance to an actor, Edward Everett Horton, with an admirable comic talent. As we all know, there is nothing wrong with movie actors, but the parallel was unfortunate and made it difficult for me, to my own loss, to take him at his true value. When my duodenal ulcer (I don't want to harp on the damn thing, but it was central in my life at the time) took me to hospital and home, Evelyn seemed more vexed at the disturbance to his staffing arrangements than sympathetic to my misfortune.

Evelyn later became private secretary to Anthony Eden, an appointment that ended in tears, not I think because of any particular temperamental differences between the two, although Eden did become increasingly and dangerously petulant as his health deteriorated, but rather because Evelyn's instinctively liberal and anti-'Realpolitik' outlook rendered him unsuitable to deal with an area of brutal realism – the Middle East.

However these things may be, I never doubted Shuckburgh's integrity and the dedication of his work earlier on the all-important North Atlantic Treaty.

The North Atlantic Treaty was signed in April 1949. Its eventual participants consisted of the Brussels Treaty signatories (Britain, France, the Netherlands, Belgium and Luxembourg) plus Italy, Portugal, Norway, Denmark, Iceland, Canada and, above all, the United States. It is impossible to over-estimate the importance of this event. It saved the world from East–West war, which otherwise would have been, if not inevitable, at least highly likely. It confronted the Soviet Union with the certainty, rather than the possibility, of a massive Allied counter-stroke, including American nuclear weapons, in the event of aggression. It is probable that without it the Kremlin, with its overwhelming superiority of ground forces, would have been tempted into adventurism. Calculations at that time were that in the event of a Soviet attack, the Red Army would be on the Pyrenees in fifty-six days maximum.

The preceding negotiations had been lengthy and delicate. With hindsight it is a wonder that security was so good, with so many parties involved. Some of the additional countries, joining the Brussels Treaty five, were most anxious to come under the North Atlantic Treaty umbrella. Italy was one of these. Others were a little coy and feared both Soviet wrath and internal trouble with their Communist Parties. I can only remember fragments of these events.

We had at the time an excellent, calm and modest Ambassador in Portugal, Sir Nigel Ronald. He approached Dr Salazar, who was running the country in a forceful and effective way, and put to him briefly and clearly the arguments in favour of his acceding to the Treaty. He reported on his conversation with characteristic brevity. The cyphered telegram went something like this: 'I approached Dr Salazar and spoke according to my instructions. After some exchanges His Excellency said that he was (corrupt group)ed.' We pondered this. Could it be 'delighted', 'astounded' or even 'horrified'? There was a hiatus in communication for some twelve hours until confirmation arrived that all was well.

Nigel Ronald was an unusual Ambassador. Most ambassadorial reports conveyed an impression of the envoy standing over the quailing foreign dignitary, devastating him with the overwhelming logic of his argument. Ronald once sent a despatch, describing his exchanges with a Foreign Minister. It ended: 'At this point I should of course have deployed the points in Foreign Office telegram so-and-so, but this did not occur to me until I was on my way back to the Embassy.' Most refreshing.

While these successful but relatively peripheral endeavours to corral useful adherents to the North Atlantic Treaty were proceeding, the far more important core of negotiation lay in Washington. Secrecy was vital. Although the American administration, including in particular General Marshall (the Secretary of State) and the President himself, was in favour of concluding the Treaty, the opposition could have been formidable in the event of a leak. We were potentially confronted by the American Isolationists, a powerful group in both Republicans and, rather less so, Democrats, and also by the unregenerate left and self-styled liberals who still professed to believe in the ultimate benevolence of Soviet Russia and international Communism. (And in Europe, of course, the left would have screamed blue murder.) Congress still had the right to reject any Treaty, but it was rightly believed to be less likely to do so after the event, and after the administration had had time to lobby and persuade.

As it happened, and to universal astonishment, there was only one leak, to an unfriendly Chicago journalist from, apparently, the Belgians. No-one could make much logical sense of this and it actually did little harm, being both inaccurate and within only a few days of the public announcement of the negotiations.

The final step was a meeting of the Brussels Treaty powers in Paris. Our delegation was small. Other than Ernest Bevin and his staff, it consisted of Jebb, Shuckburgh, Rose, George Mallaby (the amiable and able Assistant Secretary of the Cabinet) and myself. We travelled to Paris in some style on the Golden Arrow. I made friends with the Secretary of State's two Special Branch bodyguards. Even in those days, their job was no sinecure. The Irgun Zvei Leumi, the Jewish terrorist organisation, had Ernest Bevin as a prime target. They had already demonstrated their gratitude to Britain by murdering many British soldiers and Civil Servants in Palestine. Of course the traumatic effects of the Holocaust could not be forgotten, but there seemed a certain lack of chic in killing by the most treacherous methods British soldiers and civilians who had, by our declaration of war in 1939, been the means of saving the remains of European Jewry from the death camps. Winston Churchill was a noted supporter of Zionism, and I will come to his views on these matters later.

The two Special Branch men each had their particular forensic expertise, quite apart from protection. One had a deep knowledge of the detection of false diamonds. He kindly imparted it to me, but I have not yet had occasion to use it. The second knew all about abortions, then a serious back-street crime, but I couldn't stomach even his matter-of-fact account.

The ostensible purpose of the Conference was a routine Brussels Treaty meeting and the Embassy had not been fully briefed on the North Atlantic Treaty aspects. The Brussels Treaty items of the agenda were briskly dismissed. When it came to the 'Social, Cultural and Economic Questions', the Secretary of State said laconically: 'I delegate Mr Gladwyn Jebb to deal with these.' Gladwyn said: 'And I delegate Mr Montague Browne to deal with these matters.' He could go no lower. He wanted Evelyn Shuckburgh and Michael Rose to be with him at the main meetings.

Thus I found myself disposing of complications that were to take the EEC many years to consider. (Actually what we decided was not of the slightest importance, although in theory we were dealing with the equivalence of medical qualifications, insurance, and all sorts of major trade and economic questions.) Our junior sub-meeting was chaired by the admirable, distinguished and lovable Gérard André. Gérard had escaped from Occupied France and, enduring difficulties and perils, had eventually reached London. He was accredited to the French Embassy as a Third Secretary, and remained in London without a break for many years. Then, having risen progressively to the rank of Minister, he was transferred to be French Ambassador in Finland.

Gérard should have been Ambassador in London, for which position he was eminently suited. The staunchest of French patriots, he knew and understood Britain better than any Frenchman I can remember. Additionally he was persona grata with General de Gaulle (jolly difficult), to whom Gérard always referred to as Bonnie Prince Charlie, and with Marshal Lattre de Tassigny (ditto). But the Quai d'Orsay, the French Foreign Office, was not entirely free of intrigue and malice. Rather a waste of a devoted and brilliant servant of France and friend of Britain.

Gérard and I (for in those days Britain and France, in that sequence, were very much head of the European pecking-order) disposed of our agenda summarily, and hastened to rejoin the main Conference. I sometimes wonder what would have been the outcome if our peremptory decisions had been enforced? A great deal more successful than some of those of the EEC bureaucracy, I like to think.

The Conference went ahead with exemplary despatch. By the day's end the only item left was to agree identical communications to the State Department to be despatched via the five Embassies in Washington. These were to propose formally the conclusion of a treaty of mutual assistance, including, if necessary, the use of military force, and the Americans were obviously fully prepared for their reception and publication, together with their affirmative reply.

We adjourned for dinner at the Embassy. Oliver Harvey, our Ambassador, had, with his usual kindness, included the lowest end of our delegation and it was a jolly and relaxed party, with success in sight. Fragments of the conversation linger in my memory. Ernest Bevin, a Bristol man, broke a brief silence.

'I see a man has been arrested in the Cheddar caves for stealing stalakites. That's very wrong. Stalakites take 'undreds of years to grow.'

The table pondered the undoubted truth of this statement. Then someone mischievously enquired: 'Secretary of State, are stalakites the ones that come down from the ceiling, or the ones that grow up from the floor?'

Bevin also offered the company an esoteric piece of advice. 'If you are addressing a hostile audience of the Boilermakers' Union,' he said, 'You should lower your voice. They are occupationally deaf and they have to listen carefully to hear what you are saying.' I think most of us reflected that we were comparatively unlikely to address hostile boilermakers and that they would probably throw things at us if we lowered our voices.

As Bevin sat in the Embassy hall, waiting for his car to return him to the Quai d'Orsay, I noticed that he seemed pale and preoccupied. I asked him if he was all right. 'Wind under my 'eart,' he replied briefly, 'Nothing to worry about.' But it was. The intense pace of his work was even then shortening his life.

At the Quai d'Orsay, we met in the 'Salle à manger du Ministre', an impressive and stately room. Round the wall were a number of pretty little Louis Quinze chairs, upholstered in silk. A very senior member of the French delegation, seeing that his shoelace was undone, plonked his foot down on one of the chairs to do it up. It was a wet night and his shoe was muddy. Was it just preoccupation, or was it an indication of his character? I never forgot it when I met him subsequently.

Numerous drafts and counter-drafts of the vital Washington telegrams were considered; finally agreement was reached and we returned to our own countries. The telegrams were to be despatched the following afternoon and the five Ambassadors were to call on General Marshall the next day.

On returning to London, I found myself duty Resident Clerk that evening. About ten o'clock I got an agitated telephone call from our Washington Embassy. When the five Ambassadors had met, prior to their next-day rendezvous with Marshall, it was discovered that the telegrams were not identical. The French text referred to 'concluding a Treaty in the Atlantic area' instead of 'the North Atlantic area'. This may seem a trivial difference, but it was a vital point over which there had been much debate. Algeria was deemed by the French to be part of metropolitan France; 'the Atlantic area' would include it in the Treaty, and the Americans would read it as supporting French colonialism. The whole apple-cart might be upset.

I telephoned the most senior official of our delegation that I could reach. His reaction was clear and specific: 'Get on the telephone to Couve de Murville or Roland de Margerie in Paris and sort it out fast. Don't go through our Embassy. They know nothing about it and it will be too slow.' Couve de Murville was then Directeur Politique (second-in-command) at the Quai d'Orsay. He was a Protestant, and an Inspecteur des Finances (Treasury official, approximately), both of which were unusual in the Quai d'Orsay. He was reputed to be anti-British, but he was singularly able and later became de Gaulle's Foreign Minister. He came from the Island of Réunion in the Indian Ocean, and was known to his juniors as 'Le nègre blanc'.* On that evening he was out, so I spoke to Roland de Margerie, the next senior man. Roland was a very different figure, highly intelligent, full of charm and a friend of Britain. He had suffered a difficult time in the War. When France fell in 1940 he was at the French Embassy in London. The Vichy regime ordered him to China. His heart lay in England but after an agonising debate he concluded that his distasteful duty was to obey his Head of State. This had damaged his subsequent career but his obvious integrity and ability prevailed. (His son, Bobby, became Ambassador in London.)

Roland's reaction was rapid: 'Merde! We sent the wrong draft. There is no trickery in this. It will be sorted out in fifteen minutes.' I informed the Most Senior Official at his London flat and retired to bed well satisfied with myself.

The next day the Gods punctured my self-esteem. I was in the office of the Most Senior Official when his telephone rang. It was a Senior Diplomat in our Paris Embassy and I could hear quite clearly what he was saying. He was furious. The Embassy had not only been left out of our negotiations but had been bypassed on a most important matter by the Resident Clerk's telephone call. (The Senior Diplomat had apparently met Roland de Margerie on another matter and the latter had apologised for the mix-up.) Oliver Harvey was meditating a formal protest to the Permanent Under-Secretary of State. What was the use of having an Embassy, etc. etc.?

The Most Senior Official spoke carefully: 'I am extremely sorry. It was an impulsive reaction by Anthony Montague Browne. He is very young and I will rebuke him severely.'

Now, I do understand that it may have been desirable to throw me to the wolves. The M.S.O. could have, should have, said: 'Look, it's far more important that I preserve good relations with the Embassy than it is for you. Oliver is not in the least vindictive and he won't hold it against you for long.' Quite true, too. But the M.S.O. didn't say anything at all. He just looked shifty.

* The white negro.

Chapter 9

I N N O V E M B E R 1949 I was posted to Paris, to be Third Secretary in the
Chancery (the political section). The Embassy was massively over-
staffed, but not by the Foreign Office, and both the Ambassador and the
Minister not infrequently complained of the extravagance and doubtful
value of all the extraneous attachments. There were of course the Service
Attachés – a Major General of the Army, a Naval Captain and an Air Vice
Marshal, all with their junior officers, their secretaries, their cars and so
forth. No-one really criticised this. They were traditional, and some of them
were of exceptional quality and did an excellent job, notably Beville Pain,
who became a lifelong friend. Then there was the Commercial Section,
some of them regular members of the Service and many not. Sadly, they
tended to be treated as second-class citizens. Ditto the Information (Press)
Office, but with fewer 'Regulars'. Its boss, an agreeable ex-schoolmaster,
Bill Marchant, who was subsequently to become Ambassador in Tunis,
summed it up thus: 'Being Information Officer in this Embassy is like
making love to an elephant. It's uphill work, you see no results for two
years,* and you're in grave danger of being sat on.'

But this was only the beginning, and moreover the visibly useful part.
Later came two Labour Attachés, with of course cars and secretaries. (I may
be wronging them, but I don't think they spoke much French.) Then two
Scientific Attachés, to whom much the same thing applied, and who seemed
reluctant to cover for one another during absences. I am sorry to say that the
list continues. There was a Coal Attaché. There was a Civil Air Attaché.
There was an Agricultural Attaché, a rather jolly fellow who did speak
French, but quite what he did I never found out. Then, of course, there was
the Consular Section, with a real and useful function; the Visa Section, to
which the same thing applied; the British Council, out on a separate limb;
and a large and helpful administrative staff to service this extraordinary
Noah's Ark. Poor, poor taxpayer . . .

We, in the Chancery, put our little noses in the air (well, some of us) and
considered ourselves the élite. And so we were in the Ambassador's eyes, if
only because there were rather few of us and we were all regular members of
the Service. Moreover, the Chancery was the traditional centre of the
Embassy's activities, going back to the days when there only was the Chancery in any Embassy.

* To be zoologically accurate, twenty-one months.

I have tended to be lucky both with my bosses and with my colleagues. Paris was no exception. The Head of Chancery, a Counsellor who ranked third in the hierarchy, was Sammy Hood. Sammy, Viscount Hood, was a descendant of one of Nelson's greatest sea captains. It was a source of sorrow to him that ill-health, eventually leading to early retirement and death, had prevented him serving in the wartime Navy. Very tall, very calm, he never lost his temper, never showed haste and dealt effectively with emergencies in a reassuringly detached way. He had the warmest of hearts and took a lot of trouble with the young, the shy and the impetuous. (I was only two of these.)

There were five of us subordinates and we divided the world among us, in the sense of matters to be discussed or negotiated with the French. I was given North Africa, including Tangier (then still an International City) and Egypt. It was a touchy area. The French were sensitive about Anglo-American intentions in Algeria, Morocco and Tunisia, and considered, with some justification, that sooner or later subversion in these territories would be fed by the Egyptians and Libyans. It is also fair to say that there still existed a certain number of Vichy sympathisers in the French Diplomatic Service. None of them had done anything disgraceful, but their former adherence and their injured pride did not make dealing with them any the easier. In particular they saw agents of 'L'Intelligence Service' behind every bush in North Africa.

One day I was discussing the future of Tangier with the responsible French official. After a while his telephone rang. He asked me to forgive him for a few minutes and left the room. He had left some documents on his desk. The top one, read upside down, was headed 'Très Secret'. I pondered. Had it been left so plainly visible to entice me to get up and read it? And did he then plan to pop in and catch me red-handed? Or was the content of the document purposely misleading? I remained stolidly in my chair, so I never found out. In all probability Monsieur X had no sinister intentions. But in that case he was singularly careless.

An encounter with a much younger French diplomat, with an impeccable wartime record, was very different. The British were in control of Libya at that time, and had restored the King of the Senussi, whom I was to meet later with WSC, to his throne. We most foolishly subsequently withdrew, of course. My opposite number spoke to an Embassy colleague with engaging candour. 'I am instructed to ask if the British Government will allow us to leave a caretaker for our military cemeteries in the Fezzan' (South Libya). The Free French forces had incurred casualties in the area in support of the Eighth Army, so my colleague replied that he had not the faintest doubt that our Government would agree.

'Of course you realise,' our friend went on, 'that the caretaker will be a spy. But he won't be a very good spy and his concern will not be with British activities.' I am glad to say that we did agree, but it soon became obvious that the caretaker was more interested in the (then vague) possibilities of an oilfield, as well as arms smuggling into Algeria, than in his legitimate business of the upkeep of the soldiers' graves in that lonely and barren place. As my friend had said, he wasn't a very good spy.

The Quai d'Orsay did not have a Resident Clerk system and it was rather a matter of luck whom you could reach out of working hours. One night I was telephoned at my flat from the Foreign Office. Our Locust Control people in the Sudan had spotted a large swarm in the desert. The locusts were in the crawler stage, and if sprayed at once, the swarm could be annihilated before it took wing. But the locusts lay in the French Sudan and the local authorities were hard to contact and excessively fussy. Time was very limited.

I telephoned the Quai d'Orsay, but could not raise anyone useful. The Huissier* who answered the telephone was helpful. Was the matter very important? Yes. Then he would get me someone who had just gone up to the library. I waited patiently and eventually a cultivated and courteous voice asked me my business. I explained. 'I will take care of it,' he said; 'your friends can cross the frontier,' and he hung up. Who could this be, I wondered, who could so airily take over the responsibilities of the Ministère de le France d'Outre-mer (the French Colonial Office), who were most jealous of their prerogatives? I rang back and asked the Huissier. 'That, Monsieur', he said, 'was the Minister of Foreign Affairs, Monsieur Robert Schuman.'

Robert Schuman was a great man. While remaining an astute, even cunning master of diplomacy and a devoted servant of his country, he had a statesman's broad view of the world and was among the first to take practical steps towards the eventual creation of the EEC. His private life was both austere and irreproachable, a most unusual situation among politicians of the Fourth Republic. He gave away a good deal of his meagre salary to religious charities, and spent his short holidays in retreat in a monastery.

In the Pacific we and the French exercised a system of condominium in the New Hebrides. It would have been much simpler for our respective Colonial Offices to have dealt directly with each other, or indeed to have left things to officials on the spot, but as it was the Embassy dealt with the Quai d'Orsay, through a junior official (me). My opposite number had an agreeable sense of humour and we disposed lightheartedly of such prickly points as the siting of flagstaffs and post offices.

Every few months the Ministère de la France d'Outre-mer would give a sumptuous dinner party. The host was an elderly and formal colonial official, who had spent his entire career in far-off places. He greeted me with 'Ah, here is the imperial representative of England, who seeks to oust us from our Empire.' It sounded rather a large task for a minor diplomat, so I endeavoured to placate him. It wasn't easy with my malicious Quai d'Orsay friend giggling in the background.

My host mellowed with the excellent wine and started to tell me strange stories of his experiences. I remember one that shocked me. He told me that during the pre–1939 Indo-Chinese revolts against French rule, the senior captured 'Black Flags' (the equivalent of the Viet Cong, I suppose) had been

---

* Messenger/guard.

sent to a penal settlement in Kerguelen, the bleakest of islands in the far Southern Ocean. They were told that they were going to a very cold place, where they would die. Sometimes a prisoner would murder another, or even a guard, and he would be guillotined. The other prisoners would gather round and sing their compatriot to his grave. 'It was very beautiful,' concluded the narrator. Was it true? Was there ever a penal colony in Kerguelen? I somehow doubt it. I think he was pulling my leg in a somewhat macabre way in revenge for the flippancy (imaginary, I trust) with which he conceived I approached my duties.

In those days junior diplomats were expected to make their own arrangements for a house or flat, domestic staff, linen, silver, etc., and it was only in some remoter capitals that accommodation existed in a compound, or adjacent to the Embassy. One was given quite a reasonable allowance for these purposes, but at the age of twenty-six I had really no experience of running a self-propelled establishment. Luckily I had something even better; kind and diligent friends who found me a flat, a housekeeper and more or less everything I could need.

They found me a charming and unusual flat in the Latin Quarter (the oldest part of Paris, near the Sorbonne). Even more significantly, they found me Madame Doucet (Antoinette), a First World War widow. Antoinette was a Bretonne, a first-class cook and housekeeper, and she looked after me and my clothes like a mother hen. My existence was of an ease I had not experienced before or since. It seemed to me to be the epitome of luxury to be able to telephone my flat from the Embassy and say 'Oh, Antoinette, we shall be six for dinner tonight,' and to know that the dinner would be excellent and Antoinette smiling. And what a comfort never to have to bother about one's clothes, shopping, the plumbing and so forth.

The only fly in the ointment was that Antoinette, like many others, preferred working for a bachelor. I had become engaged to Nonie before leaving England, and Antoinette warned me that she could not stay in a married household. As our wedding was not to be until the next year, I just hoped for the best. The best, when it came, was rather a surprise. With amazing speed Antoinette transferred her allegiance to Nonie, who had great and unforced charm and who learnt an endearingly slangy style of French with rapidity.

This carefree background was of advantage in my next professional activity. The Ambassador was himself bilingual in French, as were his most senior colleagues (and as, indeed, most pre–1939 diplomats were expected to be), but this ability did not go far down in the hierarchy, even in the Chancery. One of my colleagues told me that his own confidential report read: 'He speaks fluent French, albeit with such a strong French accent that few Frenchmen can understand him.'

As I have said, French was one of my few strong points. Casting around for someone to do the internal political reporting, the Ambassador therefore fastened on me. This was a plum job. You were a sort of official and recognised spy, expected to travel widely, to mix with all sorts of people, from politicians to trade unionists, from editors to agitators, and provide an accurate picture of what was going on and what was likely to happen.

In 1949–50 in France, this was an activity of key importance. The spectre of a Communist/Soviet coup was very present, with memories particularly of Czechoslovakia. The Communist Party itself was powerful and well organised, and the Communist vote was the biggest single entity in the elections. The great majority of those who styled themselves Communists or supporters of Communism, however, were not hard-liners, let alone the kind of people who would support any foreign intervention by violence. One of my tasks was to attempt to form an estimate of the different degrees of red or pink in this particular spectrum. There were those like Astier de la Vigerie in the Marseilles area, who, though an educated man of some charm, had been involved in the most horrible atrocities in a wood between Toulon and Marseilles which became known as the 'Bois de l'Épouvante'.* The Super-Prefect of the Bouches du Rhône told me that they had stopped digging up the victims when the numbers reached 300. Who were these unfortunate people? Some of them were undoubtedly deeply involved with the Germans, but the great majority were minor offenders, or merely political opponents of the militants. Some were just the victims of old scores, personal and commercial. If the Left were capable of this, what might they not do later?

Getting information was astonishingly easy. Hard though it is to believe now, in 1950 the British were popular with a large sector of the French population. The Prefects were particularly helpful. They formed a remarkable Service, recruited with great care from the most brilliant graduates of the establishments traditionally feeding the Civil and Diplomatic Services. Many of them had fine war records and most of them were young, for the old Vichy-tainted Cadre Préfectoral had been largely swept away. Their powers were great, not very different from those of former colonial Governors.

I witnessed several examples of forthright action by an irritated Prefect. On a fine summer evening my wife and I, dressed and poodled to the nines, drove to the town of Blois on the way to a great reception at the Château. The streets were extraordinarily deserted. Strange on a fine evening, I thought. I started to sneeze 'Bloody hay-fever again,' I commented. Nonie began to sneeze too. Then I saw one or two gas-masked figures. Air raid practice? No. The Prefect had been vexed by a tyre-slashing demonstration and the Compagnie Républicaine de Sécurité, known as the 'head-breakers', had comprehensively tear-gassed the town. The dignitaries mounted the steps to greet their hosts weeping bitterly and complaining loudly.

That particular evening included a magnificent dinner in the Salle de Chasse of the Château de Cheverny, surrounded by the antlers of 2,000 stags. The guest of honour was a certain Monsieur André Cornu, the junior Minister for the Arts. The juxtaposition of the antlers and Monsieur Cornu† was too much for one well-wined speaker. He proposed a toast to 'Monsieur Cornu, who, as his name indicates, represents so many of the male electorate'. Jokes about horns don't fill their butts with much enthusiasm in

---

* 'The Wood of Terror'.
† Literally, someone with horns.

France. The Prefect, the official host, ground his teeth.

Another demonstration of prefectoral power caused me envy. A young and friendly Prefect was driving me along a riverside road to show me some new bridge works. A large Citroën carved us up with brutal zest. 'That, no!' said my companion. He proceeded to do a super-Fangio and forced the offender into the side. He jumped out, identified himself, took away the culprit's licence and tore it into confetti. He returned all smiles and we resumed our journey. (Could a Lord Lieutenant do this in Britain?)

A gratifying feature of French opinion at the time was the attribution of air-raid damage, which was extensive, between the Americans and the Royal Air Force. If it was a central pier neatly taken out of a viaduct, we got the credit; a ruined cathedral was put down to the American score. There was a certain justice in this, because our bombing policy in Occupied Europe was much more restrictive than that of the Americans. I cynically supposed that an American would get the opposite story, but it was not so.

This atmosphere of goodwill extended to many sectors of life. It was only five years since the Resistance had been sustained and often led by British officers of SOE (Special Operations Executive) who had been parachuted or infiltrated into France, and it was only eight years since Britain had stood alone against Germany and Italy. At intervals, investitures for the Resistance were held in the old Throne Room in the Embassy, an impressive if somewhat theatrical apartment. And the ceremonies themselves were impressive, with the Military Attachés in full dress reading out the citations, and the Ambassador, visibly moved, making the awards with appropriate dignity. The deeds of courage and self-sacrifice of the recipients were amazing. All had helped their own country and Britain at the risk of death and torture, and they were so proud of their medals. These apart, we also did as much as the Treasury would let us for the bereaved or those who had lost their homes. I kept up with as many as I could, and visited them when in their part of the country on my investigative travels. I had in fact no ulterior motive, but their friendship served me well, as their knowledge of subterranean information was often considerable.

The clearing up of some of SOE's leavings was not always so agreeable. Although in general their courage and devotion was exemplary, a few of their agents were really rascals. One, who had been parachuted into France with a large sum of money to replenish Resistance funds, had almost immediately disappeared. It was assumed that he had been captured or killed, until at the War's end it was discovered that he was living in France under an assumed name, having used the funds to buy a flourishing bicycle business.

Both sentimentally and rationally I have always been against terrorist movements, whatever their alleged motivation. The sequence of events is tragic; a couple of enemy soldiers, probably clerks, shot in the back, followed by reprisals on innocent people, followed by counter-reprisals and retaliation ad infinitum, with all the nauseating accompaniments on both sides of interrogation under torture, intimidation of families and so on. Terrorists, freedom fighters, call them what you will, can hardly ever be brought to open battle. It is not their role, and the fact that they do not wear uniform infuri-

ates their opponents. Soon the only solution the latter can see is to extermi-
nate whole areas à la Russe – or à la SS. There is no end to the bitterness, and
the scars last for generations.

Now, if these activities were truly militarily effective, there might
have been some sort of case for them. But, except during certain brief
periods, such as the Resistance attacks on trains and transport during the
Normandy landings, they achieved very little. Field Marshal Alexander,
with a candour that vastly annoyed the Italians, reported in his post-war
despatches that their Resistance efforts had been 'militarily negligible in
their effect'.

My second (and present!) wife Shelagh and her racing-driver husband had
lived in a French village, where she was admirably served and befriended by
one Marie Leroux. Marie and her family had all been in the Resistance, and
paid dearly for it. Marie herself, who was awarded the Croix de Guerre,
could neither read nor write, but had a formidable memory and safely carried
complicated messages. She had twice been arrested, put up against a wall in
front of a firing squad, and told to talk. She had replied: 'If you shoot me you
will know nothing. If you don't shoot me you will know nothing either
because I cannot read or write. What could I have been entrusted with?'

Marie summed up her views approximately thus: 'When I joined the
Resistance, I supposed that I would count trains and note their contents. I
would see and remember troop, transport and aircraft movements at Mont-
lhéry. I never thought that the Resistance would do such stupid things as
murdering little German recruits. Information was what our job should have
been.' How right she was! I later argued this point with WSC in his retirement. I felt that his order 'Set Europe ablaze' (which he never gave in those
words) was a profound and tragic mistake. Keeping up the morale of
occupied countries just wasn't worth the cruelty and terror it engendered.

At one time the perennial rumours of a Communist coup became more
specific, with information from many sources centring on an alleged hard-
core area for paramilitary action near the town of St Julien, east of Limoges in
the foothills of the Massif Central. I was due for a tour of the area anyway,
and, accompanied by our Consul-General at Bordeaux, John Brewis, visited
towns, mayors, Deputies and journalists. We also made contact with trusted
friends from Resistance days, who were dismissive of the rumours.

John was a first-class man, quiet and able. He suggested a cover for our
Massif Central foray in the shape of an inspection of a British subject's
property in a mountain village, which was the centre of a parochial dispute. (I
don't suppose anyone believed us.) Every village in France seems to have a
mayor, and this crumbling and semi-deserted hamlet was no exception. A
minor official from Limoges, who was dealing with the dispute over the
property, introduced him thus: 'Voici Monsieur le Maire. C'est un pauvre
type très arriéré.'* The Mayor smiled bashfully at this compliment, and
traced patterns with his bare toe in the dust.

---

* 'Here is His Worship the Mayor. He's a poor chap, and very retarded.'

In due course John went back to Bordeaux and I put up in a little hotel prior to returning to Paris. That afternoon I was greeted by a stout individual with a rolling meridional accent. He introduced himself and I recognised his name as one of our prime suspects. Would I dine with him and some friends and they would tell me what was going on? Certainly, how very hospitable of them. Good, dinner would be at six in the hotel.

I tried to take the precaution of ringing the Embassy, but the local telephone system was having an off day. I needn't have worried. My hosts were robustly friendly and frank and the dinner was delicious. It went on for course after course of local delicacies, with an unexpected dish of hard-boiled eggs at half-time and a blazingly coarse Armagnac. I had brought some Burmese cheroots with me and their tubercular pungency was well received all round. (I had taken to smoking these vile things under the illusion that they made me look exotically worldly. I was wrong.)

As we parted, my principal host slurred: 'You have heard of our arms dump? Yes? Would you like to see it?' I accepted with alcoholic alacrity. The following morning I was driven up a track into the hills where we climbed a winding path at a pace that did my hangover no favours. Eventually we stopped at the conventional cave mouth. My companion silently pulled two tarpaulins aside and shone his torch. There were Sten guns so rusted that they would disintegrate if you kicked them, broken boxes of grenades in the same condition and, worst of all, plastic explosive that had become semi-liquid and was oozing on to the floor. My scalp crawled. 'Let's get out of here before the whole bloody lot goes up,' I implored. 'That might be prudent,' agreed my guide.

Was this a ruse? Were there modern weapons elsewhere? Was there any real intention of armed subversive support for a coup? No, no, and possibly yes were my conclusions, but the intention was more in the nature of an unformed contingency plan.

A guarded and somewhat intermittent cooperation existed between British and French intelligence services in the field. One of the problems was the intense suspicion with which 'L'Intelligence Service' (MI6) was regarded by many Frenchmen. If their suspicions had been correct, we would have had to employ tens of thousands of agents in France alone, all malevolently francophobe, and even more in her overseas territories.

A more serious difficulty was the bitter rivalry among the different French services. There were many, and I can only recall a few. There was the DST (Direction de la Surveillance du Térritoire), roughly the equivalent of MI5, which dealt with counter-espionage and subversion. There was the SDECE (Service de documentation extérieure et de Contre-espionage, rather like MI6). Then there was the Renseignements Généraux, which reported to the Prefects, the Sûreté (police) the Deuxième Bureau (military) and so on. They all seemed to hate each other in varying degrees and we were not sufficiently Machiavellian to exploit their differences. One day a member of the Embassy had been received with extraordinary bonhomie by the boss of the DST, who was normally sour and anti-British. It was alleged that his good humour was due to a plane crash; a number of senior SDECE spooks had that day gone to Munich in their creaky old Dakota and it had pranged with fatal consequences.

Our people and the CIA were kept at arm's length at the time, and liaison was maintained via the two Chanceries. My American opposite number and I used to meet for delicious lunches, at the CIA's expense, and exchange second-hand news. After a while, we decided that this was foolish, and we asked our Intelligence representatives to join us for lunch. In due course we faded away and left them to it.

It was, of course, the flushing out of the traitors, Maclean, Burgess et al., that had exacerbated American suspicions of our security. In some cases these were well justified, but there was a tendency to throw the baby out with the bath water; it would just possibly have been less damaging if Maclean and Burgess had never been detected, or, better still, detected but allowed to continue their treason. Some of the information they handed over might actually have done good.

Judging our intentions by their own, many Russians genuinely believed that we would attack them the moment we felt we were strong enough. Gromyko, then their junior Minister for Foreign Affairs under Molotov, used to declare to anyone who would listen: 'You have a hunger for war. I know it.' I am convinced that he genuinely believed it. It points to a lack of high-level intelligence at the time, or a failure to credit it. If he had been able to study Foreign Office (and, I think, State Department) policy documents he would have found no more than a sober and reasonably efficient determination to defend ourselves and our allies. I like to fantasise that if we could have 'played back' Maclean, at any rate, and supplied him with genuine high policy information, his credibility would have increased to our benefit. But of course we would have had to cut him off from military and technical information which would have undermined his credentials, so my fantasy lacks even a toehold on reality.

The treachery of Philby and Blake was different. They betrayed gallant and idealistic men and women to torture and death, and if I had had the opportunity I would gladly have killed them, and opened a magnum of champagne afterwards. Their recruitment puzzles me. Blake's antecedents were dubious. Blake was not his name, and as far as I can recollect his background was Middle Eastern/Dutch with a good many question marks. Philby's father was St John Philby, a bitterly anti-British Arabist who took a Moslem name and influenced King Ibn Saud to point his oil concessions to the US rather than Britain. Philby père was interned for a time during the Second World War under the security measure known as '18B'. (To be fair, 18B treatment was no proof of treason. Many perfectly patriotic people were swept into that net, including the Mosleys, who would never have betrayed their country.)

The French had inherited from the occupying Germans an extensive if somewhat out-dated telephone interception system. They would have been more than human if they had resisted the temptation to bug us rotten. However, a bugging system can be a downright danger and can readily be played back at the listener. He can never tell if what you are saying is intended to be heard, and you can drop hints that cannot be openly stated, for instance: 'If only we didn't have to deal with that near-collaborator Monsieur X at the Quai, we could make much more rapid progress. He is not only full of ill-will but excessively stupid too.' But it doesn't pay to be too clever, because Monsieur X would probably read the intercept himself and cease to be your devoted friend.

Chapter 10

IN PARIS the parliamentary situation simmered and seethed. Governments came and went with paralysing effect on France's economic and international progress, and one came to see the disastrous consequences of proportional representation, even when it was decked out in the gaudiest of modifying feathers. At one time it was seriously suggested that a government of former Prime Ministers should be formed. There were seventeen of them available! I can hardly remember all the different parties. Here is a brief menu: the Communists, the Rassemblement du Peuple Français (Gaullists), the MRP (Christian Democrats), the Radicals, the Socialists, Monsieur Pleven's UDSR – and I am only just beginning.

I used regularly to attend the meetings of the Chambre des Députés (House of Commons: known as the Palais Bourbon, because that was where they met, just to the south of the Place de la Concorde), and was at once amused and saddened at their antics, as I suppose foreign observers must now be in our own House of Commons. Winston Churchill told me that he had always been opposed to the semi-circular Chamber, because it made it too easy for Members to creep gradually from right to left or vice versa without overtly crossing the floor (of which he himself had some experience). It was for that reason, among others, that he had insisted on the House of Commons, destroyed by wartime bombing, being rebuilt on the old, and in some ways inconvenient pattern.

Monsieur Herriot, the old Mayor of Lyons and leader of the Radical Party, presided over the Palais Bourbon. An impressive and rather sad figure, hunched over his desk like Rodin's brooding Minotaur. He was often referred to in the press as 'le monstre sacré du régime'.* The fandangos of the Deputies distressed him deeply. When order totally broke down, in spite of his pounding of a gavel and frantic ringing of a bell, he would as a last resort close the session with a whole one-man band, including sirens, and Huissiers and police would enter to separate the Deputies. More than once poor Monsieur Herriot wept, and once he sent a note round to the Diplomatic Box asking us please to leave rather than observe the shameful situation.

I think what had provoked that particular outburst was an assault on Monsieur Gaston Palewski, a Gaullist and a close wartime associate of the General's. A Communist Deputy had advanced on him as he spoke from the rostrum and kicked him in the stomach. Palewski was somewhat

---

* 'The sacred monster of the system.'

mysteriously alleged to be the model for the fascinating French Duke, Fabrice, in Nancy Mitford's best-selling novel *The Pursuit of Love*. Certainly he was a very close friend of hers, but he wasn't a very attractive sort of person. Louis Spears's description went thus: 'His hands were perpetually wringing each other in unexplained and inexplicable mutual congratulation.'★

At least the Deputies appear later to have improved their manners, and I am not sure that even then they were any worse than the elegant 'Yah, boo', 'Whingebag!', 'Twit', 'You're another!' style of our own lot. Were ours always like that? No, they were not. I used to get interested foreign visitors into the House to hear Question Time. Now it would be a great mistake.

For the first (and only) time my Diplomatic Service allowances were adequate, and I used to entertain extensively – nearly always politicians and French journalists. After the Palais Bourbon closed I used to take them to my flat, where Antoinette, and later Nonie, never turned a hair at the hour or the numbers, or else to the Brasserie Lip, with delicious Alsatian food and beer, which, contrary to popular belief, plenty of Frenchmen prefer to wine. The resulting flow of hard news, rumour and gossip, much of it spiteful, was well worth the effort, and gave one a degree of competence in writing the political summaries and forecasting election results. When one General Election came along I got all the multifarious parties' share of seats right to within a margin of five, and the Gaullists' smack-on at 120. My stock went up with the Ambassador, to whom I did not reveal the high proportion of luck involved, concealing my amazement at the accuracy of my predictions with studied nonchalance.

Among the journalists, who could be most useful allies, was Sam White, writing for the London *Evening Standard*. Sam was well on the way to achieving the celebrity he later enjoyed with the Crillon Bar named after him. We all worked on Saturday mornings, and I used to meet Sam for a drink, which usually became three or four, before lunch. 'Give a little, take a little' was the system, but I became very cautious after a leak of a comparatively unimportant but classified piece of information to the Czechs, via a girl in the Embassy to Sam.

White was an interesting figure, of some charm, who surprisingly spoke terrible French. He was an Australian by birth and told me that his real name was Samuel Weiss. He could deal with an embarrassing situation better than most, and it was easy to see why Lord Beaverbrook favoured him. In the late 1950s I was in the Casino at Monte Carlo having a drink with Ari Onassis. I greeted Sam as he passed by, and Ari, who didn't know him, invited him to join us. I introduced them and Sam immediately began to question Ari about his marital affairs. I reacted vigorously and told him to shut up. The conversation continued thus:

★ General Sir Edward Spears: an outstanding First World War liaison officer and friend of Churchill's. He was responsible for bringing de Gaulle to Britain in 1940, but ultimately fell foul of the General when Spears was keeping the peace in Syria and the Lebanon. A masterly writer and historian.

SAM: 'Well, of course, if Mr Onassis objects to answering questions . . .'
AMB: 'Everyone has matters that they do not wish to discuss.'
SAM: 'I don't. You can ask me anything.'
AMB: 'Very well, why are you a member of the Australian Communist Party?' (He had never revealed it, and I thought he didn't know that I knew.)
SAM: 'I'm not. I was expelled for bourgeois deviationism.'
Sam 1; AMB 0.

I referred earlier to the excessive pace of entertainment in Paris, which put me off most parties for the rest of my life. A large part of the Diplomatic Corps seemed to spend their time revolving expensively and trivially round one another. Having, yes *having* to go to as many as three parties in an evening was deadly, and one evolved a system of going into a Legation or Embassy or whatever by one door, greeting one's host and hostess, flitting rapidly round the room on one drink and leaving by another exit.

Sometimes it was fun. I was told to represent us at the Roumanian National Day. Roumania under Anna Pauker was a bastion of Communist repression and malevolence, but Oliver Harvey was a stickler for diplomatic courtesies. The food was delicious and I tucked into it with the Filipino Ambassador, who observed, somewhat cryptically: 'We are the only Westerners here.' I saw what he meant, for all our fellow guests were Comrades, with appropriate table-manners. At the buffet I stood next to Jacques Duclos. He was a fat little man, a pastry-cook by trade, who had risen to be Secretary-General of the French Communist Party. Some weeks previously he had been arrested and sent to prison for having two carrier pigeons in his possession. Clearly he was a spy! But the pigeons turned out to be for eating and dead anyway, so he was released from the Santé Prison. He looked up from his caviar and observed: 'The food is better here than in the Santé.' Georges Bidault dismissed the matter briefly by telling the Deputies: 'Les pigeons etaient parfaitement comestibles.'[*]

Poor Georges Bidault! He was a likeable man who came to a sad end when he became the head of the secret armed resistance to de Gaulle's abandonment of Algeria. He went into exile and never really surfaced again. He had been a schoolmaster, and during the War had gallantly led the Resistance in the Lyons area. He had been both Prime Minister and Foreign Minister; he was clear-sighted on many issues, and a friend of Britain. He tended however to hit the bottle and could say rather unexpected things. CSC told me that once, sitting next to her at lunch, Bidault had told her that he had been a teacher at the finishing school attended by her daughter Sarah. 'On était très bien là,' he explained 'et j'ai eu plusieurs amourettes. Malheureusement pas avec Mademoiselle Sarah.'[†]

At the British Embassy the Harveys entertained elegantly and appropriately, as I have described earlier. Walter Lees was the Comptroller, and his gentle charm and shrewd savoir-faire made things go with a hitchless

---

[*] 'Those pigeons were perfectly edible.'
[†] 'It was very pleasant there, and I had several little affairs. Unfortunately not with Miss Sarah.'

swing. The major lunches and dinners were fun and attending them was far from just a duty. At a men's lunch I sat next to Bertrand Russell, the maverick philosopher and mathematician. He was agreeably chatty and informed me that his greatest pride in Paris was having ridden a bicyle the whole length of the Champs-Elysées from the Étoile to the Place de la Concorde without touching the handlebars. He asked me which of his books I had read. The only one I could recollect was called *A Child's Guide to Einsteinian Physics* or something similar. I remembered it because, in 1940, I had whooping-cough and was in bed at home, reading the book. My father believed that vintage port was the correct remedy and I was very ready to follow his prescription. Suddenly there was a great flash and a reverberating thump. A wildly off-course German aircraft had dropped a stick of bombs down the road in the empty countryside. No-one was hurt, but it caused the occasion to stick in my memory, the association of Einstein, vintage port and bombs being an unusual one.

Had I understood the book? No, I hadn't. Russell sighed.

'That book was a failure. It did not take into account how ingrained Newtonian physics are in the average educated man. If you had asked someone in mediaeval times why a stone fell when you dropped it, he would have thought you mad. It drops because things fall down he would have said. See for yourself. And if you had questioned the matter you might have found yourself before the Inquisition. You would answer the same question by reference to the greater mass attracting the lesser, or something like that. Your generation is simply not equipped to understand Einstein – or even the Quantum Theory.'

I noted it down more or less verbatim; I later could have proved him wrong for about forty-eight hours.

Another Embassy lunch I remember was when Ava Waverley was staying there. Lady Waverley was the widow of an excellent and far-sighted diplomat, Ralph Wigram. She later married Sir John Anderson, Home Secretary and many other things, who was ennobled as Lord Waverley. She no doubt had qualities of which I was ignorant, but I found her bossy and disruptive. She ordered her courteous hosts about, and, when by chance I had given her a lift, demanded that I ferry her about Paris to do some shopping. I briskly declined and dropped her at a taxi-rank, for I had work to do. She complained to the Ambassador who sustained me.

On that day I found myself her neighbour at a large Embassy lunch. She was displeased, and so was I, but I hope I didn't show it. The pudding was a delicious cold soufflé, decorated with wax roses. Lady Waverley helped herself lavishly and began to eat the roses. I affected not to notice. Some way down the table sat Harold Macmillan (then in Opposition). Unable to attract her attention, he scribbled a note, 'Ava, you are eating wax roses!' and despatched it down the table. When it reached me I didn't see it. I didn't see it for some time, until Lady Waverley had finished her roses. She seemed little the worse, but I did feel rather ashamed, and watched her anxiously for twenty-four hours.

The average tour of duty to be expected at an Embassy was then about three years. I think that this was a mistake, particularly as far as internal reporting was concerned, for one was just reaching a reasonable working knowledge and had made a number of professionally useful contacts when one was called away to start again. My companions were gradually turned over. Sammy Hood was succeeded by the equally able and charming Tony Rumbold. When I consider some of my ex-colleagues, I realize how lucky I was. But the intelligent, patriotic, unselfseeking gentleman diplomat was not then unusual; perhaps because the pre-1939 members of the Service were usually quite well off and enjoyed the agreeable life, and often the experience of strange and wild places, while serving their country with considerable ability and without much cut-throat personal ambition.

A contemporary member of Chancery I missed was David West. He was brilliant, a term I use with care. He had a way-out sense of humour and considerable judgement, but he did not altogether hit it off with the Ambassador. This to neither's discredit; they just had different points of view. He later resigned from the Service for the most respectable, in the literal sense of the word, of reasons, so that one of his children could have proper continuing medical care in England. A real loss.

David was one of the few people I know who laughed so much at jokes (mostly his own excellent ones) that he was sometimes compelled to lie on the floor. He went further. In 1951 General Eisenhower came over to take command of the NATO forces. The Communist Party put on a maximum effort, flooding Paris with hostile demonstrations. A section of the mob gathered outside the Embassy, filling the narrow Rue du Faubourg St Honoré. They were reasonably well-behaved, but noisy. David said: 'I've had enough of this racket. I shall put the finger on them.' What could this mean? We soon found out. Clad in black jacket and striped trousers, David went out on to the little balcony with the flagstaff and surveyed the crowd austerely. Suddenly his face lit up: 'Aha, c'est vous!'* he exclaimed, pointing at an imaginary ringleader, and writing in his notebook. 'Et vous, et vous aussi! Je vous reconnais.'† The crowd were torn between anger and laughter, the ringleaders between apprehension and disbelief. It did no harm.

In pursuit of my duties, I took to the streets quite frequently at that time, suitably dishevelled and hoping to pass for a student. I wanted to know how spontaneous and how organised the demonstrations were. On that night I was all too successful. To get their cohorts through the police cordon round central Paris, the Communists had sent their people in by the Métro (Underground) hoping to pop up behind the police. The latter were well aware of this, and at the exits of the Métro a posse waited to turn the demonstrators round and punt them down the stairs again.

On my Haroun Al Rashid rounds I was nearly goal-kicked down the Rond-Point station steps, and having evaded this disagreeable fate decided to walk home to the Latin Quarter. It was reasonably quiet until I got near

---

* 'Aha, so it's you!'
† 'And you, and you too! I recognise you.'

the Sorbonne, where the students had been having some quiet fun. Near my flat two policemen were banging a girl's head against the pavement by her hair. 'Stop, you'll kill her!' I yelled, advancing in a knightly way. They turned to me with night sticks raised. 'And you too,' one of them said. I produced my orange diplomatic identity card with the haste of the hero's crucifix in a Dracula film. They relented. One said, 'Before you interfere you should know what she was throwing: this.' He produced a bottle. 'Sulphuric acid,' he said. It smelt like the truth. The girl was led away to the *panier à salade** and I went thoughtfully home.

Over three thousand arrests were made that night. It sounds like anarchy, but it wasn't that bad and no-one was killed. In fact, the scale of the demonstrations gave no true indication of the feeling of people at large. Most were frightened of the Soviet Union and delighted to see proper steps being taken to defend the West. The military arm of NATO got quite rapidly into its stride. At least, the administrative side did, at Versailles. It was called Supreme Headquarters Allied Powers Europe: SHAPE. The current riddle was 'Why is NATO like the Venus of Milo?' 'Because it's all shape and no arms.'

All of us at the Embassy pooled our luck, and I was not confined to internal reporting. Being Chancery Duty Officer produced as many variations as the Resident Clerkery. Most were trivial: drunken Brits who had lost their passports and their money and couldn't find the Consular Section, lunatics with inventions or grievances, people who felt that they were unjustly excluded from the Embassy's parties, and so on. One Saturday afternoon in 1952 I was working in the Chancery when the guard on the gate telephoned.

'We've got two ladies and a baby here, sir,' he said; 'they insist on seeing the senior diplomat available.'

'They must want the Consular Section,' I replied, 'send them round there.'

'No, they don't want the Consular Section,' he persisted, 'and I really think you had better see them.' He was a sensible and experienced man, so I went down.

In the waiting room was a veiled woman in black, and a second holding a baby. After asking my identity in excellent English, the first, who was clearly in charge, threw back her veil. 'I am Queen Zain of Jordan,' she said. 'Here is my passport. My husband King Talal has long been unstable and is now totally mad and violent. Look at my throat.' It was black with finger-tip bruises. 'I am in fear of my life and ask for your protection for myself and my child.'

This was delivered much as I have rendered it. The formality of expression – and its purport – made me feel like a bit-player in a B historical romance. Could this be a joke? No, it couldn't. The passport was too genuine and I knew that King Talal had the reputation of being dotty and having an intelligent and strong-charactered Turkish wife.

* Police van.

'But Ma'am,' I ventured, 'why haven't you gone to the Jordanian Embassy?' After all, Jordan was a totally independent country and was represented diplomatically in France. 'Because the Ambassador is afraid of the King and will do nothing. Also, once the King realises I have gone he will follow me with his bodyguards. He himself is armed.'

I told the Chancery guards to close the heavy wrought-iron gates and not to admit anyone without my instructions, gave my visitors that universal British panacea, tea and biscuits, and retired to my office to telephone and to inform the Foreign Office with a brief cyphered telegram. I located the Ambassador staying with the Comte de Billy in the country. Open line or not, he had to know what was going on. I suggested hospitality in the Embassy, at least temporarily until we could find out if the French authorities were prepared to take action against a violent madman, even if he was a King. (They weren't.) The Queen was in visible distress and most probably in physical danger. The Ambassador's reaction was robust.

'I certainly won't send a frightened woman from my door. Get Walter Lees to put her up in the Embassy and I will return to Paris.'

When I returned downstairs two things had happened. A Mercedes had drawn up and three Arabs had got out and demanded admission. This was refused through the closed gate and they had gone away. The Lady-in-Waiting had taken further fright and fled. (Clearly the Embassy could not detain people against their will.) The Queen was calm and confident that the child would suffer no harm; she had prevailed on the Lady-in-Waiting/ nurse to go to a large international hotel and await instructions, rather than return to the Trianon Palace Hotel at Versailles where King Talal was staying.

The stalwart Walter Lees took charge of the Queen, which presented no problems since the Embassy (the correct title for the Ambassador's residence) was next to the Chancery building and connected by a hole in the wall. The Embassy was a magnificent building bought by the Duke of Wellington from Pauline Borghese, Napoleon's attractive and wayward sister, for £40,000 with a gold plate dinner service and the whole contents of the building thrown in. Much of the furniture was of museum status, and some pieces unique.

Thereupon King Talal returned and thumped on the Embassy gate with the butt end of a pistol. Walter wagged a negative finger and went about his business. The French police guard on the pavement watched stolidly. This annoyed me. Where was all this diplomatic immunity, then? I rang the Quai d'Orsay, then the Ministry of the Interior, without effect. Were the French secretly delighted to see us potentially embroiled with Jordan, our former client state? After all, they were permanently sore about the loss of the Lebanon and Syria, which they attributed to us. Were they trying to negotiate an arms deal with Jordan? Or was it just Saturday afternoon? I never knew.

My personal involvement ended at this point. The Jordanian Prime Minister was then in Paris, but was unwilling, or unable, to act, so the

Defence Minister, also in Paris, took over. The Crown Prince, Hussein (now King) was sent for. He was a sixteen-year-old at Harrow, but he immediately displayed the courage and decisiveness which was characteristic throughout his reign (not always coupled with the best judgement, unfortunately). Hussein confronted his father, who promptly blacked his eye. (I rely on a witness for this; I did not attend the meeting.) Talal was subsequently persuaded to leave for Amman, where men in white coats received him as he got off the aircraft. Queen Zain, meanwhile, had left for Switzerland with her child.

A not so Ruritanian but funnier episode took place in midsummer. Most of the senior diplomatic staff were away, and I was bidden to meet Sir Stafford Cripps, the Chancellor of the Exchequer, and his family off the Golden Arrow at the Gare du Nord, give them dinner at the Embassy, and put them on a train at the Gare de Lyon, where they were to accompany Monsieur Petsch, the Finance Minster, to stay in the South of France. I duly turned up at the station, but no Crippses got out of the first-class carriages. Odd, I thought, and went exploring at the far end of the long train in the second-class carriages, which were outside the station's shelter. As I did so the heavens opened and my tropical suit was reduced to a clinging film of cloth. There indeed sat the three Crippses in a second-class carriage. I didn't understand this, and thought it Socialist ostentation. Cripps was a rich man, as well as Chancellor of the Exchequer.

We drove to the Embassy, Cripps discoursing the while on the possible effect of the release of Soviet gold reserves. Then I went home to change and joined the Chancellor, his wife and their daughter for dinner. We sat in the Throne Room as the dining rooms were being redecorated. The thunder rolled theatrically and all the lights went out. By the light of a single candle the Crippses, determined vegetarians, crunched carrots and drank Evian water, while I ate an entrecote and drank a bottle of Oliver Harvey's Château Pape Clément. More thunder, a puff of wind, and the candle went out. In the darkness the Chancellor's daughter asked:

'What is your hobby?'

This must mean me. 'I don't think I have one,' I replied. 'What is yours?'

The answer was brief: 'Christianity.' I thought that this was rather patronising to the Almighty (but perhaps she was pulling my leg?).

At the Gare de Lyon, Monsieur Petsch was not having any of this second-class nonsense. A complete coupé carriage awaited the party, with a pleasant drawing room and bar. I stayed for a drink before departure, and a female member of Petsch's party, assuming I was travelling with them, made various suggestions to me for the night's journey. She had, I think, dined rather well, but it was most flattering.

Paris was the frequent centre for international conferences, in which the Embassy was rarely directly involved. One of the longest-running shows, probably about disarmament (it nearly always was), was at the Palais Rose. Our representative was the Labour Government's junior Foreign Office Minister, Ernest Davies. He had an engaging and unusual Private Secretary, Heath Mason, whom I had known well in the Western Department.

'Unusual' is perhaps an understatement. Heath was a cherubic New Zealander, who looked about fifteen. Early in life, in fact when he was fifteen and must have looked ten, he had gone to sea on an island schooner. The boatswain was a hairy, bullying brute. He made a dead-set at Heath, who was finally driven to retaliate. He hit the boatswain with one of those long bars of ship's soap, used for scrubbing decks. Retribution was terrible. The boatswain debated carefully and did the worst thing he could think of. Flogging? Keel-hauling? No: he reported Heath to the Seamans' Union for conduct derogatory to the dignity of a boatswain.

'I had to leave the schooner,' Heath went on, 'so I came to England and became mate of a barge on the Medway.'

'That was quite a jump in promotion – cabin-boy to mate. What was the crew of a Medway barge?'

'Two. Later I was sacked for running it aground three times in one afternoon.'

Heath had then joined the RAF, but his eyesight prevented him from flying, so he learnt Russian and became Assistant Air Attaché in Moscow. I asked him if he ever met Stalin. He had, several times. 'What was he like?' Heath pondered: 'A nice, grey, grandmotherly little figure with a hint of murder in his eyes.' (Arthur Koestler described him as 'the pock-marked Georgian with the assassin's eyes').

Heath piloted Ernest Davies about in an effectively urbane sort of way. Ernest Davies needed a bit of piloting. He was under a certain amount of strain and liked to relax, and indeed let off steam, when not working. It is interesting to reflect that even in 1950–51, when there was nearly forty years to go to the thawing of the Cold War, the West took disarmament totally seriously. Thank God we recognised the Soviet Union's rather different approach, and took the very ordinary precautions we did! In the evening, Ernest Davies, Heath, Nonie and I, and sometimes others, used to go out to jolly little bistros and chansonniers.* Ernest would cheer up temporarily, but usually relapsed. He gave me one piece of advice I have always followed: 'Don't ever marry an American, Anthony. You can't call your soul your own.'

I sat in on one of the interminable Palais Rose sessions. Some of the Soviet observations had stung Ernest Davies and he delivered a polite but firm little homily. While this was being translated, he went back into his notes. Gromyko replied briefly. The interpreter said, in his even drone: 'Mr Gromyko says that Mr Davies is a cannibal.'

E.D. looked up in astonishment and exploded: 'That's a bit hard, Gromyko! I was brought up a vegetarian.' But this was one of the very few light interludes in those dreary and fruitless exchanges.

As my tour of duty in Paris (1949–52) drew to its close, the political atmosphere was gradually changing. The internal Communist threat, if threat it ever was, began to diminish, and though the Fourth Republic Deputies continued to flit, fight and fulminate like demented fruit-flies, a

---

* Miniature music-halls.

more confident under-swell became faintly perceptible. The frustration of the electorate began to make the reappearance of Mon Général something more than the remote possibility nearly all had considered it.

Had we – the British, the Americans, much of NATO and many of the French themselves – been wastefully obsessed by the Communist threat? We certainly hadn't been in the case of the Soviet military danger; as I have said, it was estimated that the Red Army could be on the Pyrenees in fifty-six days. But we had devoted much money and human resources in our endeavours to counter Communist propaganda. We and the Americans, in reverse order, had subsidised the movement 'Paix et Liberté' and this was only the tip of the expensive iceberg, of which Marshall Aid was by far the most effective overt manifestation.

There was certainly a case for saying that left-wing support in the French electorate was not particularly meaningful, and stemmed from the old tradition of 'pas d'ennemis à Gauche'.* On a trip to the South I had met seed-growers, the most prosperous of French farmers, in the St Rémy-de-Provence area, and they claimed to vote Communist with persistent solidarity. I couldn't see them as destructive street-fighters. And yet, and yet . . . The Commune of 1871 was still a living memory and in that revolution, so admired by Karl Marx, 20,000 people had died in the restoration of order in Paris, not counting the many murdered by the Communards. The atrocities and fanaticism had been appalling. In the recent Liberation, tens of thousands had been executed or murdered by their own countrymen. An official investigation had spoken of 'twelve thousand executed without any guarantee of justice' and everyone knew that this was a minimal figure. La belle France could and sometimes did turn tragically into the 'Black Hunter' of Victor Hugo's poem, capable of insane, cruel and large-scale violence. So I think our insurance premium was well justified.

A more significant long-term manifestation was the gradually increasing momentum towards some form of united Europe. Jean Monnet had been one of the most active progenitors of the movement, and France had fastened on to it for a whole variety of motives. The least charitable interpretation is that France saw in the various organisations – the Coal and Steel Pool (1950), the Green Pool and so forth – a crutch to raise her again to an international position that her own efforts could not justify. Some Frenchmen may have foreseen the loss of Empire, in particular North Africa, and were already looking for a new field for the expansion of their undoubted national genius.

Britain was invited to join the Coal and Steel Pool. Notice for acceptance or refusal was minimal. I met the Foreign Minister's Private Secretary at a cocktail party and reproached him. How could he expect Britain, in a very different situation from France and most other West European countries, to give a swift reply to so fundamental a question? What about our still immensely powerful coal and steel trade unions, the Commonwealth, etc., etc.? Clappier (I always remember his name, because it means 'rabbit hutch'; he

* No enemies on the left.

later became Governor of the Bank of France) smiled pityingly. 'My dear colleague,' he said 'what on earth makes you think we want you to join? You would only slow everything down and the initiative would be lost in a welter of committees and parliamentary debates.' Plus ça change ... The Dutch, who were then rather friendly to us, suggested that we should say 'yes' and argue later. But that was not our way, and now we do it rather clumsily.

Few of the people I then met are still around. One who is still most visible is François Mitterrand. He was then (1951–2) an ambitious younger Socialist politician, who did not especially stand out. His patron was Gaston Defferre, the mayor of Marseille, and a most powerful figure of the old godfather style. Nonie and I first met Mitterrand at a small, rather jolly lunch party, and the conversation flickered rapidly to and fro – rather too rapidly for poor Nonie; as I have said, she acquired colloquial French with gallant rapidity, but on this occasion found it tricky to keep up. Madame Mitterrand had been talking of a little motor cruiser they had on the Seine and had then switched to the maiden voyage of the French Atlantic flagship the *France*. Nonie, her mind on the river-boat, asked if Madame M. had done the cooking? Deep puzzlement all round. Mortification of Nonie (quite unnecessary because the laughter was benevolent; most people are civil to a pretty and engaging girl who is doing her best in a foreign language), who fell silent and mournful. She and I were in black; somewhat ridiculously the Embassy was in mourning for, I think, the King of Sweden. Monsieur Mitterrand asked if Nonie had lost somebody dear to her? I replied 'Yes' and left it at that.

Then, on a Friday morning in September 1952, I received the summons I have described in the Prologue. When I telephoned Nonie with the news, she was pensive. Paris had been a happy place for us both and the thought of such a rapid departure was painful. In the event, the forty-eight-hour timing for arrival at Number Ten was mitigated to two weeks. There was not enough time for the usual farewells and I made a rapid handover to my successor, Sir Anthony Meyer, who did an excellent job on the internal political reporting, but followed it up with a political career in which he himself must have been the object of a number of interesting internal political reports from foreign Embassies in London.

An outstanding problem was Min, our stray cat. Min had been treated for pneumonia by our vet, who described him on a label in rather derogatory terms as 'chat vulgaire tigré'* and decreed that it would kill him if he ever went into quarantine. Nonie loved animals, and especially Min. On an unexpected visit to London when we were engaged, I had found her in her flat making a late-night scrambled egg for a stray Earls Court cat, as she had nothing else to offer it. That bright star of Belgian diplomacy, André de Staercke, came to the rescue. He was his country's Ambassador to NATO and lived in an enormous treble-flat (thirty-nine rooms, I think) in solitary bachelor state. He was a convinced alurophile and joyfully adopted Min, who finished his days at a great age and vastly inflated on Belgian food.

And so I left Paris, to embark on more troubled waters.

* Common tabby cat.

BOOK THREE

———— ❧ ————

Number Ten
1952–1955

Chapter 11

---- ❧ ----

NUMBER TEN DOWNING STREET has, as all the world knows, an unimpressive front door in a cul-de-sac. Downing was something of a jerry-builder and the whole structure seemed in constant need of attention. It was a miracle that it hadn't collapsed from near-misses in the wartime bombing. Beyond the modest facade is a passage to the main building, which is reasonably extensive and can be seen from Horse Guards Parade, behind the garden shared with Number Eleven. In those pre-Clear Air Bill days, cheerful coal fires burned in the rooms. The staff of Messengers were experienced, beautifully mannered and quietly efficient. The house was definitely welcoming.

This atmosphere was put to the test when I arrived at the beginning of October 1952, because no-one was expecting me and my Club bedroom had been double-booked. The Prime Minister was staying with the Queen at Balmoral, and on the evening on which I was supposed to report, the duty Private Secretary had gone home. The permanent staff rose admirably to the occasion and immediately provided a comfortable room, a drink, and even a short speech of welcome.

After dinner at my Club, I went to an early bed. I was awoken by the telephone at about 4 a.m. Shades of the Resident Clerkery, I thought, I bet it's the Admiralty. It was. Our first nuclear weapon test at Montebello Island had been a success and they wanted the Prime Minister to be informed. I had never met Winston Churchill, but I surmised that he might not like 4 a.m. telephone calls. Anyway the explosion would presumably still have been a success at nine, so I waited until I had eaten breakfast before telephoning the news, which was received without much surprise, except at the identity of the announcer. When WSC returned, I was not to see him for ten days, while I was indoctrinated by my colleagues.

It must be remembered that the Prime Minister does not have a Department. The senior staff at Number Ten at that time consisted of four Private Secretaries plus the Appointments Secretary, who dealt mainly with ecclesiastical patronage. When WSC returned to office after the 1951 General Election, he had taken one look at the current Private Office and stated that he did not want any of 'Attlee's leavings'. This was unfair, and it did not take much persuading by Sir Edward Bridges, the formidable Head of the Civil Service (and the Treasury) to get him to change his mind. As WSC well knew, Private Secretaries were not political appointments, and served Prime Ministers of different hues with notable impartiality.

However WSC, at the age of seventy-seven, did cling tenaciously to old faces, a trait which had both helped and hindered him throughout his life. He wanted Leslie Rowan, who had been number two in his Private Office during the War, but Leslie, a man of the strongest character and a very warm heart, had become indispensable at the Treasury. WSC then demanded, and got, Jock Colville (see note on p. 2 above), who had been a wartime member of the Private Office, and was then serving in our Embassy in Lisbon.

Jock later wrote extensively about his experiences with WSC. *Footprints in Time* and *The Churchillians* are admirable works, illuminating, lapidary and elegant. He also kept an exhaustive diary, extracts of which he published under the title of *The Fringes of Power*. This, although his major work, is not his best. It is, inevitably I suppose, too full of social engagements, which are out of proportion to the historical content. Nevertheless it is a seminal work on WSC and his two prime ministerships, and far from dull. It also tells one a good deal about the author.

The Prime Minister wanted Jock to be his Principal Private Secretary. Not unnaturally, if he was to be at Number Ten at all, Jock shared this view. However, there was already a Principal Private Secretary in situ. David Pitblado had only recently been appointed in the Attlee regime. He was a highly competent and conscientious Civil Servant, later holding a number of responsible senior positions with effective ability. He was also an agreeable, tolerant and humorous colleague. A compromise was reached by which Colville and Pitblado became Joint Principal Private Secretaries. It sounded all right, but it didn't really work very well, in spite of the civilised good manners of both those involved.

Broadly speaking, Colville was to deal with foreign affairs and defence, and Pitblado with home affairs and economics. The trouble was that the Prime Minister was not deeply interested in home affairs and economics. It was true that he had been in his time both President of the Board of Trade and Chancellor of the Exchequer (and of course Home Secretary and many other things) but these experiences had been heavily overlaid by the War. Then, of course, WSC had concentrated on military success, on world statesmanship and on the morale of the nation, and the costs thereof had been secondary, perhaps too secondary, for our cavalier financial attitude with a weak Chancellor of the Exchequer (Kingsley Wood) and our excessively generous attitude to our Allies had made no small contribution to our post-war penury. The net effect of the Private Office arrangement was that Colville was closer to the Prime Minister by old association and affinity, and this position was reinforced by the tasks which he consequently undertook. He also knew many of the Ministers from past association, and they knew him. Thus Pitblado was relegated to a less exciting, less intimate and indeed less significant role than was desirable and his due.

The third Private Secretary was Peter Oates. Oates had been a wartime expert on degaussing (the alteration or neutralisation of the magnetic fields of ships, to protect them from magnetic mines). He was responsible for

Parliamentary Questions, among other things – a distinctly tricky job, for a Minister can be made to look a fool more easily at Question Time than at any other point. Moreover, WSC was not always meticulous in learning his lines, and Tuesdays and Thursdays, the Prime Minister's days for Questions, must have been a cause for deep anxiety, particularly as WSC was quite apt to exclaim, as he entered the House: 'Remember, you are responsible!' When I had to accompany the Prime Minister on these occasions, I much disliked it and was as jumpy as a kitten, but Oates took it in his stride. The House was not so boorishly vulgar then as it is now, and WSC undoubtedly commanded respect. But no mercy would have been shown to him if he had blundered.

Peter Oates lived some distance from London, but never grumbled at the late hours. He told me that when he first arrived at Number Ten, Miss Stenhouse, one of the three senior (and remarkable) permanent staff, had said: 'I hear you have a large family of young children, Mr Oates. That experience should be of considerable assistance to you in dealing with the Prime Minister.' I was sorry when Peter Oates moved on. Smells are very evocative, and for some reason a faint aura of fresh fish and chips brings back memories of him. Pleasant and reassuring: perhaps we ate them together.

My predecessor, who took pains to brief me, was David Hunt. He came from the Commonwealth Relations Office, later to be amalgamated with the Foreign Office. David had a distinguished career as a wartime Staff Officer and later as a don, and ended up as Ambassador to Brazil. He told me rather ruefully that it was difficult to get on close terms with WSC. Once he thought he had succeeded. He was on evening duty, and mentioned to the Prime Minister that he had just attended his own birthday dinner party. WSC congratulated him warmly. 'We must have a drink together,' he said. Then, summoning a messenger: 'Bring Mr Pitblado a whisky and soda.'

I am not attempting to give an exhaustive survey of the staffing of Number Ten, but having mentioned the splendid Miss Stenhouse I must tell of the equally splendid Miss Davies. These two ladies, together with Miss Minto, were the backbone of the Prime Minister's Office. Omniscient, powerful, self-effacing and kind, they had apparently been there since the beginning of time. It was even alleged that Lloyd George had once chased Miss Davies round the Cabinet table. Behind them was a staff, almost entirely feminine, of clerks, shorthand typists, telephone operators and others, some known collectively as the Garden Room Girls, for that area of the ground floor was their headquarters. Without any exception that I can recall, they were ultra-efficient, agreeable and often pretty as well. When one wanted an obscure file it appeared as if by magic, unlike the Foreign Office where a request to the Registry was usually met with the answer: 'The file is in the Department.'

The telephonists were a dream. They seemed to be able to find anyone anywhere in the world, with minimum delay. I once asked for a certain James Thompson in Aberdeen, with no more background than that. After ten minutes (a most unusual delay) he was on the line speaking from Liverpool, where he had lived for fifteen years. The Number Ten switchboard could also cut in on any conversation: a boon if you were in a hurry and your wife was gossiping, but people got unaccountably irritable at being deprived willy-nilly of their conversations. I have already spoken of the Messengers. They too were superlative, and reliable to their finger-tips. They were presided over by Mr May, silver-haired, dignified, imperturbable.

The Prime Minister had brought with him his personal secretaries after the 1951 election. The two longest-serving in my time were Elizabeth Gilliatt and Jane Portal. Liz was the daughter of Sir William Gilliatt, the distinguished gynaecologist, and Jane the daughter of a regular soldier and niece of R.A. Butler, the Chancellor of the Exchequer, and Peter Portal, the wartime Chief of Air Staff. It is unnecessary to add that it was not for their family connections that the Prime Minister had recruited them. Their efficiency was undoubted and their discretion and personalities endeared them to WSC on a permanent basis.

Serving both WSC and CSC with effective devotion before, during and after the War was Grace Hamblin. Grace is a remarkable person of charm, kindness, modesty and outstanding efficiency. Her work, though well known and appreciated by the Churchills, deserves greater public recognition. Her final role was to be the first Curator of Chartwell for the National Trust.

Finally, there was the Appointments Secretary, Tony Bevir. Tony really deserves a chapter to himself. When I enquired how I should know him, I was told: 'You can't fail to recognize him. He is a Dickensian character. He is covered in snuff and looks as though he had slept in his waste-paper basket.' Tony's knowledge of the Church was encyclopaedic. The clergy dubbed him 'Heaven's talent scout'. He spent a good deal of time travelling and knew every Bishop, Canon and Rural Dean, and most of the rest of the Church. His recommendations for bishoprics, Crown livings and much else were models of care and good sense. Tony had a mild weakness for good wine, and would retire at intervals to rest at the Kildare Club in Dublin. An odd choice.

WSC was very fond of him, as were we all. At one of his superb birthday parties, he spotted Tony sitting alone on a sofa. He advanced on him ponderously, handed him a bottle of vintage Pol Roger and a glass and addressed him solemnly: 'Treat these like Bishops, Bevir – bloody carefully.' WSC was determined to get him a well-deserved knighthood. The Civil Service found reasons to demur, so the Prime Minister prevailed on the Sovereign to award Tony her personal honour, Knight Commander of the Victorian Order (KCVO). Whitehall was vexed, particularly as Tony had on the previous day lost all his official keys. Expensive and annoying to all. The comment on the new KCVO was 'Keys Can Vanish Overnight'.

When Bevir was away, I was co-opted to deal with his work. I much wanted to advise the Prime Minister on the appointment of a Bishop (then the PM's responsibility to the Queen) but I never got the chance. I think that it would not be unreasonable to conclude that WSC was not deeply concerned about ecclesiastical appointments. I once ventured to quote to him

Lord Melbourne's complaint on choosing new Bishops: 'I believe they die to vex me.' WSC was furious: 'That is untrue and unfair. I take a great interest in these matters.' Well . . .

On minor decisions, I took the advice of Bevir's two efficient, elderly and erudite female assistants. One sometimes had to discuss Crown livings with the presiding Bishop and then I spoke from a closely reasoned and persuasive brief provided by the two. Only once did it go wrong. Reading from my prompt, concealed on my desk, I said: 'We think that X would be a good appointment for your Diocese.' The Bishop shook his head and tut-tutted. 'Oh dear me no. That would never do. Remember the sad affair at Appleshore.' I had never heard of either the place nor the incident. When His Grace had departed, I sent for the two advisers and recounted the conversation. 'Oh dear,' they said in chorus, 'We had forgotten all about the sad affair at Appleshore.' What it was I never discovered.

Chapter 12

REVERTING TO November 1952, in due course I was summoned for my first meeting with Winston Churchill. He worked sitting at the baize-covered Cabinet table – not the modern coffin-shaped conference type, but a simple, rather narrow rectangle. Behind him was a portrait of Walpole, the first Prime Minister.

My first impression was of his size, and his eyes. He was much smaller than I expected (it usually is the case with public figures, the notable exception being General de Gaulle) and his eyes were of a striking blue, in a healthy pink complexion. He wore his usual black jacket and striped trousers, and a dark blue bow tie. His soft collar was a size too big, a deliberate and sensible habit. He pointed silently to a chair immediately beside him, and gazed at me. The silence lengthened. Anyone who has stood for the Armistice Day two minutes will know how long it can be. I deliberated. Was it up to me to speak, to declare how honoured I was to have been chosen and so on? I have very often regretted what I have said, and rarely regretted silence, so I kept quiet. Should I manfully return his gaze, looking him squarely in the eye? No again. It would have resembled a children's game and I would have blinked first. I deliberately unfocused my eyes, which on consideration must have given an impression of myopia, simple-mindedness or intoxication. Finally he spoke: 'I dare say we will get on very well together,' he said doubtfully, and dismissed me. As I reached the door, he addressed me again: 'You worked for Orme Sargent. A good man. A good deal better than most of the Foreign Office. Why was he called Moley? There didn't seem to be anything particularly subterranean about him.'

I explained.

WSC snorted: 'It is an unsuitable nickname.'

It took me a long time to feel at ease with WSC. Frankly, he intimidated me. Moreover, I was so anxious to get things right that I was at serious risk of becoming a fuss-pot, because it is much easier to make mistakes in small matters than in larger ones.

In due course I had a stroke of luck. The Prime Minister called, at very short notice, a Ministerial meeting. He wanted a Parliamentary figure, and the obvious one was the Lord Privy Seal, Harry Crookshank, who was also Leader of the House. The meeting was to be at 2.30 and neither his own office nor I could locate Crookshank. I therefore got the Chief Whip, Patrick Buchan-Hepburn. At 3.25 Crookshank telephoned: 'I hear you have been trying to get hold of me. What is it?' I explained, adding that there was no point in his coming now, as the meeting was about to break up, which it did five minutes later.

Shortly afterwards WSC's manner to me, which was beginning to be more cordial, changed to freezing, mistrustful, almost hostile. I searched my conscience, but could find no answer. Then suddenly, the sun came out. I was bidden to dine alone with WSC on my night on duty and his formidable charm and wit entranced me. I was delighted but puzzled. Then I heard the explanation. Crookshank had apparently approached the Prime Minister in the House of Commons and said something like this: 'I know you don't like me, but I will not tolerate being excluded from important meetings. I telephoned your Private Office at 2.45 and was told that the meeting was over. It lasted another forty-five minutes. That's what happened. Don't let them tell you anything different.'

WSC was not unnaturally perturbed that his newly arrived Private Secretary should wantonly sow discord among the Cabinet, particularly as his relations with Crookshank were not very good. It was clear that I would have to go. He spoke to Jock Colville, and here was where my luck came in. 'But Prime Minister, I was in the room when the Lord Privy Seal spoke to Anthony. It was nearly half past three, and the meeting was breaking up.' The one certain way to raise someone in WSC's esteem was to run them down unfairly. In any case, he disliked outside interference with his Private Office. Hence the astonishing change of climate.

Crookshank was an honest man and would never have made such a misleading démarche deliberately. But WSC had never liked him, although he ultimately recommended him to be appointed a Companion of Honour. His letter to Crookshank was a model of irrelevance. It ran, approximately: 'In making this recommendation to Her Majesty, I am mindful of the fact that you were blown up in the First World War and buried for two days.' Subsequently WSC saw a report of a speech in which Crookshank had made a little joke: 'They call me the Lord Privy Seal, but I am neither a Lord, nor a Privy, nor a Seal.' WSC's comment: 'He's wrong about one of those.'

Though I don't think I consciously sought to ingratiate myself with the Prime Minister, which would anyway have been totally counter-productive, it is much more agreeable to feel that one's work is appreciated and that one is trusted to undertake significant business. But gaining WSC's trust was a long-term process, and the game was snakes and ladders. The reward was that, if ultimately given, trust was accompanied by undemonstrative affection and was difficult to destroy.

The Prime Minister's regime was unusual for a hard-working statesman of international renown in a world beset by appalling problems, rebellions and near-wars, with an unreliable and union-ridden domestic economy and the ever-present lowering threat of Soviet aggression.

WSC breakfasted in bed about nine o'clock. It was a proper English breakfast, ornamented in season with cold grouse or cold partridge, but the quantities were small. It was followed by a cigar and a very weak whisky and soda, that was scarcely ever drunk but used as a throat moistener. ('When I was a young subaltern in the North West Frontier wars, the water was not fit to drink. To make it palatable we had to add whisky. By diligent effort, I learned to like it': WSC circa 1920.) He was attended by Rufus, his poodle, who had a breath like a flame-thrower, and later by his budgerigar Toby, who chattered like a schoolgirl at a picnic, perched and laid droppings on visitors' heads, fought with his own reflection in the silver pepper pot and generally made an endearing nuisance of himself. Meanwhile WSC read the newspapers – all of them, from the *Daily Worker* to *The Times*. He had already read the first editions of the same papers before going to bed the previous night, delivered by despatch rider by the newspapers themselves (well, probably not the *Daily Worker*). He was unrepentant at reproaches that this was a waste of time: 'I get far more out of them than out of the official muck,' was his rejoinder.

The Private Secretary on duty, who for continuity's sake had also been on duty the night before, would meanwhile have read the official incoming papers and in particular the Foreign Office telegram distribution, and would sit with WSC going through anything urgent and discussing the day's programme. If there was no Cabinet, which usually took place at 11 a.m., or other significant meetings, the Prime Minister would work in bed until it was time to dress for lunch. He even carried on his flow of comment, questions or instructions from his bath, with a somewhat disconcerting habit of submerging totally just when an answer was being delivered.

During the morning, Ministers (or those he knew well enough) were received at his bedside. R.A. Butler ('Rab'), the Chancellor of the Exchequer, had a large bald head that Toby found particularly attractive as a perch, with inevitable avian consequences. Butler mopped his head with a spotless silk handkerchief and sighed patiently: 'The things I do for England ...'

Ministers who sought to call on WSC were not always welcome, particularly if he was working on a speech, a task on which he lavished more concentration and more anxiety than any other business. On my way up to WSC's bedroom on one such morning, I was intercepted by Butler and Anthony Eden, the Foreign Secretary, who had just come in unexpectedly. 'We must speak to Winston urgently,' said Eden. 'We'll come up with you.' They stopped outside the open bedroom door while I went in. 'The Foreign Secretary and the Chancellor are here and say they must see you urgently,' I announced portentously. WSC looked up irritably: 'Tell them to go and bugger themselves,' he ordered and returned to his speech notes. As I retreated, pondering on a suitable paraphrase ('The Prime Minister hopes that you will forgive him for the moment as he has reached a crucial point in his speech', perhaps?), a shout followed me from the bed: 'There is no need for them to carry out that instruction literally!' From the faces in the corridor it was all too clear that they had heard both messages.

On an ordinary working day, the Prime Minister would lunch with Mrs Churchill (as she then was; WSC did not accept the Garter until 1953) and usually a small number of guests. If there was a business content, which there usually was, one of the Private Office attended. And of course from time to time there would be a large formal luncheon in the State Dining Room. I much enjoyed such invitations as came my way. The food and wine were superlative, both on smaller occasions when the Churchill's own cook, Mrs Landemare, was in charge, and on the larger ones when the Government Hospitality Department were responsible. Cream featured plentifully. WSC said: 'You should eat plenty of cream. It coats the sheaths of the nerves,' though with what scientific justification I know not.

Although out of historical sequence in this narrative, I would like to recall here one of the grander lunches. The Crown Prince of Japan, now the Emperor, was the chief guest. Only men were present and the Prime Minister enlarged on our former close and friendly relations with Japan, ended when the Anglo-Japanese Treaty was not renewed in the 1920s (mainly because of American pressure). Had this not happened there was a reasonable chance that Japan would not have joined the Axis Powers (Germany and Italy). For what it is worth, my own opinion is that Japanese economic-military imperialism would have impelled them into an aggressive course in China and elsewhere in any case.

However that may be, the luncheon went swimmingly. Perhaps too swimmingly, for when the time for toasts arrived, the Prime Minister rose and proposed the health of the Emperor of Japan before that of the Queen. I choked on my glass of port and saw Rob Scott, a senior Foreign Office official who had been captured and grossly maltreated by the Japanese, turn pale with mortification. It was of course an aberration which had the virtue of greatly pleasing the Japanese.

During her travels with her sick husband, WSC's mother, Lady Randolph Churchill, had acquired in Japan two splendid bronze horses, sixteenth-century, I think. They were about eight inches high, and represented a mare in season and a stallion, a separate piece, gazing at her. WSC sent for them to show them to the Crown Prince. 'To me,' he said, 'they represent sex in bronze.' There was much translation, then the Crown Prince took the bronze mare, turned her over and gazed at her intently. The Prime Minister muttered 'He won't find it there . . .'

It occurs to me that the expression 'swimmingly' could be misinterpreted. I should make it clear that although WSC enjoyed his drink, during the twelve and a half years I spent with him I never saw him the worse for wear, although he once said he was.

When Parliament was sitting the Prime Minister would usually go down to the House of Commons after lunch. He answered Questions on Tuesdays and Thursdays and would afterwards go to the Smoking Room to chat to Members and to find out how he had been received. 'How did it go?' was a question repeatedly asked by WSC after a speech. The Parliamentary picture was faithfully reported to him by Christopher Soames, married to his youngest daughter Mary. Christopher was Member for Bedford and the Prime Minister's Parliamentary Private Secretary. But WSC wanted a view from almost everybody when he had delivered anything significant.

I suppose that this concern over opinion is both normal and necessary in a public figure, particularly a politician or indeed a statesman, but I thought

WSC carried it to extremes. The reason is not hard to find; he was deeply sensitive to criticisms, voiced and unvoiced, private and public, that he was past it, that he was not suitable as a peacetime Prime Minister and that he should hand over to a younger man. At that stage (1952) very few in the Conservative Party were bold enough to speak out. Some hoped that some-one else would bell the cat, or even that bad health or death would solve their problem. Generous souls, but there were few of them and the majority of the Party revered him.

Returning to Number Ten, the Prime Minister would have a nap. This was no ordinary nap. Undressed fully to his nightwear of a long silk vest, he would take a very small sleeping pill and go to bed for one or two hours, awaking refreshed and ready for dinner and work.

I asked him if he had had many sleepless nights in the war. 'Only two that I can remember,' he said. 'When *Repulse* and *Prince of Wales* were sunk by the Japanese, and when Crete fell to the German parachute troops.' How did he manage it? 'Well, I just turn out the light, say bugger everybody, and go to sleep.'

The afternoon nap was a mixed blessing for the Private Office. It enabled us to catch up with our work and it enabled the Prime Minister to work on after dinner until almost any time. I am told that his wartime hours were even worse and I am not sure if he was right in his contention that it enabled him to get the last ounce of intellectual or physical effort from his extraordinarily robust frame. Field Marshal Montgomery went to bed at 10.30 or so, battle or no battle, having left suitable instructions with his Staff, and he didn't do too badly.

When on duty one sometimes dined with the Prime Minister. This was always fun and gastronomically agreeable, and WSC was at his best. He was a generous and entertaining host, and he did like to see his guests enjoying themselves. Irrelevant snatches of conversation remain in my mind.

> WSC, after dinner, in a sudden silence: 'Have another glass of champagne?'
> AMB: 'No thank you, Prime Minister, I've had plenty.'
> WSC: 'Have some more brandy.'
> AMB: 'No thank you, I've done very well.'
> WSC: 'Well, have a cigar.'
> AMB: 'Thank you again, but no.'
> WSC, grumpily: 'It's a great mistake to miss doing yourself good while you're still young. This is very good brandy. It was very nice of Jean Frémicourt to leave some for his héritiers.'

I should explain that the brandy in question was labelled in manuscript 'Héritiers de Jean Frémicourt'. It was the best I have ever drunk. Pale golden, gentle and uplifting, it had an aroma like the faint smell of tulips.

My only grumble, and indeed that of CSC and certainly the domestic staff, was that WSC sat too long after dinner and thus postponed the end of a long day, when one could go home, having usually snatched a rapid dinner earlier and left one's wife to return to Number Ten. After dinner the Prime Minister

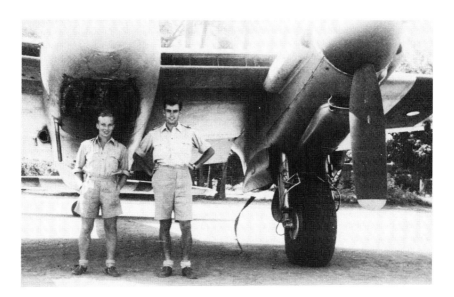

Frivolity and flying. *Above*, Anthony Montague Browne (right) with Flight-Sergeant George Price beneath their Mosquito, 1945. *Below*, The end in Burma: photograph taken by AMB of Rangoon Jail – with its message 'JAPS GONE' – on 2 May 1945.

10, Downing Street,
Whitehall.

The bearer of this pass,
Mr. A.A.D. Montague-Browne, is
a member of the Prime Minister's
Staff and should be given every
facility.

John Colville

29th September, 1952.

AMB's Downing Street pass, 1952.

Churchill, with AMB, leaves Downing Street for the House of Commons,
May 1953.

Churchill with Lord Beaverbrook at La Capponcina, 1957.
(Photograph by AMB)

Aboard Aristotle Onassis's yacht *Christina*, Monte Carlo, 1957. In front of
AMB are Aristotle Onassis and Emery Reves; to his right is Tina Onassis;
Wendy Reves is talking to Churchill.

The visit to Eisenhower, May 1959. *Above*, In the helicopter on the White House lawn en route to (*below*) Eisenhower's farm in Gettysburg.

Returning to London from the USA, 1959: to the left is Churchill's detective,
Sergeant Edmund Murray.

Jane Montague Browne, AMB's daughter, greets Churchill at London Airport
on his return from the USA, 1959.

returned to the Cabinet Room to work and finally, as already described, to read the first editions of the next day's papers. Among other things, this enabled him to surprise Ministers by a billet-doux with their breakfasts, based on information that they had not yet got. Thus: 'Minister of Works. What is this that you are doing in Kensington Palace Gardens? It is a wicked thing to cut down a living tree.' This is authentic, and referred to a letter in that morning's *Times*, complaining of the urban deforestation.

When the Prime Minister eventually went to bed, it was considered wise to accompany him to his room to field any Parthian shots for the morrow, rather like the Petit Coucher of the Kings of France. Just before going to sleep he would, in his own words, unbrush his hair, say charmingly, 'Good night, my dear,' and that was that. And so, at last, at last home to bed.

My long-suffering wife, Nonie, put up stoically with these bizarre hours. We had rented a small house in Maunsel Street, not more than ten minutes' drive from Number Ten. Proximity apart, it was far from perfect. If an apartment is called a flat, this house should have been called a vertical: steep narrow stairs with one or two rooms on each floor. This proved a major and damaging fault when our daughter, Jane, was born in 1953. She was a happy and smiling baby (and grew into a sunny and loving daughter), but babies do require a lot of running to and fro by their mothers, and the stairs gave Nonie a thrombosis of the leg.

Our landlord too was not exactly ideal. Sans peur he may have been, but he certainly wasn't sans reproche. In severe winter weather the water tank, placed with true British plumbing aplomb on the most exposed part of the roof, froze solid. I could not get at it because it was actually on my landlord's own roof, adjoining ours. My urgent requests for action, namely unfreezing the tank and repairing the broken-down shack in which it sat, received the airy answer that it was not worthwhile because it would only freeze again. To be in a small house with a baby, her young mother and no water supply is something one tends to remember.

About every third week I went down to Chequers (the official prime ministerial country house, presented to the Nation by Lord Lee). I enjoyed it. Though architecturally it seemed to owe more to Edwardian stockbroker than to the original ancient pile, it was a quiet and pleasant place to work, high in the Chilterns, with fine views and walks. It was staffed by highly competent members of the Women's Auxiliary Air Force, and life was made as easy as possible. I was surprised on my first arrival with the Prime Minister, as usual late for dinner on a Friday, to have my bag unpacked, dinner jacket laid out and bath run. My room was next door to WSC and he toddled in (if this accurate verb may be forgiven), clad in a dressing gown, to enquire if I was comfortable.

WSC's preference was very strongly for Chartwell, his own house near Westerham, but the opening and shutting of it and the domestic arrangements, on top of Number Ten and Chequers, were more than CSC could bear. One conversation went thus:

WSC: 'I shall go to Chartwell next weekend.'

CSC: 'Winston, you can't! It's closed, and there will be no-one to cook for you.'

WSC: 'I shall cook for myself. I can boil an egg. I've seen it done.'

Amazed silence on all sides. The threat was not carried out.

Being the junior Private Secretary, I tended to get the less exciting weekends, for they were almost always devoted to business in some shape or form, and it was on these relaxed occasions that major policy decisions were often taken. Even with the limitations imposed, some weekends could be absolutely fascinating, for the discussions were of an informal nature, at the luncheon or dinner table, and one was rarely required to take official minutes, a task which I much disliked and which seemed to me to distract one from one's real business of following the drift of the Prime Minister's views and seeing that they were translated into appropriate action – or at least taken on board by the Departments involved, which was not quite the same thing.

My memories of Chequers, though happy, are intermittent (like most of those recalled in this book). Among them is that of the three Chiefs of Staff arriving for a military lunch on a Saturday. The Prime Minister, of course, had also been Minister of Defence and this was the side of things he most enjoyed, together with foreign affairs. The Chiefs, Harding for the Army, McGrigor for the Navy and Dickson for the RAF, were all remarkably small men and on arrival they advanced to greet the Prime Minister like the last survivors of the Seven Dwarfs. WSC was not a giggler, but on this occasion he got a distinct spasm. He didn't make it any better by indicating Dickson, and enquiring in what he imagined to be a whisper: 'Let's see, that's the intelligent one, isn't it?' Actually he was quite right, but a better way to put it would be to say that Sir William Dickson probably had the most imaginative of three absolutely first-class Staff brains.

WSC's increasing deafness was a severe handicap and, as I have said, was later misinterpreted as senility. He hated hearing aids, and although his seat on the Front Bench of the House of Commons was wired for their reception, and his telephone equipped with an amplifier, it was apparent that he did not hear readily in a buzz of conversation. If one was alone, and spoke clearly, he could follow perfectly without the voice being raised, particularly if with someone he knew.

WSC was not above making use of this disability, though never with the devastating effect of Bernard Baruch,* who used to turn off his old-fashioned box-receiver with great ostentation if he was bored. The wartime Assistant Military Secretary of the Cabinet recounted that at one meeting a rather prosy boffin was droning on about buffer-stocks against an emergency. The Prime Minister was becoming visibly impatient. Finally he exploded:

'What is he talking about?'

'Buffer stocks, Prime Minister.'

'Oh, I thought he said butterscotch.'

The deafness was the root of one of the most resoundingly tactless remarks

* American financier, highly influential Presidential Adviser and close friend of WSC.

I have ever encountered. At Chequers the dining-room table was a large oval. Silence fell for a minute at his own end, and WSC called out genially: 'What are you talking about down there?' The reply came: 'We were discussing which would be better, to be blind or deaf, if you had to choose one.'

w s c: 'What?'
End-of-table repeats remark forte and then fortissimo.
w s c: 'What did you decide?'
End-of-table, in a glass-shattering roar: 'We decided that it would be better to be blind, because if you are blind, people are sorry for you, but if you are deaf they think you are bloody stupid and they hate you.'
w s c: 'I see . . .'

Journeys to and from Chequers, thirty-eight miles from London in the Chilterns, were normally made at top speed. 'You're a sportsman, Winston,' one of his friends had said to him, 'You always give the train a chance to get away,' and thus it was with appointments. Preceded by a police car, the Prime Minister's car had a police bell (these were pre-siren days) and an illuminated Metropolitan Police sign that could be raised and lowered. Trying to read small print as you rocketed round corners, and enveloped in cigar-smoke – and Rufus the poodle's breath – tried even my stomach, which I thought years of low-flying had rendered invulnerable. WSC was immune.

One Friday evening, more and more odds and ends delayed departure for Chequers. 'We won't get there for dinner,' WSC decided. 'We'll dine in the Savoy Grill.' I suggested Boodles, quieter and on the way out of London from Downing Street. When we stopped in St James's Street, WSC asked if he could bring Rufus in.

'I'm afraid not.'

'Why?'

I could only think of the most foolish school-boy answer. 'Because we would have to re-christen the Club Poodles.' Strangely, this went down quite well.

Quite early in my time at Number Ten WSC had remarked to me, out of the blue: 'I blub an awful lot, you know. You'll have to get used to it.' At the top of Boodles' stairs I got an example. WSC stopped, and contemplated the Roll of Honour of members of the Club who had been killed in two World Wars. Then he wept silently and muttered 'Coronel'. Admiral Cradock's name was on the list. He had had his last dinner at Boodles, before sailing to intercept Von Spee's squadron off South America in the First World War, and had gone down with his ship in that battle. WSC was First Lord of the Admiralty at the time.

I saw – and see – nothing wrong in a man weeping. Nelson wept copiously. So did Bismarck. And in the eighteenth century men took a positive pride in weeping. 'I am a man of sensibility,' they would explain. Anyway, WSC recovered briskly and we had a jolly dinner, sitting afterwards in the bow window on the ground floor that juts into St James's Street. Passers-by did remarkable double-takes at the sight of the familiar profile a few feet away.

By chance I recently came across the bill. It came to £8 for a menu of oysters, whitebait, lamb cutlets, ice-cream, a savoury, a bottle of Veuve Clicquot 1943 (for £2) and sixteen brandies. This last item excited some comment when I recently sent the Club Chairman a copy of the bill as a souvenir. It wasn't quite as bad as it looks. WSC had indicated the last two diners left and said: 'Let us do the civil. Could you ask those two old gentlemen to have a drink? They seem very interested in us.' They were the Club's Vice-Chairman and Secretary, and at least twenty years younger than WSC, and we drank only two large brandies each.

A snatch of our earlier conversation that evening has stuck in my mind.

> WSC: 'I do like this Club. Most of your members are decent country gentlemen.'
>
> AMB (looking round the room): 'Well, of the six I can see, I think three are stockbrokers.'
>
> WSC, indignantly: 'You shouldn't say such things about your fellow-members! Really, my dear, you must avoid this penchant for pessimistic judgement.'

Considering that his much-loved brother Jack had been a stockbroker, I thought that this was a bit much.

My last memory of Chequers travel was a quiet Friday evening. I was about to dine at home with Nonie when the telephone rang and an unmistakable voice said: 'I need you after all. It would be helpful if you would come down for dinner.' It was then seven o'clock and Chequers was usually an hour and a half from Central London. Moreover I hadn't changed and the Prime Minister most definitely expected you to do so. Help was not slow in coming. One of the telephone angels at Number Ten had monitored the call, and within less than five minutes a police car drew up, Nonie flung my dinner jacket and sponge bag through the window, and we were on our way. The police drivers, I think, enjoy an opportunity to show their paces. We raced through London, bell ringing continously, going across red lights and on the wrong side of the traffic islands. Passers-by gazed at the strange spectacle of a speeding police car, apparently carrying a lunatic in the back seat who was attempting to take off his clothes.

I have never returned to Chequers; I suppose it is now much more geared to rapid communication, and certainly that the security system is more onerous. One summer afternoon I was working with the Prime Minister, sitting on the lawn. Earlier he and CSC had taken on Clement Attlee and his wife at after-lunch croquet. I reflected that the spectacle of the Leader of the Opposition playing croquet with the Prime Minister was unlikely to be found elsewhere. (Did Kinnock ever play croquet with Mrs Thatcher?) I had gone into the house to fetch a document, and on returning was surprised to see a dumpy little woman in earnest conversation with WSC. I approached, and heard her say: 'You see, Mr Churchill, they control me by wireless.'

'Come and tell me all about it,' I urged, 'the Prime Minister is awfully busy.' She followed me docilely. We were pursued by a shout from WSC.

'No-one is to be unkind to her. She is to be given a pound and a piece of cake and taken home.' She was. It turned out that the duty Special Branch police officer was in his bath. There's no accounting for bathing hours.

It is the custom for an outgoing Prime Minister to plant a tree at Chequers. I asked WSC what his choice would be. He rolled a blue eye towards me and said:

'Well, what do you suppose I would choose?'

I thought. 'An oak?'

'An *English* oak.'

It would make a good guessing game to imagine trees suitable for different Prime Ministers. The only two I know are Chamberlain and Attlee; a yew and a hornbeam respectively, which seem eminently suitable.

At Christmas 1952, I was detailed to be on duty at Chequers. Not only was I the most junior of the four Private Secretaries, I was also the only one without children at that time, so it was eminently reasonable. Nonie went down to her mother in Gloucestershire, and I prepared for rather a jolly three days. Not so. At about 6.30 on Christmas Eve, the Prime Minister turned to me, presented me with a box of very serious cigars and two bottles of brandy and spoke: 'It is a shame to keep you from your family. I will get on quite well without you for two days. I have ordered a police car to take you immediately to London. You can keep in touch by telephone. Happy Christmas!'

It was far too late to get to Gloucestershire, and anyway I had to be close to Number Ten. Everyone I knew was out of London. I repaired to my Club, Boodles, for a solitary but bibulous dinner, for the wine list was remarkable. Boodles was shut, but a notice invited us to go to the Carlton Club just down the road. There was fog in the chilly dining room, just as there was outside. One melancholy old man was dining. The atmosphere was not exactly festive, indeed it was positively suited to Scrooge's Christmas Eve, but I tried my best and ordered boar's head, with visions of cheerful gleemen carrying in a smoking dish head-high. The waiter looked surprised and brought me some cold brawn.

On the way home, I thought it appropriate to call in at Westminster Abbey. It was locked. I eventually found a Roman Catholic church near my home, open, warm and enlivened by three drunks. So ended Christmas Eve.

Chapter 13

T HE PRIME MINISTER's relations with his Ministers would fill a whole volume, indeed several. But as a signpost in my meandering tale it may be right to touch on them here. Central to the whole matter is the question: 'Should Churchill have undertaken his second prime ministership?' Certainly CSC believed that he should not, but her view was strongly influenced by the formidable stresses she had endured over the years, and by her anxieties that WSC's health would not stand up to the strain. He had already suffered a stroke in 1949, kept amazingly secret by Max Beaverbrook, with whom he was staying in the South of France. Would he break down? She later told me of her nightmare that WSC would collapse in the midst of a speech, become incapable of conducting affairs and end his life as his father had done, 'the principal mourner at his own protracted funeral', though from very different medical causes. (I cannot add anything positive to the controversy over the nature of Lord Randolph's illness, but quite early in my service WSC said to me: 'You know my father died of locomotorataxia, the child of syphilis.' The significance of this remark lies, of course, not in whether WSC was right or wrong, but in the fact that this was what he believed.)

I myself would have concluded that he should not have been Prime Minister again in 1951, but for two things. And they are massive 'buts'. In the first place he had an animal vigour, a reserve of resources and a resilience of more dynamic resolution than I have ever encountered. After his second severe stroke in 1953, his powers were indeed diminished. But not more than eight weeks after, I was standing alone with him before dinner at Chequers. He put his feet together and did a standing jump on to a low stool. 'Not bad for a man who's had two strokes?' he observed.

The second 'but' is of more national and indeed world significance.

Who else was there?

WSC once said that the job of Prime Minister was sui generis. You couldn't tell how a man would do until he had done it and you might easily be surprised: 'Even a grub will grow into a Queen if you feed it on royal jelly.' On that basis there were several figures who might well have risen to the supreme occasion and done it better than Anthony Eden. But consider the circumstances in 1945. Churchill loomed over the national and international scene on an awe-inspiring scale. To much of the world, and indeed to much of his own country, he was Britain. When the General Election took place on 5 July 1945, the war against Japan was in full swing and in the Far East we voted by proxy. I was astonished to find that quite a number of aircraftsmen, who weren't at all badly educated, supposed that they could vote for Labour and still retain Winston Churchill. Perhaps they were rationalising a new coalition Government.

And then Churchill's Party was resoundingly defeated. If he had retired from politics on that note, it would have been a crushing blow to the Conservatives, and dashed their hopes of a recovery and a victory over the Labour Party before too much damage had been done – vain hopes, as it turned out. Moreover, it just did not lie in his character to admit defeat and slink away from the battle. He most certainly was deeply saddened by the apparent indifference of the electorate to him personally. But he was capable of putting bitterness behind him, and sufficiently politically sophisticated to realise that people do not usually cast their votes on the basis of gratitude (though they do, sometimes, on that of rancour), but on calculations of personal or factional advantage. WSC sometimes philosophised on this theme. His romanticism led him to hope that nobler feelings would guide the vote. He was convinced that in 1940, when defeat stared us in the face, the country would have opted overwhelmingly for defiance. But he added: 'If it is a choice between attraction and repulsion, it is usually the latter that carries more weight as an electoral motive – in normal circumstances. Nineteen-forty was not precisely normal.'

Retirement in 1945 was ruled out both by personal predilection and by bitter anxiety for the future. The Soviet threat was looming ever darker and the British Empire, still covering one quarter of the Earth's surface, and the United Kingdom's grievously damaged economy were in largely inexperienced and possibly malevolent hands. How could Churchill retire?

This being accepted, how could Churchill not lead the Conservatives in the next General Election? If they won, how could he not then head the new Government?

These inevitabilities did not however necessarily make for a united Cabinet. The first and greatest weakness was the understanding that Anthony Eden was to be the next Leader of the Conservative Party. Constitutionally the position of Deputy Prime Minister has no particular validity: it is only an indication that the Deputy would be expected to take over temporarily in case of incapacity or death; but it was universally recognised that Eden's anointing was of much greater significance, and for a Prime Minister, particularly an old man, to create an heir apparent is an act of political self-castration. Politicians (and, to be kind, much of human nature) are such that sails are trimmed to the new wind, whether it is blowing in the right direction or not.

But for his devastating ill-health, both before and after his first gall-bladder operation, could Eden have made a good Prime Minister? I think not. He had considerable virtues. To read his account of his First World War experiences is to see a courageous, effective and totally honest young man, shouldering great responsibilities with success and ease in a situation that sorted out the competent from the useless with brutal and final efficacy, at least in the lower echelons of the fighting services. Other qualities facilitated a remarkably rapid ascent of the ladder to become Foreign Secretary in 1935 at the age of thirty-eight: a first-class intellect, distinguished appearance, charm of manner and a dedication to his profession, which was rather that of foreign affairs than a rounded ensemble of the national political, economic, social and parliamentary spectrum.

One can well understand Eden's frustration at the repeated postponement of WSC's retirement. The Foreign Office is of all the Departments of Government, and certainly of the major policy-forming ones, the most likely to be dominated by the Prime Minister of the day. The issues with which the Foreign Office deals are after all of final national importance. Thus it was not only that the Prime Minister kept postponing his retirement, but that he also was able and willing to look over Eden's shoulder and comment, not always tactfully, on his handling of affairs.

During the War Eden had rebuked Harold Macmillan, then Minister Resident in the Middle East, with the words: 'We already have two Foreign Secretaries: I really can't manage a third,' and here he was back in the position of playing second fiddle in the area of his own responsibility and expertise. On top of this, whereas in the War the Prime Minister and the Foreign Secretary had thought very much alike, now there was a gulf between them on the renegotiation of the 1935 Suez Canal Treaty and on the timing and desirability of a Heads of Government meeting with the post-Stalin Soviet regime, to mention only two matters.

It is no part of my business to speculate on the flaws that led to Eden's disastrous failure as Prime Minister. R.A. Butler said of him: 'There he goes! Half mad baronet, half beautiful woman.' (Eden was descended from the notoriously dotty Sir William Eden.) The remark may have been inspired by jealousy, but it contained an element of truth. When Eden resigned from Chamberlain's Government in 1938, his motives seem to have been as much pique at Chamberlain's by-passing him on foreign affairs (notably in his direct communication with President Roosevelt) as on the great issue of appeasement of the dictators. And his vehement antipathy to Mussolini and Ciano seemed as much personal as moral and political.

Embittered by his prolonged secondary role, and later gravely damaged by his illness, Eden's demeanour seemed to be more and more conditioned by vanity and wounded pride. WSC was certainly conscious of this and the repeated postponements of his resignation as Prime Minister were caused more by his waning confidence in his successor than by an old man's selfish conceit.

WSC's disenchantment with Eden, so apparent to those in his own entourage, led to a whimsical misunderstanding. Descending the stairs to dinner, the Prime Minister announced: 'A man of great charm, of ability and intellect and of unquestionable patriotism, but not the stuff Prime Ministers are made of. No.'

In the uneasy pause someone asked: 'But would Rab [Butler] be any better?'

WSC looked astonished: 'Whatever are you talking about? I'm referring to Melbourne.' He had been reading *Lord M*, David Cecil's fascinating account of Queen Victoria's first Prime Minister.

But at that stage, whom else could WSC have chosen? There were some who had the guts and the vision to have risen to the occasion, Alan Lennox-Boyd and Oliver Lyttelton for instance, but they were not names of sufficient national, let alone international weight. The only possible contender, as far as the Conservative Party was concerned, was R.A. Butler, and WSC held him in low regard – wrongly perhaps, but Butler's character had little affinity with his own. Moreover, he looked on him as a Munichois, a crypto-pink, a man who had built an easy career on the fortune of his wife (a Courtauld). Much of this was unfair; but there was a degree of truth in it all. WSC had a John Bull's rough and ready but deeply perceptive understanding of what the country would or would not approve. 'People like winning,' he used to say, and he did not feel that Butler was capable, in the broadest sense, of 'winning'.

Butler was an intriguing character. Vain he certainly was, but then so are most politicians. He used to tell, with some satisfaction, how as an undergraduate at Cambridge he had applied for the post of summer tutor to some of the French Rothschildren. His application, out of a great many, had been selected. I later heard the Rothschilds' explanation. They had received so many letters that they had put them all into a waste-paper basket and thrown them from a top-floor window. The first to reach the ground had been chosen.

Once, while waiting to see the Prime Minister, Butler asked me: 'What quality do you think a Chancellor of the Exchequer most needs in this country?'

I couldn't think of an intelligent answer: 'Luck?' I hazarded.

'No,' said Butler, 'verve. And that is what I've got.' Well, he had a lot of qualities and those who knew him well were often not only admiring but deeply fond of him, but I did not feel that verve was quite his strongest point.

Not the least significant reason for WSC's chilliness towards Butler was an aborted manoeuvre in 1947, when he was in hospital undergoing a hernia operation. 'Perhaps the surgeon's knife will accomplish what the 1922 Committee* has failed to do,' commented a warm-hearted and grateful back-bench Member of Parliament, later to be a junior minister. Butler, Crookshank, Lord Salisbury and from the Labour side Hugh Dalton were reported to have tentatively discussed the question of a coalition Government, with Ernest Bevin as Prime Minister and Churchill either excluded or offered a minor role. Both Eden and Macmillan had declined to consider any such plot, and WSC was soon informed of it. He bore no rancour, but he did not forget it.

It is hard to identify the motives of the three Conservative figures involved. Of one thing I am certain: Salisbury's actions were in no way

* The official Conservative organisation for backbenchers (non-Ministers).

dictated by personal considerations. He was totally honourable and deeply patriotic. But he did get it wrong, and not all that infrequently. As the French Ambassador remarked unkindly, à propos of Salisbury's reactions to certain foreign policy questions: 'History has finally been given the chance to prove that at least one member of the Cecil family can make a fool of himself.' WSC himself remained cool towards Salisbury. Asked on one occasion if he should be invited to attend a major meeting, be replied 'No. He'll either be ill or obstinate.'

The manners of Churchill's Ministers varied, but one and all seemed to have a far greater stock of sang-froid and courtesy than apparently exists now. What a lubricant such qualities supply to controversial business, and how remote seem the chances of their return! Was it because (is one allowed to say such a thing?) they were gentlemen? Lord Salisbury himself furnishes an example. He had given me rendezvous in his room in the House of Lords at 4 p.m. Naturally I was punctual, but the room was deserted. At ten past, there were pounding footsteps, and Salisbury appeared running; he had been delayed at the wedding of his page, and having fixed the time of a meeting, this grand and elderly figure had felt it wrong to be late. (And if anyone asks if WSC would have run, the answer is, why no; but he was sui generis.)

To digress a little, Salisbury also bears witness to WSC's somewhat puckish attitude to names. Salisbury was known to his family and friends as Bobbety, but WSC spurned this rather affectionate style: 'It's too childish,' he said brusquely and usually referred to him as Old Sarum. Some names for no logical reason seemed to irk him. Telegrams in the Foreign Office distribution from our High Commissioner in Pakistan, a perfectly respectable diplomat called Grafftey-Smith, were always greeted with a curled lip and a muttered 'Grafftey? Why Grafftey??' Selwyn Lloyd (then Minister of State at the Foreign Office, later Foreign Secretary and finally Speaker of the House of Commons) became 'Celluloid'. The US Senator Kefauver became 'Cowfever'. John Foster Dulles, the US Secretary of State, was referred to as 'Dull-duller-Dulles'. The *New Yorker* magazine tended to be 'the New Porker'.

The Ministers in the 1951–5 Government, apart from the leading figures, who might be involved in the succession, did not see the Prime Minister with any great frequency outside working meetings. Although gregarious, hospitable and friendly, WSC had very few intimates outside his own family and staff. His wartime 'Overlord' system, by which senior Ministers were given the oversight of several Departments, had rapidly proved unsatisfactory in a peacetime administration, and the former trusted but ageing figures had mostly gone.

There remained Professor Lindemann, now Lord Cherwell: 'the Prof.'. He was not a ministerial figure and didn't want to be, whatever his official title (actually Paymaster General). He remained an expert adviser who would be called upon to speak with a scientist's knowledge. Drawing on the Central Statistical Office, and with the frequent unsheathing of his slide-rule, he would give lapidary views on which he did not welcome contrary comment. I once made the mistake of twitting him on his wartime advocacy of aerial wire-and-mine fields, which had proved a noisy, ineffective and expensive nuisance. The Prof. had a positively Sicilian memory for a slight, but he did forgive me. At a Chequers weekend, talk at the luncheon table had been on the nuclear deterrent. WSC poured a pinch of salt on the table and asked:

'Prof., if this were X [some nuclear substance – thorium deuteride, perhaps?] and it was detonated, what would the effect be?'

'Winston, it couldn't be detonated.'

'Never mind. Just suppose it could.'

A brief consultation of the slide-rule, then: 'We should be severely burned,' he said primly and put away his slide-rule with a snap. As we left the table, he addressed me:

'It's shameful how little you people know of science and mathematics. Do you not even understand the basics of the Quantum Theory?' (shades of Bertrand Russell).

'No.'

'Well, I need some air; come for a walk with me and when we come back you will.' And I did – for almost a week. Jock Colville had had much the same experience.

The Prof. was the firmest of vegetarians, removing even the yolks of eggs. A non-smoker and a teetotaller, he allowed WSC to persuade him to drink precisely 20 cc of brandy after dinner. His origins were German and Alsatian and his substantial family fortune came from water-works. Randolph said he was Jewish. CSC, who was fond of him, and used to play tennis with him, was uncertain. WSC quite rightly said it didn't matter, and the Prof. himself kept mum on the subject. I was only interested in the question in so far as I sought an explanation for his almost paranoiac hatred of the Germans.

I found him an enigmatic and somewhat sinister figure. He once told me that during the War he had considered the clandestine introduction of botulin into the canned fish supplied in quantity to Germany by Sweden. Pointing to the goldfish-bowl-sized brandy glasses, he said: 'Botulin is far more lethally effective than a nuclear bomb. That quantity of the pure crystal would be enough to destroy all mankind.' Discussing the first atomic bomb, dropped on Hiroshima, he told me that the possibility had been considered of first releasing some vivid pyrotechnical device, to ensure that as many people as possible were looking upward when the bomb detonated at 1,500 feet. Was he just trying to make my flesh creep? I think he was, and succeeded.

If I have painted a somewhat sombre picture of the Prof., it should be recorded that many of those who knew him well were devoted to him. Roy Harrod, an intimate of his at Christ Church, Oxford, where he lived and worked, described him as a saint. He certainly served Britain with unswerving dedication. Towards the end of his life he suffered stoically from angina. Norman Brook, the Secretary of the Cabinet, reporting on a visit to him, wrote: 'I found the Prof., somewhat characteristically, sniffing a phial of dynamite.' The Prof., moreover, did have a lively sense of humour. The talk had fallen on who would be the next Pope, and Cardinal Spellman of Boston was mentioned. 'No,' said the Prof. firmly, 'You couldn't possibly have an American-speaking Pope.'

'Why not?'

'Well, you can't have the Pope "guessing" infallibly.'

A strange and quite out-of-context quirk of the Prof.'s was his dislike of Lester Piggott, then a very young and very successful jockey. 'He's so conceited,' he said. I don't think he had ever met Piggott, and he certainly did not go racing.

Field Marshal Lord Alexander of Tunis had become Minister of Defence in 1951. WSC had wanted Lord Portal, the wartime Chief of Air Staff, but he had declined the offer. Alexander was the type of man who appealed strongly to the Prime Minister: courageous, straightforward, debonair, resolute in defeat and modest in victory. His career needs no adorning from me. Sadly, as Minister of Defence he was a flop. His contributions to Cabinet meetings were increasingly uninspired, and consisted all too often of reading a brief from his staff officers. 'King Log,' sighed WSC.

Unfortunately the briefs themselves were frequently of a low quality. In peacetime there is inevitably a constant battle between the proper provision for defence of the realm and the need for economy. This is often complicated by competition between the Services for the funds available. In the St James's Park lake at that time lived three pelicans. They were known as the Chiefs of Staff, because two, not always the same two, were usually in a corner plotting against the third, and they were invariably fighting over their rations. WSC became increasingly disillusioned and contemplated again taking over the Ministry himself, but was dissuaded by almost universal advice to the contrary. Ultimately Harold Macmillan succeeded Alexander in 1954.

One of the side-effects of Alexander's decline was to cause Field Marshal Montgomery to rise higher in the Prime Minister's personal regard. He had always had great respect for Monty as a fighting soldier, but the latter's egocentric and somewhat naïvely outspoken self-regard had kept him at arm's length, at times at least. 'Montgomery? In defeat unthinkable; in victory unbearable,' he is alleged to have exclaimed (a remark sometimes attributed to Eddie Marsh). Gradually he came to reassess him at his true worth, not only as a master of the battlefield but as a world strategist. However, he remained watchful of Monty's remarkable tactlessness and lack of political savoir-faire.

WSC objected to denigration of almost anybody, unless he had originated the attack himself. At a Chequers luncheon, some rather snide remarks about Monty were being passed and sniggered at. The Prime Minister's reaction ran thus: 'I know why you all hate him. You are jealous: he is better than you are. Ask yourselves these questions. What is a General for? Answer: to win battles. Did he win them without much slaughter? Yes. So what are you grumbling about?' Silence of sniggerers.

In the midst of his second administration WSC remarked: 'I have three competent Ministers: Macmillan, Monckton and Macleod.' This was, of course, not to be taken seriously. There were among the seventy or so (I can hardly believe the number) Secretaries of State, Ministers of State and Parliamentary Under-Secretaries of State, all of them politicians, a great many of competence and more, but they did not much fill the Prime Minister's eye. Among the more senior, there were men who might have left a real national and international mark, and often did so in a more restricted field. The pyramid of Government narrows very sharply.

I have already mentioned Lennox-Boyd and Lyttelton, both tough and practical, and the former imaginative as well. Lyttelton's comparatively undistinguished parliamentary performance let him down on occasions. Nevertheless he had among other qualities a great sense of aptitude, and of fun. On being offered wild duck, which was not wild at all, he commented: 'This is a mallard imaginaire.' When he was Chairman of the London Tin Corporation and a friend asked: 'But Oliver, what do you know about tin?' he replied loftily: 'L'Étain, c'est moi.' Both Lennox-Boyd and Lyttelton held the post of Colonial Secretary at different times; both were well suited to such an exacting and powerful office, and both acquitted themselves with distinction, courage and humour in a situation where the tide was running against them.

Lord Beaverbrook commented thus of two of the three 'competents': 'Ah yaas, Macmillan and MacLeod: the West Highlanders, the dirk in the stocking.' (Beaverbrook is usually quoted as beginning his shafts with 'Ah yaas . . .'. In my experience he very often did.) Perceived success in housing, Macmillan's field, depended largely on the number of new houses built. If the figure exceeded expectations, there were headlines. He was gaining ground all the time, but was not then considered by WSC as a serious contender for the leadership. He had a good First World War record and as Minister in the Middle East and North Africa during the Second World War he had been workmanlike and adroit. A modern cloud hangs over his reputation in respect of the forcible repatriation to torture and death of anti-Tito Yugoslavs in 1945. This episode remains a foul blot on our national record, but it would be unfair to pin responsibility on Macmillan on the basis of such conflicting evidence as has been brought forward. As Minister of Housing he was a great success and WSC was proud of his achievements.

Walter Monckton was Minister of Labour. He was a dear, with an impeccable record as a soldier and a lawyer at the highest level of professional engagement, and many other qualities. It was impossible not to like him for his kindliness and his humour. Competent he certainly was, but in a dangerous direction, for, strongly encouraged by WSC, he was conciliatory to the point of damaging appeasement of the trades unions, whose appetite for power, and indeed tyrannical power, was increasing every day. Many of the steady old Dobbins were being replaced by younger and less principled men, some of whom had clear links with the Soviet Union. The patriotic discipline of the War (and even that was totally disregarded by some unions) had long gone, and the powerful and determined figure of Ernest Bevin was also no more. Thus the combination of a charming and conciliatory Minister of Labour and a Prime Minister bent on good relations with the Unions even at a very high price was disastrous – not immediately, but increasingly in subsequent Governments.

I look, and looked, on labour relations as one of WSC's greatest failures. He himself seemed oblivious to the harm he was doing. Did this derive from his genuinely liberal past, e.g. his attitude to insurance, his Early Closing Act, his Labour Trades Board Acts of 1909, and so many other humane impulses? Of course, he inclined to the Whig aristocrat style (though paradoxically he was well aware that old-fashioned Tory paternalism was usually kinder than the Liberal industrial employers' ethic), but I think that his romanticism, so apparent in so many areas, blinded him to the truth: that he was no longer dealing with the decent representatives of an unquestionably decent and patriotic workforce. 'To get the poor people home for Christmas,' the instruction to Monckton in the face of a major railway strike, was an inadequate motive for the policy that led to the ever-growing and almost mortal damage that was to be done to our national economy in later years.

I think that WSC's weakness on strikes was as much a product of old age and deteriorating health as it was a reflection of genuine feeling on organised labour. He was daunted by the spectre of a general strike and of the iron determination and huge organising energy needed to counter it if it came. Nineteen-twenty-six still haunted him. If he had had the necessary personal resources to subdue the increasingly truculent menace of the worst unions, could he have convinced the country to subject themselves to the necessary discipline and deprivation?

It is always agreeable to pat one's own back for prescience, so I venture to record part of a memorandum I wrote to Christopher Soames in 1953. It was addressed to him because it was well outside my responsibilities, because it had strong domestic political emphasis, and because at that time I was too much in awe of the Prime Minister to address him directly on matters outside my concern. But of course I intended it to be seen by WSC.

Minding my own business as usual, I am writing to you about Trades Unions. You may remember we talked of the possibility of amending Trades Union legislation to diminish the tyranny of the Unions and you said at the time that it was impossible and possibly not desirable, and that public opinion would not wear it. I believe that the atmosphere has now changed.

The main features might be the repeal of the Act of 1906, which broadly speaking makes the Unions immune from legal suit for damages, and the restoration of the Trades Disputes Act of 1927 whose two main provisions were that if a Union were to contribute to a political party individual members had to contract in to do so, rather than contract out, and that political strikes to coerce a Government were illegal. (This Act, as of course you know, was repealed by the Socialists in 1947 and never replaced.)

If these two steps were taken, coupled with a provision that unless a majority of all the members of a Union voted for a strike in a secret ballot that strike would be illegal, then the most dangerous aspects of Trades Unionism would be at an end.

The 1906 Act was passed in an atmosphere very different from today: the Unions were struggling and the danger of hard-faced employers was a real one. Now the Unions are the Fourth Estate and form the most irresponsible part of the country. It is hard to blame employers for being weak, as in the dock dispute, when they get no real lead from the Government.

It is a matter of opinion how drastic action of this kind would affect votes. I myself believe that it would rebound to the advantage of the Conservative Party, because many of the saner Trades Unionists very much dislike the irresponsibility of their lower grade leaders which constantly threatens their family budget.

Christopher was civil but discouraging. I do not think he showed it to WSC and I can well see why. I reintroduced the point to him in May 1962 but to no greater avail. It is interesting to reflect on the effect on our national fortune if legislation of this kind could then have been passed.

In 1931 WSC had contributed an essay to a book entitled *If It Had Happened Otherwise*. It was called 'If Lee had not won the Battle of Gettysburg' and it was a charmingly imaginative historical structure. He rather liked building an ephemeral but fascinating narrative on the radical consequences of a different single political or military decision. In his old age I brought up with him the possible consequences of a more robust labour policy. WSC was unwilling to discuss the matter, which obviously he found worrying and even painful, so I dropped the subject. Perhaps the old accusations of using troops against the miners of South Wales, subsequently proved false in a court of law, and the left-wing hatred inspired by his successful organisation of counter-measures to the General Strike of 1926 still weighed with him. After all, his great hope had been to be seen for what he indeed was, a man of peace and goodwill. Nevertheless, the failure to resist the unions in 1951–5 and increasingly later was to have the direst economic and social consequences, which it was left to Mrs Thatcher partially to remedy many years later.

The Chairman of the Trades Union Council at the time was a good egg, Sir Tom O'Brien, a Labour Member of Parliament and boss of the quaintly styled 'Kinematographic Workers' Union'. He was an emotional man and he congratulated WSC warmly on the appointment of Walter Monckton. 'That was a suggestion straight from the Holy Ghost, Prime Minister,' he said. WSC's reply surprised him: 'From an even higher source than that,' he said with a grin. When we in the Private Office asked him for an explanation, he told us that George Christ from the Conservative Central Office had originally suggested the appointment.

Chapter 14

T HE MOST crucial of the Prime Minister's relationships with his colleagues was of course that with Anthony Eden. It was bedevilled by three main issues: the timing of the succession, the question of a Summit meeting with the Soviet Union and our policy in the Middle East, particularly in respect of our relations with Egypt. These differences inevitably spread to the respective Private Offices, which instead of playing the correctly emollient role between their masters, often found themselves the conduit for intemperate messages from Eden and somewhat patronising rejoinders from WSC. Those from Eden, not infrequently conveyed personally by telephone, were wont to end: 'And tell Winston that I'm at the end of my tether.' (Our internal philosophical comment, with a sigh, was: 'The Foreign Secretary's at the E. of his T. again.') WSC, in any case, did not hold the Foreign Office in high regard. His dinner-table comment: 'A lot of scuttling rabbits. And the Treasury are a lot of mean swine' – (grin) – 'always excepting my Private Office of course,' was enlarged on more seriously in these terms: 'The Foreign Office is probably the best educated of the Departments of State and in many ways the most agreeable. I hold many members in high personal regard. They are adept at analysing a foreign power's views and explaining why we should fall in with them. They are not nearly so good at the reverse process, which is why in negotiation we more often than not come out below our minimum needs. All might be well if they were imbued and led by a strong guiding spirit, but this is not so.'

Monty, who was present at this dissertation, commented: 'The Foreign Office are wet, weak and need a weed-killer.'

These differences on vital policy, and indeed the pressures on WSC to retire, fostered in him a mood of determination, perhaps obstinacy, not yet to give place to a man in whose judgement he placed ever-waning confidence. Eden's ill-health, culminating in his operations in 1953 (one of them botched), confirmed him in his assessment, and the Foreign Secretary's ever-increasing nerve-twanging petulance added further weight to this view. With characteristic tact, I remember remarking to Eden's Private Office: 'The difference between us is that I work for a great historical figure, and you work for a great hysterical one.'

Christopher Soames, doing his duty as a Parliamentary adviser, took the temperature of the backbenchers and told his father-in-law: 'Quite a lot of them want you to go.'

WSC replied: 'Tell them that I won't go until things are a lot better, or I'm a lot worse.' And behind this lay a most significant further feature: Winston

Churchill so deeply wished to be, and to be remembered as a peace-maker. When he was awarded the Nobel Prize, I remember vividly his early and touching joy, which turned to indifference when he learned that it was for Literature and not for Peace. He did not attend the ceremony in Stockholm and CSC represented him there. Albert Schweitzer, fresh from Lambarene, and several highly distinguished scientists were his fellow prize winners. WSC's comment to me on his non-attendance was deliberately outrageous: 'I'm not going to stand up there with those chemists and a catch-'em alive-o' (Schweitzer!). It was of course said with provocative humour. He could not go anyway, because of the Bermuda Conference. And Schweitzer did not attend either!

I have no doubt that WSC's genuine yearning to be considered a peace-maker was an extremely powerful motivation of his policies. He had bitterly resented the Socialist election campaign slogan of 'Whose finger on the trigger?' which sought to portray him as a sabre-flourishing and aggressive militarist. At dinner one night Anthony Head, the Secretary of State for War, was telling the story of his appointment in 1951. WSC had sent for him and told him that he would either get the War Office or another appointment. Thereafter Head had been removed to hospital for an emergency appendectomy. Barely conscious from the anaesthetic, he was told that the Secretary of the Cabinet had to speak to him urgently on the telephone.

Norman Brook wasted no words to tell Head what his Department was to be. 'It's War,' he said briefly.

Head's dazed reaction: 'What, already?'

WSC was far from entertained.

The vexations with Eden's Private Office had unfortunate side-effects. Evelyn Shuckburgh, the Principal Private Secretary, did little to help. As I think his own book *Descent to Suez* shows most clearly, he was not the right man for that most exacting and stressful job. An agreeable Embassy would have been much more his cup of tea.

All sorts of silly incidents, large and small, became time-wasting irritants. The Prime Minister, as I have indicated, received a distribution of Foreign Office telegrams (incoming and outgoing cypher communications with Embassies and other Missions) to enable him to keep abreast of affairs. It was our job, and specifically mine, to filter the telegrams and where necessary to add marginal explanatory notes. (For instance, I once felt it necessary to explain the significance of a Burmese figure improbably named U Tin Kunt. The Prime Minister accused me of having invented him.) To do this, I often had to ask the Foreign Office for minor information. Rather than go through the laborious routine of bothering the Private Office I would usually go direct to the 'Desk Officer' (forgive Americanese) responsible, whom I often knew personally. To expedite this reasonable process I asked for a Foreign Office internal list. It was refused with vehemence.

A more serious consequence befell over secret intelligence. One of my earliest jobs within the Foreign Office had been the distribution of this material to the appropriate departments. Scrutinising what was sent to the Prime Minister, I realised that both the quality and the quantity of papers were diminishing. I made representations to the appropriate quarter, and was rewarded by an increase in quantity, but not of quality. One delivery even contained some rather *Boys' Own Paper* clandestine photographs. At Chequers that weekend the Prime Minister commented adversely on the bland diet he was being fed. I told him of my conclusion that information was being withheld from him. His reaction was explosive: 'Send for C [the head of MI6] and I'll sack the shit.' I was reasonably sure that the clandestine gentleman in question was not responsible. He reported to the Foreign Office. But it took an awful lot of persuading to postpone and eventually avert action of so drastic a kind.

I duly conveyed WSC's displeasure in a highly edited form, but direct to our intelligence people and not via the Foreign Office. They were grateful, and confirmed my hunch that the inadequacy of the information reaching Number Ten was none of their doing. The motives of those responsible might have been their distrust of WSC's discretion. They would have been partially but only very partially right, for he obviously was capable of keeping perfectly silent when it mattered. During the War the sanctity of Enigma, Ultra or Boniface (according to taste: cryptography) was totally respected. Again, they might have felt that comparatively raw intelligence was misleading, and should be predigested by themselves. Or again, if you have a suspicious mind, perhaps 'they' did not want the Prime Minster to be over-informed and thus more prone to interfere?

On that occasion WSC's thwarted retaliation simmered down to a petulant note, thus: 'C. It would be helpful if the disagreeable information you send my way were not written in blue ink on blue paper. Contrast in this matter is usually considered important, as in black on white. P.S. Is "Fluff" [a code word] really a well-chosen term? It is not a good policy to seek notice by doing foolish and unhelpful things.' I managed to suppress this too, this time without much effort. I seemed to spend a good deal of time suppressing or trying to suppress written outbursts. Actually it wasn't as difficult as it sounds, because WSC with his enormous wealth of experience and his essential kind-heartedness did not often push his anger à outrance.

Two more non-delivered missives lie before me as I write, both composed when WSC was in charge of the Foreign Office during Eden's illness in 1953.

Foreign Office

This draft Parliamentary Answer is not of the highest quality. References to 'my good friend Mr Foster Dulles' would be neither apposite nor truthful. Do you not know that in the United States one's mistress is often so styled? The whole tenor of this excessively long, dreary and uninspiring screed is redolent of a second class mind.

And to one of our Ambassadors:

Your telegram No. 127 of May 10. You use the expression 'Giving the French a much needed shot in the arm'. Will you please explain whether you contemplate the use of firearms or of a hypodermic syringe? The latter is not a recognised process of British diplomacy. Have you found it beneficial yourself?
    WSC

Shortly after the intelligence incident I received a visit from a senior official of the Customs and Excise. What had I been smuggling, I wondered? He soon put me at ease as his manner was clearly that of a supplicant and not an inquisitor – the only time I have ever met a Customs Officer in that mode. In those days, drug smuggling was not a great problem. Diamond smuggling, however, was rampant. The miscreants (potential accusations of racism make it imprudent to identify them) concealed the gems in various parts of their bodies. The Customs Officers found investigation singularly disagreeable (can you blame them?) and the smugglers sometimes produced their rather slimy lawyers to allege assault. All this could be much improved by the use of a special X-ray screening machine, but they were exceedingly expensive and the Treasury wouldn't cough up ('mean swine'). Could I enlist the Prime Minister's sympathies? After all, he was First Lord of the Treasury. I could and successfully did, to the extent of two machines. I have always hoped that this will stand me in good stead when I come to grief with a detected illicit half-bottle of duty-free. The Treasury never knew of my intervention and were somewhat puzzled by a remark dropped by the Prime Minister to the Chancellor about 'how unpleasant it must be to have to spend one's day gazing up smugglers' arses, when a small expenditure could deal with the matter both more efficiently and more aesthetically'.

On the other hand the Foreign Office, unfortunately, were only too well aware of who had rumbled their vetting of intelligence data and this did not improve relations. I should, however, make it clear that the Number Ten Private Office's problems, and particularly my own, extended to only a very few in the Foreign Office. Nevertheless, the sky at the summit remained lowering and relations between the Prime Minister and the Foreign Secretary were never to regain the instinctive understanding and warmth of the War years. With the great bulk of my colleagues, however, I remained on friendly and happy terms, and it was not difficult to do so: they were intelligent, hard-working and dedicated people and much easier to like and admire than not.

I am well aware that the incidents I am recounting are out of historical sequence. This should teach me to keep a diary. But if they appear desultory, then that is what they were, and chronology would not alter their interest or insignificance.

At Number Ten I thought that my contacts with the Paris Embassy had been permanently severed, but it turned out not to be entirely the case. Oliver Harvey was retiring, and the Foreign Secretary had recommended him for a peerage. At a Chequers weekend the Prime Minister was ruminating: 'Harvey is a good man, a creditable war record and lifelong and effective service. I'll do better for him than a peerage.' I was startled. What more could he be given? 'I'll make him a Privy Councillor. Anyone can have a peerage and any Minister can be a Privy Councillor, but for a career diplomat or a civil servant it is a true distinction.'

I reminded WSC that Bismarck had said that you could underpay an able man all his life as long as you called him Privy Councillor. Oliver Harvey had sons (this was before the days of life peerages); I was quite sure that he would prefer a peerage. WSC snorted: 'Well, you're wrong. But if you feel so strongly, ask him which he would prefer.'

Easier said than done. Harvey was in a remote part of Wales and had no telephone. The matter was urgent. Telegrams were then efficient, so I sent one: 'Which would you rather have, a peerage or a Privy Councillorship?'

Back came the brief reply like a boomerang: 'Peerage, please.'

I was relieved to be right, but I thought what fun it would have been if he had replied: 'Both.' The no doubt apocryphal story of the origin of the Diocese of Bath and Wells hangs on a similar tale. The two bishoprics were formerly separate, and they both fell vacant at the same time in Queen Elizabeth I's reign. She had a favourite old Somerset priest at Court. She sent for him, and spoke thus:

'Sirrah, I am minded to make you a bishop. There are two Dioceses vacant. I cannot recollect which they are, but you will no doubt know. Which would you like?'

The old man had a powerful Somerset accent. 'Baarth, ma'am', he replied. The Queen was somewhat startled.

'Both? Both?? Well, you have served me faithfully, so I suppose that can be done. So be it.'

I don't believe a word of it, although I was told the tale by Heaven's talent scout Tony Bevir.

I had two further contacts with Paris while still at Number Ten. Arriving rather late one morning, I was told that WSC wanted a message to go immediately to Anthony Eden, who was in Paris for a conference. My two senior colleagues were too busy, and it was urgent. WSC briefed me in a low voice while the Cabinet was sitting. I was to take a written message to the Foreign Secretary. If he accepted the suggestion therein, well and good. If he didn't concur, there were two alternative oral messages. This was big stuff, and I was thrilled.

A police car took me flat-out to Heathrow, where the first flight was held for me. I had no ticket or passport but that had been arranged. The British European Airways staff were less than pleased at the delay; the flight in question was called Silver Wing, Sovereign, or something similar, BEA's answer to the railway's Golden Arrow. Moreover, on board was Sir Arnold Overton, a new member of the BEA Board, and it was his maiden flight as a Director. I was seated next to him. He was friendly and we had a relaxed flight, drinking plenty of champagne with lunch.

On arrival I was whisked directly from the aircraft to the Embassy. Anthony Eden was in his most charming mood and my errand was rapidly accomplished. At Le Bourget Airport the manager of BEA's Paris office greeted me. He was an old friend from Embassy days. 'There's lots of time,' he said, 'come and have a glass of champagne.' We did rather better than that, and the time passed rapidly. Suddenly my host looked at his watch. 'My God,' he said, 'we must run. Your flight is about to leave and Sir Arnold Overton's on board.' Run we did, and I plopped into a seat next to the still courteous Overton. We drank some champagne together over a sort of high tea.

Back at Number Ten, the Prime Minister was dining alone with CSC. I went in to report to him. 'You must be tired, my dear,' he said. 'Have some champagne.'

Paris was, of course, an important Embassy, second only to Washington and well in front of Moscow, where communication was greatly circumscribed by Soviet suspicion, and it was not infrequent that our Ambassador to France would intervene in matters that were not exclusively Anglo-French in interest. Gladwyn Jebb, who had succeeded Oliver Harvey, rather overdid it. His communications, often marked for the Prime Minister personally, arrived in and out of season. WSC had become increasingly irritated. One evening after dinner, he looked at Gladwyn's latest screed and announced: 'I've had enough of the gibbering, jabbering Jebb. Send for a young lady.' A shorthand typist appeared and WSC dictated:

'Following personal for Sir Gladwyn Jebb from Prime Minister. Too many geniuses are attempting to play a leading part in present affairs. There are not sufficient leading parts for all the geniuses. Pray reflect on this. Winston S. Churchill.'

He sat back with a satisfied air, then glared at me. 'What are you looking so po-faced for?' he demanded irritably.

'It will break his heart,' I replied, rather pompously.

'Nothing of the sort. I know him much better than you do. He's as resilient as a rubber ball. Now be a good boy and send it off.' Nose in air, like an offended butler, I withdrew.

The Prime Minister hated working alone. After ten minutes he sent for me.

'Have you sent off that telegram?'

'No, Prime Minister.'

'Why the hell not?'

'Because a Foreign Office messenger has not yet come to pick it up.' This was perfectly true, but he hadn't come because I hadn't sent for him.

A contemptuous snort: 'Oh, very well. Tell Kirkpatrick to write him a rude letter.'

The following morning I called on Kirkpatrick, by then Head of the Service (Permanent Under-Secretary of State) and read him the aborted telegram. A wintry smile crossed his face. The only other people I told were Jock Colville at Number Ten and Robin Johnston, Jebb's private secretary at the Embassy in Paris. To my surprise the telegram was quoted almost verbatim in the Londoner's Diary in the *Evening Standard*. Whodunit? Not me. Certainly not Kirkpatrick.

It is hard to give accurate priorities to the problems confronting the Prime Minister. He had a tendency to concentrate on one major issue to the exclusion of other matters, which though not of world importance were nevertheless significant and often urgent. It was the Private Office's job to make sure that the secondaries were dealt with, and as it was an unpopular task, often provoking the Prime Minister to irritation, I, as junior, got the greater part of it.

Sometimes, being cajoled into reading Foreign Office reports on smaller countries, WSC would break into schoolboy verse:

> 'The Czechoslovaks
> Lie on the flat of their backs
> Emitting loud quacks.'

Then, turning to events in Yugoslavia:

> 'The Yugoslavoks
> All die of the pox.'

Such high poetic flights did not in fact reflect enmity or contempt. They did not reflect high esteem either, and he resolutely avoided their social engagements. Denmark was an exception. Someone said of that country, which WSC liked, that the Germans had been 'kind to the Danes' in the Occupation. This provoked the reply 'Huh. The murderer's canary.'

A question sometimes raised about Churchill's second prime ministership is: What went on with regard to European Unity? The answer is: 'precious little'. The issue had come to be of major importance to politicians only when they were out of office and had no other cards to play. The unspoken instruction in the Foreign Office under the Socialist regime was 'embrace destructively'. When the Conservatives returned the climate was not as bad as that, if only (to be unworthily cynical) because there was too great a backlog of support for the movement, from WSC's Zurich speech to the activities of his son-in-law Duncan Sandys. It was true that there just wasn't time for an active Minister to pursue a 'hobby enterprise' (which, incidentally, is what Ari Onassis called his control of Olympic Airways and the Monte Carlo Société des Bains de Mer) but the disregard went further than this, led by Anthony Eden and generally supported by WSC. Instead of being in the van of European unification, we ultimately missed the bus. I fear that I was as guilty as any, in my minor part in those affairs. In the interim we tended to send political second-raters to Strasbourg.

Some old friends and associates – notably Violet Bonham Carter and Count Coudenhove Kalergy, one of the founding notables of the European Movement – urged the Prime Minister to espouse a more positive role towards Europe. They were treated civilly, but no more. WSC said that he had quite enough over which to fall out with Anthony Eden, without adding an issue that was not of urgent importance, and he was unwilling to receive delegations on the subject. This gave offence. People find it very hard to recognise that a Prime Minister, especially an old man, has to ration his time with the utmost strictness and conserve his energies with a reasonable amount of relaxation. Harold Macmillan read Trollope. Winston Churchill played Rubicon (six-pack bezique) and at weekends watched movies in the evening if he could.

Bezique was to become rather central in my life, because in his long retirement it was WSC's major entertainment and I was his most frequent partner.

It is an excellent game, not particularly difficult, and with a gambling aspect to it, but in the end I felt like that character in Evelyn Waugh's book who was marooned in a remote area of the Upper Amazon and condemned to read Dickens aloud to his captor for the rest of his life.

When I had been at Number Ten about six months WSC decided that I must master the game before my next duty weekend at Chequers. Jock Colville was instructed to teach me, and we sat cross-legged on the floor in the Private Office, occasionally referring to the rule-book, somewhat mysteriously written by one signing himself Squeezers. Occasionally a visiting Minister passed through, and was puzzled, if not contemptuous, at the sight of the two Foreign Office Private Secretaries apparently gambling on the floor in working hours. Only one commented: 'You look like two Arabs bargaining in a souk.'

Thereafter, during or after our games, WSC became more relaxed and even chatty. Here are some fragments:

'Do you speak Welsh?'

'No, Prime Minister. Do you?'

'Yes. I can say "All Wales is a sea of song." Lloyd George taught me. But I've forgotten it.'

And:

'Are you a Freemason?'

'No, Prime Minister.'

'I am. Here, I'll show you the Mason's grip.' Various fumblings followed, which I presume the Masons would deplore as horribly indiscreet, but this time it is I who have forgotten the conclusion.

'Do you enjoy Madame Tussaud's waxworks?'

'Yes, indeed.'

'I haven't been there for many years, but it used to be great fun. As a child I was taken there and I thought it was Madame Two Swords. It sounded frightening. Your deal.'

When attending what I always called the 'Petit Coucher' (after the French Kings' retirement to bed, at which privileged courtiers were present) I used to be horrified at the extravagance of the Battles of the Socks. WSC would frequently have a problem removing his elegant black silk evening socks, and after a brief struggle, his valet would be instructed 'Cut the bastards off!' Wandering about his bedroom, while I fielded last-minute instructions, WSC became invigorated by his plans, and the wander turned into a stride. Inevitably he stubbed his bare toe most severely. He leapt into the air with a string of pure bargee's despair and hopped round the room with almost indecent agility for one of his age, eventually subsiding with: 'My poor bloody toe . . . No doubt my language was regrettable, but it did make me feel so much better. Goodnight, my dear.'

In mid-bezique:

'Do you get indigestion?'

'Yes, all the time, Prime Minister.'

'There is no need to do so. I suffered much until I learnt these exercises.'

And he put down his cards and demonstrated. 'I'm not sure if I got them right. I taught them to Christopher: ask him, and you won't get indigestion.'

I did; Christopher kindly put on a demonstration and I still got indigestion.

A job that fell not infrequently to my junior lot was representing the Prime Minister at memorial services. He was bad at going himself. It was obviously true that he was exceedingly busy, but there were some that he definitely should have attended in person, and his absence from which gave offence.

The occasions I remember best are, inevitably, the ones when something went wrong. One of these was the service for Chaim Weizmann, the first President of Israel, and a friend of WSC's since the latter's days as Minister of Munitions in the First World War. I was told at short notice to represent. I borrowed a black tie from the Messengers, a top hat from Tony Bevir and wearing my overcoat I thought all was well. It wasn't. Tony's hat was much too big for me and I had forgotten that I would have to wear it in the synagogue. The service was long, the address moving, the singing superb. I had balanced the hat on my ears, and they gradually began to give way. This alarmed me. Would they be permanently unstiffened? Would I be lop-eared for the rest of my life? The fact that I was also bonneted and in darkness was secondary. The situation was made no better by Monsieur René Massigli, the French Ambassador, who sat directly behind me, and at intervals murmured: 'Faites attention à votre chapeau! À mon Dieu, ou avez vous trouvé ce chapeau?'*

The Papal Requiem – three hours' worth – in Westminster Cathedral was not much better. Representing the Prime Minister, I was seated in a most honourable position in front of the congregation and behind the Duke of Norfolk, representing the Queen. That's all right, I thought, I don't know the ritual, but he certainly will. He didn't. We were both bobbing up and down at the wrong time, kneeling when we should be standing, sitting when we should be kneeling. It was embarrassing, but worse for the Duke than me. After all, he was the lay leader of the British Roman Catholic community and I was only a heretic.

Not all one's missions were so innocuous. Displeased by the ideas of a female member of the Government, WSC despatched me to instruct her to vary her plans. 'And tell the old cat to do what I say or I'll sling her up by the tail,' was his parting shot (incidentally totally inappropriate, as he was notoriously soft-hearted to animals and had a genuine streak of anthropomorphism which I found exceedingly endearing). My message was not well received; indeed, it provoked a flood of tears, even when delivered in the most emollient style I could contrive. This was followed by a blank refusal to comply. I returned crestfallen to Number Ten and reported. WSC was contemptuous. 'That's no good at all, send for the Chief Whip.' I did. Patrick Buchan-Hepburn received his riding orders and set off confidently. An hour later he was back, looking shaken.

* 'Be careful of your hat. Good God, where did you get that hat?'

'She said no,' he explained. 'She meant it. I thought she was going to weep again so I left.' She won, but the incident did not increase WSC's love for women in politics, never one of his greatest passions.

The Minister of Education, Dame Florence Horsbrugh, usually had a cigarette stuck to her lip. This displeased the Prime Minister, who nevertheless felt that he could not advise on anything so personal. Finally his opportunity came. At a Cabinet meeting on a hot day, the Secretary of State for Scotland, James Stuart, asked plaintively:

'Prime Minister, do you think we could have the window open?'

WSC meditated, then: 'I don't see why. The Minister of Education is not smoking.'

James Stuart (later Lord Findhorn), was a man of great charm, courage and ability. He was also so laid back as to be almost horizontal. He was addressing the House on a hot afternoon. The subject was technical and dull, and the Secretary of State was getting through it as rapidly as possible.

'Speak up!' shouted an Honourable Member.

'Oh, all right,' drawled Stuart amiably, 'I didn't think anyone was listening.'

On another occasion Stuart was attending a mildly hostile constituency meeting. A question was thrown at him from the back of the hall, and he was seen to speak to his wife.

'Don't ask your wife!' screeched the questioner; 'Speak for yerrself, mon!'

'Well, if you must know,' Stuart confided, 'my wife said: "Don't look so bored, James," and I said: "But I am so bored." '

My most embarrassing mission was quite simple. The Brigade of Guards were rehearsing the Queen's Birthday Parade on the Horse Guards just outside Number Ten. Reasonably enough, the bands were thumping enthusiastically. The Cabinet Room windows were open and the Prime Minister was holding a meeting. He summoned me: 'Go out and tell them to stop that noise.' I goggled at him speechlessly. Could he really mean it? He could. I had a Bateman cartoon vision of a small civilian figure accosting the mounted military swell in charge of the Parade and telling him to be quiet. No, it was really too much. I took refuge in bureaucracy. The correct channel of communication must be via the Private Secretary to the Secretary of State for War. He would then, of course, contact the Military Secretary's office, who would in turn address the GOC London District, who would of course carry out his duty and arrange for the officer commanding the Parade to be less noisy. I explained all this to the somewhat astounded Private Secretary. I need not really have bothered, for the Parade ended ten minutes later, and the band went oompahing back to their barracks.

Chapter 15

————— ❧ —————

ONE OF the first questions I asked after arriving at Number Ten was: What do I do if the Prime Minister is taken ill? The reply was: 'Send for Lord Moran, and he will send for a doctor.' This was not nearly as nasty as it sounds. Moran was a specialist of specialists; he knew who was best at what, he was not going to take any chances, and he was ready at any hour of the day or night to drop anything to call on his August Patient. And the A.P. was exceedingly demanding, not to say valetudinarian, sometimes with cause and sometimes without.

I often pondered on this. WSC was undoubtedly endowed with fiercely proud courage. He was certainly not afraid of death. Yet minor ills could provoke nothing short of a fuss. Was it always so? Was it simply the care of the owner of a machine of wonderfully high performance, who sought to keep it at the highest pitch? This puzzle I did not resolve, except to conclude that age had a great deal to do with it. That and the anxiety of appearing to be failing before jealous eyes.

Thus Moran had a good deal to put up with. One morning on going up to the Prime Minister's bedroom, I found him with a thermometer in his mouth. This was not uncommon, but what followed was. Nodding an abstracted good morning to me, he picked up the telephone and spoke to Moran. 'Charles, my temperature is sixty-six degrees.' An agitated and incredulous quacking noise came from the receiver. 'No, Charles, you heard what I said: sixty-six degrees Fahrenheit.' Further quacking. 'What the hell do you mean, in that case I'm dead?' A long pause, then: 'Well, that is to say ninety-six, but I would still like you to come round.'

Moran was somewhat querulous socially and found it easier to deprecate than to approve. (And who is to say he was wrong?) He had had a distinguished career, winning a Military Cross in the First World War as a battalion doctor, writing an interesting book on morale, *The Anatomy of Courage*, as Dean of the great teaching hospital of St Mary's Paddington, and as President of the Royal College of Physicians. He was brought in as physician to WSC on Brendan Bracken's recommendation during the War.

It is a pity that Moran's reputation has been marred by his publication, after WSC's death, of a vast and highly readable tome of reminiscences of his relations with him. It aroused a good deal of anger in the Churchill family as an outrageous breach of professional confidence. Moran maintained that WSC had given him permission to publish. In that case he was singularly imprudent not to get some brief written evidence and not to have told CSC,

Christopher Soames or some other family member, or indeed one of us in the Private Office. He was not popular with his fellow-doctors, who had dubbed him 'Corkscrew Charlie', and they fell on him for an apparent betrayal of the Hippocratic Oath.

Many tales have been told to his disadvantage: his demand to the Prime Minister that he should be made Minister of Health, his request that his rank should be increased to Viscount, and a further request that he should be made Provost of Eton; his reproaches of ingratitude to WSC when none of these were granted. I think these stories are true, but they dwindle in significance in comparison with the undoubted judgement and care with which he watched over his patient. Moran put people's backs up with his jealous insistence on being present on journeys and occasions when his professional services were not needed, but again he might conceivably have been needed, and we should now give him the benefit of a favourable weight in the balance.

Moran was blessed with a charming and devoted wife and two sons, one of whom served ably in the Diplomatic Service and remains a friend of mine, in spite of the review I wrote of his father's book for the *Sunday Express*. I wanted to call it 'The Noblest Moran of them all' (I like anagrams) but John Junor, the Editor, wouldn't let me.

Moran attracted somewhat two-edged remarks from his patients. 'Charles takes his own pills with the melancholy air of one who knows better' (WSC). 'He is good at telling you what you are dying of and asking you to get on with it' (CSC). 'Ah yaas, he's the fellow who doesn't believe in medicine' (Beaverbrook). But a fair question is: 'Would Moran have been kept on if he was no good?'

Old friends of the Prime Minister sometimes complained of wounding neglect. In this, I think they were unrealistic. During a public life stretching back to the beginning of the century and covering many strata of society WSC and CSC had accumulated a vast baggage-train of friends, close friends, and acquaintances who felt that they had the right to be something more. Both the overwhelming weight of office and CSC's liking for privacy made it impossible to keep up with all but a very few. Desmond Morton (Intelligence), Louis Spears (a most colourful and likeable figure) and even Brendan Bracken were gradually to see less of the Old Master, as Brendan sometimes described him.

However, Brendan flitted snipe-like across the scene and was always made welcome. He was by his own choice a mysterious figure. Southern Irish by birth, some people believing him to be Australian, the legend had got about that he was WSC's illegitimate son. Brendan never made any such claim, but he did not actively discourage the story and had a photograph of WSC by his bedside. He had very early attached himself to WSC and had been closely involved with him in the 1930s and even before. During the War he had made a success of the Ministry of Information, where Duff Cooper had failed (WSC's comment: 'It proves that you can't put a thoroughbred to pull a muck cart') and had gone to the House of Lords, but parliamentary politics were not to his taste. His flamboyance, his quicksilver wit, his flood of conversation amounting to verbal diarrhoea, had not endeared him to CSC, who suspected his influence on WSC. She was almost certainly unfair in this respect, later rather grudgingly accepted Brendan, and ultimately felt real affection for him, both for his assiduous championing of WSC in the 1930s and for his undeviating help as a Trustee of the original Chartwell Trust. She still, however, did comment when he was coming to lunch or dine: 'Oh dear, he is so noisy.'

Noisy he definitely was, and his polemical onslaughts were well worth hearing. One tirade, addressed to Nye Bevan, who in spite of his tub-thumping left-wing politics was much attached to the good things of life, began: 'You lounge lizard Lenin, you Bollinger Bolshevik,' and went on from there. In an exchange with Bracken, Bevan shouted: 'You never listen to what I say,' to receive the reasonable rejoinder: 'You never encourage me to.' Brendan was not universally trusted. An opponent said, looking at his shock of red hair: 'Everything about that man is false. Even his hair, which looks like a wig, is real.'

In spite, or possibly because of his peculiarities, WSC was very fond of Brendan. So were many others. He was kind to the young and devoted a considerable proportion of his large self-made fortune to charity. His knowledge of the Church, and of cathedrals, churches and great houses was unrivalled; to sum up, it was quite impossible to ignore him. I never was befriended by him: I think he was uneasy about anyone (unless they were old friends) he felt was close to WSC, whom he genuinely loved and revered.

WSC has been accused of basing some of his friendships, or perhaps it would be better to say relationships, on what our nannies called cupboard-love. There is a little, but only a little truth in this. On submitting one of the innumerable minor drafts for his signature, thanking someone for a present, I had used the phrase 'I am most grateful to you for [etc.].' WSC struck it out and substituted 'I am indeed obliged to you for . . .' adding to me, 'I am not most grateful under £500.' This was a jest, I trust and believe.

On the other hand, when reproached for his close relationship with Philip Sassoon, the enormously rich parliamentary scion of that family, whose entertaining was renowned, WSC replied: 'It is no bad thing to attach a restaurant car to your train when you are starting on a journey of unknown duration.' Now this and other somewhat ruthless sallies I have quoted could easily be misunderstood as both cynical and ungrateful. They were neither of these, but said tongue in cheek, often in the presence of the individual targeted, who understood them for the rather affectionate rough raillery they actually were. When WSC was informed that his last contemporary present at the cavalry charge at Omdurman had died, leaving him the sole officer surviving, he replied: 'How very civil of him!' But he in fact held the man in question in considerable regard and looked on him as a friend. This should not need explaining, but I do see that bald repetition of a bon mot could lead to total misunderstanding of WSC's essentially genial nature.

Max Beaverbrook and Violet Bonham Carter were notable exceptions to the relative eclipse of some old friends. (The latter's vehemence earned her the sobriquet of Ultra-Violet: I suppose since they were so definitely at opposite ends of the spectrum that Beaverbrook should have been dubbed 'Infra-red', though certainly not politically.) Violet had known WSC since well before the First World War. The daughter of the Prime Minister Asquith, she had admired and indeed loved the young, brilliant and adventurous Churchill, though I don't think WSC had ever paid her any marked attention. He was fond of her, but no more. CSC told me, somewhat complacently: 'When Violet heard that Winston was going to marry me, she fainted.' Violet was a first-class public speaker, and wrote eloquent and forceful letters in a strong, clear hand. The opinions expressed were equally strong and clear, and when conveyed orally were delivered from closer and closer range. One inevitably retreated, and I once backed into a coffee table and brought all crashing down. She was a welcome visitor, and must be numbered among the true and valued friends of WSC's, but her violent Liberalism (if this is not an oxymoron), in effect a form of political ancestor-worship, made it difficult to fit her acceptably into the social occasions at Number Ten, for she would dominate and polarise the conversation all too easily.

Lesser satellites abounded. There was the Fish Man. WSC kept an aquarium of tropical fish at Chequers, and the Fish Man was invited to lunch to advise on their well-being. WSC found solace in sitting contemplatively by the tanks. In this he was in advance of modern dentists who sometimes keep tropical fish in the waiting room to soothe their patients. One must add it to the long list of his inventions, such as the tank, Mulberry Harbour, the zip or siren suit, and the sticky band wound round cigars to prevent dribble. Once, as we were leaving Chequers, WSC was heard to remark to a particularly endearing fish, called, I think, a black guppy: 'Darling, I do love you. I would make love to you if only I knew how.'

On the question of the Prime Minister's inventiveness, which, though sometimes prompted by outside advice, was nevertheless formidable, CSC had an unkind story to tell. She said that when visiting WSC in 1908, when he was President of the Board of Trade, she found him playing with a metal and cloth device on his desk.

'What is that, Winston?' she enquired.

'Oh, it's a crank invention that someone sent along. It's of no real use,' was the reply. It was the first zip. WSC hotly denied the truth of this.

In 1952 WSC was still engaged in the last volume of his history of the Second World War, and various military swells, known as the Book Syndicate, used to call on him at regular intervals to advise and, to a limited extent, to ghost sections, on which the Prime Minister invariably put his own final imprimatur. A barrister, Denis Kelly, was the secretary of the syndicate. I was fond of Denis; he was rather a sad figure and tended to be accident prone, but he showed great loyalty to WSC and his historical work.

To Chequers also came Oscar Nemon, the sculptor. The Queen had wanted a bust of WSC for Windsor Castle, and Nemon had been chosen to do it. It was an inspired choice – an absolutely first-class head. Nemon went on to execute a number of further statues and busts of WSC, but they never achieved the success of the first, often consisting of the same head transplanted on to another body. While he sat for Nemon, WSC returned the compliment by sculpting the sculptor in plasticine. It wasn't at all a bad first – and only – effort; but Nemon embellished himself later, which was rather a pity.

Apart from the regulars, and of course his family, WSC was constrained by business, personal regard or expediency to see far more people than he wanted. Even so, I think he saw far fewer than subsequent Prime Ministers. He managed to get away with it because of his renown, his mystique, his prestige. People who might have been importunate with lesser figures seemed not to feel too aggrieved that they were not personally received.

Important official visitors came in plenty. John Foster Dulles, the US Secretary of State, was not one of the Prime Minister's favourites, as I have indicated. WSC quite early concluded that he was anti-British and objected to almost everything about him, in particular his lack of humour and his 'great slab face'. When Dulles came to lunch I was on duty and took him up to the dining room in the little Number Ten lift. Dulles was a large man, and we were uncomfortably compressed. The lift stuck. An almost visible thinkbubble hung over Dulles' head: 'Nothing works in this country, not even the elevators.' We breathed heavily over each other, while hastily summoned technicians wound and unwound the lift-cable, with shouts of 'Bit further, Bill'; 'No, it's stuck again'; 'Back to you for two feet.' The Prime Minister didn't make it any better with irritated cries of: 'Oh do hurry up! What on earth are you doing in there, Anthony?' I don't think the incident really helped Anglo-American relations.

In September 1953 Éamon de Valera, the Irish Republic's Taoiseach (Prime Minister) came to Number Ten. I was on duty, and relations with Southern Ireland were a subject on which I held strong views. I remembered that during the War the Irish had refused us the use of their ports, so that the escorts of the Atlantic convoys, which included cargoes for the Republic itself, were forced to steam much greater distances, and operate from decent, long-suffering, patriotic Northern Ireland or from Liverpool, with consequent heavier losses of life and ships. In spite of the fact that many gallant Irishmen had fought for us, de Valera's wartime Government had been friendly to Germany; indeed, it had presented condolences to the German Embassy on the death of Hitler. Above all, de Valera had been deeply implicated in the cowardly murder of unarmed British Officers during the Troubles. I contemplated a Citizen's Arrest for murder when the Taoiseach crossed the threshold, but opted for a blank refusal to be in the building when he came. The Prime Minister took it in his stride, merely remarking: 'I will do violence to no man's conscience,' but he later read me a short lecture on overcoming personal prejudices in public affairs. He referred to the criticism he had incurred when his letter to the Japanese Ambassador in 1941, declaring war on Japan, had ended: 'I have the honour to be etc., etc.' His reply had been: 'It costs nothing to be civil to a man if you intend to hang him later.' I reflected that there was no chance of hanging de Valera, and contented myself with the sort of silly joke WSC sometimes appreciated. 'I hope the Taoiseach [pronounced Teashock] is not followed by an unpleasant supper surprise.'

To read some recent Churchilliana, one would suppose that their family life was deeply unfriendly and as fraught as the Oedipuses'. This was very far from the truth. The bonds of family love were fundamental. In particular, the suggestion of alienation between WSC and CSC is both absurd and hurtful to their memories. Given the frantic pace of WSC's earlier life and his diversity of occupations and interests, it is not at all surprising that he should have seen less of his wife than a City commuter, or indeed a country squire, would have seen of his. But in any case upper-class spouses in those days did see less of each other, and indeed of their children, than is the case today. Children were produced, washed and brushed and accompanied by their nannies, for reasonably short periods and then vanished behind green baize doors. That doesn't mean that they were any the less loved. WSC told me in touching terms of the death in infancy of his daughter Marigold. 'She said: "So tired" and closed her eyes. And I thought that Clemmie would die in the violence of her grief. She screamed like a creature under torture.'

Though he had taken with philosophy the social ostracism that his defection to the Liberal Party had brought down on their heads, he did not forget the pain that it had caused CSC and the remarkably spiteful inventions of the gossips. 'They said that I beat Clemmie and that you could hear her crying as you passed our house. They said that I drugged, and if you rolled up my sleeve, my arm was a mass of piqûres. We were cut by people we had known well and had looked on as friends. Once when I passed Lady Londonderry in the Park, I bowed politely and she did this.' And he raised his nose and snorted like an offended sea-lion.

Mary Soames has discussed her parents' relations in detail in her biography of her mother, *Clementine Churchill*. The book is a masterpiece and there is really nothing to add, except to note the impact made on this particular observer. Quite early in my time at Number Ten I was amazed and perturbed at a storm blowing up out of nothing on a quiet afternoon at Chequers, culminating in CSC beginning quietly: 'Winston, I have been married to you for forty-five years, for better' and concluding fortissimo: 'AND FOR WORSE!' and sweeping out. The Prime Minister looked at me silently for a moment and then observed solemnly: 'I am the most unhappy of men.' This was so manifestly absurd that I could not help bursting into an unseemly peal of laughter, which WSC did not seem to mind. By dinnertime peace had returned. WSC and CSC, and indeed their children, inevitably lived under a public spotlight and incidents which would excite little outside comment in an ordinary family became the subject of speculation and exaggeration. It is only fair to add that in the case of some, there was little need for exaggeration.

CSC had always hated the South of France; she had not over-enjoyed political dinners, the sudden influx of exacting guests at little notice, and all the distractions and strains of active public life. She was highly strung, imbued with the strongest moral principles and almost morbidly sensitive to noisy vulgarity. Looking after her extraordinary husband had been a great strain, which lavish financial means or modest tastes were not there to mitigate. So it was that when the hurly-burly of the prime ministership was over, she shied away from the new and equal stress of WSC's gradual but perceptible physical and mental decline. Living on the brink of a nervous breakdown, she sought rest and quiet, both terribly difficult to achieve while maintaining, as she never failed to do, a watch over her husband's care and comfort, though perhaps not so much over his entertainment. It was never neglect; it was exhaustion.

At first at Number Ten I avoided her as much as possible. Frankly, she scared me, and at times irritated me too. During one of the Commonwealth Conferences, it had fallen to me unexpectedly and unwelcomely to be landed with seating the Prime Ministers of the Commonwealth at dinner, the Commonwealth Relations Office's *placement* having been rejected out of hand by CSC. In those days there weren't so many Commonwealth Prime Ministers (thank God), but there were quite enough to give one pause. Relations between India and Pakistan had been bad but there had seemed to be a degree of warming between the uneasily arrogant and sulky Nehru and the Pakistani Prime Minister at the earlier stages of the Conference. Might it not be furthered by seating them next to each other, for each was unwilling to make the first move; if the idea did not work, then the clumsiness of Britain could be blamed for a chilly meal? Well, no, not in CSC's view. My table plan was torn up and I was upbraided in civilised but cutting terms for interfering in high matters of State. I grumpily left the matter in the hands of Government Hospitality, and retired hurt.

Although it is out of sequence in my tale, I must record that Clementine Churchill became over the years a loved and deeply respected confidant and friend.

My knowledge of, and friendship with other members of the family developed slowly. I got off to a bad start with Randolph. WSC's relations with his brilliant, brave, generous but sometimes recklessly irresponsible only son have been told and retold by both friendly and spiteful pens. Randolph said of his father: 'Nothing grows under the shadow of a great tree.' WSC sometimes said of his son: 'I love Randolph, but I don't like him.' Neither statement was really true. Randolph sought desperately to be admitted as an ally and intimate of his father, working closely with him as Christopher Soames, WSC's son-in-law, actually did. His father sought for peaceful and affectionate relations, where there was no risk of an explosive outcome to an important dinner, as there had so often been, nor of a torrent of reproaches. The facts seemed to me to be that, temperament apart, Randolph had first been dreadfully spoilt and encouraged in precocity, and later, when this early fruit had turned bitter, he had been rejected and ignored with unnecessary bluntness.

One Chequers weekend in 1953, Randolph had come down for a rare lunch and afternoon visit. In the early evening I had changed (we always wore dinner jackets) and had been working with the Prime Minister in his bedroom, where he was having a pre-dinner rest. The principal object had been to get him to read a weeded Foreign Office telegram distribution, which he was apt to neglect on the premise that anything important would be brought to his attention anyway. Correct premise too, but there was a wealth of significant background; the intellect should not live on headlines, particularly that outstanding intellect. Among the contents of the despatch box was a letter from President Eisenhower, received earlier in the week and brought down to be digested for a reply. Randolph had been bonhomous and affectionate and had just spent some fifteen minutes bidding his father goodbye before the latter retired to his bath. Presently he came to join me in the office over a whisky and soda.

'My father has told me that I should read Eisenhower's letter. May I have it?'

The letter seemed to me to be of no great consequence, but it was marked 'Top Secret and Strictly Personal. Eyes Only' and Randolph held no official position. I became a stuffy bureaucrat and demurred, on the grounds that the Prime Minister had instructed me to reseal the letter, lock it up and not show it to or discuss it with anyone without his personal agreement. I offered to go up and seek instructions from WSC in his bath. The atmosphere deteriorated rapidly, with witty schoolboy exchanges on the lines of 'Are you calling me a liar?' 'No, not yet,' and so forth. Finally, Randolph exploded: 'I can't stay in the same room as you.' As the office was mine, I politely held the door open and he departed with a final volley of general reflections on my character and ability.

I was saddened both because of my genuine regard for Randolph and more because a friendly meeting with his father had been derailed. I hastened to tell the Prime Minister.

'Did you finally show him the letter?' he asked.

'No.'

'You were right.'

I have no doubt at all that Randolph believed that he had been authorised to see the letter and that WSC had either been misunderstood or had changed his mind.

I have related this incident at some length as it illustrates the sad frailty of Randolph's relations with his father. It was tragic that two such remarkable and fundamentally mutually loving natures should almost invariably strike such damaging sparks.

My own relations with Randolph remained formal and cold for some months. Finally, one night, just as I was about to go to bed in our flat in Eaton Place, Randolph rang and asked me to join him for a drink in a friend's house. I declined, citing the hour. This provoked such an exaggeratedly melancholy reproach that I did go. The matter Randolph wished to discuss was not particularly significant but good terms were restored, and Randolph invited me to lunch at Whites the following week.

When I arrived at the Club Randolph greeted me somewhat uneasily. 'Evelyn Waugh is joining us,' he said. 'He can be extremely rude to people he doesn't know.' I refrained from saying look at who's talking, and prepared a shaft just in case. I had no occasion to use it as Waugh was agreeable and interesting. (My unused quip would have been to propose a toast to the Peace of Vereenigen. I expected this to elicit surprise and questions, to which I would have replied: 'It was the end of the Boer War.')

In later years Randolph invariably showed me kindness and hospitality at his house at East Bergholt, and sometimes the services of his pet osteopath in Ipswich. CSC's cousin, Sylvia Henley, was very fond of Randolph. She said: 'One can have the most pleasant weekend staying with him, but it is advisable to keep your car with the engine running at the door.'

Randolph himself was capable of launching shafts that could be brutal as well as witty. A well-known figure had leased his house in London. She later reproached him thus:

'Randolph, I will never lease a house of yours again. There was nothing but a series of tradesmen demanding payment of their bills, mostly for drink.' Which elicited the following rejoinder:

'You shouldn't talk of drink. Your father died of drink. Your brother is dying of drink' (both true); then, leaning forward to inspect her mildly swarthy countenance: 'and what's more, you haven't shaved today.' Much as one may deplore such horrible manners, it certainly put an end to that conversation. On a gentler note, he once observed: 'You know, when the Devil comes to earth, he needs some sort of human habitation. If he is intent on major mischief, then he puts up in Max Beaverbrook. If on minor, then he chooses Evelyn Waugh.'

One day he telephoned Lord Beaverbrook at his Arlington House flat. Max's valet had his own style of address and replied:

'Mr Churchill, I fear that the Lord is walking in St James's Park.'

'On the lake, I assume,' said Randolph.

Randolph's wit did him little good politically. His dislike of Anthony Eden amounted to an obsession and extended from policies to personality, in spite of Eden's marriage to Randolph's first cousin Clarissa. He was going to accompany Eden, as a journalist, to a Washington conference and was dissuaded on a number of grounds, including the argument that he would be persona non grata with the British delegation and Eden especially. 'Oh well, I suppose you're right,' he sighed, 'I would be the last camel that broke the straw's back.' And finally, when he applied to the Selection Committee for the candidacy of the Bournemouth West Constituency, a Committee member asked him the usual question: 'Mr Churchill, if we chose you as our candidate, would you live in the constituency?' He received an immediate answer: 'No! I promise you I won't do that to you.' He wrote a highly critical, indeed scathing book on Eden's failings, of which he gave me a copy inscribed to 'Anthony (M.B. to avoid confusion) from Randolph'.

Christopher Soames had been an Assistant Military Attaché at the Paris Embassy when he married the youngest Churchill daughter, Mary, a most lovable figure, who was certainly the best balanced of that remarkable brood. Her father loved her deeply and was delighted by her giving birth to no fewer than five children. 'She's a very serviceable animal too,' he told the somewhat austere and astonished Sir Alan ('Tommy') Lascelles, the Queen's Principal Private Secretary, when the latter had expressed his admiration for Mary.

Lascelles came from a mould that now seems to be broken. In some ways he resembled Moley Sargent, whom he admired. Like Moley, his sense of patriotic duty was omnipresent, his contempt for those who fell below his own very high standards total, and his personal ambition very small outside his work; and, like Moley, he declined a peerage when he retired. I admired him from a distance, but seemed destined, quite inadvertently, to ruffle his feathers. First there was the missed Royal luncheon (see Chapter 5); then a matter of Tudor history. Lascelles had read *The Daughter of Time*, which sought to rehabilitate the nasty reputation of Richard III, claiming that Shakespeare as a Tudor PR man had done a hatchet job on him. Lascelles was much impressed by the book and sent it to the Prime Minister for his opinion as a working historian. WSC was busy, bade me read the book and draft an answer. I did so, consulted an Oxford don, and drafted accordingly, thanking Lascelles 'for his interesting historical aberration'. He was miffed at this unceremonious dismissal of his pet theory, but WSC was amused and did not give me away.

Christopher Soames became Member for Bedford and, as Parliamentary Private Secretary, rendered remarkable service to WSC, which the latter recognised and appreciated more and more as he grew older and more detached from his few contemporaries and his political colleagues. I am not sure that there would have necessarily been the same appeal in all earlier circumstances, but horses for courses – in more ways than one, for Christopher caused his father-in-law to take up active participation in racing and his horses were a source of happiness and interest to him long after his retirement. After all, he had been a cavalryman. Of the famous, and probably fatuous, however gallant, cavalry charge at Omdurman he said: 'Oh yes, it was most exhilarating. But I did reflect: "Supposing there were a spoil-sport in a hole, with a machine gun?"' And of the St-George-slaying-the-dragon cavalry memorial near Hyde Park Corner, he reflected: 'It is entirely appropriate that an obsolete animal should commemorate an obsolete arm.'

His remarks about his racehorses could be equally trenchant. His most successful stallion Colonist II had gone to stud, his last race having been a flop. WSC explained it thus: 'I said to Colonist, "This is your last race. From now on you will spend your life in agreeable female company." I fear that his mind was not on the race.' And more briefly, when asked if Colonist was still racing, he replied: 'No, he has given up racing. He is now rogering.'

In a later conversation he commented on the persistence of racehorse-owning in families.

'My father had a horse called "Abscess on the jaw",' he said.

'??'

'Well, that's what the bookies called her. Her real name was Abbesse de Jouarre.'

I told him that my grandfather, born in 1832, had owned sixty blood horses and hunters, none of them much good. He had also charged with the

Heavy Brigade at Balaclava in the Crimean War, and had fathered fourteen illegitimate children and eight legitimate ones. WSC was rather admiring, but finally concluded doubtfully: 'He must have been rather an immoderate sort of man?'

Christopher had a down-to-earth, indeed earthy approach to matters. However much I disagreed with him, and that I sometimes did most heartily, the most important point was that he was totally devoted to his father-in-law and that this affection was deeply reciprocated. Relations between Randolph and Christopher were, on the whole, neutrally friendly. I cannot remember Christopher ever attacking Randolph, of whose intemperate tongue he was wary, but Randolph could not always refrain from speaking his mind. Once in the Private Office, with Christopher standing somewhat jaw-dropped, he addressed the ceiling thus: 'Then take the Master of the Horse. He hasn't opened a book in his life, but he's shrewd, very shrewd. He'll get on whatever side of the Tories predominates.' Unfortunately the high philosophical tone degenerated into a pointed critique of Christopher's career that left an embarrassed and sad audience.

The brightest star, though only an occasional visitor, was Sarah. Her looks, her charm, her dancer's elegance were linked to a generously impulsive nature, a romantically imaginative mind and a delightfully husky voice, with a tinge of mid-Atlantic accent. It is strange that women acquire this trait of voice-matching far faster than men. It must be protective colouring, like the chameleon or the lemon sole. I expect that the Sabine women were speaking Latin with a Roman accent within weeks of being carried off. WSC referred to Sarah as 'the Mule'. I asked him why. He said: 'Because she's bloody obstinate and she won't breed.'

This thumb-nail sketch of the family background is obviously superficial. These were first impressions and my knowledge of and affection for most members of the family were to grow with the years.

It is undoubtedly true that WSC loved his family deeply. It is also undoubtedly true that they came second to his purposes and his political work. How could it be otherwise?

Chapter 16

WITH MEMORIES of his wartime association with Roosevelt still fresh, it was obvious that the Prime Minister would and did set more store by Britain's and especially his own association with the United States and its President than by any other aspect of foreign policy. This was both natural and sensible; but the extreme, almost desperate emphasis that WSC placed on the 'Special Relationship' was neither of these.

The Special Relationship's life had not been a long one and it had been a sickly child, doted on by its British parent and increasingly neglected by the American side. It had only flourished in the earlier days of the War and had lost its appeal to the US administration as their country's material contribution to the battle overtook our own.

I was not guiltless in harbouring the illusion that the US were our natural, staunch and permanent friends. My meticulous flying training by the US Navy (which undoubtedly saved my life) and my eight months' wartime sojourn in America had left me with abiding feelings of gratitude and affection which endure to this day. But on joining the Foreign Office in 1946 it did not take me long to realise that a substantial part of the State Department at least was fundamentally anti-British. Not only that, the long-standing practice of appointing Ambassadors for political services and the Isolationist tradition had produced a service of patchy ability. Our older regulars were often head and shoulders above their American colleagues in professionalism, historical experience and sheer intellectual horsepower. The best US diplomats were very good, but the bulk of them were vin ordinaire. Thus we not only seemed to be arguing against prejudice but sometimes also against ignorance and stupidity. I could name the most visibly anti-British members of the State Department, but it would be a long list, and I prefer to remember the others.

Could the Prime Minister be convinced of anything even approaching the real situation? No, he couldn't. In WSC's eyes people like Dulles, Jefferson McCaffrey (US Ambassador in Cairo at the time of Suez) and Byroade, mysteriously dubbed 'Colonel', at the State Department were unfortunate exceptions. Tongue in cheek but not entirely so, I once suggested that our meagre intelligence resources would be better deployed against our Allies, and particularly the Americans, than against our potential enemies; after all, we knew what the latter intended anyway, whereas the former were always springing unpleasant surprises on us. WSC was genuinely shocked and annoyed. He very definitely was not a student of Niccolò Machiavelli, and he rejected the maxim, so dear to General de Gaulle, that no nation can afford to show gratitude. He didn't even particularly accept the eighteenth-century Lord Halifax's dictum that 'public affairs are a hard business and good nature is a bungler at them'.

Not even the American offer to the Russians at Yalta to discuss the future of Hong Kong without the presence of the British could substantially change WSC's tenacity, though it is not clear when he became aware of this remarkably unfriendly suggestion. And if further proof is needed it rests in General Wedemeyer's account of his briefing by President Roosevelt when being despatched to the Far East at the end of 1944 to succeed General 'Vinegar Joe' Stilwell as Military Adviser to Chiang Kai-shek. He quoted Roosevelt as saying 'with all the force of which he was capable' that he was determined to eliminate the European Empires in the Far East. But this was not revealed until General Wedemeyer published the story many years later, and I suppose that one must make allowances for the fact that Roosevelt was within a few months of his death. Nevertheless I am convinced that it represented his true attitude.

WSC's persistence in blind trust of the US was surprising, as he was a hard-headed realist in so many ways. But apparently as far back as Tehran in November 1943, the Prime Minister's advisers, including the Chief of the Imperial General Staff, were suggesting that he should not put too much reliance in Roosevelt's support, and it soon became obvious that the latter was determined 'to come to terms with Stalin whatever the British might say' (Harry Hopkins, Roosevelt's friend and personal representative). Such warnings fell on stony ground. Lord Moran, who was present, records:

> Winston is puzzled and distressed. The President no longer seems to the P.M. to take an intelligent interest in the war; often he does not seem even to read the papers the P.M. gives him. Sometimes it appears as if he had no thought-out recipe for anything beyond his troubles with Congress. Nevertheless, though we have moved a long way since Winston, speaking of Roosevelt, said to me in the garden at Marrakesh, 'I love that man', he is still very reticent in criticism. It seems to be dragged out of him against his will. And with half a chance he will tell over dinner how many divisions the Americans had in a particular show against our handful, and how their casualties in that engagement dwarfed ours, and things of that kind.

Against such a background of determined devotion, it is not hard to see how miscalculations could later arise.

When the US Presidential election took place in 1953, WSC privately adopted, and used the Republican slogan: 'I like Ike'. He later met and admired the Democrat contender, Adlai Stevenson, whose charm, intelligence and warmth were indeed memorable, but he saw in Eisenhower an old comrade-in-arms, who had quite often deferred to his judgement. Surely it could happen again? No, it couldn't, but WSC never gave up hope. He made considerable changes in Volume VI of his war memoirs, then nearing publication, to remove any criticism of Eisenhower. In particular, the wilful failure to take Berlin before the Russians, and the subsequent withdrawal of Allied troops from huge areas of Central Europe, which led disastrously to the Communist position of strength in the Cold War, had been criticised in civilised but scathing terms in the earlier draft. The published version was mild. A pity, I thought. History is history, and you don't do much good by failing to illuminate the grosser errors. To which the reply is, of course, that you don't do much good by offending the new US President either.

With this background, it is not surprising that the personal communications between WSC and Eisenhower ranked very high in the former's scale of importance of events. I was not present at their meetings in Washington or Bermuda, but these have been well documented and discussed, and I am here referring to their exchanges of letters. The styles were very different, as one might expect, but so were the contents. WSC's letters were almost entirely his own composition; Anthony Eden would be shown drafts, and he no doubt in turn showed them to senior Foreign Office figures, but the final version, though making some concessions and additions, was unmistakably Churchillian. Whatever the topic, the underlying message was always the same: if Britain and the US stick together, then all will be well. The language and argument were not particularly high-flown, but heavy on historical logic and steering an adroit course between patronising explanation and assumption of knowledge that probably was not possessed by the recipient. With the exception of pressure for a Summit meeting with the Russians, which may have been premature, WSC was nearly always subsequently proved to be right.

The President's replies were bland, and generally negative. They bore the mark of several drafters and it was not difficult to sense the old editorial wish that 'this correspondence should now cease'. The exception, again, was the opposition to an early Summit, where the arguments were cogently and clearly expressed.

In spite of all this, the Prime Minister looked forward with almost childish excitement to the arrival of the President's missives. This got me into trouble. WSC had gone to an official banquet at the Savoy when a messenger and guard arrived from the US Embassy with a letter from the President. It was, of course, double-sealed and the inner envelope marked 'Top Secret: Eyes Only'. Reasoning that the Prime Minister could not be extracted from the Savoy and that the letter might be truly urgent, I opened it, as it was indeed my duty to do. The contents were neither urgent nor particularly significant. When the Prime Minister returned, he was indignant. He pointed speechlessly to the 'Eyes Only' inscription. I was rather hurt and said, in effect, that if I was not trusted, then I would do more harm than good at Number Ten (I suppose I might anyway). WSC took this in silence. Half an hour later he summoned me and delivered judgement: 'The question of whether you should have opened the letter is moot, but I do accept that one might well conclude that you should have. In any case, I will always forgive mistakes towards the enemy' (i.e. overdoing it, rather than taking inadequate action).

I still felt a little ruffled, but got an unusual opportunity to score off the Prime Minister a day or two later. He had for some time taken exception to my not wearing a hat. This culminated in: 'You should wear a hat in this weather. It is imprudent not to.' I had a plentiful crop of hair at that time, and commented that I preferred to be bareheaded. 'That is somewhat dégagé,' he rejoined severely. So I bought a hat and carried it when with him. A few days later I accompanied WSC to the House of Commons, and he was in a bad temper, having had rather a dusting at Question Time. Driving down Whitehall he considered my bare head with distaste and asked after my hat. I raised my hand silently, holding the thing.

'Why don't you put it on your head?'

'Because we are passing the Cenotaph, Prime Minister.'

He removed his own, with a glance that said 'Don't do that too often.' I felt as though I had teased a bull-dog in its basket.

When we reached Number Ten he determined on retribution, and accompanied me into the Private Office seeking whom he might devour. His eye fell on a pile of letters I had dictated and which were awaiting signature. The date was given in the form (for example) '14th September 1953'. WSC's eyes lit up. 'It is not the fourteenth September,' he said triumphantly. 'If anything it is the one thousand nine hundred and fifty-third September. You should express it either as "the 14th of September" or as "September 14".' I meekly acquiesced.

As I have said, I did not accompany the Prime Minister to Bermuda or Washington, these ventures being reserved by Jock Colville and Pitblado. However, I did inadvertently throw a minor long-range spanner in the works at Bermuda in December 1953.

The French had been responsible for repeated postponements of the Conference, on which WSC set great store, by their failure to form an enduring government. There had even been discussion of the 'Empty Chair Policy' of going ahead without them in various areas. WSC's birthday was on 30 November and I had given him a copy of a book by C. S. Forester, a brilliant account of an English rifleman cut off from the army in the Peninsular War and operating with the guerrillas. WSC found it absorbing and even read it at the table when dining with Eden on the aircraft to Bermuda. He continued to do so on the verandah of the Mid Ocean Club, where the Conference took place. Unfortunately the press managed to photograph him with the title blazoned all too visibly. It was *Death to the French*.

Seeing WSC off on his departure for the Conference I garnered one of his typical remarks. Asked by the newspapermen how he expected to weather the seventeen-hour journey (he had had his major stroke the previous June), he replied: 'Well, I shall take a sleeping pill and either wake up in Bermuda or Heaven – unless you gentlemen have some other destination in mind for me?'

The Bermuda Conference strolled loftily over the great problems of the world but had little practical result. President Eisenhower warned that if the North Koreans resumed an offensive against the South, he would authorise the local use of atomic weapons. WSC assented to this suggestion with surprisingly little reflection. He seemed at that point briefly to share Eisenhower's view that the nuclear development was only a further extension of conventional warfare, a conclusion very different from his often expressed conviction that a whole new dimension and philosophy of conflict now glared upon the world.

The European Defence Community was discussed, with WSC urging it on the reluctant French but in the form of a 'grand alliance, with all nations standing in line under a unified command' and very specifically including West Germany. In view of modern attempts to enlist the long-dead Winston Churchill in arguments for or against a federal Europe, a united Europe or, in de Gaulle's words, 'l'Europe des patries', I will, in their proper place, attempt to deploy his views such as I knew them. But it is on the whole a vain exercise, for conditions during his later lifetime bore no resemblance to those now pertaining. The interest is historical and to a considerable extent academic.

The main heft of the Conference lay in WSC's passionate conviction that a Summit meeting with the USSR was essential and the Americans' equally determined view that it was highly undesirable. Eden and the Foreign Office sided with the Americans, in a reasonably muted and diplomatic style. The only constructive outcome of the Conference was to illuminate with clarity how far the views of the Prime Minister and the Americans differed.

WSC did not give up easily, and to the end of his tenure at Number Ten he nursed the vision of a meeting with Stalin's successors. He was totally concerned with avoiding the final horror of a nuclear war, while still maintaining his confidence in the weapon as a total deterrent, if only people knew what its use would entail. He had read with fascination and awe Nevil Shute's book *On the Beach*. Set in Australia after a major war, it depicted conditions as the nuclear contamination gradually spread over the Southern Hemisphere, inexorably and painfully eliminating all life, so that euthanasia was forced on the whole country. WSC wished to have it translated into as many languages as possible, especially the Slav tongues, and sent to the countries' leaders with his personal appeal that they should read it.

Similarly, after a briefing on the potential nuclear delivery of the US Strategic Air Command's B-47 and B-52 bombers, and of our Canberras, against a very limited Soviet defence capacity, he discussed a series of peaceful but unopposable high-altitude forays over Soviet bloc territory. 'Red beads' (quite literally) would be dropped over large areas to bring home the potential annihilation. Was he serious? It is very hard to say, as he threw out ideas like sparks from a Catherine wheel, but he certainly brought the matter up on many occasions.

Some time after the Bermuda Conference, I was alone with him after dinner. He reverted to his desired 'Summit meeting' (not a term then in common use). 'I will take you with me,' he promised. Warming to his soliloquy, he decided to broach the idea of a solo mission to Moscow, unaccompanied by his Foreign Secretary. Eden was contacted on a scrambler telephone. His reaction was not unexpected. 'But Winston, they'll think I've been liquidated,' came back in agonised tones. I don't think that the Prime Minister was just teasing him.

At the time I felt that WSC was right in so persistently seeking a meeting with the new Soviet leaders, and that the Americans', and indeed the Foreign Office's, opposition was based on flawed reasoning, if not on jealousy of the Prime Minister's hogging the international limelight as far as President Eisenhower and Eden were personally concerned. Now, with subsequent knowledge available, I reluctantly conclude that such a venture would have been too dangerous, in that any perceived success could have weakened the Western Alliance's resolve without actually securing any real counter-balancing Soviet withdrawal from their aggressive intentions.

When it came to Europe, the Prime Minister had a somewhat complicated ambiguity of purposes. He profoundly wished for détente with the Soviet Union, but he was determined to maintain a stoutly defensive military posture against the Communist bloc. He said of Stalin: 'He never broke his personal word to me,' which seemed an almost incredible misreading of events by a great historian. I was astonished, and when conversational opportunity offered, mostly after WSC's retirement, I discussed the question with him at length.

It will be recalled that after the Germans had invaded Russia in 1941, they had later found at Katyn the mass graves of some 12,000 Polish officers. An international team of inquiry, convened by the Germans, had concluded that the deaths had taken place well before the German invasion, but we had nevertheless blamed the Nazis. Had WSC known the grisly truth, I asked? He replied:

'It was an agonising decision. The Nazis were not noted for veracity and had concealed many crimes. Had the international investigation been suborned or duped? I could not allow myself to believe that our allies were responsible. I put it behind me.'

'Do you regret it?'

'I regret many things.'

He went on to indicate that what he had then feared the most was a separate peace and a second Nazi–Soviet alliance on the lines of the Molotov–Ribbentrop pact of 1939. Before the Japanese attack on the US in December 1941, Britain would have been confronted by Germany, the Soviet Union, Italy and possibly Japan with no fighting allies, except the Commonwealth. That Russia was capable of making a separate peace is certain. We now have evidence from the captured German Foreign Office documents of the 1939–41 offers of Soviet assistance to Germany, and after they were at war there were exchanges in Stockholm.

I have never been able to explain WSC's remarkable blind spot in judging Stalin. Did it spring from his 'great man' theory of history, and his belief that all could be settled by a few at the summit? Psychologists have suggested that WSC's neglect by his father, and his early passionate longing to stand well in his eyes, account for this almost automatic admiration of a great figure, be it a King, a President or an all-powerful and ruthless despot. Churchill was unwilling to volunteer much information in this area and I felt that intrusive questions would have been indecorous and out of place, even when I had been with him for many years.

This cast of mind did not diminish WSC's bulldog grip on military reality, but he sometimes slipped in his recollection of past events. In 1954 he informed the Commons that in the last stages of the advance into Germany in 1945 he had sent Montgomery a telegram urging him to retain captured German arms so that they could again be issued to the Germans if the Russians continued their advance beyond the agreed frontiers, and in the intoxication of victory sought to settle matters once and for all with the West. A sensible precaution, indeed; but although Monty loyally said that if the Prime Minister stated that such a telegram had been sent, then it indeed had been, no such missive had actually been despatched. It caused a row in the House, it encouraged those who said that WSC was past it, it infuriated the Russians and their British toadies, but it encouraged the Germans quite a bit.

There is no doubt that WSC had a high regard for the Germans all his life. His distinction between the German people and the Nazis was clear, though it did not stop him from acquiescing in the mass destruction strategy of Bomber Command, initially on the grounds that it was the only way that we could strike back at Germany at that time. One has only to read his essay on Hindenburg and Ludendorff in *Great Contemporaries* to see his feelings for their astonishing Fatherland. He used to recite a poem: 'The German foot goes seldom back where once it firmly trod.'

He often discussed his theory for a peace settlement for Greater Germany after 1945, and indeed after 1918. The country should be divided horizontally. The northern section, principally Prussia, should be subjected to a severe but correct regime of control. The southern section should have a much looser degree of intervention and more lenient terms, and the Habsburgs should be restored to the Austrian throne. I couldn't quite follow the logic of this; after all, the Nazi movement had its origins in Bavaria.

WSC had disliked the German war-crime trials. He would have preferred something much more summary, and much shorter. One can sympathise. The trials went on for too long and there was something very unpleasant in seeing well-fed lawyers hounding desperate men to a predetermined doom. I came to sympathise with Goering for his indomitable courage and presence of mind under cross-examination, and his final defiant suicide (Hartley Shawcross, the then Attorney-General and chief British prosecutor, told me that his sympathies had also been aroused.) But what alternative to the trials was possible? Something had to be done, and if justice was short and summary how could it be fair between, say, the concentration camp guards who in some cases stayed at their horrible duties and those more cunning who had fled? I'm so very glad I was not involved in it.

WSC's instincts were nearly always chivalrous – 'In victory, magnaminity,' in his own words – and he did not appreciate the victors trampling on the conquered, particularly if the former had not been combatants. A kinsman serving in our army of occupation in Germany wrote to him complaining that the Hunt they had organised, presumably a fox-hunt, had been forbidden to ride over German farmland. The letter got short shrift, but was ultimately sent to the Foreign Office with a scribbled 'Foreign Secretary, here is a truly important international matter for you to settle.'

When it came to France, ambivalence was again evident. WSC's love of France was sentimental and long-standing, based on personal experience in peace and war. His greatest heroine, or indeed hero for that matter, was Joan of Arc. But this did not deter him from taking a firm line with the French if he felt it was required, and he told me that after 1940, and their breaking of a solemn agreement not to sue for a separate peace, he never felt the same about them.

In the 'general post' – fan-mail, letters from inventors, lunatics and many decent but puzzled citizens – there was always a number of hate letters from France on the anniversary of our sinking of the French ships at Mers-el-Kebir in 1940. I asked WSC about it at dinner in France after his retirement and noted his reply.

'It was horribly painful. But they did not then deserve all that much consideration. Admiral ... I can't remember his name [it was Gensoul] did not send a complete signal of our terms. We had their cyphers. All he told was the alternatives of sinking themselves or being sunk. That was not the full issue at all. We offered them the honourable choices of fighting at our side for the liberation of France, of sailing to a French West Indian port, or to the United States and being disarmed, or of sailing to a British port with reduced crews who would be repatriated. If all these were refused, then we demanded that they should scuttle their ships. Their truculent reaction was perhaps the creature of their shame at their country's surrender. I was most unhappy at the attack and it was not particularly well carried out. But it spelled out to the world our determination to fight on AT WHATEVER COST!' And here his voice rose to a shout, startling Beaverbrook's white cat who was sitting on his lap.

WSC's attitude to de Gaulle was half-amused and half-indignant (I am speaking of 1951–5, when Churchill was in power and de Gaulle wasn't). He told me with a rueful smile that during the War he had set up what amounted to a public relations campaign in Britain to assist de Gaulle when the General's stock was particularly low. He had staunchly withstood Roosevelt's plans to oust the General, and stood by him in and out of season. Duff Cooper's advice had then been very helpful, though in other matters 'Duffy could be a goose'. after a certain length of time de gaulle had become too much of a symbol of French resistance for us to ditch him, however badly he behaved – and some of his behaviour was shameless. 'He may be a bastard, but he's our bastard and we're stuck with him,' seemed to sum it up in many people's minds.

I had rather hoped that WSC would pay some attention to the information I had on contemporary France – after all, I had just returned from three years of reporting on the country – but it was not to be, and perhaps that was fortunate because I, in company with nearly everybody I knew, did not believe that the French people would again turn to de Gaulle, save in the direst emergency. Proportional representation had shown its most futile aspects, but the situation could hardly be described as a dire emergency, though North Africa might be so categorised. We underestimated the power of prolonged irritation and frustration. The French are an impatient people.

Chapter 17

EGYPT WAS an issue on which the Prime Minister and his Foreign Secretary differed profoundly, and which damaged their relations permanently. Hawk and dove, when the renegotiations of the Anglo-Egyptian Treaty of 1935 came on the agenda, both WSC and Eden deployed every argument they could muster. The battle swayed to and fro, punctuated by Eden's six-month absence from the Foreign Office after his three gall-bladder operations and WSC's stroke in June 1953. The focal point of the issue was the Suez Canal, where some 80,000 British troops were stationed, mainly taking in each other's washing. But troops in peacetime always appear to be doing this; it is hardly their fault. Scattered down the west bank of the Canal were repair-shops, stores and airfields. It was a formidable complex, built to sustain the wartime armies in the Western Desert, to support our presence in Iraq, Jordan and Palestine, and to hold the vital arterial link with India and the Far East. The safety of oil transit from the Gulf was then a major factor, as the super-tankers that could not pass the Canal were not yet in common use.

The Prime Minister considered all these factors, but was much more conscious of the political and strategic influence of the base, which he saw as a powerful stabilising factor for the whole area – an earnest of British will and ability to keep the peace and secure our interests and those of our client states. This concept may ring rather oddly in today's little Britain, but then we were still a great power and WSC believed vehemently that our influence was unequivocally for the good in the world. He was not blind to the dwindling of the national will and vigour necessary to back up such a stance. 'I can defend the British Empire against anything except the British people,' he said, and he quoted:

> We sailed wherever a ship could sail
> We founded many a mighty State.
> Pray God our greatness may not fail
> From craven fears of being great.

The military, and some Cabinet Ministers, initially backed the Prime Minister, and in the House of Commons the Conservative 'Suez Group' were stalwart, but gradually the tide turned. My cynical view is that many of those whose opinions had changed were simply trimming their sails to the new wind and the heir apparent, Eden. The pretext for abandoning the base was given as its irrelevance in the nuclear age. But the same argument could be used for almost any military or naval establishment, and the Suez base, important as it would have been in the event of hostilities with the USSR, had also a totally different function quite unconnected with war between the great powers.

Egypt's revolution had removed King Farouk, who although no friend of Britain was a comparatively stable factor, and thrown forward first Neguib, a not unreasonable figure, and then Nasser. Nasser can be compared with a less bloodthirsty Saddam Hussein, and his interference and adventurism were a most dangerous element in the Middle East powder keg. Once committed to a course of weakness and appeasement, Eden was stuck with it until the final tragedy of 1956. By that time he was bitter and disillusioned with Nasser, in whose regime he had placed considerable confidence.

I watched with pain and foreboding the Prime Minister's gradual retreat to acceptance of a grossly inadequate revised Treaty with Egypt, leaving our vast base guarded by Egyptian civilian watchmen. If it had not vanished in the 1956 fray, it would soon have been looted out of existence anyway. Even a trip-wire of British troops might have prevented Nasser's seizure of the Canal. The events of that time sowed the seeds of 1956 which accelerated Britain's gentle decline into a vertiginous plunge. The hinge of fate indeed.

I did not refrain from impertinently intruding my views, orally and in writing, on anyone who would listen. The Prime Minister was kind enough to do so, mainly I think because I shared his deep misgivings over our 'scuttle' (his own words) on the Canal issue. I wrote memoranda, I importuned my colleagues and Christopher Soames. I lobbied my own friends in the Foreign Office. It availed nothing, but it did not escape the attention of the most vigorous of the Foreign Office scuttlers, notably two members of Anthony Eden's Private Office, who squeaked with indignation. It even earned me a rebuke from the Foreign Secretary himself, which ran approximately thus: 'You are not doing your duty. Your job is to further Foreign Office policy with the Prime Minister, not to oppose it.' I replied that having been seconded to the Treasury, and thus to the Prime Minister, my job was to serve him. I wished to add that if the Foreign Office's policies were foolish and cowardly and potentially disastrous, which was indeed the case on this issue, then my duty was to oppose them tooth and nail. But for once I kept quiet.

The Prime Minister was often unwontedly silent as the Middle East scene deteriorated, though from time to time the lava overlipped the volcano's edge, and he expressed himself in vehement and melancholy terms. To one tirade he added, as if in answer to the unspoken question 'Why don't you put a stop to this disgraceful capitulation, since you see its consequences so clearly?' the following deeply sad conclusion, spoken in calm and meditative terms. 'You must remember that the Office of Prime Minister is not a dictatorship, certainly not in peacetime. I am surrounded by hungry eyes. Poor Anthony' (not me – the other one).

A lengthy, philosophical discourse of self-justification in a patchwork of reminiscences is distinctly boring. However, since the point subsequently was the reason for my declining the offer of the post of a Private Secretary to the Queen, I here inflict my views on the reader.

I firmly believed, and still do, that British influence in the world was, in the words of *1066 and All That,* a Good Thing. What matters is not who rules you, but how they rule you. It is very difficult to decide if a country is happy or unhappy, but certainly some ingredients of the formula must be positive answers to these obvious questions: Are the people being kept alive? Is their government protecting them from external aggression and internal disorder? Is it doing its best to cope with famine, flood and pestilence? Is its justice accessible and incorruptible? Is medical and educational improvement a real part of its policy? Is progress being made to greater involvement of the population in the process of government? Many, many more could be added, but let us stay simple.

If I had been a Gaul, I would have regretted profoundly the collapse of the Roman Empire, even though its rule could be brutal, especially in the earlier stages of conquest and occupation. When I came home from my work, I could expect to find my family alive, my house intact and a market for my goods. There was a good chance of a first-class water supply, good roads and a judge who was locally incorruptible. Above all there was law and order. After the Roman departure came the Dark Ages, where none of these things applied. (And what about central heating?)

Mutatis mutandis, the same arguments apply to the British Empire and, to a varying extent, to other empires. I am not suggesting that we could or should have stayed in India, but I am aware that our rule brought order to a fragmented subcontinent and that the benevolence of the Indian Civil Service, Indian Medical Service, Forestry, Transport Services and so much else is well recognised today by a great many Indians and Pakistanis from all levels of society. Under the Raj, a few dedicated men would rule an area the size of Wales with admirable impartiality. They could be severed for years from their children, sent home to Britain to avoid the high chance of fatal diseases, and they themselves would often leave their bones in lonely graves. If the few troops who garrisoned a population of say, 400 million, opened fire on a mob, it was world headlines. Now? Every day one reads of twenty, fifty, a hundred killed in communal strife. And the deaths in the partition of 1947 ran into one or two million; choose your own number, for no-one knows.

Africa is a much clearer case. Food-producing areas are now starving. Tribe fights with tribe and genocide raises few eyebrows. Democracy there is defined as 'one man, one vote – once, and never again', and financial and material aid is filtered through so many corrupt hands that little reaches those who need it most. Winston Churchill said: 'The epitaph on decolonisation may be taken from the Book of Isaiah: "Thou host multiplied the nations and not increased the joy." '

Perhaps the most poignant observation is that so much misery could be avoided if the new countries did not spend such huge sums on modern armaments. They certainly shouldn't need them. If only aid could be made conditional on a reduction of military spending. If only the arms-producing powers could agree not to send them anything more lethal than a catapult. Utopia, Utopia . . .

George Santayana, the American philosopher, poet and historian, wrote of British rule: 'Never had the world had so sweet and just a master.' WSC never entertained visions of hegemony, but he did firmly believe that it was our duty to rule and guide. For him Kipling's exhortation 'Take up the white man's burden' (addressed to the United States over the Philippines) was both relevant and wise.

I have referred earlier to President Eisenhower's attempts to deflect the Prime Minister from a Summit meeting with the Soviet leader, and it is perhaps appropriate to quote from one letter here, together with part of WSC's reply.

In 1954, referring to WSC's desire to meet the new Russian leaders, Eisenhower suggested that this sprang from 'a very deep and understandable desire to do something special in your remaining period of active service that will be forever recognised as a milestone in the world's tortuous progress toward a just and lasting peace'. He went on to suggest that Winston Churchill should conclude his career with a speech on how colonialism, which is 'on the way out as a relationship among peoples' should be phased out.

WSC's reply to this particularly ham-fisted suggestion was as follows:

> I am not looking about for the means of making a dramatic exit or of finding a suitable curtain. It is better to take things as they come. I am however convinced that the present method of establishing the relations between the two sides of the world by means of endless discussions between Foreign Offices, will not produce any results . . . I read with great interest all that you have written me about what is called Colonialism, namely: bringing forward backward races and opening up the jungles. I was brought up to feel proud of much that we had done.

WSC notes that Eisenhower's feelings are in full accord with the policies being pursued by 'all the Colonies in the Empire', but added:

> In this I must admit I am a laggard. I am a bit sceptical about universal suffrage for the Hottentots even if refined by proportional representation. The British and American Democracies were slowly and painfully forged and even they are not perfect yet. I shall certainly have to choose another topic for my swan song: I think I will stick to the old one 'The Unity of the English-speaking peoples'. With that all will work out well.

The offensively patronising line of Eisenhower's suggestion, and his sheer crass ignorance, not only of WSC's nature but of world history, took one's breath away.

Apart from WSC's well-founded objections to the new Egyptian Treaty, based on general strategic, political and historical grounds, there was a further element in his long-standing support for Israel, and his fear that the removal of the British forces in the Canal would encourage Egypt to attack across the Sinai Desert. And, as he himself put it: 'I have not always been wrong.' His close links with the Zionist leaders dated back to the First World

War, when he had openly supported their cause, including the Balfour Declaration of 1917, which gave the British Government's support to the setting up in Palestine of a national home for the Jewish people, without detriment to the existing Arab inhabitants. The Declaration never explained how this impossible squaring of the circle was to be achieved: it demanded superhuman sacrifices from the Arabs and angelic forbearance from the Jews. However, at that time both sides were very different from what they are now, and I suppose there was some sort of chance of accommodation before the massive enforced exodus of Jews from Europe of the thirties and forties.

WSC's support of Zion had however been severely tested by the terrorist attacks on our people by the Irgun and the Stern Gang. When members of the latter had murdered Lord Moyne, our Minister in the Middle East, in 1944, WSC had told the Commons:

> If our dreams for Zionism are to end in the smoke of assassins' pistols and our labours for its future to produce only a new set of gangsters worthy of Nazi Germany, many like myself will have to reconsider the position we have maintained consistently and for so long in the past. If there is to be any hope and successful future for Zionism, these wicked activities must cease and those responsible for them must be destroyed root and branch.

Alas, Zionist leaders' promises of the rejection of terrorism were not to be fulfilled, but by 1953–5 the pendulum had swung, and the threat of aggression came from the Egypt revolution.

I served subsequently for a short time in the Middle East Department of the Foreign Office, and I noted that it is almost impossible not to be branded as either anti-Jewish or anti-Arab, sometimes both at the same time. I suppose that to call one anti-semitic would have had a better chance of accuracy, since both Arabs and Jews are Semites, and can be equally exasperating. But in fact I was only pro-British, and deeply regretted our abdication of responsibility in the Middle East, both for our own sake and for that of the region's inhabitants, left to flounder in war, murder and sterile hatred, the motives for which one can understand only too well.

Incidentally, WSC disapproved of 'strokes at the head', i.e. assassination or military action directed at an enemy leader. This was strange, because he had vigorously encouraged SOE's activities and on a philosophical level he would quote, with broken continuity of memory: 'In the darkness gleams but one light: the red star tyrannicide.'

In early 1955, when WSC's much postponed resignation as Prime Minister had a firm date on it, the new Egyptian Treaty was in place. When one looks at present-day Egypt, which has largely reverted to its sensible and peaceful traditions, it is hard to realise how far the excesses of Nasser were to go. The kidnapping of dissidents, the use of mustard gas in the Yemen, the ramshackle but potentially dangerous (and Russian-supported) imperial designs, the union with Syria – these were indeed threatening to all our peaceful interests. In March 1955 I had occasion to call on Kirkpatrick, the Head of the Foreign Office and the Diplomatic Service. He had by this time mellowed towards me, and paid me the compliment of discussing our policy on the Suez Canal, concluding: 'You don't like what is happening, do you? No more do I, but we must obey our political masters. Anyway, if you were in a position to influence events, how would you deal with the present situation?'

I replied that I would try to influence the Israelis to advance over the Suez Canal to the Sweetwater Canal just beyond, and to declare that they would be the guardians of free passage of the Canal until an effective international set-up (not the United Nations) could take over. Their armed forces were capable of the action, and we and the French, and with any luck the United States, would hold the ring. Kirkpatrick smiled and made no comment. At that time the suggestion made some sense. A successful Israeli coup would have unseated Nasser, and between the Sweetwater Canal and the Nile stretched many miles of desert. In later years I wondered if my words had sowed appalling seeds? Hardly likely, but in any case I had not envisaged the almost unbelievable ineptitude of what took place in 1956.

In policy towards Middle Eastern countries other than Egypt, there was a greater degree of agreement between the Prime Minister and his Foreign Secretary. The toppling of the permanently pyjama'd and weeping Mossadeq, who had temporarily ousted the Shah, had been the result of a coup orchestrated by the CIA with British assistance – or the other way round. But when it came to the expropriation of the great BP refineries at Abadan, the Americans had been totally unwilling to condone direct action, let alone assist us. Surely this should have pointed some sort of moral in the disastrous planning of the Suez operation?

WSC's opinion of the Shah was unfavourable. To some rather grandiloquent pronouncement on the dynasty, he commented: 'The Shah gives himself howling airs, but he's only a sergeant's son and he hasn't got his father's courage, let alone his abilities. His father was another Mustafa Kemal. When Mossadeq took over, this man ran, until our Ambassador in Baghdad turned him round and pointed him home. That's why he'll probably never forgive us.' He was right, but I think that the animosity sprang more from the joint Anglo-Russian wartime occupation of Iran, from which we withdrew most scrupulously. At all events, when Carl Foreman was making his film *Young Churchill*, based on WSC's *My Early Life*, he contemplated shooting the Omdurman battle scenes in Iran with the (paid) assistance of Iranian cavalry, but was brusquely turned down.

Later events in Iraq were both more significant and more tragic. When Nuri Said's government was overthrown by the Ba'ath party in 1958, he, the young King and Abdulillah the Regent were horribly murdered. Both men, and particularly the gallant Nuri, had been staunch friends of Britain. For a short time the issue hung in the balance, and the Commander of the substantial Iraqi force at Habbaniyah, close to Baghdad, asked our Ambassador what course he should adopt. He was told that Britain was neutral, and within a short time our Ambassador was shaking the bloody hands of the murderers.

WSC was horrified. I noted what he said: 'The Middle East is one of the hardest-hearted areas in the world. It has always been fought over, and peace has only reigned when a major power has established firm influence and shown that it would maintain its will. Your friends must be supported with every vigour and if necessary they must be avenged. Force, or perhaps force and bribery, are the only things that will be respected. It is very sad, but we had all better recognise it. At present our friendship is not valued and our enmity is not feared.'

I felt bitter. Nuri Said had shown me kindness during his visit to Britain and he was a warrior and a man of honour. After a small luncheon at Number Ten he had said to me:

'Young man, if you want to understand the Middle East, listen to this fable. A frog sat on the banks of the Euphrates. A scorpion accosted him and said: "Will you ferry me over the river on your back, because I can't swim?" "Certainly not," replied the frog, "I know you scorpions, and you would lose your temper and sting me." "Be reasonable," pleaded the scorpion, "if I did that, I would drown." The frog was a good-natured chap, so he agreed. Half-way across, his helpless back was too much for the scorpion, who plunged his sting into it. "Why?" gasped the dying frog. "The Middle East," replied the drowning scorpion.'

I have later heard that this fable exists in many lands and in many forms, but it does seem to make the point.

Nuri had brought WSC a present of a desert leopard cub. Now such a gift would seem appalling – the imprisoning of a big cat of an endangered species – but forty years ago ecological concern was far less widespread or even recognised. The young leopard was brought in its crate to be opened on the Cabinet table. I was on duty. The cub emerged, an adorable fifteen-pound ball of fluff, steaming with justified fury. 'Pray examine it and tell me its sex,' instructed the Prime Minister. The cub clenched chubby paws with a glint of steel in them and gave me the sort of look that the Ayatollah might have given Salman Rushdie. I politely suggested that as it was his leopard, he should conduct this indelicate investigation himself. He declined. The cub, named Sheba, went to the London Zoo for quarantine and at intervals I visited her with my wife and baby daughter, who was usually appropriately left in the care of the Curator of Mammals.

Another Oriental potentate who was entertained by the Prime Minister was the Emperor Haile Selassie of Ethiopia. That visit went off rather well. WSC respected Haile Selassie and the latter spoke warmly of the British campaign for the liberation of his country. In these operations the talented but dotty Orde Wingate had first come to the fore and the Emperor spoke of him and, affectionately, of Wilfred Thesiger the explorer. He had a long memory and an unusual elegance of gratitude to Britain. The Crown Prince of Ethiopia was the Duke of Harar and I narrowly avoided a diplomatic incident when I found that his place-card was made out for the Duke of Horror.

I sat next to Selwyn Lloyd, the Minister of State at the Foreign Office. He was in a deeply depressed mood, and did the excellent wines full justice. While not best pleased to be seated next to the junior Private Secretary, he was affable and unburdened himself. 'I started my career as a little Liverpool attorney, and that's the way I'll end it,' he confided. 'Anthony no longer trusts me, and Clarissa thinks that I'm disloyal.' He had taken a robust line on the perpetual Egyptian wrangle and his views had been ill-received. I later reflected that his career was not to flourish too badly: Chancellor of the Exchequer, Minister of Defence, Foreign Secretary and Speaker of the House of Commons would satisfy most people.

Not all post-Imperial matters, however, were tinged with gloom. During one of the Commonwealth Conferences I was sent to see the Prime Minister of Australia, Robert Menzies, at the Savoy. Like many before and since I fell under the spell of his charm, not smooth, not flattering, but humorous, warm and down-to-earth. It was about six in the evening and Menzies decided that it was time for a drink. He was celebrated for his dry martinis, and on this occasion he decided that the shaker was not large enough, so he emptied a flower vase and made them in that, dry and paralysingly strong. He then delivered a careful, brief and vivid review of the non-progress of the Conference, answered the questions I had been sent to ask, and dismissed me with: 'Why don't you come and live in Australia? You're young enough.' I think that in another ten minutes he could have persuaded me.

WSC's opinion of Menzies was sky-high. I was present at a later dinner where WSC set out with apparent seriousness to persuade Menzies to leave Australia, enter the House of Commons immediately, and soon succeed the incumbent as Prime Minister.

After dinner on that night WSC and Menzies recited poetry, ending with an Australian ditty in which each recited alternate lines. The fragments I remember went like this:

> He jumped upon his bloody horse
> And rode upon his bloody course
> The bloody creek was bloody floody
> The bloody track was bloody muddy
> [Presumably taking to the water on his horse]
> Said he 'It's sink or bloody swim
> It's the same for me as bloody him
> It's all too bloody sickening. Bloody'
> The bloody horse was bloody drowned
> The stockman reached the bloody ground
> Ejaculating 'Bloody, bloody, bloody, bloody.'

There was a long pause. Then WSC drank some brandy and said: 'And that seems to me to be a most adequate summary of the world situation.'

Certainly the Prime Ministers assembled for the Conference were beset with problems, of which the Commonwealth situation was about the least bloody. India, or at least Nehru, was always to take an anti-British line, but the old Commonwealth was different. It was still an era when Menzies could say: 'I'm British to the boot-straps.' And Sid Holland, the Prime Minister of New Zealand, awakened to comment on the Suez operation in 1956 of which we so idiotically had failed to warn him, said as reported: 'I don't care what the problem is. We're on the side of Britain.' How remote it seems – and not just in time. Canada was rather different; the influence of the likes of Lester Pearson was beginning to cast its shabby shadow and Pierre Trudeau was not far over the horizon. (I was later, in an impromptu and intemperate speech to Canadians in Alberta, to describe Trudeau as 'that all-dancing, all-singing, neon-lit draft dodger'. What is it about French Canadians – or quite a lot of them, at least? They hate Britain; they hate English-speaking Canada; they dislike the United States; they don't even like France.)

But back to the early 1950s. At that same Commonwealth Conference I went to a grand party. Oliver Lyttelton, the admirable Colonial Secretary, was talking to Nehru. As I passed, with typical courtesy he waved me into the conversation, which was about the Mau-Mau rebellion in Kenya. He was seeking, with truth and eloquence, to persuade Nehru, who of course gave moral support to Mau-Mau, of the vile nature of their activities. (WSC, on reading the Mau-Mau oath, said: 'I've never encountered that particular degree of filth before.') Lyttelton was saying: 'And of course the atrocities are horrible beyond description.' Lady Mountbatten, who had paused to listen, chirped brightly: 'On both sides, of course.' Lyttelton's struggle to control himself was visible: Mau-Mau's activities were almost beyond belief, the burying alive of elderly Britons being only a minor manifestation. The Press description of them as 'bestial' was quite wrong; no animal behaves like that.

Chapter 18

A CONSTANT chore at Number Ten was the answering of G.P. (general public) letters. They all were answered, and swiftly, unless they were wildly abusive or plainly lunatic. Towards WSC's birthday time (30 November) letters increased to a flood, and he wrote a short message: 'Thank you so much for your good wishes. Winston S. Churchill.' This was reproduced in facsimile on Number Ten paper. I am not sure if I approved; I saw a good many of these messages enshrined in frames in worthy people's houses. But what was the alternative?

With the volume of birthday correspondence, mistakes were bound to occur. It was, I think, a Florida State Senator who addressed an exceedingly self-important letter to the Prime Minister indicating the sort of treatment he expected when he visited Britain and dropping a few condescending hints on WSC's conduct of affairs. By error he got a facsimile 'Thank you so much ...' reply, which he recognised for what it was. Stung to fury, he put his thoughts on Britain and the British in a long memorandum to his secretary, bidding her forward it to Number Ten. He was not going to condescend to correspond direct. The secretary obeyed and added a few shafts of her own. (I believe she was Southern Irish: certainly her prose gave that impression.) The correspondence was given to me to sort out by the apologetic girl responsible. I comforted her, and having always been bad at withstanding temptation, I found the shrill, raw, semi-literate abuse irresistible. I sent another 'Thank you so much for your good wishes'. I don't suppose it did much for Anglo-State-Senatorial relations, but in this case they were past salvaging anyway. And with any luck I may have given either the Senator or his secretary a stroke.

We had a lengthy list of numbered formulae to use in responding to the G.P. letters, e.g. 'The Prime Minister has taken note of your complaint regarding your local hospital and has asked the Ministry of Health to look into the matter and answer you direct'; 'The Prime Minister regrets that he is not in a position to finance your perpetual motion machine' (here we had to be careful: the first serious suggestion for a jet engine is said to have been a G.P. letter); 'The Prime Minister is grateful to you for letting him see your poem, but regrets he cannot have it set to music to replace the National Anthem.' Americans usually wanted signed photographs, and here there were never facsimile signatures. Spaniards usually wanted cigars.

A flood of presents accompanied WSC's birthdays, particularly his eightieth. One of the less welcome gifts was from both Houses of Parliament:

it was Graham Sutherland's portrait. The first stages were auspicious. After the early sittings the portrait was nearing completion. It was, for reasons I can't remember, in Lord Clark's (of *Civilisation*) house, and Lady Churchill went over by invitation to see it. After a first inspection, Clark apparently called to Sutherland, who was not in the room: 'It's all right. She likes it.' Alas and alack, WSC did not. His actual comment was: 'I look like a down-and-out drunk who has been picked out of the gutter in the Strand.' But his reaction was melancholy rather than angry and he certainly did not instigate the picture's destruction. It was put away in the Muniment Room at Chartwell and I doubt if he ever knew what had happened to it.

It was much later that CSC told me about the destruction, with what I can only describe as a nervous giggle: 'Anthony dear, I'm going to tell you something rather awful. That Sutherland picture made Winston so unhappy. It spoiled his eightieth birthday. I had it cut up and I burnt it.' I was taken aback, and barely credited it at first. But then I realised that there was nothing I could do about it anyway. I think CSC was horrified that her earlier judgement had been so misplaced.

I believe that the culprits were really the Parliamentary Selection Committee. A picture of this kind is in effect a State Portrait, and should be sufficiently representational for future generations to see what the subject really looked like. It should not be solely an opportunity for the artist to show off his pirouettes. It was not a pleasant picture, and the colour was an ugly sepia. There is a remarkable sameness in Sutherland's portraits. Beaverbrook said: 'The fellow's a caricaturist,' and, of his portrait of Somerset Maugham: 'Maugham looks as though he had died under torture.' No doubt one can acquit Sutherland of deliberate malice, but can the same thing be said for some members of the Selection Committee?

WSC really enjoyed dressing up, and indeed did look very fine in a white tie and the fruit-salad that went with it. Accompanying him to a dinner, I was much taken with the spectacle. 'You do look good!' I said, without any intent of flattery, but in spontaneous reaction to the presence and innocent self-satisfaction of the PM in all the colourful Orders and decorations on his genially pouter-pigeoned front. He contemplated himself thoughtfully: 'I have many medals for adventure, but none for bravery,' he said sadly.

I had been sorry that he had ultimately accepted the Order of the Garter. It would have been more fitting if, having declined a Dukedom, he should go down in history, like Pitt the Younger, as the Great Commoner, and I think CSC shared this view. Impertinently I quoted Melbourne: 'I like the Garter. There's no damned merit about it.' This did not go down well, but after an initial outburst WSC subsided and said: 'The two highest awards in Britain are the Victoria Cross and the Garter. In that order. It would be a very sad day if the order were ever reversed.' Actually I have a feeling that the George Cross, for the highest civilian and non-combatant gallantry, comes before the Garter. If it doesn't, it should.

In the same vein, I did not like WSC's acceptance of the rather sycophantic suggestion that he should wear a pilot's brevet (Wings) on his honorary Air Commodore's uniform. Wings are not an award; they are a badge of proficiency, or at least of former proficiency, and in spite of WSC's early adventurous flights, he had never been a pilot.

WSC had almost unqualified respect for military prowess, but he did not care for it being publicised and he did not approve of the foundation of an association for the holders of the Victoria Cross and George Cross. He told Brigadier Jackie Smyth, one of the founders, of his view. His actual words were: 'It is very difficult to fault such men. But I think it would have been better for them to stand in, er, silent grandeur. Unrecognised in public houses.' I felt that he was mistaken: flaunting it was not, and it gave humble people, and those like the many Gurkha VCs, a feeling of renewed recognition.

Although a 'King's Man' all his life, WSC disapproved of the award of a Military Cross to the then Prince of Wales (Duke of Windsor) in the First World War. He felt that it devalued the great courage of those who had received the MC for genuine fighting prowess. 'When everybody's somebody, nobody's anybody.' His attitude to Honours and decorations was somewhat unpredictable. He once described a blueprint for a future peerage. Each generation should descend one peg, unless the incumbent of the peerage should render such national service as to justify retaining his father's rank. Thus the undistinguished son of a Duke would be a Marquess, and his equally undistinguished son an Earl and so on, until in WSC's words, they would be not only undistinguished but extinguished.

I was puzzled and reminded him of his reverence for ancestors, not all of them of the quality of 'Soldier John', the first Duke of Marlborough. His reply was to quote somewhat cryptically from Byron's poem 'The Bastard', with its line: 'No tenth descendant of a foolish face'. He then told a story of Soldier John: he had apparently been caught by Charles II hiding in the cupboard of one of the King's mistresses, Louise de Kérouaille. The King had merely dismissed the understandably disconcerted gallant with the words: 'I have nothing to say to you, my poor fellow. You do this for your advancement.'

'Mark you,' added WSC, 'I don't blame the girl. He was a handsome fellow. I once saw two Australian women looking at his portrait at Blenheim and one said: "Well, he could put his boots under my bed anytime he chose." '

WSC pursued this earlier theme further. 'If the archives are to be believed,' he said, 'at one of the Führer Conferences Hitler said that a great strength of the British was "that the good blood of nobility returned to the people" because of our primogeniture, whereas on the Continent a title spawned a dozen or more of its own meaningless kind.'

The Prime Minister's attitude to awards over which he exercised some control was inconsistent, and often dominated by sentiment. He proposed to give Noel Coward a Knighthood. He had to be reminded by Tony Bevir that during the War, when all holdings of foreign assets had to be declared for the country to buy munitions and food under the US 'Cash and Carry' laws,

Coward had failed to reveal a substantial sum of dollars, and had been charged and convicted in Court. 'You are right,' said WSC. 'I had forgotten. It would be like decorating a subaltern who had run away and then cheated at cards.'

Political honours were another matter. Surprise was expressed at a particularly undistinguished figure being sent to the Lords. 'It isn't just a peerage,' explained the Prime Minister, 'it is a disappearage.'

From decorations it is an easy step to the Crown: the fount of all honours. WSC's position is very easily summarised: he was the staunchest Royalist and he adored the Queen.

For his regular Thursday Audience he wore a frock-coat, hardly ever seen even in the fifties, and it was quite evident that he thoroughly looked forward to these occasions. Did he perhaps have visions of achieving the same relationship as that Melbourne, her first Prime Minister, maintained with the young Queen Victoria? It is impossible to say, for although forthcoming to his Private Office in most secret matters, WSC kept pretty mum about his Audiences, unless the subjects discussed required action. Certainly his relations with the Queen did not reach the level of comradeship they had attained with George VI. Given the difference of age they could hardly do so, but I did sometimes feel that the level of regard and affection was somewhat one-sided, although WSC was always treated with the greatest respect. It was believed to have been Prince Philip, probably at Lord Mountbatten's instigation, who had wished to change the Royal Family's name from the House of Windsor to the House of Mountbatten. WSC was strongly opposed to the idea. The only time I mentioned the subject to him, he merely said that to change the name would have been a great mistake. And in this he was surely right, for the country would not have liked the change merely to add a further dimension to the already over-puffed Mountbatten bosom. The Admiral was certainly the greatest public relations man of our generation, but he only had one client.

I have always liked the story of the Kaiser's reaction to the Royal assumption of the name of the House of Windsor in the First World War, to accord with the anti-German hysteria sweeping the country. Cruel idiots are even said to have stoned dachshunds, and German Shepherd dogs to have been renamed Alsatians to protect them. On hearing the news, the Kaiser is alleged to have demanded a Command performance at the Berlin Opera of *The Merry Wives of Saxe-Coburg-Gotha*.

The Coronation was the apotheosis of WSC's love and reverence for the Crown. Dressed for the part, in the unique and bizarre uniform of the Lord Warden of the Cinque Ports, and with his Orders and medals, he was an unforgettable sight. The Duke of Wellington had lent him the Iron Duke's 'Great George' part of the Garter Regalia, and accompanied by CSC he drove in the Royal procession in a horse-drawn carriage. He caused a certain amount of confusion when, on the return from Westminster Abbey, the horses became over-excited near Admiralty Arch and he ordered the coachman to pull out of the procession. The Crown Equerry, John Miller, who ran that part of the proceedings, was distinctly put out.

I had been invited to be a Gold Stick – an usher in the Abbey – but had declined. I don't quite know why. The cost of acquiring full-dress diplomatic uniform? (I had the Court sword.) An innate distaste for elaborate ceremonial? A dislike of getting up at 4 a.m.? Probably just a curmudgeonly nature, and a feeling that such showy rejoicing did not fit in with our lamentable national decline.

The Prime Minister gave a number of grand parties, to one of which he invited the Glaoui, the Pasha of Marrakech. He was a picturesque old bandit, a true war-lord of the Atlas in his younger days, but with a sinister reputation when it came to dealing with his opponents. After dinner a few of us set out from Number Ten to watch the firework display from the Air Ministry roof. Downing Street was blocked by a jolly and friendly crowd, and when they spotted the Prime Minister in the first car, they began to rock it, while he grinned at them benevolently. The Glaoui later misunderstood the crowd's mood. To my consternation, he put his hand inside his robe and I saw the butt of an automatic pistol emerging. 'No, no, Excellency!' I shouted, politely holding his arm, 'these are very nice people.' He looked doubtful but subsided. He had a pretty miserable Coronation in other ways. His seat for the procession was in an uncovered stand, and he had to walk there in pouring rain from the Savoy. He had been invited to a garden party at Blenheim Palace and, assuming that it was in London, had left for it at 5 p.m., eventually arriving at Woodstock just as the waiters were clearing up the last crumbs. And finally, the gold and emerald crown he had bought as a present for the Queen had to be returned under the strict Palace protocol rules. Cartier had valued it at £13,000. Most of the emeralds were flawed.

My most vivid memory of the Prime Minister's feelings for the Queen is seeing him gazing with great tenderness at a charming photograph she had given him, with a warm inscription. It showed her laughing and happy as she returned from the Opening of Parliament. 'Isn't she a winner?' he said.

My daughter Jane was born in August of the Coronation year. When WSC was informed he sent for me, gave me about a quarter of a pint of 'Héritiers de Jean Frémicourt' and a cigar and questioned me closely. ('Will your wife suckle her?' was one unexpected enquiry.) I will always be grateful for both WSC's and CSC's unfailing and lasting kindness to my family. It was very warming, but it must not be supposed that my relations with the Prime Minister ran a universally smooth path.

There was a distinct hiccup when the Prime Minister was working at Chequers on some predetermined Government changes of junior Ministers. I was intrigued, and was quite ignorant of the number of Ministers allowed, which could not be exceeded – but which the new list did exceed, quite substantially. Woe! There was a lot of unscrambling, a lot of words to be eaten and a number of missiles hurled at my ears from the various quarters. Nor was this all. Angry with himself as well as me, because after all with his vast experience he should have had a clear idea of ministerial limitations, he fell on my prose style. In a letter to the Queen's Private Secretary, Sir

Michael Adeane, I had referred in the context of the ministerial changes to informing 'the people concerned'. 'That is an off-hand way to describe them,' he said, 'It is indecorous.' A rather absurd discussion on the right term then took place. 'Personalities', 'Candidates', 'Members', etc., were all in turn rejected. Finally 'those concerned' was agreed to be adequate. 'Let us now leave the matter alone,' WSC sighed.

Two further setbacks occurred in quick succession. VJ day, commemorating the end of the Far Eastern war, fell when WSC was at Chequers. I was in London on secondary duty and did not expect him to come up to the capital. He did, however; found no Private Secretary at Number Ten and demanded me in no uncertain terms. It took me no more than ten minutes to reach Downing Street, where the Prime Minister was marching up and down, accompanied by Tony Bevir. When he caught sight of me he trumpeted with rage. I kept silent; Tony, quietly but clearly, said: 'Prime Minister, you are behaving like a rogue elephant.' I don't know if WSC heard him, for the storm continued unabated for some minutes. Then he saw that I was wearing a black tie.

'What is that for?'

'Prime Minister, it's VJ day.'

'Oh, it's for your dead comrades. I see.' And silence fell.

WSC had his own method of calculating by-election results. After the Central Office (Conservative Headquarters in Smith Square, London) produced the final canvassing figures, he would take all the 'Yes' Conservative votes and deduct 10 per cent from them. Then he would take all the 'noes', the 'don't knows' and the 'abstains' and add them together. The two figures often turned out to be a surprisingly accurate prophecy. There was a by-election in West Wycombe to which the Prime Minister attached considerable importance as a barometer. The canvassing figures came in after dinner and I was told to produce the results by WSC's system. Flustered by the heckling, my mental arithmetic, normally good (flying had taught me) deserted me. The figure I gave showed a good Conservative victory. Elated, the Prime Minister telephoned the Central Office, who had predicted a narrow result, and told them that they were a pessimistic lot of no-gooders. They should believe him in future. Then doubt struck him, and he calculated for himself, finally turning to me to say bitterly: 'You have let me down.' I slunk away. But in the morning, something had got into the West Wycombe electorate and my flawed figures turned out to be correct. Finding WSC in a good mood, I reminded him of Napoleon's question when an unknown officer came up for promotion: 'Is he lucky?' This only drew a pensive stare and: 'Perhaps. But once is enough.'

WSC's relations with the Central Office and the Conservative Party machine were a sensitive area. In some ways he had always lacked a true power base. The old Conservatives had a lingering distrust of him, going back to the double changing of sides and the adventurism of which they suspected him. R. A. Butler had had enough to do with the Research Department, among other things, to have left his imprint, inimical to WSC and

distinctly Wet, spawning in its turn similar constituency selection committees and Conservative candidates.

WSC was well aware of the position, but he was too old and preoccupied
with national affairs to take the root-and-branch action the situation
required. He relied on some Central Office stalwarts, like George Christ, but
to a damaging extent he ignored inner Party politics. As Harold Macmillan
accurately said: 'He was not interested in Party politics as such,' and CSC
supported his feeling that it would be wrong and degrading to use his record
and his vast prestige for purely Party ends.

But sadly it is not possible for a peacetime Premier to neglect his Party, for
by doing so he forfeits so much patronage and so much power. WSC once
spoke of the question in a historical context. He began ironically by saying
that he envied Stalin, and went on to explain that the latter had been
Secretary-General of the Communist Party and therefore was in a position to
assert his authority from within as well as from above. The very real damage
of a drift into the weakest policies could have been scotched, and later
Butskellism avoided – the amalgam of the policies of Hugh Gaitskell, Leader
of the Socialist Opposition from 1955, and the Butler supporters.

The House of Commons was a totally different matter. WSC's much-
quoted words 'I am a child of the House of Commons' represented his
precise feelings and he enjoyed the House in a way which I, who have never
been in Parliament, found inexplicable. Moreover, the success or failure of
his appearances at Prime Minister's Question Time and his few major
speeches in the House was unquestionably of great importance. Their composition was a lengthy and arduous task, as was the case with all his major
speeches. A draft or drafts might be demanded from Departments; Jock
Colville and (much later) I myself were told to prepare sections; but the final
product was usually pure Churchill. He went to ground with his two personal secretaries and was reluctant, even dangerously reluctant, to be disturbed. Perhaps he had once been a spontaneous speaker, but he was not
when I knew him, though his repartee could be devastating well into old age.
When the speech was complete, it was tried out on many – professionals,
family, staff or visitors; copies would be sent to significant ministers for
comment; and eventually it would be typed out on small sheets in what was
known as 'Psalm form'. If it was to be an afternoon speech in the House,
WSC would if possible lunch in bed, drink half a bottle of champagne and set
off for his critical rendezvous pale and irritable. The last step was a short
interview with Mr Punt, an eminent throat specialist, who would squirt his
vocal cords with a spray. The Prime Minister would sing a brief scale and
depart. If it was an after-dinner speech, usually of less significance, I used to
feel sorry for his neighbours, who would get little enough from him until he
had delivered it.

It is easy to see why there was such tension. Churchill's oratory was after
all world-renowned and historically enshrined. A flop would be as damaging
to him, particularly in his last years, as a series of tone-deaf performances
would be today to, say, Placido Domingo. His speeches were his opportunity

to demonstrate to his colleagues, the House, the Party and the world that he still had the capacity and the will to govern.

That WSC enjoyed being Prime Minister is indisputable (wouldn't anybody?).

'I used to wake up feeling that there was half a bottle of champagne inside me.'

'Don't you now, Prime Minister?'

'Only sometimes. That bloody stroke . . .'

But on a fine morning at Chequers he declaimed: 'I shan't work today.

> 'I hate my books, I loathe the State
> I'll wrap my lunch in Livy
> I'll put the Great Seal in the grate
> And the Privy Seal in the privy.'

But the end was approaching remorselessly, and he knew it.

Meanwhile the steady procession of Government business continued, against an ever-increasing background of the impatience, well or ill controlled, of some senior Ministers. After dinner one evening Eden and Macmillan were standing behind the Prime Minister, waiting for him to conclude his admittedly over-lengthy monologue so that they could depart. They both made schoolboy winding-up motions, casting their eyes to heaven. Funny? Perhaps.

The Cabinet were undoubtedly in awe of him. For one thing he seemed to have been there for ever. His first ministerial appointment was in 1905. Summoned by his buzzer, I went into the Cabinet during a meeting to field some query. The Prime Minister was addressing his colleagues, and I was somewhat startled to hear ' . . . and as I told the Cabinet in 1854 . . .' For a moment nobody's expression changed; subconsciously I suppose they did not feel the statement to be improbable. Then as raised eyebrows appeared round the table, WSC went on without altering his tone: ' . . . that is to say, in 1954'.

Changes in ministerial appointments were rarer than they later became, and the Prime Minister saw a great deal less of junior Ministers than he should have, but he could be friendly and whimsically interrogative when meetings did occur. To Anthony Nutting, Minister of State at the Foreign Office: 'Are you anti-semitic?' and, before the surprised Nutting could reply: 'I'm not, but you have a perfect right to be, just as you have to join the Primrose League.' (The Conservative Primrose League had been founded by Disraeli, himself of course Jewish, so I suppose there was some inner meaning, but neither Nutting nor I could unravel it.)

Visitors continued to be a problem. Churchill had become a national or even an international monument. Many felt that their position or former friendship justified their claim to being received or even lunched or dined, but it was just not possible. Business pressure apart, the old do tend to fall back on a smaller and smaller circle. (I now feel this myself.) We softened his rebuffs as much as possible but still, I fear, sometimes gave offence.

Rather unexpected people were sometimes seen and Billy Graham, the American preacher, was one of them. I was on duty, WSC was delayed, so I conversed with Graham for half an hour. Had I any hints, he asked? I said be clear, be brief and don't talk to the press if the Prime Minister asks you not to. I took to him. He seemed to have a genuine simplicity of faith and goodwill. WSC kept him a good deal longer than expected. When he emerged they were both grinning. The press were waiting outside Number Ten but Graham told them nothing. When I asked WSC what they had discussed, he continued to grin and said: 'I shan't tell you.'

A year or two ago, I met an acolyte of Graham's who was again in Britain. I asked him to give Graham a letter, in which I suggested that with his vast audience and his eloquence he could do so much good by devoting even a few sentences to man's duty of kindness to animals, our unfortunate involuntary companions on earth. I got a brush-off letter from an assistant. Well, I suppose animal welfare is neither glamorous nor commercial.

> T'would ring the bells of heaven,
> The wildest peal for years,
> If Parson lost his senses
> And people came to theirs
> And he and they together
> Knelt down with angry prayers
> For tamed and shabby tigers
> And humbled dancing bears
> And wretched blind pit-ponies
> And little hunted hares.

To which sentiment Billy Graham, the Roman Catholic Church, and in particular the deplorable Archbishop of Bologna, who preached that cruelty to animals is not a sin, could afford to pay some attention for the good of their souls.

All this time WSC's popularity in the country was probably undiminished and his vitality remained, though more spasmodic than the public supposed. His stroke in June 1953, which took place at a dinner for the Italian Prime Minister, de Gasperi, has been well documented. It was kept most effectively secret; we were all anxious that when Churchill left the scene, it should be of his own volition. In his worst differences with Eden he had spoken privately of going to the country on the issues involved, but he never meant it. Meanwhile he could still surprise with succinct wit. In one of the last Parliamentary Questions he answered, Woodrow Wyatt, Socialist member for a Birmingham constituency, had asked if he would comment on the 'empty chair policy' (going ahead without France) and received the brief reply that the Hon. Gentleman should be more concerned with the empty seat policy, Wyatt's constituency having just indicated that they would not readopt him. Parliamentarians are never unhappy to see a colleague disconcerted, and the laughter on both sides of the House was loud and long.

His comment to President Eisenhower on the Communist witch-hunt by Senator McCarthy and his bully-boy lawyers was equally brief: 'He's

spoiling a good cause.' It was at that time still possible to discuss race relations without being called a Fascist. WSC said that he took his stand on the
principle that 'prejudice should go but choice should remain.'

These minor examples could be multiplied and bettered, but they were the
background to undeniable decline. One of the first to underline this for
public attention was *Punch*, under Malcolm Muggeridge. A cruel cartoon
showed a slumped Prime Minister with mouth twisted by paralysis. The
caption was 'Man goes forth unto his labour . . .' WSC was bitterly hurt. It
must be conceded that the decline of a Prime Minister's powers is a proper
subject for comment, but to jeer at physical infirmity is not very creditable.
In Churchill circles the editor was henceforth known as Buggeridge. (The
beautiful and witty South African actress Yolande Finch had long since
coined the phrase 'as smug as a Muggeridge').

WSC generally enjoyed cartoons. His favourite, rather mysteriously, was
'Useless Eustace' in the *Daily Mirror*. He thoroughly approved of Michael
Cummings of the Express Group, disliked Giles ('there's something
unpleasant about him') and detested David Low's politics, while admiring
his skill. Low was a New Zealand Communist who was a favourite of Beaverbrook's. I found his employment inexplicable. In his own quirkish way
Beaverbrook was a true patriot, yet he employed people like Frank Owen,
Michael Foot and, appropriately below all, Low. Competent and talented
they undoubtedly were, but the harm they did in opposing Britain's
rearmament against Hitler is appalling. One of Low's cartoons depicted
Colonel Blimp, his favourite Tory butt, exclaiming over our belated, inadequate but desperately needed arms programme of the late 1930s: 'Gad Sir, if
we want to keep our place in the sun, we must darken the sky with our planes.'
I would like to have confronted these gentlemen with the sight of one of our
stricken airfields in the Battle of Britain. Would they have adopted for their
own use Churchill's earlier saying: 'I have often eaten my own words and
found them on the whole a most nourishing diet'? I doubt it.

'Recrimination can be of much use as a guide to the future' is a phrase
attributed to WSC, but he very rarely indulged in it publicly unless unbear-
ably provoked, and that is what he undoubtedly was by Opposition taunts
that he could not control the American use of the nuclear weapon, of which
after all we had been the progenitors before the Americans took over with the
Manhattan Project. The Quebec Agreement, drawn up at the wartime Conference in 1944 and initialled by President Roosevelt and the Prime Minister,
stipulated among other things that neither country would make use of the
nuclear weapon without the other's agreement, and that research would be
pooled save in the matter of the peaceful use of atomic energy. Although
never enshrined in a formal treaty, it was a simple and conclusive document.
It had always remained secret and it had been bargained away by the post-
1945 Socialist Government. It constituted a complete and devastating
answer to the left-wing charges of ineffectual weakness in controlling any
wild American impulses to make use of the weapon, which is the way the left
saw them, and one is bound to say with a degree of justification.

WSC therefore decided to publish the Agreement as a White Paper. He duly informed Attlee first, and on 5 April 1954 he addressed the House of Commons. He had a straightforward and impregnable case, but the Opposition saw their danger and mounted a raucous clamour to shout down the Prime Minister. It was unquestionably a put-up job, but by whom? I cannot believe that Attlee was responsible, though he may have been relieved at the outcome. He was a gentleman. Nowadays such ugly caterwauling is commonplace, but then it was not. WSC was taken by surprise and knocked off his oratorical perch. If only he had put down his notes and addressed the simple issue again and again: that the Socialists had thrown away a priceless agreement and were now blaming the Conservatives. In days gone by he could have achieved this with ease and his counter-attack could have been devastating. But in 1954, he couldn't and didn't. Looking stricken, white-faced and old, he ploughed on through his notes, his voice barely audible above the din. It was a triumph for falsehood over truth. It was also the all too visible beginning of the political end of the Prime Minister.

Anthony Eden was to wind up the debate. He told me that two Ministers had advised him not to attempt to salvage the Prime Minister: he was down, let him stay down. To his everlasting credit Eden rejected this loyal advice and did his best. But it was too late.

I remember thereafter reflecting on what an odious system of government we had that threw up such characters as were all too visible on both sides of the House of Commons. Now, of course, they appear to constitute the majority – a sort of political Gresham's Law. WSC's often-repeated view on Parliamentary democracy ran something like this: 'Yes, it is an appalling muddle, riddled with faults, dangers, unfairness and contradictions. It is also a perpetual popularity contest. The only trouble is that when you consider alternative systems, they all turn out to be worse.' (And of course at that time he hadn't seen the US Presidential elections by television.)

WSC liked to bat about various broad themes, which he did not seriously wish to put into practice. He suggested a new electoral system. Everyone of age would have one vote. Those with a wife and children (i.e. more responsibilities and more of a stake in the country) would have a second. A householder would have another; an employer of a certain number of employees another; a man with a university degree or a high professional qualification another; one who had served his country and been decorated for it another. Intriguing, but distinctly complicated and controversial.

In the Private Office at Number Ten we we all had our pet hates among Members of the Commons. A few of the Opposition were certainly straightforward agents, conscious or unconscious, paid or unpaid, of the Soviet Union, but there weren't many of these. I think the total of the truly disaffected, used in its broadest sense, was about thirty-six. Others were perfectly loyal citizens, but personally obnoxious. One of my unfavourites was Colonel George Wigg, who was to become Lord Wigg. He looked like a badly bred potato, with huge ears (Ear Wigg?) and a barrack-room lawyer's approach to life. He made great play with his military career, which was quite genuine, but he overdid it when he claimed to have 'carried a rifle more than any member of the Government'. I thought 'carried it, but not fired it at the enemy,' and when I made investigations with the War Office, so it proved. Colonel Wigg's major line of wartime service had been in the Army Bureau of Current Affairs, a number of whose members were thought to have made good use of their position to propagandise for the left. I told the Prime Minister the facts, but he characteristically never made use of them in the House. I had thought that even in that high temple of phonies a man should not be allowed to mislead so grossly; the bounds of good taste might justifiably be broken to bring him to book. WSC contented himself with a derogatory remark about Army Schoolmasters, which was most unfortunate; the old Army Schoolmasters were a thoroughly decent lot and did a first-rate job. Wigg made an unattractive speciality of publicising opponents' private misdemeanours under the pretext of security. He himself was ultimately charged with kerb-crawling.

WSC's decline in Parliament was far from consistent: he could still pull rabbits out of hats and startle, even dazzle his listeners. In an excellent and telling speech on weapons procurement, his theme had been that timing was of the utmost importance and extremely difficult. Was it right to order a new design of aircraft or tank now, or wait until something better, only on the drawing-board, was proven? Suddenly he departed from his notes and, looking over the heads of the Opposition, quoted. It was to the effect that we all regard our actions as being only stepping-stones to something better. It is only when we reach the end of our lives that we realise that we have lived them ad interim. Sitting in the Official Gallery, level with the floor of the House behind the Speaker, it was my duty to check the Prime Minister's speech against his notes. If necessary, one went up to the amiable and able Hansard editors and made minor corrections. All Ministers made use of this harmless facility, and it was only the mean-minded who objected. On this occasion Hansard had, most unwontedly, missed a word or two, and I was in no position to help them. I asked WSC what his quotation had been. 'Surely you recognised Schopenhauer's essay "On the Vanity of Human Existence"?' he asked with genuine surprise. Of the minor degree of heckling he had suffered in the debate, he said: 'I always like hearing a lot of old gentlemen making a shindy about nothing at all.' Old gentlemen?

WSC once asked his daughter Sarah how she felt at the end of the run of a play. 'Don't you hate it when the show is over?' Sarah agreed emphatically, and once the date of his resignation in April 1955 had been settled, it was painfully clear that the Prime Minister shared her feelings. Part of this was undoubtedly personal pride. To contemplate the end of a career of such unsurpassed length, variety, defeat, victory and overall magnificence must be almost unbearable. During this twilight time WSC was markedly subdued. He quoted (actually heavily misquoted) Milton as rendered by Melbourne on his own decline:

So much I feel my genial spirits droop,
My hopes all flat.
Nature within me seems in all her purposes weary of herself . . .

When asked how he intended to occupy his time in retirement, he told the story of the old woman who had spent her entire life working for other people. On her deathbed she spoke thus:

I'm going to do nothing for ever and ever.

These sombre and painful personal reflections were exacerbated by foreboding on Britain's future and on the competence of Anthony Eden. In his diary Jock Colville recounts WSC's final exclamation, late at night before his resignation: 'I don't believe Anthony can do it!' The Prime Minister had nevertheless consistently sought to establish Eden's claim to the succession, however much he clung to his own timing for his repeatedly postponed exit. When Eden's first gall-bladder operation took place, WSC had sought to edit the communiqués put out through the Foreign Office News Department. This led to an unseemly argument with Eden's wife Clarissa, of whom WSC was fond. I found myself pig-in-the-middle. WSC's only purposes, in his own words, were 'to safeguard Anthony's position and to emphasise that his absence from affairs was temporary'. In the light of the repeated delays in the handover, Clarissa was visibly suspicious of her Uncle's motives and was determined to control the announcements herself. 'Uncle Winston is not to interfere,' she told me with strong emotion on the telephone. Her vehemence was understandable but unnecessary. The unfortunate junior in the News Department was blown hither and thither, but was more concerned with the danger of offending the Secretary of State's wife than going against the wishes of the distant Prime Minister. WSC was at that moment inaccessible, and since his intentions and Clarissa's were actually the same I concluded that it was best not to argue, even though I was aware that I should be berated a day or two later for lack of determination, perhaps even in WSC's severest phrase for 'having fallen below the level of events'.

So, whatever his misgivings, in 1955 the Prime Minister was irretrievably committed to the succession. The last days were full of ceremonial and farewells. The Queen offered Churchill a Dukedom on the Palace's understanding from Colville that he would refuse it. Why this proviso was necessary I really cannot see; however, WSC duly did turn it down. Later I asked him what title he would have taken if he had accepted. 'Can't you guess?' he said. I couldn't. 'The Duke of London,' WSC said firmly. He added that at the time he thought a peerage would embarrass Randolph's potential political career, sadly never to materialise. Moreover, WSC felt that a Dukedom without a great estate could be an embarrassment. 'I suppose I could have been the Duke of Westerham,' he said. 'Then Randolph would have been the Marquess of Chartwell and little Winston Lord Bardogs' (a farm on the modest Chartwell estate). 'It really wouldn't do.'

His declining the Dukedom had been qualified by the request that 'if I felt the work was too hard [continuing as a member of the House of Commons] I would be very proud if the Queen chose to reconsider Her proposal.' He never did ask for the proposal to be reconsidered.

Right up to his final departure, WSC had persevered in the business of State and in particular with defence matters, since it was no longer of any real use to argue with Eden on foreign affairs. Following the ousting of British forces from our Suez Canal base, headquarters had been set up in Cyprus. It was huge – at least in numbers of staff, if not in military capacity – and I drew the Prime Minister's attention to the numbers, reminiscent of Mountbatten's absurdly extravagant headquarters in wartime Ceylon. WSC was outraged. He instructed me to take a number of 'test-bores' on the numbers employed respectively on non-combatant and combatant duties in various areas of the armed forces, the figures to be compared with 1939, and the number which could be deployed for action within three months to be stated. He was well aware that the nature of armed forces had changed vastly with technical advance and was prepared to make allowances. When he had sufficient data he proposed to set up a small committee: himself as Chairman, General Templer and Norman Brook as the sole members and myself as secretary. The committee would inflict economies on the Armed Forces without right of appeal and the economies would fall on the tail not the teeth. Utopian?

In the event such statistics as were produced were pretty horrifying, the Royal Marines coming out best as far as I can remember. The Navy had proved to be one of the worst examples. If my memory hasn't failed me totally, we had seventy-eight admirals and one hundred and forty-two ships, many of them auxiliary. During a discussion of the blocking of the Dardanelles in time of war, Monty had suggested to the highly unamused Mountbatten: 'Block them with admirals, Dickie. You've got enough of them and that's all they're good for.'

And then WSC's timing of his resignation became irrevocable, so nothing came of the intended economies. According to Martin Gilbert's official history: 'On the morning of April 6 (1955) Churchill received [from me: AMB] his last document at 10 Downing Street about the economies achieved in the Cyprus Headquarters under the most recent set of proposals.'

A press strike was in progress when the resignation day came, which saddened the Prime Minister: he would have liked his departure to be suitably floodlit, and why not indeed? The final hours were moving as Churchill presented each member of his staff with a dated silver V for Victory. But through all the sentiment and forced gaiety, one could perceive the dark and tragic set of the tide of our national decline, against which Churchill had stood in vain, and which he had sometimes unwittingly and unwillingly abetted.

When I took my leave of him, he was unexpectedly brief. 'I won't say goodbye. It is au revoir. We shall be seeing each other quite soon.' Little did I realise what this portended.

BOOK FOUR

———— ❧ ————

Late Afternoon
1955–1965

Chapter 19

————— ❧ —————

SHORTLY AFTER his resignation in April 1955 WSC set off for a painting holiday in Sicily, accompanied by CSC, the Prof. and the Colvilles. It was not a success; the weather was wet and WSC's spirits low. The anti-climax of departure from power and above all the prospect of long days as an observer of events were deeply depressing. True, he was going to stand again for Parliament in the forthcoming (May 1955) General Election; true, he was going to proceed vigorously with his *History of the English-Speaking Peoples*, initiated many years ago, before the Second World War; true, he had his family, his painting, his friends and almost universal affection and admiration. But all these were as nothing against the departure of the urgencies of Government, the telephone calls on high matters of State, the red boxes with their 'Most Immediate' labels, the Cabinet meetings, the deferential ministerial colleagues, advisers and experts, and the journeys on great national purposes.

WSC had one real power left. His approbation of his successor's policies was largely taken for granted, but if he had delivered a speech of severe criticism, even of disavowal, it would have been a thunderbolt. Like the use of the nuclear weapon, so extreme a step could not credibly have been taken, but WSC was well aware of its existence and it gave him some illusory comfort.

Did he dream of a return to power, his health miraculously improved and old age rolled back? Not really. But he more than once recounted the legend of the Holy Roman Emperor, Frederick Barbarossa, drowned in a river on his way to the Third Crusade. The story had it that he had never died, but slept in a cavern in the Harz mountains, his beard overflowing his chair. Once every hundred years he would awake and ask a passer-by if the ravens still flew about the mountain. Answered 'yes', he would relapse into slumber. Should the answer ever be 'no' he would arise, for he knew that the Holy Roman Empire and Germany must be in peril, and would descend from the mountains to save them. 'There do not appear to me to be any more ravens,' WSC added, with a twinkle, 'but I do not think that I will descend from the mountains. Anthony [Eden] wouldn't like it.'

With WSC's departure from Number Ten, I returned to the Foreign Office. I was well aware that Anthony Eden would sooner have appointed a crocodile to his Private Office than retain me, but in any case I had done my three-year stint. I was sent to the Middle East Department, to deal with Syria, the Lebanon and Iraq. The three countries in my remit, later such a

187

wasps' nest, were at that time comparatively tranquil, and I seem mainly to have been concerned with the nationalisation of British public utility companies and the like. It was not a particularly memorable time, but it did feature the only occasion on which anybody has offered me a bribe. The would-be briber was a well-known figure and the actions he wished me to take were in any case impossible. I rapidly concluded that he was suffering from a nervous breakdown, as subsequently proved to be the case.

My humdrum existence was interrupted one morning by a telephone call. An unmistakable voice said without preamble: 'I am staying with Max at La Capponcina' (Beaverbrook had an enchanting villa on the sea at Cap d'Ail just outside Monte Carlo). 'I do need your assistance, and it would be very nice if you could come down for a week. Max says that he would be glad to have you, and your ticket will reach you today. I will expect you tomorrow afternoon. Goodbye.' This did not leave much room for argument, so with hasty explanations, ill-received at the Office and kindly at home, I set out.

I was greeted warmly and established in a sort of Wendy House, comfortable, white and with a dazzling view, on one of the garden terraces overlooking the sea. The only snag was the hot-water geyser, a menacing and malicious antique with which I never came to terms. You opened the hot tap and there was a hiss of escaping gas. This was supposed to ignite immediately, but it didn't. You were then faced with the dilemma of turning it off, leaving the Satanic machine full of unlit gas, or persisting until it exploded with an appalling bang which brought twigs down from the trees, frightened the birds away, and once even detached a large piece of plaster from the ceiling.

Although not too steady on his feet, WSC had accompanied me down the steep hill to my quarters, and enquired searchingly and with charm after my comfort. I was touched and flattered. The regime was far from arduous, the surroundings beautiful and the company and food excellent. Beaverbrook took considerable pride in his wines and his Swiss chef, and liked a lively dinner-table. WSC had acquired two secretaries, Doreen Pugh and Jill Maturin, of whom the former was to serve him devotedly until the end of his life, later partnered with no less effective devotion by Catherine Snelling. They looked after the routine – and more than that – with perfect competence.

With that background and in that climate it was all too easy to slip into a lotus-eating mood, lulled by the fact that some of one's tasks were undoubtedly significant. But only some. Quite early on, I began to reflect that, like Napoleon's description of a rear-guard, I was achieving my purpose not by doing, but by being. However, I assumed that it would only be for a week or two and that I should shortly return to that temporarily slumbering volcano, the Middle East, or to be exact to the Department dealing with it. After all I was only just thirty-two and had packed quite a lot into my nine years in the Service.

It was not to be. After further summonses South, I eventually received a letter from Harold Macmillan, the Foreign Secretary. I reproduce it below, because it indicates his relaxed style and the casual way in which my fate altered:

Many thanks for your note of August 2. I dined with Winston on Friday night. I thought him in good form – better than I expected. He is extremely grateful for all the work you gave him, and I hope you will be able to go on doing so. Christopher Soames came in later in the evening. Altogether I felt rather relieved. But I suppose it is natural he should have ups and downs. This evening was certainly one of the ups. I do not know what you are doing for leave, but if you are in the Foreign Office on Monday, August 15, you might look in for a moment and see me. I shall be up for a Cabinet.

Not unnaturally I did 'look in for a moment'. The Foreign Secretary spoke thus: 'Winston needs you. He is going to travel extensively and as you know he is already deep in correspondence with Ike, with Adenauer, de Gaulle and I don't know who else.' (This was not exactly true: WSC was scrupulously careful not to embarrass his successors.) 'Moreover, the Middle East Department is not one that one can flit in and out of like a weekend cottage – I know it's not your fault. So I'm going to second you to Winston. You'll continue to be a full member of the Service, and we'll pay you as before. Winston will reimburse the Treasury.' Then, gazing into my eyes, he added: 'In the nature of things it will be two years at the most. And we won't forget you.' I think that even at that moment I realised (though I would of course be the first to agree that there are shining exceptions to the rule) that if a politician says 'We won't forget you' you should write yourself off totally and without delay.

Soon after I was again at Cap d'Ail. CSC was there but left before long and Beaverbrook returned. His hospitality was munificent, but I don't think he either liked or trusted me. Night after night at dinner we had worse and worse arguments, indeed rows. When I said goodnight to WSC in his bedroom, he used to observe, rather doubtfully: 'You get on very well with Max, don't you?' In all honesty I could not confirm this.

Finally I decided that the situation was untenable. I could not go on quarrelling vehemently with my generous host, a man old enough to be my grandfather. Alone of the company, I used to breakfast on the terrace. I composed a short note, thus: 'Lord Beaverbrook, I am most grateful to you for your hospitality, but I am leaving today for the Hotel Hermitage. I will make appropriate arrangements with WSC later this morning.' I summoned Beaverbrook's excellent and charming butler, Meade.

'Will you please give this note to his lordship when he has had breakfast?' I said.

'Certainly, Mr Montague Browne,' Meade replied, 'but there is a note for you from his lordship. Would you like to read it first?'

I opened it, fully expecting a 'get out and don't darken my doors or spoil my dinner again'. In fact it ran: 'Anthony, I forbid you not to argue with me at dinner tonight.' I hastily destroyed my own epistle. One can't leave in the face of such a jolly invitation, an elegant olive branch even if it was offered more to keep the peace with WSC in the house than as any personal compliment to me.

From that night things improved. I had always had mixed views of

Beaverbrook, but now, in an atmosphere of increasingly relaxed relations, I began to see more of his virtues than his vices. Kindness by stealth was one of the former: many people who were not his natural friends or allies were treated with considerable and discreet generosity. Only some acknowledged it. I was touched to find him late one night walking up the steep Cap d'Ail road in driving rain. He was going to visit one of his small grandsons – or was it grandnephews? – who was ill, in a *pension* above the village. He was then already an old and not a well man.

His presents to my four-year-old daughter Jane were imaginative and accompanied by touching notes. Cynical I may be, but I do not believe that such things were done for calculated motives. In my own case, I could do Beaverbrook little good, and could certainly do him no harm, even if I'd wanted to: WSC's fondness for him was far too deeply rooted to be affected one way or another.

Beaverbrook's conversation was nearly always stimulating and his turns of phrase unexpected. The conversation touched on the Moderator of the Church of Scotland.

'No, I don't like him,' said Lord B. 'He's a tiresome fellow.'

'Why not?'

'He calls me petulant names.'

'What does he call you?'

'He says I'm Satan.'

Chorus from round the crowded table: 'Aren't you?'

A grin from our host: 'Ah yaas, and you're all tiresome fellows too. You've had too much champagne.'

Beaverbrook's communications with his newspapers were frequent and incisive. He claimed that he no longer controlled them, and his remarks to various editors often began: 'This is just the view of an old reader,' but I have the feeling that the old reader's views were infrequently ignored.

When he wanted to speak to whomever was running things, his opening shot was sometimes: 'Who is in charge of the clattering train?' WSC, close by at the time, seemed displeased at this harmless gambit. Later I asked him why. He replied: 'Max took it from me. Of course he has a perfect right to use it, but I had it first.' He told me that it came from a poem, he thought originally published in *Punch*. He, WSC, had intended to use it as a peroration for one of his most eloquent speeches of warning of the oncoming war, delivered in the House of Commons in the mid-1930s. He had never actually used it, because there was such a row when he had concluded his argument that anything more might have been an anti-climax. The poem ran:

> Who is in charge of the clattering train?
> The axles creak and the couplings strain,
> And the pace is hot, and the points are near,
> And sleep has deadened the driver's ear,
> And the signals flash through the night in vain
> For death is in charge of the clattering train.

I reflected that it was lucky that none of Beaverbrook's editors appeared to know the last line.

Looking back on the many intemperate (on my side anyway) arguments I had with Beaverbrook, I think the worst was, of all things, over the standing of Rudyard Kipling. This was rum, because I have always held Kipling extremely high in the literary pantheon. *Kim* is one of the finest short novels in the English language and shows an insight into Indian life that many Indians have said that they could not equal, particularly given the stratification of the caste system. And if I were asked to name the greatest short story in our language, I would unhesitatingly say 'The Miracle of Purun Bhagat'. But if I revered Kipling, Beaverbrook worshipped him, and any qualification of praise was anathema. (I rather think that I had said that the worst of Kipling's poetry was like great music played by the village brass band.) Beaverbrook later told me that Kipling, his hero, had turned his back on him after the Irish settlement of the early 1920s and refused to speak to him again in spite of many overtures.

Strangely, WSC had a very similar story to tell. He, too, admired Kipling enormously and quoted him copiously. He, too, had been rebuffed after the Irish settlement. In his case Kipling had not always been totally friendly and WSC felt that there had been elements of himself intended in the poem beginning:

> Paget M.P. was a liar
> And a fluent liar therewith.

A wide variety of visitors came and went at La Capponcina, including on WSC's side his wife and his children, in so far as their lives allowed of it, and more frequently his literary assistants restarting work on his monumental *History of the English-Speaking Peoples*. This was to be his last literary effort and it is patchy in quality. The portions that he wrote himself are often up to his very highest standard. It is difficult not to be moved, for instance, by the last sentences of his chapter on Richard Coeur de Lion:

> The King laid siege to this small, weak castle. On the third day, as he rode daringly near the wall, confident in his hard-tried luck, a bolt from a crossbow struck him in the left shoulder by the neck. The wound, already deep, was aggravated by the necessary cutting out of the arrow-head. Gangrene set in, and Coeur de Lion knew he must pay a soldier's debt. He prepared for death with fortitude and calm, and in accordance with the principles he had followed. He arranged his affairs; he divided his personal belongings among his friends or bequeathed them to charity. He sent for his mother, the redoubtable Eleanor, who was at hand. He declared John to be his heir, and made all present swear fealty to him. He ordered the archer who had shot the fatal bolt, and who was now a prisoner, to be brought before him. He pardoned him, and made him a gift of money. For seven years he had not confessed for fear of being compelled to be reconciled to Philip, but now he received the offices of the Church with sincere and exemplary piety, and died in the forty-second year of his age on April 6, 1199, worthy, by the consent of all men, to sit with King Arthur and Roland and other heroes of martial romance at some Eternal Round Table,

which we trust the Creator of the Universe in His comprehension will not have forgotten to provide.

The archer was flayed alive.

I was told that the American Civil War chapters were at one time compulsory reading at West Point. WSC had paced many of the battlefields and felt profoundly and emotionally involved in the heroism, the romance and the horrible tragedy of that most bloody conflict. In between such high points, however, there were chunks of perfectly adequate but rather dull bread and butter, because WSC was under contractual pressure to finish the four volumes and his personal energies were declining. Bill Deakin had helped him greatly and later Dennis Kelly and Alan Hodge, the latter a professional historian and co-editor of *History Today*, had borne the brunt.

Even I was pressed into service and on a mountain holiday in Switzerland was told to write the chapter on 'The Rise of Germany' in the nineteenth century. This was fun, and I was rather proud of the result, particularly as WSC's own proof-reader and critic Mr (Literary) Wood (to distinguish him from Mr (Accountant) Wood) noted on the galleys: 'Masterly writing and grasp of detail'. Alas, the mice got at the cheese and the professionals put a lot of water in my wine on the grounds of incompatability of style with their own efforts. WSC generously gave me £1,000 for my chapter, a large sum in those days, with the remark: 'This is a present. It is not for the taxman.' The taxman thought otherwise.

In a passage on the German siege of Paris in 1871, I had described 'the spirited peripatetics of Gambetta', the gallant French statesman who had escaped from the encircled city in a balloon in a vain attempt to raise new forces on the Loire. A broad smile spead over WSC's face: 'We musn't be irreverent to Gambetta. Some might consider it unfilial.' He went on to explain that one of the many bizarre stories circulated about himself was that Gambetta was his natural father. How anyone could possibly sustain this, taking only the obvious Spencer Churchill features of WSC, it is hard to understand.

Beaverbrook himself came and went. In his absence WSC sent him spasmodic reports on events in his household. One ran: 'Your white cat has just killed a beautiful rat, and brought it to me at the dinner table.'

The choice of Beaverbrook's own visitors was on the whole subordinated to the well-being of WSC. Quite a number of them were inevitably from the newspaper world, and with only one exception that I can recall they preserved discretion on the very open conversation of the dinner-table. The exception was the late James Cameron. I noticed that he was scribbling on fragments of paper and mentioned it to our host. 'Ah, no,' he said, 'he won't let me down.' But he did, in at least two highly imaginative articles. The presence of Churchill, who did not give interviews, was like a bowl of cream in front of a hungry cat.

Lord Rosebery (Harry) was a fairly lengthy visitor. Beaverbrook referred to him irreverently as 'Lord Razzberry'. In what passes for research on this book, I came across a letter that Rosebery addressed to me dating from that general period. It referred to Robert Rhodes James's wish to write about Rosebery's celebrated father. Rosebery had consulted WSC who had given Rhodes James 'a favourable chit', and this was Rosebery's follow-up. It ran as follows:

> Many thanks for your letter. I have a copy of Winston's reply to me on Jan. 15th last year; but I wanted to make sure whether he had any further information or second thoughts about Mr Rhodes James. Personally I do not think that a new 'Life' of my father would create much interest at the present time.
>
> I am very annoyed with [Roy] Jenkins' book on Dilke. Presumably he real-ised that he could only sell it by exploiting his divorce to the full. To do so he had brought the ridiculous charge that my father, who was not only a great friend of Dilke's but also a great friend of Crawford's, engineered the divorce. Imagination could hardly rise higher. I have Dilke's letters to my father which show that the idea of this plot is quite untenable.
>
> I had thought of writing an article contradicting the book, but I did not want to advertise it in any way; but it makes me loath to lend my father's letters. I think I shall write to Mr Rhodes James and tell him that I do not think a 'Life' of my father at the present time would make any practical appeal to the public.*

The imp of mischief undoubtedly sat at Beaverbrook's elbow and he was quite inclined to tell mildly malicious stories about his friends, and rather stronger ones about his opponents. He related that Rosebery père was stay-ing with friends, accompanied by his son Harry. When leaving he was asked to write one of his elegant dicta in the Visitors' Book. He pondered long, pen poised, until Harry said:

'Oh come on, father, you know exactly what you're going to write. I saw you trying out various phrases on scraps of paper last night.'

At which his father shot him a look of hatred and observed to the air: 'I like a manly man and a womanly woman, but I can't abide a boily boy,' his unfortunate progeny being afflicted by adolescent spots.

In spite of this badinage, Beaverbrook was much attached to Rosebery, who finally gave the address at his memorial service in St Paul's Cathedral in June 1964.

Back in England Beaverbrook telephoned me one morning. 'Have you seen Roy Jenkins lately?' he asked without preamble. I replied that I had, at a publisher's cocktail party. 'Did you tell him what you were doing?' Rather surprised, I said that in answer to his question I had told Jenkins that I was still working for WSC on secondment. There was no secret about it. Beaver-brook said: 'Well, he's going to put down a Parliamentary Question on why a member of the Foreign Office is working for a private Member.' Nothing happened: I was told that Jenkins had been dissuaded, but it wouldn't have mattered. The answer drafted but unused would have said that it was in the country's interest that WSC should have official assistance, and it was not costing the taxpayer a penny, as he was reimbursing the Treasury.

* Lord Rosebery later overcame his mistrust of Rhodes James and gave him every help. Rhodes James and his wife became close friends of the later Roseberys.

During one of the later stays at Cap d'Ail, Beaverbrook had several times broached the subject of a lunch with Joseph Kennedy, the father of JFK, Robert and Ted Kennedy, and the US Ambassador to Britain from 1937 to 1940. Kennedy had rented a house on the coast, halfway to Nice, and Beaverbrook, who had always maintained connections with him wished to please him. I could not understand why: Kennedy had been bitterly anti-British during and after his Embassy days, and had confidently and almost gleefully prophesied to President Roosevelt Britain's early and contemptible defeat by the Germans. During the German air onslaught on Britain in 1940, he had taken himself to safety in the country at night and was dubbed 'Yellow Joe'. (This seemed to me unreasonable: why should the Ambassador of a neutral country expose himself unnecessarily to bombs?) I demurred at the proposal and urged WSC not to be seen consorting with an enemy of our country, who had sought to harm us in our hour of greatest need. An argument ensued, and WSC concluded it by saying: 'If Max attaches importance to it, I will go. But it must not appear in the press.'

Kennedy made himself as agreeable as bad food and worse wine, his reputation, and his toothy tendency to smile as mirthlessly as a dogfish allowed. I have only met one other smile so unappealingly shark-like and that was on the face of Mr Ivan Boesky of insider dealing fame. Nothing appeared in the British press, but it did in the USA.

I would have sought to prevent another outing if I had known more about the host at the time. Beaverbrook suggested that it would be diverting to lunch with one Arpad Plesch and his wife at their large and pretentious house at Beaulieu. Plesch was either German or Central European and something of a mystery man. Later investigation produced many stories about his vast wealth, none of them to his credit. He was said to have married an elderly heiress to part of the IG Farben fortune (the German chemicals giant) and on her death to have married her daughter. Although Jewish, he remained persona grata in Nazi Germany until quite a late date. During the war it was alleged that he procured blockade-running sugar for the Axis powers from Cuba. How was it, I asked when my enquiries dredged up these unpleasant suggestions, that Plesch managed to live in great style in France, and to own racehorses in England? The answer was cynical in the extreme.

However, what really put me off when the luncheon duly took place was our host's persistent endeavours to interest WSC in his pornographic library. He claimed that it was the third greatest in the world, after the Vatican and the 'Enfer' at the Louvre. It was housed, he said, in a room designed to reproduce in miniature the magnificent library at the Abbey of Melk on the Danube.

Plesch's last wife had previously been married to an Esterhazy and he told us that when they got married, Esterhazy, with Hungarian humour, had sent his bride a brief telegram: 'God Plesch you.'

That evening, although I was still in general ignorance of Plesch's background, I took my courage in both hands and berated Beaverbrook for furthering such an unsuitable meeting. I expected an explosion, or at least a cold reminder that he had known WSC very much longer than me, in all sorts of weathers, and was more capable than me of judging in such matters. However, his reply was both mild and cryptic: 'Anthony, you can meet people on the Riviera whom you wouldn't recognise at Ascot.'

I often wondered what Beaverbrook's motives could have been. Mischief? But he was undoubtedly devoted to WSC. Probably he just thought that his old friend might be diverted by the meeting. However, I knew that any knowledge of it would blow a hole in CSC's fragile good relations with Beaverbook, so I kept my misgivings to myself.

A sortie of my own produced exaggerated opposition from my host. Tina Onassis had invited me to come on a short cruise to St Tropez, Hyères and Corsica. Ari was away on business and she wanted to invite some 'young and jolly' friends who might have bored him. I cleared my absence with WSC and informed Beaverbrook with all proper formality that I should be absent for some days, and hoped I might be allowed to return to La Capponcina thereafter. The reaction was unexpected: 'Ah yaas, I know all about that cruise. It's for juvenile delinquents. I'd rather you didn't go.' Juvenile delinquents? Who could he mean? I was in my thirties and the other guests sounded perfectly respectable. I twigged finally. He didn't want to be tied down all day by his principal guest and he didn't want to leave him alone. I reminded him that the literary team were on their way so WSC would be fully and agreeably occupied. To no avail: 'Ah yaas, you'll be a most interesting co-respondent and my newspapers will duly report that fact,' was the response. But I went. Nothing unseemly occurred, though we did all bathe nude from a deserted coast in North Corsica – from quite widely separated male and female beaches.

Back in Britain, I was to enjoy Beaverbrook's hospitality both in London and at his country house Cherkley. It was always fun, but one had to be careful not to admire things too much, in case, as in classical Arabia, your host would present you with them. It was not infrequent, having commented on a particularly good claret, to find a case in the boot of your car when you got home. He had what seemed to me an admirable idiosyncrasy regarding wine. At his larger dinner parties, there were sometimes different wines for different people. With a considerable staff and decanters and napkin-wrapped champagne bottles it was not difficult to arrange, and the distinction seemed to be based not on rank but on whether the drinker was interested in wine or not. I am not absolutely sure of all this, but the different shades of say, old and less old champagne are definitely detectable.

It is tempting to meander on about Beaverbrook. He was a fascinating character, and I don't think any biographer has really done him justice, nor indeed has he revealed much about himself in his own highly idiosyncratic writing. I felt warmly towards him; it is difficult to resist charm, and generous kindness to one's family, as in a party-dress sent to my small daughter Jane, with a manuscript note: 'To the most beautiful girl in London, Max'.

I was to have the privilege of seeing him, and later his second wife Christofor, right up to that final gallant but chilling speech at his last birthday party on 25 May 1964. I will never forget the last passage: 'This is my final word. It is time for me to become an apprentice once more. I have not settled in which direction. But somewhere, sometime soon.'

He died very soon thereafter and did not complete his writing. He had told me that *The Age of Baldwin* was to succeed *The Decline and Fall of Lloyd George* and that the works were to be completed by *Churchill's War*. He had previously always referred to it as 'Churchill's Victory' and I never knew what caused him to change his mind. Perhaps the same realistic pessimism that was now increasingly affecting WSC himself.

There seemed to be plenty to do, back at La Capponcina, and time passed agreeably enough. Nonie came down to stay. WSC treated her with charm and warmth, and she enjoyed herself. But I was always conscious of the lotus-eating nature of my existence. I was doing absolutely nothing to advance my career and was progressively losing touch with the real world, cocooned in easy comfort and beautiful surroundings, and slipping all too easily into the Riviera social life. Everyone has an infection of that grossly over-estimated quality of personal ambition (and if it is a quality at all, why do those heavily endowed with it take such pains to keep their gift secret?): I think that I am lucky to have escaped the most virulent strain, but even so I did feel that, however analgesised by the greatest of luxury living, remarkable food and wine and excellent, even brilliant company, I still had something to offer on a rather different stage. It was the icing without the cake.

WSC accepted without much demur this phase of his retirement. His interest in current affairs could be illuminated readily in conversation at lunch or dinner, but otherwise became more and more desultory. I received a Foreign Office distribution of telegrams brought by a Queen's Messenger whom I intercepted at Nice airport on his way to Rome. But WSC skimmed through them like a newspaper holiday-reader on the beach. In fact the London papers were of more interest to him, but this was no great change. Only the possibility of a political intervention, a visit to a statesman or to the United States, or the thought of a speech (but never in the House of Commons) could kindle a little of the old fire.

In an (unusual) philosophical discussion at dinner on the nature of happiness, I suggested that it consisted of having a number of small things to which one looked forward. WSC made no comment, but when going to bed he remarked: 'What you said is true. But it is melancholy, and only applies when you are on the shelf.'

In these circumstances it is possible to suppose that WSC's appreciation of alcohol would be increased, in short that he would drink more. The reverse was the case. It has always irritated me to hear the exaggerated tales of his consumption. I never saw him drunk, but enlivened, stimulated, sometimes eloquently impassioned in a theme after dinner. Once when alone at La Capponcina, where I dined with him à deux for thirteen consecutive nights, he decided that we should eat at the Hotel de Paris, where he was invariably treated like a deity come to earth. The night was balmy, the dining room magnificent and the food and wine sans pareil. We drank pink champagne and WSC's conversation was a wonder and a delight. Indeed during all those solitary meals, he was never, ever dull. When we returned home, we had to negotiate the long flight of Capponcina steps. WSC said: 'Give me your arm, my dear, I'm a bit boozed.' There was absolutely no objective sign of this.

Chapter 20

I T I S from here on that my chronology must become even more desultory. The formal sequence of stays in the South of France, in London or at Chartwell has no major significance, and any interest lies in WSC's reactions to current affairs, progressively to become less active, and his comments on matters past.

Lord Moran remarked: 'Winston's old age will not be a happy one, for he is not interested in other people.' Coming from a physician with many years of intimate knowledge of his patient, this is a surprisingly imperceptive observation. I think that WSC had as much interest in others as most old people, but this had been conditioned by his concentration on great events, and thus by the part that the individuals were playing on that stage. And with old age the whole picture was gradually dimming. Yes, he was unhappy in his old age; not really for Lord Moran's reasons, but because he foresaw many of the melancholy events that were to affect our country and sat down every day with the knowledge that he could do little to influence things and that his intellectual and physical resources were slowly running out.

WSC's conversation touched on these matters both obliquely and directly. His admiration for Clemenceau is well known and he spoke with sympathy of his unhappy old age. He had visited the old tiger and found him sitting alone in front of an unlit fire, wearing white cotton gloves. Clemenceau told him without apparent emotion of his decline. Moved, WSC asked him:

'But what have you left?'

Clemenceau suddenly quickened: 'Il me reste mes griffes,'* he growled.

'What will you do with them?'

'Nothing. I shall live until I die.' And WSC nodded several times to underline the point.

Inevitably WSC considered foreign affairs and defence more than other issues: they were after all what had always interested him most and also the areas in which he still had up-to-date inside information via the Foreign Office telegram distribution. His distaste for the Foreign Office was by no means diminished by his reading and I came in as a handy Aunt Sally for his reflections, regardless of the fact that I shared most of his views on issues and some of them on personalities. I so often seem to have found myself defending causes in which I do not really believe, but I was quite sure that the vast

---

* 'I've still got my claws.'

majority of the Diplomatic Service were thoroughly decent and patriotic people, well above average intelligence and often far more interesting characters than their Home Civil Service counterparts. WSC spoke thus: 'Well, you know them better than I do, but I have known them far longer. It is true that the Foreign Office is probably the most intelligent of Government Departments. It is also the most feminine. No, you are not to smile! I don't mean Anthony [Eden], but he is a prima donna, isn't he, and donnas are women, aren't they? Our diplomacy tends to turn the other cheek to the wrong people, and sometimes it turns all four.'

WSC's table conversation had always tended to have a philosophical and certainly a poetical side, and in those post-resignation days it became more predominant. I tried to encourage his reminiscences, not just because they were truly fascinating but also because they could avert his falling into sombre reveries and sunken silences, which I was empirically quite sure were bad for him physically. It was interesting that quite often he repeated the exact words he had used much earlier, sometimes indeed in his own books or speeches; it was as though he had polished a phrase to convey his exact meaning and saw no point in changing it. His extraordinary powers of memory were well known, going back to his schooldays when he won a prize at Harrow for reciting the whole of Macaulay's 'Lays of Ancient Rome' without missing one of the 1,200 lines, and although more recent events and people were dimming, this remarkable gift could reappear aptly and sometimes disconcertingly.

The two World Wars were an obvious area in which to seek his evening thoughts, from the great questions of international policy and military strategy to the personalities involved, whom he had known so well. Were we right or wrong to go to war in 1914 and 1939? Should we have compounded with the Germans in 1940? One would predict that WSC's answers would be thunderous on both points, but they weren't quite as clear-cut as all that. Perhaps dinner-table talk can be a better guide to true feelings than public pronouncements, for it is expressed under no pressure of the long-past events and has no need to accommodate public opinion. 'Emotion recollected in tranquillity' . . .

I reminded WSC of his letter to *The Times* of 7 November 1938. It ran in part: 'I have always said that if Great Britain were defeated in war I hoped we should find a Hitler to lead us back to our rightful position among the nations.' I expected an explosion, but the answer ran thus:

'Well, that's all right if you choose to take it out of context. You could also find that I had said even more favourable things about Mussolini and I had met him personally. I was exerting all my power to avert war, and Hitler's earlier policies did indeed raise Germany from the dirt. Of course he was poisoned by anti-semitism and intoxicated by visions of conquest and I made plenty of references to that too, didn't I? I think my summing-up in my book is the best I can do: "Into this vacuum [Germany] strode a maniac of ferocious genius – Corporal Hitler." You might also consider that the letter you have chosen to quote is an answer to those who claimed that I sought war because it would bring me to office in a way nothing else could.'

Pursuing the same topic, he showed an ambivalent attitude to Britain's guarantee to Poland which made our declaration of war on Germany in September 1939 inevitable.

'It was a gamble on two factors and the odds were against us. One was that Hitler would be deterred from further aggression, the other that the Poles would not take advantage of our guarantee to be dangerously provocative. But I had to endorse any message that Britain would fight for something. Yes, the alternative would have been worse, if worse there is than the destruction of some 55 million human beings.'

Nobody knows for certain how many people lost their lives between 1939 and 1945, but on the Prime Minister's instructions I had asked the Central Statistical Office to prepare an estimate including military and civilian deaths in all theatres. To my astonishment the figure was in the broadest terms about 35 million. Corresponding figures for the First World War were thought to be between 17 and 22 million. Of course, our own military casualties were infinitely higher in the first than in the second war.

On 1940 I played the Devil's Advocate. Leaving aside the appalling issue of the extermination camps, which was then not evident, would it have been better if we had joined the New Order, as a substantial part of France was then inclined to do? Would the monstrous tyranny of Stalinism have been brought to an end, for Hitler most certainly would have attacked Russia and, unharassed in the West, almost certainly would have won? Would the equally monstrous tyranny of the Nazi regime have been mitigated or abbreviated by the influence of Britain, whom Hitler had always respected? Would we have kept our Empire and our financial strength?

WSC's reply was brief: 'You're only saying that to be provocative. You know very well we couldn't have made peace on the heels of a terrible defeat. The country wouldn't have stood for it. And what makes you think that we could have trusted Hitler's word – particularly as he could soon have had Russian resources behind him? At best we would have been a German client state, and there's not much in that.'

I was aware that he liked to discuss historical fantasy, but this seemed the wrong stage, and the conversation risked disturbing WSC more than stimulating him.

WSC, during his often-described late-night supper with Stalin in the latter's cottage within the Kremlin, had covered a great many points, some mentioned in his memoirs. What was the worst time in Stalin's life, he had enquired? Was it when the Germans were sweeping forward and their lead tanks could see the spires of Moscow? No, Stalin replied, it was during the liquidation of the Kulaks (the deliberate starving to death of some two million independent small farmers by the Soviet Government). This was the first time that the Soviet authorities had ever admitted that the 'famine' was in fact mass murder.

WSC reverted more than once to the shame of Singapore. How could our forces have been so easily overwhelmed? I asked him about the heavy guns installed as seaward defence. 'Well, whatever was said at the time, they wouldn't have availed much against a nimble enemy. And it isn't easy to install guns of that calibre with a 360-degree traverse.'

The fall of Singapore to the Japanese in 1942 was one of the worst disgraces ever suffered by British armies. Some 35,000 relatively lightly equipped Japanese had forced the surrender of more than 90,000 British, Australian and Indian troops. The Japanese had command of the air and had sunk the new battleship *Prince of Wales* and the battle cruiser *Renown* without too much trouble. WSC told me that before the war Bomber Harris had been on the planning staff as a comparatively junior officer. Admiral Tom Phillips, who went down with the *Prince of Wales*, was his naval opposite number. After a vehement discussion on air power versus capital ships, Harris had concluded the meeting by saying: 'Tom, there is no reasoning with you. One day you'll be on the bridge of your ship and you will be hit by bombs and torpedos dropped from the air. And as you sink you'll swear it was a mine.'

Who had told WSC this story?

'Harris, I think.'

'What did you think of him?'

'I admired his determination and his technical ability. He was very determined and very persuasive on his own theme. And the Prof. backed him up. You must remember that for a long time we had no other means than Bomber Command of hitting back. The public demanded action and rejoiced at our counter-blows at German cities after Coventry and so many other towns. And the fact undoubtedly was that large numbers of German aircraft and vast resources of manpower and material were tied up in their air defence. But it did go on too long, and I pointed it out to the Chiefs of Staff. Such destruction tends to acquire its own momentum and those who hold weapons are apt to use them. That worried me about nuclear. Of course Harris was under-recognised at the end and so were his gallant men who suffered the heaviest casualties of all. I did something for him when I got back to power but it wasn't much.'

'What about Harris's personality?'

'A very considerable commander. I said so many times. But there was a certain coarseness about him.'

WSC's long-standing and deeply ingrained military and naval knowledge came out time after time and technical terms fell easily from his mouth. He asked about the rate of fire from the fighter-bombers I flew. I said it worked out at about forty 20 mm shells a second. 'All those shots fired in anger,' he reflected. 'Were you angry when you fired them?' I replied no: as far as I could recollect, concentrated, ballistically interested and sometimes frightened.

Conversations on individuals merged inevitably into discussions of historical issues, and vice versa. WSC had said of Lawrence of Arabia, whom he admired and had befriended: 'He had the art of backing uneasily into the limelight.' Had he really believed that *The Seven Pillars of Wisdom* was factually accurate? 'No. But it was a remarkable work. He was a stylist. And his operational reports to Allenby did not indulge in fantasy. Allenby would not have been taken in, in any case.' What about Lawrence's masochistic homosexuality? WSC expressed strong distaste, but added: 'At the end of the road he was a very remarkable character and very careful of that fact.'

WSC's personal reminiscences of Lawrence were entertaining but not of major historical significance. He related how, during the Jerusalem Conference in 1921, the Emir Abdullah, later King Abdullah of Jordan, had vanished overnight. A serious breakdown of negotiations was feared, and Lawrence was sent to bring him back. It transpired that he had merely felt the cold in Jerusalem and was going home to get some more clothes and blankets. Or so he said.

When CSC was staying I asked them both about Curzon. The Foreign Office had a fund of rather malicious stories about him, mostly centring on his stress on a short 'a' in his pronounciation. Thus, on seeing his office when he became Foreign Secretary in 1919, he exclaimed: 'When I was Viceroy of India, my inkwell was silver and crystal. This thing is bräss and gläss. And those curtains! Ghăstly, quite ghăstly.' Visiting the troops in France during the First World War he was taken to see a mobile bath unit. 'I never realised that the lower clăsses had such white skins,' he is alleged to have observed.

I had always felt that these stories tended to spring from members of my Service who had suffered Curzon's chilly arrogance when young, but CSC's informed accounts were undoubtedly true. She told me that she practically never told a lie. I believed her totally. She added that if she did feel compelled to tell a lie, it was a jolly good one. I believed this too.

Apparently Curzon, accompanied by his second wife, had come to dine with the Churchills in the 1920s in their house in Hyde Park Square, then considered to be ON THE WRONG SIDE OF THE PARK. Their finances were under strain, which was far from uncommon, but CSC, who had superb taste, had achieved her usual tour de force with decoration and furnishing. Curzon advanced into the drawing room, looked round, and exclaimed to his wife, whom he had preceded through the door: 'But my dear, this is really quite nice.'

Referring to his second marriage, he said, according to CSC: 'I wooed her in three weeks, and polished off the honeymoon on the voyage home.' CSC's final shaft was a recollection of walking round the garden at Kedleston while staying with Curzon. A bowler-hatted, waistcoated individual approached.

'That' said Curzon, 'is my head-gardener. He is under notice of dismissal.'

'May I address your Lordship?' asked the bowler-hatted one.

'Yes, my man.'

'I just wanted to say that you are the most awful cad I have ever met.' And he withdrew.

When I asked WSC for his summing-up of Curzon, the proconsular Viceroy of India, the orientalist, the courageous traveller, the indefatigable Foreign Secretary, he said briefly: 'George wasn't much.' This dismissive view from a man well known for generosity of outlook bewildered me and influenced my opinion until I read Kenneth Rose's masterly biography of Curzon, *Superior Person*, which, coupled with accounts from Shelagh, my (second) wife, who was born in India, of Curzon's extraordinary and successful efforts there, inter alia to preserve and restore the subcontinent's heritage and monuments, more than restored my confidence in my early view. She reminded me that Clemenceau had said of the more arrogant and less intelligent memsahibs: 'Your women will lose you your Indian Empire.' Curzon himself had noted that the greatest threat to British rule in India was 'the racial pride and the undisciplined passions of the inferior class of Englishmen in this country'.

WSC's reminiscences did not of course come tumbling out in a constant stream, nor were they usually the fruit of Boswellian interrogation. Circumstances in conversation, or a reference in the newspapers or the books that WSC read more and more, sparked off reflections and animadversions.

Ireland was then not so wretchedly tormented by the activities of the disgusting psychopaths of the IRA, but it was quite often in WSC's thoughts, prompted by his work on the *History of the English-Speaking Peoples*. He said he'd always had a soft spot for the Irish (we were speaking of the Southern Irish), while he looked on the people of Ulster as 'part of our flesh and bone'. I told him that my father, an Ulsterman, had warm feelings for the South in spite of the fact that the IRA had not only tried to murder him while he was a serving soldier, but had also fired a burst from an early (American-supplied) tommy-gun through the door of a room which contained only my mother, our nanny and a child in arms (my sister Jeanne). And they knew who was in the room, for they had put them there. My baby sister is said to have exclaimed 'Pop!'

Did WSC's affection spring from his many Irish friends, his stays as a guest with spirited and entertaining members of the Ascendancy or from historical roots, I asked? 'Not really from any of those,' he replied. It came from the many Irish soldiers who had served us so well. That had also been my father's view.

I was particularly curious to hear WSC speak about the incidents of 1913–14. The Liberal Government, in which he was First Lord of the Admiralty, was attempting to force Irish Home Rule down the throats of the Ulster Loyalists, who, not unreasonably, greatly feared and resented the idea of being swamped by the Southern Irish and ruled by Dublin. They looked on the Ulster Catholic minority as superstitious, primitive, treacherous and murderous barbarians, anti-British to the core. Plus ça change . . . The Liberals' plans had been thwarted by the action of three-quarters of the Officers of the Cavalry Brigade, stationed near Dublin, who had threatened to resign their commissions en masse rather than move to Ulster to coerce the Loyalists. Churchill had despatched warships to Lamlash, on the west coast of Scotland, with orders to sail to Belfast to prevent the seizure of arms depots by the Loyalist volunteers, if necessary by gunfire.

Had he seriously contemplated the Navy opening fire on British patriots, I asked him, with deliberate provocation? There was a real explosion. How could I believe he would contemplate any such thing? It was a terrible suggestion, a most unworthy question. Of course I accepted his denial and apologised. My object had been to rouse him from melancholy lethargy, and I had been all too successful. In his novel *Savrola* he had written of a city being over-awed by the guns of the fleet. And at the heart of the Dardanelles adventure lay the belief that if the Narrows had been forced, the Navy could have sailed through the Sea of Marmara and forced Constantinople to capitulate under threat of bombardment. But the final conclusion must be, with the utmost certainty, that he would never have fired on 'our own flesh and bone'.

WSC's religious views have often been discussed without any clear conclusion being reached. I fear that I cannot do more than record what he said, and said more than once. 'Whether you believe or disbelieve, it is a wicked thing to take away Man's hope.' 'The Sermon on the Mount is the most perfect expression of ethics ever conceived. And the Benedictions are of God-given eloquence and beauty.' Once, in the presence of the Prof., he lectured the table on the probability of the life of the soul, basing his argument on the conservation of energy. And he did say, quite clearly and many times: 'I believe that man is an immortal spirit.' But that, after reflecting on his many comments, some jocular, on death and the hereafter, is the best I can do. Would it be fair to record him as an optimistic agnostic?

Suicides beset the Churchill family. Their eldest daughter Diana, CSC's brother, Randolph's second wife, June (after WSC's own death), and Sarah's second husband, Anthony Beauchamp: all killed themselves. WSC's views on the matter were clear: 'It is only justified by intolerable and incurable pain, or by the knowledge that great evil to others could be averted by death. And of course in certain circumstances of war.' And he declaimed Kipling's lines:

> If you're lying out wounded on Afghan plains
> And the women come out to cut up what remains,
> Then roll to your rifle and blow out your brains
> And go to your God like a soldier.

Had he ever contemplated suicide? 'No. Well, only philosophically.' If we had lost the war and he faced capture, what then? 'Certainly not!' Well, I don't suppose anyone would doubt that he would have taken as many of the enemy as he could with him. It is well recorded that when travelling by sea in the War, he had insisted that the lifeboat allotted to him should carry a machine-gun.

He went on to reflect on the execution of Nurse Edith Cavell. She had stayed in German-occupied Brussels in the First World War and had been court-martialled and shot for helping British prisoners of war to escape. 'What a chance of immortality the German officer commanding the firing-squad missed! He could have stood in front of her and commanded the soldiers to shoot him first.'

This particular snatch of conversation was followed by the information that the only beverage that went with artichokes, which featured on the menu, was water. WSC added that his own appreciation of cooking was diminished by his failing sense of smell. 'I am deaf in my nose.'

One morning I found him silently contemplating his budgerigar, Toby, who, as usual at liberty, was elaborately embroidering the edge of a sheet of writing-paper. 'Answer me this,' WSC said: 'how is each feather clever enough to know that it should grow green, yellow or black so precisely according to its position on Toby's anatomy?'

Answer came there none, but the post did, with an invitation to go to Aachen next May (1956) to receive the Charlemagne Prize and to make a major speech. The award would be made by the first post-war German Chancellor, Konrad Adenauer, for whom WSC had considerable respect. After a brief period of reflection and enquiry into who had previously been awarded the Prize and what it was for, WSC accepted. He later courteously, ex post facto, asked the Foreign Office if they thought he was right to do so, and they, with equal courtesy, replied in the affirmative. The Prize was awarded by the City of Aachen (Aix-la-Chapelle: site of Emperor Charlemagne's Court) to a person who had contributed outstandingly to European cooperation.

As the date approached, WSC's post-prandial conversational rumbles centred on (a) that he was not going to Aachen after all, and (b) what he was going to say when he got there; (b) prevailed. He decided that he would not make the expected speech, welcoming Germany back into the European family and praising the undoubtedly worthy Adenauer. This would have been a fitting sequel to his Zurich speech of 1946, when he had appealed for the creation of 'a kind of United States of Europe' and stated that 'the first step in this direction must be a partnership between France and Germany. In this way only can France recover the moral leadership of Europe. There can be no revival of Europe without a spiritually great France and a spiritually great Germany.' Momentous words indeed at any time from Winston Churchill, but in 1946 . . .

However, instead of pursuing this theme and enlarging on Britain's part in it, WSC concluded that it would be more helpful to offer an olive branch to post-Stalin Russia. European unity was not flavour of the year with Anthony Eden, nor indeed with the Foreign Secretary, Harold Macmillan, in 1956. This left a rather empty terrain and I endeavoured to put a clearer plan before WSC. He was determined not to embarrass his successors, and thus the only reasonable procedure for this particular occasion was to speak of his hosts and of the rapprochement between West Germany and her former enemies (the Federal Republic was now a member of NATO), and to offer muted encouragement to the new Soviet rulers. Anything stronger would upset both the US Government and Anthony Eden.

WSC rather grumpily agreed, with the words: 'All right, you write the bloody speech then.' So I did, and keeping it short both for apprehension of the physical strain on the speaker and because if you are forced to be rather bland, it is better to be rather brief. At the last minute WSC demanded a warning to West Germany not to pursue its rightful aim of reunification with too much vigour. If the Soviets' almost paranoiac fear of German reunification were fanned beyond a certain point, the results would be catastrophic. It was easy to add a passage to this effect, particularly as I shared WSC's apprehensions. The passage in question eventually told the audience that if the West Germans sought unity by excessive means, they might have it indeed, but it would be a 'unity of ashes and death'.

When the speech was made, attention focused on this rather purple patch of a phrase. There was a chilled and disconcerted silence and the faces of the German dignitaries were interesting to watch. However, the speech as a whole was well received and although the press wrote up 'ashes and death', no harm was done in the West. In the Soviet Union, the reaction was distinctly favourable. Nine years later, CSC, writing to Harold Wilson, then Prime Minister, said: 'In other directions too he [WSC] sought to improve our situation for instance by his persistent friendly references to Russia being part of Europe. After his Charlemagne Prize speech at Aachen in 1956, there were, I am told, some of the first indications of the post-Stalin thaw.'

On reflection, WSC's favourable references to Russia in his speech had something of turning the other cheek. In April, the month before Aachen, Bulganin and Kruschev had visited Britain. They had distributed largesse, graded according to the rank of the recipient. The swells got Russian cameras, allegedly made by the unhappy technicians of Zeiss, formerly of Iena, and now transported to the Soviet Union. Nonie and I, to our vast gratification, got no less than seven pounds of Beluga caviar. WSC also got some caviar, but his principal gift was a large number of bottles of liqueur from different parts of the Soviet Union. The bottles came in red velvet cases. I was the only person to sample one, and that once only. It tasted like alcoholic hair-oil. WSC thought that the gift might have been a calculated jeer, on the lines of the insulting gift of tennis balls from the Dauphin to Henry V.

The circumstances surrounding the Aachen speech were somewhat fraught. The hotel in which we stayed was not of the grand luxe category to which WSC was accustomed. The beds, notably, were rather austere, the mattresses being divided into three separate parts, just like the British military ones known as 'biscuits'. (Perhaps they were?) WSC slept ill and this added to his normal pre-speech tension. As we departed, the smiling hotel manager presented his autograph book for signature. 'I'd gladly sign your passport to hell,' was the muttered response. But he did sign, and the proprietor spoke no English.

As we drove to the Hall, WSC said: 'How good is your German?' I apologetically replied that while I could read some, my conversation was limited to a few phrases. 'That's no good,' he snapped, 'I can say "Du bist ein Esel"* perfectly well for myself.' I was rather pleased at this acerbity, reminiscent of earlier years.

---

* 'You're a donkey.'

When we were seated, I looked through my copy of the speech notes, completed in 'psalm form' just before we left the hotel. I turned to stone: three pages were missing. This was awful: WSC would dry up in mid-speech and now he was unlikely to be nimble enough to recover. I sent up a brief prayer. It was answered. The three pages dealt with a single self-contained passage, of no great importance to the speech. No-one noticed.

After the ceremony we drove in a convoy with Adenauer at break-neck speed to Bonn. Road conditions were not good, and I was dismayed to see one of the large group of motorcycle outriders disappear over the verge. The convoy did not stop.

In Bonn we stayed with the able and friendly Derek Hoyer-Millar (our last High Commissioner and first Ambassador to West Germany, later Ambassador in Washington and retiring as Lord Inchyra). WSC was tired and asked for a whisky and soda. Derek brightened.

'I'm rather proud of my whisky, Sir Winston. Anthony, will you pour it out? You know how he likes it.' I did as I was bidden, adding the soda from small bottles on ice. WSC spluttered and put it down:

'Proud of your whisky? It's the nastiest concoction I've ever tasted!' Derek gave me a reproachful look, took the offending drink away, and replaced it by one of his own mixing. Further spluttering:

'Good God, this one's even worse! I'm going to my bedroom to have a rest.' Exeunt Senior Statesman and Ambassador. I examined the drinks: we had both given him whisky and tonic.

After that things looked up. WSC's conversations with Adenauer were constructive and cordial, and his genuine admiration for the genius of the German race shone forth.

We then flew up to Celle, near Hanover, to stay with his old regiment, the Fourth Hussars. As was to be expected, their welcome was superb. That night in the mess, WSC made a brief speech and Colonel Kennard, commanding the regiment, an excellent answer, alternating his sentences from English to German for the benefit of the German guests. A first-class result for Anglo-German relations.

The following morning, as we bumped along in an Army vehicle for WSC to review the troops, he addressed me over his shoulder:

'Should I say something to them?'

'Yes.'

'Well, write me something quickly.' This really was asking too much. The truck was lurching from rut to rut; I had nothing to write on and no time in which to write it.

'It would not be right to read something to the soldiers,' I bellowed over the noise of the engine; 'do speak impromptu!' A doubtful sideways look as we stopped, but the words he spoke were so much better than anything I could have written.

After the trip WSC was disturbingly tired, and I wasn't sorry to see the Meteors of 615 Squadron, of which he was Honorary Air Commodore, rising to escort us at the Kent coast.

Chapter 21

———— ❧ ————

READING WHAT I have written, one might suppose that WSC now
lived in the South of France and only occasionally visited England,
which of course was not so. But I did see him with greater continuity
when he was abroad, living in the house and having virtually every luncheon
and dinner with him.

In England he normally spent the week at 28 Hyde Park Gate. No. 27 also
belonged to him and it was here that my office was set up, airy, agreeable and
accessible, with the Misses Pugh and Snelling and CSC's secretary adjacent.
At weekends and when Parliament was not sitting, WSC would rejoicingly
go to Chartwell, and I would either commute or stay the night there if the
visits were of any duration. Meanwhile my connection with the Foreign
Office became increasingly tenuous, although I was in due course promoted
to the rank of Counsellor and continued to get my distribution of telegrams
and a cubby-hole in which to read them. They provided little comfort.
Events in the Middle East were moving inexorably to disaster. Nasser had
undoubtedly caught the tide of rampant Egyptian nationalism, and was rapidly becoming the oriflamme of unreasoning Arab pride in other countries.
Here at last was a true leader who could put the West in its place and revive
Islamic glories and conquests. The Americans were not particularly helpful,
encouraging Nasser, among much more serious gambits, by the probably
inadvertent but almost incredibly ham-fisted gift of a pair of pistols, immediately interpreted as symbolical by the recipient. When aid for the High
Aswan Dam was cut off because of Nasser's association with the ever-ready
and ever-mischievous Russians, the reaction was the more dramatic. In July
1956 Nasser nationalised the Suez Canal, all too obviously left open to such a
feat by our foolish agreement to withdraw our forces two years previously.

Anthony Eden's deteriorating health had added to his endemic feverish
petulance. He was the more enraged because he had been the author of his
own misfortune and Britain's tragedy. He had trusted Nasser and now felt
that he had nurtured a viper in his bosom. And, as P.G. Wodehouse says,
nothing makes a man more annoyed than the knowledge that his bosom has
been used as a viper nursery.

Every known detail of the lead-in to the Suez operation by Israel, Britain
and France has been hashed over again and again. Every diarist, informed or
uninformed, impartial or axe-grinding, has discussed his part in it. I can
only write of what I know and despairingly saw: the end of Britain as a Great
Power.

By this I do not mean that I had the prescience to foresee that we could be politically so inept, militarily so dilatory and indecisive and nationally so disunited, even gutless, nor could I believe that the Americans would turn on us with such joyful malevolence. Rather, I felt as the storm gathered that we had been offered a chance to redeem some of the years of retreat and surrender and restore our position in the Middle East as a firm presence whose friendship was to be valued and whose enmity feared, with all the world-wide benefits that this implied. Nevertheless, I had misgivings about what I knew both of our plans and of the personalities involved. Above all, in the words of the Irishman giving advice to a traveller lost in a maze of roads: 'I wouldn't have started from here at all.'

At the beginning of August 1956 WSC, after Harold Macmillan had dined with him at Chartwell the previous night, went to see the Prime Minister at Chequers. En route he dictated a short appreciation of the Egyptian situation to Miss Pugh, his accompanying secretary. His doubts of what he knew of our plans were evident:

> The military operation seems very serious. We have a long delay when our intentions are known. The newspapers and foreign correspondents are free to publish what they choose . . . The more one thinks about taking over the Canal, the less one likes it. The long causeway could be easily obstructed by a succession of mines . . . Cairo is Nasser's centre of power.

WSC went on to express confidence that we would make use of our armoured forces based at Tobruk, close to the Egyptian frontier, rather than rely on the lengthy and laborious process of an amphibious landing on a hostile shore. This had been Monty's idea, as expressed to WSC at lunch at Chartwell and, I had always assumed, put forward officially too. 'Our object is to knock Nasser off his perch,' the Field Marshal had said, 'and it shouldn't take too long to do that going overland from Tobruk to Cairo.' Of course, in the event we did no such sensible thing, the pretext being that it would antagonise the Arab world by involving Libya, then peaceful and reasonably friendly under King Idris of the Senussi, and suspicious of Nasser's ambitions.

As the inevitable climax approached, it became evident that the Americans were backing away from their support of Britain and France. After all, the use of the Canal by all peaceful nations was not much to ask, and if this had been agreed by Nasser there would have been no need for military action. Many reasons have been advanced for the Americans' desertion of their allies: jealousy of long-standing influence in the Levant, Egypt and the Middle East as a whole; the US oil companies seeing a chance to clip BP's wings and establish themselves as an alternative (when the Iranians had seized our great refineries at Abadan in 1951 the US had very carefully stood back from supporting us against Mossadeq, whom they were later to dislodge with our assistance by an engineered coup); the forthcoming November (1956) Presidential elections, in which friendship with the wicked colonialists, British and French in that order, might lose votes. Whatever the reasons, everything that Dulles, the US Secretary of State, said was increasingly at variance with his initial friendly stance, and President Eisenhower went along with it without any apparent misgivings, and later with the rancour roused by 'being cut off from information of developments by the British'.

The net effect of all this was quite simple. Nasser was encouraged to pursue his adventurist course and Britain and France were equally forced to pursue a course of independent action.

I was kept in touch by communications from Freddie Bishop, the Prime Minister's admirable Principal Private Secretary, some in writing and some oral, but none of these gave any exact indication of imminent armed intervention. Freddie was under-estimated by the Prime Minister, but he was an absolutely first-class and sensible man, and was correctly careful not to give away operational information even to Winston Churchill via myself. However, it did not take an Intelligence genius to deduce that something serious was afoot; the procession of sand-camouflaged tanks on their way to the ports was sufficient in itself.

Towards the end of October, I received a summons from the Prime Minister to call on him the next day. I notified WSC, went to my rendezvous and was received alone in the Cabinet Room. Eden seemed a different man from my previous meetings, friendly, exhilarated, almost light-hearted. 'You are to promise not to tell anybody except Winston until this is all over,' he began. Intrigued and surprised by this somewhat schoolboyish opening, I naturally assented. The Prime Minister went on to tell me of the plans for the immediate Anglo-French assault on Suez. Little was said of the 'separation of the antagonists', the overt reason for intervention following Israel's invasion of Sinai. He then despatched me to see Norman Brook (Secretary of the Cabinet), who would give me details of the military operations involved. Just as I was leaving, the Prime Minister stopped me.

'I want to ask you this. If I offered Winston a seat in the Cabinet without portfolio, would he accept?'

I was astounded. I simply couldn't imagine anything less likely. Finally I said: 'I do not believe that he would like the opposite of the harlot's prerogative.'

This was not so cryptic as it might now appear. Referring to the Press Lords, Baldwin, when Prime Minister, had said: 'They seek power without responsibility, the harlot's prerogative throughout the ages,' a phrase suggested to him by his cousin Rudyard Kipling.

I thought I had gone too far as I saw a flush mounting in the Prime Minister's cheek, so I hastily added: 'Well, Prime Minister, you did ask me for my opinion. I will of course convey your offer to Sir Winston today.' I was dismissed quite civilly and went to see Brook. In a world-weary voice he informed me that the first step would be to 'take out the Egyptian air force', the first time I had ever heard that phrase. But surely, alerted by all the military brouhaha, they would have already dispersed? They had.

I informed WSC of what I had been told. He listened without comment and without surprise until I reached the Cabinet offer, which I gave him verbatim. Here he did indeed manifest surprise and asked me to repeat the exchange slowly. Then a broad grin spread over his face: 'Well, I must say, you do take a lot on yourself. Turning down the offer of a seat in the Cabinet without even asking me!' I hastily reiterated that I had only answered the question of my opinion. The matter was of course for him alone to settle. Did he want to speak to the Prime Minister on the telephone? No, he didn't; but he must have later, as no more was heard on the subject.

The background of WSC's health at this time is of interest. On 20 October he had suffered a stroke, or more accurately, perhaps, a 'spasm', in the South of France, where he was staying with Wendy and Emery Reves. He recovered sufficiently rapidly to travel home a few days later, and just four days after the incident he was walking in the garden. He seemed to have these 'spasms', minor strokes in effect, as other people catch colds, and to suffer extraordinary little harm from them, though one must suppose that the cumulative effect, after the stroke of 1949 and the much more severe one of 1953, must have been considerable. Certainly on this occasion WSC's intellectual powers seemed none the worse and his interest in the development of the Suez crisis remained lively.

I was the more surprised when, on 2 November, WSC said that he felt too tired to draft a public message of support for the Goverment's action. The Private Office at Number Ten had asked me to convey this request from the Prime Minister. Did WSC not wish to support the operation? Yes, he said, he definitely did want to support it. Would I please draft in that sense? I reproduce below the result, addressed to the Chairman of his Constituency Party, Alderman Donald Forbes. It was published on 3 November:

> I think that my constituents may wish to have a brief statement of the reasons that lead me to support the Government on the Egyptian issue. The British connection with the Middle East is a long and honourable one. Many of the States there owe their origin and independence to us. In peace we have assisted them in many ways, financially, technically, and with our advisers in every sphere. In war we have defended them at great cost. Above all, we have endeavoured to confer on them the benefits of justice and freedom from internecine wars.
>
> In the last few years the United States, France and we ourselves have been principally concerned with keeping the peace between Israel and her neighbours. In spite of all our endeavours, the frontiers of Israel have flickered with murder and armed raids.
>
> Egypt, the principal instigator of these incidents, has openly rejected and derided the Tripartite Declaration by which we, the French and the Americans sought to impose restraint. The last few days have brought events to a head. Israel, under the gravest provocation, erupted against Egypt. In this country we had the choice of taking decisive action or admitting once and for all our inability to put an end to strife.
>
> Unfortunately, recent months have shown us that at present it is not possible to hope in this area for American co-operation on the scale and with the promptness necessary to control events. Her Majesty's Government and the Government of France have reacted with speed.

I regret profoundly that the Egyptian reaction has forced the present course on us. But I do not doubt that we can shortly lead our course to a just and victorious conclusion.

We intend to restore peace and order to the Middle East, and I am convinced that we shall achieve our aim. The American alliance remains the keystone of our policy. I am confident that our American friends will come to realise that, not for the first time, we have acted independently for the common good.

World peace, the Middle East and our national interest will surely benefit in the long run from the Government's resolute action. They deserve our support.

The Prime Minister wrote:

My dear Winston, I cannot thank you enough for your wonderful message. It has had an enormous effect, and I am sure that in the US it will have maybe an even greater influence . . . These are tough days – but the alternative was a slow bleeding to death.

Thereafter everything came to pieces. I find it painful to recall the details of our decline and tail-between-legs retreat. WSC sank into a mood of deep melancholy, the symptoms expressed mainly in a slow but progressive withdrawal of interest in public affairs.

Certain incidents during the collapse of the Anglo-French campaign did stimulate him to old-style fury. 'Rent-a-Mob' had made one of its earlier appearances in the demonstrations against the Government's actions and against Britain itself. On hearing that a large section of the crowd was composed of foreigners, WSC exclaimed: 'I would never have believed that we would allow that gutter-muck to come to insult us and dictate our national policies in Trafalgar Square.' He was horrified that Gaitskell, the Leader of the (Socialist) Opposition, after an initial stout-hearted and sensible speech such as one would have expected from Ernest Bevin or Clement Attlee, should have gone into reverse and sought to make political capital out of our national danger. 'I shall never speak to him again,' WSC said, 'He's a vile coward to give in to the dregs of his Party.'

I was to see Eden twice more before our capitulation and noted 'The triumphant trumpet peal died fitfully away'. It was tragic to witness his struggle with increasing bad health, his temperature reportedly rising without warning to 104 degrees, and faced with the absolute certainty of defeat and disappearance from the political scene, perhaps in ignominy. With all his faults he did not deserve that.

On 23 November the Prime Minister flew to Jamaica to stay in the house of Ian Fleming of James Bond fame. If he had not done so, he would have collapsed totally. The Suez crisis was still fully with us and Eden's departure was very ill received. A vicious cartoon by Osbert Lancaster showed his leading figure, 'Maudie Littlehampton', gazing at the departing aircraft and observing: 'I think that I could bear anything except that brave little smile.' Monty wrote to WSC of the Jamaica holiday: 'Under such conditions the captain of the ship does not go sea bathing – he dies on the bridge.'

WSC said sadly: 'I never thought that we would be Jamaica-ed.' Many versions of his subsequent obiter dicta on the Suez operation have been circulated. What he said to me was this: 'I would never have done it without squaring the Americans, and once I'd started I would never have dared stop.'

For Eden it was Greek tragedy. The hero, who through his folly and weakness had made some violent dénouement both possible and necessary, in his belated flash of ill-considered resolution was brought to ruin.

Two years later, when WSC lunched with General de Gaulle to receive the decoration of Compagnon de la Libération, the conversation touched briefly on the Suez episode. As we rose from the table de Gaulle addressed me: 'Quelle maladresse! Quelle chute! Massu ne vous pardonnera jamais.'* General Massu had been the French Commander at Suez and France had shown a considerably greater inclination to carry on than we had. In 1956 our stock fell to the lowest point in Europe, and particularly in France, that I could remember.

As I have said, the Suez fiasco was a hard blow to WSC, obviously for its effect on our national destiny, but also because of the collapse of Anthony Eden. WSC had known him for so long, had admired him so much in the 1930s – indeed, had felt an almost paternal affection for him. I think Jock Colville was deeply mistaken in suggesting that towards the end of his tenure WSC had felt 'a cold hatred' for his successor. It was more irritation at being under pressure to depart and grave doubts about the consequences.

WSC was above all a historian of extraordinary gifts. He believed profoundly in Britain's enduring capacity for good in the world and he saw with horrified clarity the effect of our almost unbelievably rapid decline. 'It is no good being wise and benevolent if no-one listens to you and if you are not in a position to enforce your will.' This was the gist of many weeks of post-Suez ruminations.

Yet despite the severity of the blow, WSC's powers of regeneration and his refusal to admit defeat showed through, and showed constructively and practically, even in his health-stricken eighty-third year. His first thought was to repair the breach in Anglo-American relations, and when he had recovered from his indignation he was quite extraordinarily forgiving. Magnanimity has been recognised by all who knew WSC as a most powerful ingredient of his character. And in any case it was not in the West's interest to prolong and exacerbate the rift. As early as late November 1956 he wrote to President Eisenhower. To quote from Martin Gilbert's official history:

> The theme of the letter, as first drafted by Colville, then substantially redrafted by Montague Browne, and finally accepted by Churchill, was that whatever the arguments put forward in Britain and in the United States 'for or against Anthony's action in Egypt', it would now be an act of folly, 'on which our whole civilisation would founder', to let events in the Middle East come between the two countries. The only country who would gain from that would be the Soviet Union.

* 'What clumsiness! What a collapse! Massu will never forgive you.'

The President's rejoinder was not helpful. Referring to the Suez operation, he said that it was 'not only in violation of the basic principles by which this great combination of nations can be held together, but that even by the doctrine of expediency the invasion could not be judged as soundly conceived and skillfully executed'. WSC certainly agreed with the last remark, but he was saddened and vexed by the unrepentant tone of the President. He felt, however, that it left the door open. He sent a copy of both letters to the Queen, who replied in a somewhat neutral vein: 'It is most interesting to learn his [Eisenhower's] appreciation of the situation, and I hope it means that the present feeling that this country and America are not seeing eye-to-eye will soon be speedily replaced by even stronger ties between us.'

Thereafter WSC withdrew from that particular field, though he never wavered from his intention to use whatever powers remained to him to further an Anglo-American rapprochement. He let the matter substantially stand for two and a half years, because he felt that further wooing would be not only undignified but unproductive. Insistence on dignity actually worried him very little: 'No-one ever improved his dignity by standing on it,' he said.

By early January 1957 it became apparent that Anthony Eden would have to relinquish the prime ministership. No man could continue in office after the devastating damage that his policies had inflicted on the country; but this apart, his rapidly deteriorating health would in any case have settled the matter. On 9 January he resigned. It is strange that quite a number of contemporary recorders expressed surprise at his departure. Certainly WSC had been convinced that it must happen. Even though he remained loyal to Eden in his more general social meetings, he had privately been considering what the new options might be. This is not to say that he considered himself an arbiter of the Cabinet's decision (for it must be remembered that this was the way the new Leader was to be recommended to the Queen, whose prerogative it theoretically remains to send for anyone she chooses; only later did it become a matter of Party vote). But WSC was perfectly aware that any public preference he expressed, or that was attributed to him, would be powerfully persuasive, and he was scrupulously careful. He did talk about the succession 'in my circle', which of course included Christopher Soames and a very few other Members of Parliament, and naturally CSC. I was also brought in, and with my usual incautious certainty gave an opinion strongly in favour of Harold Macmillan. The only other horse in the race was R. A. Butler, and of the two Macmillan did seem, in one of Randolph's favourite phrases, the better man with whom to go tiger shooting.

At that point I knew nothing of the 'first in – first out' accusations levelled at Macmillan's conduct over Suez,* and WSC never did. They might have given him pause, but Macmillan would have got the Cabinet's vote in any case – unless perhaps WSC had given a contrary view publicly, which he

---

* Macmillan is said initially to have been a keen hawk and subsequently to have urged our surrender on the grounds of the depletion of our foreign reserves and the American-supported run on sterling.

would not have done. As it was, of course, his support went to Macmillan. Anthony Eden had made no recommendation for a successor.

It seemed, and still seems to me that a new Prime Minister should go to his lonely post with the maximum of unity and approval, the more so in time of deadly crisis. Thus it was important that WSC should be seen publicly to have been consulted by the Queen. It is by no means abnormal for the Sovereign to consult senior figures, and WSC was something very much more than that. If his views had not been taken, the omission might have been interpreted as indicating his disapproval of the Queen's choice.

I waited for a message from the Palace, but none came, so I rang the Queen's Principal Private Secretary, Sir Michael Adeane, and made my point. Adeane was under considerable pressure and was somewhat brusque. 'I really can't do business like this,' he said, and went on to suggest that he should come to Chartwell to receive Churchill's views. I demurred, both because I did not feel that this would adequately indicate the thoroughness of consultation and satisfy public opinion, and, I must confess, because I knew what a stimulant such a summons would be for WSC. The country, and its Sovereign, owed him full and proper recognition and at the lowest valuation it could do no harm.

Adeane listened somewhat testily, and ended the conversation. I was much relieved when he rang back half an hour later. 'I'm afraid I was rather shirty,' he began, with his characteristic straightforwardness. I was pleased by the use of this agreeably archaic term, and the more so when he gave WSC rendezvous to call on the Queen the next day. He was duly photographed doing so, and I don't think it did the handover any harm.

It was WSC's last significant act on internal policy.

Chapter 22

✲

AT CAP D'AIL Lord Beaverbrook encouraged WSC to treat the house as his own and invite whomever he wished to lunch or dine. In late 1955 there came his long-time literary associate Emery Reves and his fiancée Wendy Russell, later to be his wife. The following day WSC lunched with them at their house, La Pausa, at Roquebrune some six miles east of Monte Carlo. The connection was to have an enduring and benevolent influence on WSC's well-being and happiness in his last years.

Emery was of Hungarian Jewish origin and had first met WSC in the 1930s, when he placed the latter's political articles in Continental and American newspapers, at one and the same time giving wide circulation to his warnings of the rise of Nazism and the probabilities of an aggressive German war, and replenishing the ever-hungry Churchill coffers. WSC had always correctly considered himself to be a professional writer – with some forty books and innumerable newspaper contributions to his credit – and had said of the Chartwell estate: 'All this came out of my pen.'

During the war Emery had moved to London, where he was injured in the Blitz, and then to the USA. His literary connection with WSC extended to all his later subsequent books, the six volumes of *The Second World War* and the four of the *History of the English-Speaking Peoples*, dealing mainly with the foreign rights with notable skill and dedication.

La Pausa was an outstanding house by any standard. Originally a lavender farm, it stood some six hundred feet above the sea, with panoramic views of the coast to the Italian frontier and westwards to beyond Monte Carlo. In the 1920s it had been given by the then Duke of Westminster to his mistress, Coco Chanel, who had built it in substantially its present form. Emery and Wendy had transformed it into a treasure house of pictures, statuary, furniture, carpets and objets d'art. The breadth and richness were extraordinary, the taste remarkable and the effect breathtaking. The pictures were mainly Impressionists and included Cézanne, Renoir, Gauguin, Bonnard, Toulouse-Lautrec, Monet, Manet, Pissarro, Van Gogh and many others. Some of the sculptures were by Rodin. The furniture and carpets were museum pieces.

WSC was much taken by the beauty of the house, its serene and peaceful surroundings and particularly by the warmth of his hosts. He gladly accepted an invitation to stay there in 1956. It was to be the first of many visits over the next years, substantially replacing, but never displacing, the stays with Beaverbrook. The Reves took endless pains for his comfort and

216

entertainment, and it was their dedication to his happiness that drew so strongly. I myself was received with hospitality and kindness and spent all too many lotus-eating days there as WSC's work, first political and then literary, diminished and tailed away.

Emery was an interesting character. He had been a child prodigy at the piano, and all his life he had enlarged his knowledge and appreciation of beautiful things, among which I must include his wife. WSC's taste in music was lively, albeit somewhat basic. Military marches, solemn and well-remembered hymns and late Victorian music-hall songs pleased him, and Emery set himself to build on this foundation from his comprehensive collection of gramophone records. Music after dinner became a regular feature when there were no guests, and WSC acquired favourites among the classics with surprising readiness, mainly Brahms, Mozart and Beethoven, with an occasional sortie into Sibelius. The passage in the fourth movement of Brahm's First Symphony, of which Wagner is said to have exclaimed: 'Here we hear the gates of heaven opening' particularly held WSC's attention, and he sometimes demanded its repetition out of context.

On reflection, I should perhaps not have been surprised at the success of Emery's experiment. WSC's mother had been a talented pianist and he himself once told me that as a boy he had wanted to learn to play the cello. On the same occasion he told me that he had considered going into the Church. 'What do you suppose would have become of me then?' he ruminated. I suggested that he would have crossed the floor and become Pope, an idea that rather pleased him. When the music was over he assisted in walloping the cushions back into shape, which was a surprising manoeuvre, as he profoundly believed in Belloc's axiom:

> It is the duty of the gentleman
> To give employment to the artisan.

Indeed, he went further; one of my earliest recollections of him was being told:

> Put your finger on the bell
> And make it ring like bloody hell

when he wanted a whisky and soda. I was rather saddened by his attitude to servants (I know that this is a term not much in general use today, but I don't quite know how else to express it. Anyway, WSC was a Victorian.) He was not unkind to them, and if he knew of their troubles he could be warmly generous, but he certainly could not be called considerate, or even particularly polite.

Apart from his publishing activities, Emery had an acute interest in politics and history, and had written an incisive work that deserves to be better known, *The Anatomy of Peace*. His approach was more philosophical than direct, and indeed one felt that he would have made a remarkable university don.

Wendy was quite a contrast. A Texan beauty of great vivacity and sparkling style, she had been a top model, early married and early divorced, and had assimilated from those with whom she had associated not just a veneer of learning but a deep knowledge of some subjects, notably art, where her taste and flair were remarkable. Most of this, though far from all, had come from Emery, for Wendy was totally frank, and if uninformed asked questions until she found out what she wanted. She devoted herself unreservedly to WSC, whom she had always admired and now loved.

I use the word 'love' with care. Wendy's feelings for WSC, and the affection which he returned her, held nothing whatever to justify the leering prurience of Noel Coward's remark that WSC was 'absolutely obsessed with a senile passion for Wendy'. To anyone who knew WSC – and Wendy – it would not be necessary to make this point. To me it underlines the perils of having spiteful people in your house. 'There is nothing more dangerous than an intelligent man who will say anything for a laugh.' Reflecting on Coward's bitchiness, I wondered if it derived from knowledge of WSC's part in his omission from the Honours List? It might have comforted him to know that in 1953 WSC had written a warm, almost affectionate, and certainly laudatory letter to Charlie Chaplin, whom he had known personally in the 1930s. The letter referred to Chaplin's 'dear native land' (Britain) and had been suppressed when the author's attention was drawn to Chaplin's publicly expressed views on his own dear native land, to his distaste for paying taxes anywhere, even in wartime, and to some of his rather unusual personal tastes. It is intriguing that such brilliant clowns as Chaplin and Peter Sellers, who parodied with such extraordinary talent contemptible human vices and absurdities, should have embodied some of them quite seriously in their own lives.

This is not to say that the visits of Coward and his confrères were disagreeable. They were certainly an entertaining lot. Coward himself was always willing to sing 'Mad Dogs and Englishmen' or whatever, beating time with a fork. He was accompanied by his host Edward Molyneux, the couturier, who had a beautiful and exceptionally cuisined house at Biot, and obviously loved Coward. Molyneux was a most estimable man. In the First World War he had lost an eye and won a DSO; during the Depression, when others were sacking their employees left and right, Molyneux kept on his staff, paying their wages from his own pocket.

Another visitor of the same general persuasion was Somerset Maugham. Here again WSC and CSC had known him socially for many years. His house on Cap Ferrat, La Mauresque, is too well known to need description. I was delighted to be invited to lunch there, not once but quite frequently. I looked on him as the second-best writer of short stories in the whole of the English language, and only marginally so, to Kipling. He showed me his study, which looked out on another part of the house, rather than on the wide and brilliant blue. He explained that it was hard enough to write without the distraction of scenic beauty. As I pen this, I look on to a lovely wind-swept landscape of woods and fields. May it be an excuse.

Maugham's guests were fun, his table of the highest standard and his conversation, even in his old age, vivid and mordant. He made a point of drinking excellent dry Martinis before meals as an effective answer to those who claimed that they spoiled your palate. At my first luncheon, we had avocado ice-cream. Avocados were then something of a novelty and Maugham explained that he grew his own, having smuggled the original stones or plants from Mexico (or was it Brazil?) in his golf bag. It was not clear whether it was an offence to smuggle them out, or into France, but at least the penalty could not have been as drastic as that imposed by the tyrants of Zanzibar, after British departure; there the forfeit for smuggling cloves was death. Maugham didn't like diplomats: 'They have the uneasy air of one who knows that he is not as other men are, coupled with the apprehension that other men are not aware of this.' (Cribbed, I think, from one of his own books.) This was possibly exacerbated when in 1940 he had apparently not been allowed to take more than a fraction of his outstanding picture collection with him when the evacuation of British subjects from the South of France was being organised.

I asked his good friend and secretary, Alan Searle, why I was so privileged. He was frank. 'Willy invites you for a number of reasons. He wants to be invited to La Pausa to meet Winston again, who he thinks dislikes him. He wants to hear gossip, which he thinks you know. [I didn't.] Finally, you always leave before he gets tired and therefore before he wants you to.'

Ultimately I received a letter: 'I don't want Sir Winston to think me a crashing bore, but if he would care to come to lunch here one day with you it would give me great pleasure. I would send a car to fetch him and take him back to the Hotel.' The lunch was a success and later Maugham came to La Pausa. Relations between him and WSC, never close but always agreeable, did not noticeably improve, and one day on hearing that Maugham was coming, WSC burst into somewhat off-key song:

> Oh W. Somerset Maugham,
> Oh why, oh why were you born?
> Oh W. Somerset, W. Somerset, W. Somerset Maugham.

Not his greatest composition. I don't think the subject ever heard of it, but he did later remark: 'If you think I'm senile, you should see Winston' (who wasn't).

Part of the reason for Maugham's somewhat acerbic and bitter nature may be found in his devastating stammer. He would sometimes stop in mid-speech and emit a low whirring sound, like an alarm clock running down. Then he would snap his fingers, which apparently broke the spell. He told me that at grand Edwardian tables, to which he had been invited as a play-writing lion, his hosts would think it funny to seat him adjacent to an unfortunate who had an equally distressing but different speech impediment, and the guests would rock with honest laughter. Could people really be so cruel?

I never asked WSC for his views on homosexuals, but he did express them from time to time, though in the context of the effect of homosexuality on other conduct. Commenting on the Burgess, Vass and other security cases he said, in effect, that 'homosexuals might indeed be a security risk, not so much because they might be subject to blackmail, but because they often feel themselves alien and apart from the mainstream of the country, like a black in a white country, or a white in a black one.' (This might also apply to other ethnically separate minorities.)

His more general remarks on sexual proclivities (I'm trying not to hurt feelings) were as robust as might be expected. Of the egregious Tom Driberg he exclaimed: 'That's the fellow who brought sodomy into disrepute;' and, when he heard that Driberg had married a somewhat plain wife: 'Well, buggers can't be choosers.' Both these sallies were attributed to the Smoking Room in the House of Commons, coupled with another on the late Mr Ian Mikardo, a Labour Member who looked like a malevolent octopus. WSC studied him carefully, enquired as to his identity and, on being informed, observed: 'Oh. They tell me he's not nearly as nice as he looks.'

Reverting to the visitors to La Pausa, the Reves were careful to choose only those who would be agreeable and diverting to their august resident. They subordinated their own way of life to his tastes in a truly unselfish way for which they have received little recognition. Some suggested scornfully that it was to keep Emery's principal author under his eye and influence, but I have no doubt that this was untrue. WSC would have continued his literary association with Reves in any case, for it had proved satisfactory and profitable over many years.

WSC's family were invited at frequent intervals, but for a variety of reasons they did not often come, with the notable exception of Sarah.

CSC talked to me at length about her lifelong distaste for the Riviera. I noted one remark verbatim: 'I was so unhappy there [pre–1939] and unhappy about Winston's liking for it. It epitomised to me the shallowest side of his character.' Moreover, she never felt well there, and did not find either congenial companions or interesting occupations, particularly as she had for many years abandoned tennis, at which she had excelled. A further factor in her distaste was her concern at the attractions of the Casino; but with WSC at La Pausa she need not have worried, for the Reves disliked the place as much as she (or, for that matter, I) did. WSC did go there from time to time to play in small figures at one of the roulette tables in the Salon Privé. He was received with the utmost courtesy, and gawking tourists were kept at a discreet distance, but even so the atmosphere was unattractive and claustrophobic.

I used to fancy that the glittering-eyed and rather pathetic old harpies who sat at the Casino tables from opening time to late at night would fly up to the ceiling when the lights were put out and hang there like bats, to flop back on to their places the next afternoon. The ceiling itself was notable, with scantily draped Junoesque ladies improbably shooting at pheasants with bows and arrows. Renoir had tendered for the commission, but he had been turned down in favour of the actual artist, who incidentally was more expensive.

Once when I had accompanied him to the Sporting Club, an annexe of the Casino proper, WSC was waiting for his car at the entrance when Frank Sinatra bounced up to him and wrung him by the hand, exclaiming: 'I've wanted to do that for twenty years.'

WSC, who didn't like to be touched, bellowed: 'Who the hell was that?' I told him, but he said he was none the wiser.

Other members of the Churchill family came to La Pausa, but it was difficult for those in active careers, or occupied with their young families, to stay for more than a short time, whereas in England it was easy to drop in at Hyde Park Gate or Chartwell. This, and CSC's aversion to the Riviera, were potent factors in the eventual breakdown of the La Pausa regime, which had given WSC, in his own words, 'months . . . which were among the brightest in my life.' This, however, was some time in the future.

WSC had quite a pantheon of highly regarded individuals, historical and present, and it was unwise to reflect unfavourably on the former, however well-founded subsequent negative evidence might be. I was blasted into orbit with exuberant intellectual energy for making some disparaging remarks about Napoleon and, what was worse, casting doubts on the accuracy of some of the Joan of Arc legend. The living icons were not quite so taboo. One of them, whose merit was in any case not questioned, was Field Marshal Smuts. Although he had died in 1950, it was not until after WSC's retirement that a monument to him was suggested in Britain. The idea came from Clement Attlee, which was an interesting comment on the Leader of the Labour Party's attitude to South Africa, and an endorsement of his innate good sense on a good many issues. He suggested that WSC and he should write a joint letter to *The Times* appealing for funds to set up a British memorial to Smuts in the form, I think, of a garden or a park on his beloved Table Mountain. WSC liked the idea and left for La Pausa. The letter was duly published. It earned me a rather intemperate letter of rebuke from Colin Coote, former editor of *The Daily Telegraph*. How dare I permit the letter to go to *The Times*, that apostle of appeasement, when *The Daily Telegraph* had always supported WSC and he, Coote, had been a close friend of Smuts? I could only reply in a cowardly way that *The Times* was Attlee's idea and that it was rather a historically conventional way of airing one's views – indeed, Lord Randolph Churchill had used that newspaper to announce his resignation as Chancellor of the Exchequer, before telling the then Prime Minister! In vain. Coote was far from gruntled and I reflected that newspapermen yielded little to operatic prima donnas in strength of professional defensive sentiment.

Meanwhile La Pausa, dubbed Pausaland by WSC, was to continue to be his much enjoyed winter residence for long periods at a time. Apart from myself, the longest-staying visitor was Sarah, whose presence was a great joy to her father. She became a close and much valued friend of mine, and her wit, sparkling charm and warmth contributed enormously to the atmosphere of the house. Her sense of fun never left her. When she became engaged to Henry (fourteenth Baron) Audley she sent me a telegram: 'Hence forth my life will be more Audley' and she recounted, with giggles, her mother's somewhat tart comment on hearing of her engagement. 'Well, darling, at least you are finally marrying a man with his own name.' (Sarah's first husband, Vic Oliver, was born Samek and her second, Anthony Beauchamp, was originally Entwistle.)

Alas, the dark shadow of alcoholism was soon to spread over her. Clinics and cures were of no avail. At her parents' request, and with her own agreement, I arranged for her to enter a renowned Swiss establishment. Sarah accepted the suggestion calmly, but added: 'Anthony, you are really wasting your time. Alcohol is part of my life.' She was a totally truthful person, and this pronouncement, sadly, was no exception. Her decline was the more tragic because, in the words of her agent, her acting abilities had reached a point when she would have been a success without the name of Churchill. Moreover, her poems had been published and her painting was achieving more than promise, assisted by the advice and encouragement of Wendy and Emery. Sarah outlived her father and died indomitably. I shall always mourn her.

At La Pausa personalities came and went, mostly to lunch or dine, with the common factor of being bidden because they were considered to be of interest to WSC. Nonie came out and was her usual considerate and entertaining self, WSC making it plain that he enjoyed her company. The Prof. (Cherwell), who followed her visit, was not so easy a guest. At my hosts' request I sent him a telegram asking how long he would be able to stay; reasonably enough they liked to plan ahead. I received a reply saying in effect that if he wasn't welcome, he wouldn't come at all. Mollified, he did arrive, to spend much of his time marching up and down in the brilliant sun, dressed in a London suit, overcoat and bowler hat. The Reves were puzzled.

WSC was continuing to work on his *History of the English-Speaking Peoples* and was now ending the fourth and final volume. His critical faculties remained alert, and although most of the spadework of what had not already been written by WSC before 1939 was done by Alan Hodge and Denis Kelly, he was well capable of originality of thought and composition and trenchant criticism. I had tried my hand at a passage and inserted what I thought were suitable Churchillian adjectives. 'Remember the dynamic noun!' was his marginal comment.

In 1957, a single-volume edition of the War Memoirs was in the course of preparation. It was to contain a terminal essay rounding up events after 1945. There was great pressure of time, and it was to be worth £20,000 to WSC, which he definitely needed. Denis Kelly and I were bidden to draft it. It was great fun, but the result was not particularly distinguished, and provoked a disagreement with Emery. I had drafted a passage condemning in strong terms the activities of the Jewish terrorists in Palestine, which included the blowing up of the King David Hotel in Jerusalem with the loss of ninety-five British lives, and the hanging, and subsequent booby-trapping of the bodies of two British sergeants. Emery demurred but WSC said the passage must be included: 'It is a fact and a very sad fact, and must be recorded,' he said. 'But the Jewish people know well enough that I am their friend and always have been.' He had in fact spoken out in the House of Commons during the War in even stronger words on the assassination of Lord Moyne in Egypt by the Jewish Stern Gang, comparing their conduct to that of the Nazis. Emery accepted the point and withdrew gracefully.

The social traffic was by no means all one-way. The Reves had numerous friends, though as I have said, they did not bring them into WSC's life unless they were sure he would want to meet them. In his own words in a letter to CSC: 'They ask the guests I like and none I don't.' The Churchills' own associations with those who lived there, mostly British, and those who holidayed there went back many years. Monte Carlo was not really a place for the young.

Among the most agreeable sorties were lunches and dinners with the Prefect of the Alpes-Maritimes, Pierre-Jean Moatti, and his vivacious wife. They lived and entertained on a splendid scale in the old palace of the Kings of Savoy in Nice. Pierre-Jean was a lively, indeed positively fiery figure. He had been decorated in 1940 for gallantry in a forlorn hope and had an impeccable record during the Occupation. French Prefects still had very considerable powers in those days, and Pierre-Jean exercised his with panache. 'I will put up with those pederasts,' he once remarked, jerking his head in the direction of Cap Ferrat. 'They are a fact of life. But if they continue to pick up little boys in Villefranche, I will expel them within twenty-four hours.' France exercised a sort of tutelage over Monaco and the Prefect is rumoured to have once informed the Monegasque authorities that if they did not comply with his proper requirements, he would cut off their water supply.

WSC, the Reves, Sarah and I were bidden to lunch by Prince Rainier and his wife Princess Grace, whom Sarah had known in Hollywood. On arriving, we were placed in a salon until our hosts came to greet us. WSC did not mind this in the least, but Pierre-Jean got to hear of it and was outraged. 'Rainier should have been at the door to receive Sir Churchill,' he exclaimed indignantly. Nevertheless I thought very highly of Princess Grace; she had persuaded her husband to abolish the cruel 'sport' of competitive shooting of live pigeons, released from traps by the harbour.

Pierre-Jean was a reasonably talented amateur painter (I have one of his pictures and it is gay and colourful). At one visit I asked him how his painting was going. 'Never again,' he said sadly. He went on to explain that Chagall had been staying with them, and had persuaded the reluctant Pierre-Jean to show him his paintings. After walking round them in silence, he said: 'Well, my dear friend, I will give you my opinion.' Pierre-Jean waited hopefully. 'They're shit,' pronounced the great man.

Later another guest, a well-known art critic, was staying. He had heard the story and persuaded the now even more reluctant amateur artist to let him see his work. 'Chagall is notorious,' he said. 'He can't bear anyone but himself putting paint to canvas. Let me look; I'm a professional critic.' So he too walked round in attentive silence. Then:

'What did Chagall say?' he asked.

'He said they were shit.'

'Well,' mused the critic, 'I think that he flattered you.' So Pierre-Jean resolved never to paint again.

Chester Beatty, the great mining magnate (among other things), lived above Monte Carlo on Mont Agel near the golf course. (It is curious how a golf course brings instant suburbia even to remote places.) He was a delightful and entertaining host and told tales of his early copper-mining adventures with an air of gentle innocence. Once, prospecting in, I think, Arizona when the West was still quite wild, he was informed that a rival had sent two gunmen to kill him. He had asked them to call on him and received them at his desk, on which lay a heavy calibre revolver. 'Gentlemen,' he had said gently, 'I just wanted to remind you that murder is not a monopoly.' They took the hint. WSC was vastly pleased with the story. 'And I have no doubt you meant it,' he commented with satisfaction. Beatty smiled cherubically.

And then there was Daisy Fellowes. The daughter of a French ducal family and heiress to the Singer sewing-machine fortune (or, as I inadvertently put it to Emery, 'the Sewer singing-machine'), she had been a striking figure of panache, chic and somewhat heartless beauty in the early 1920s. WSC told me that when he was at the Versailles Peace Conference after the First World War, she had asked him to tea, 'to see my little child'. When he reached her house, there was no little child, but his hostess lying on a tiger skin in a chaise-longue – à la Elinor Glynn. WSC had fled.

Daisy had first married the Prince de Broglie, then WSC's first cousin, Reggie Fellowes. He had suffered from prolonged and incurable ill-health, and Daisy had looked after him with exemplary care. In her old age, made the more endurable by great wealth, she lived at a beautiful, but in a strange way rather sinister house on Cap Martin, 'Les Zoraïdes'. It had an atmosphere of 'La Belle et la Bête' and a huge shallow swimming pool of which flower petals coated the surface. She was an entertaining guest and a superlative hostess, and WSC enjoyed her company in small doses. Not so the Reves, though they dutifully made her welcome, and not at all CSC.

Daisy showed me personal hospitality, as an odd man is often a convenience, and I enjoyed her parties. At one I met Greta Garbo for the first time, who, I am proud to say, became a friend. She used to spend the summer at a villa on the Pointe des Douaniers, which she shared with George Schlee, a White Russian banker whom she called 'Schleeski'. Like everyone I know, I was knocked flat by her charm, which had nothing to do with her age. On that occasion we sat down four, and I remember the menu: iced carrot-juice and vodka, more vodka and caviar, grouse. This on the Riviera in August.

I should be, and am, grateful to Daisy for her hospitality, but it shocked me – and I am certainly no Socialist – that a woman of her advanced age could spend £2,000, at the prices of those days, on a single model dress. There was quite a lot of very visible poverty not far away. Moreover she certainly played her part in propagating any malicious gossip going about La Pausa and, I fear, embellishing it.

I don't think that WSC had previously met Greta Garbo (GG or Miss G as she was known), but when he did see her he was greatly taken by her calm charm, and she equally by his interest in her. Lunching, I think, at the Château de Madrid, the super-luxurious restaurant overlooking the sea from the High Corniche road between Nice and Monte Carlo, Miss G started to squirm and wriggle to the point of contortion in her chair. I thought that she was having a seizure; but she explained that she had put on thick woolly underpants and, as it was now too hot, she was taking them off. George Schlee was a pleasant and urbane figure, but I think even he was rather taken aback. She invited me to lunch with them at the Pointe de Douaniers. I found my hostess looking thoughtfully at the rocks where, some two hundred yards away, a man was bathing nude. 'That is the first naked man I've seen for seven years,' she said.

GG was an entertaining and frank conversationalist. The talk had fallen on broken romances (quite a lot of them were visible on the Riviera). GG asked me if I had ever heard of her great affair with John Gilbert, the actor of silent film days. I had. She said that when she finally ran away with him, heading for Mexico by car, her doubts had grown by the mile. Finally, when he stopped to take on petrol, she walked through the filling station, out the other side and hired a car to drive home.

I treasure (or treasured, because I can't find it) a rather scruffy bit of paper torn from the bill-pad of a bistro in Portofino. It read: 'Come and join us for a few days on "Christina" here in Portofino. The Piaggio [amphibian aircraft] will pick you up and take you back. Love Ari' (Onassis). Underneath was: 'Yes, do come. G.G.' and a lipstick kiss.

It would be tedious to recite all the illustrious visitors to La Pausa, and in any case I can't remember them. The Duke and Duchess of Windsor came to tea. Nothing of note took place, but when they had left I noticed WSC chuckling. 'I was thinking of the copy of one of my books, which I sent him some years ago,' he explained. 'He wrote to thank me thus: "Dear Winston Thank you so much for sending me a copy of your latest book. I have put it on the shelf with all the others."' Then WSC's face saddened: 'He became such an empty man,' he said. 'He showed such promise. Morning glory.'

Chancellor Adenauer, holidaying in the South, came to pay his respects. This led to a minor incident with the press. The local newspaper *Nice Matin*, inevitably known as 'nice morning', wrote a highly imaginative article describing an altercation over whether WSC should call on Adenauer, or the other way round. In fact the contrary was true, WSC saying that he was a private citizen and should go to see the Chancellor, and the latter, with his usual perfect courtesy, insisting on calling on the older man. It took a lot of effort to get the reluctant Editor/Proprietor to put the matter right.

Dealing with the press was not always easy, particularly on the occasions when WSC was in bad health. Editors invariably assumed that each illness must be the last, and they despatched distinguished correspondents to be in at the kill, which is how WSC himself described it. He was attended by a British doctor, Dr Roberts, who was conscientious and prompt. I don't think Lord Moran much liked anyone but himself so much as laying a thermometer on his August Patient, but he did not come out unless summoned and this was infrequent. CSC tried in vain to get Dr Roberts some sort of official recognition, not so much for his attentions to her husband as for those to the British community. The medical bulletins should most properly have been issued and signed by Roberts, but WSC insisted on seeing and indeed editing them himself, and told me to give them to the press at the Hotel de Paris in Monte Carlo. This inevitably exposed one to a hurricane of questions from hungry and frustrated journalists from all over the world. They were on the whole both understanding and agreeable, and I established lasting friendships with one or two, notably the able and amicable American correspondent of the *Herald Tribune*, Don Cook. The late Mr René McColl was not quite so benevolent: 'If you don't give us something, there'll be helicopters over in the morning.' His proprietor, the late Lord Rothermere, was an old and valued friend of WSC, so I had few anxieties.

The French correspondent of a local paper had the habit of making rather snide interjections at such get-togethers. They were more in the form of statements than questions and were generally misleading and spiteful, especially when aimed at the Reves. He spoke no English, so I retaliated by giving my news solely in that language until his French colleagues told him to shut up. This provoked a bitter little paragraph that I treasured. It was in the middle of an article on the award of some local prize, and read: 'I would like to propose the award of the Prize of the Lemon to Monsieur Anthony Montague. This gentleman wears ox-blood coloured trousers [did I?] and loves to lead the press into ignorance and errors.'

Actually he had a point. The serious press, both French and international, was a fact of life and generally acceptable, but the local paparazzi and stringers were a bore, always managing to turn up and buzz about like unzappable armoured bluebottles wherever WSC was going. Clearly someone was tipping them off and presumably being remunerated for doing so. I therefore told the suspect, and him alone, that the following day we were going up high into the mountains to a remote village for lunch. The next day was very hot. I waited until noon, when the French police guard came to find out our plans, and told them that we were lunching at the villa. They later regaled me, rocking with laughter, with stories of the fury of the paparazzi, who had toiled up the remote and narrow mountain roads on motor scooters in the boiling sun. I think the mole must have had a thin time in the bar that evening.

Very welcome neighbours and visitors were Jim Lees-Milne, of the National Trust, the superb and entertaining diaries and many other things, and his wife Alvilde, the daughter of an old friend of WSC's, General Sir Tom Bridges. They lived just up the hill in a long low house, styled the Wagon Lit, with a truly beautiful garden, the work of Alvilde. Sarah and I used to pop up there for a drink and a relaxing gossip, and WSC enjoyed their return visits, with the remembrance of the great houses and gardens he had known so well. At the bottom of the same hill were Lord (Langton) Iliffe and his beautiful wife Renée. They were quietly and happily hospitable and added to the variety of those in whose company WSC took pleasure.

Having covered only some of the social scene, I should record that most of the time WSC preferred to stay at the Villa, working on his books, playing endless games of six-pack Rubicon bezique, painting and sitting quietly with his hosts in the lavender garden, smoking his cigar and admiring the view. He certainly did paint quite a number of pictures and gave several to Wendy and Emery. One or two were really good, but on the whole the vigour that imbued his earlier work was not there. He got angry with me when I told him that in his landscape of the bay of Menton, the sea appeared to go downhill. When I last saw the picture, it still did; but it was nevertheless a wistful and romantic scene.

Dinner conversation and obiter dicta at the bezique table could still be memorable. On the then still open question of capital punishment, WSC was clear. 'In the present state of human development it is a regrettable necessity. I am not convinced that it is not a deterrent. Very few people do not weigh the possibility of hanging in their calculations. And in any case the Home Secretary only lets a very limited number of death sentences reach their conclusion.' He went on to describe how, when he was Home Secretary, a large calendar stood on his desk with the proposed dates of executions ringed in red, so that they could never be absent from notice. He said it was a very lonely decision, for no other Minister was involved once sentence had been passed and legal appeal over-ruled, though Home Office advisers naturally played a large part.

I recalled that the then Home Secretary, David Maxwell-Fyfe, had rejected a recommendation for mercy in the Bentley and Craig case, during WSC's prime ministership. Craig had murdered a policeman in the course of a robbery, and could not be hanged as he was only sixteen. Bentley was already in custody when the shot was fired, but was condemned to death as an accomplice. He had shouted: 'Give it to him, Chris,' to Craig, who then carried out the murder. I remember Maxwell-Fyfe's stricken face during the time he had to reach his decision. Was he right? WSC said 'Unquestionably, yes.' The verdict was correct. Both the criminals had had weapons (a knife, I think, in Bentley's case); no-one seemed to care for the decent and courageous policeman, or for his bereaved family. When WSC had appointed Gwilym Lloyd George (later Lord Tenby) to be Home Secretary, he had taken into consideration whether he would be sufficiently robust to take these terrible decisions and had reached the conclusion that 'he would hang them all right if he had to.'

I cannot over-emphasise that remarks such as these were not callous; they were the blunt conclusions behind which lay a lifetime of anxious thought and sad experience. Anyone who knew him soon realised that WSC was a truly humane man.

An unverified tale of WSC at the Home Office entertained me. The Home Secretary is the Keeper of the Sovereign's Conscience and is responsible for the Sovereign's speeches. WSC, on receiving a draft from the King's Private Secretary, read it through hastily, and scribbled: 'Excellent. But should perhaps refer to A.G.,' and then departed to Scotland. Worried officials concluded that there was some deep legal significance in the speech, and that A.G. must mean the Attorney-General. This legal luminary studied the speech and wrote a learned treatise concluding that there was no harm in it. On his return WSC was bewildered: 'All I meant,' he explained, 'was that the King might refer in passing to Almighty God.'

This particular dinner conversation was brought to a close by an off-stage interruption. WSC had at the time a Scottish valet, a large jolly man who liked his drink, but did not on that account fail in his duties in the slightest degree: he was after all an ex-Guardsman. At that particular moment he could be heard descending the steep marble stairs leading to WSC's bed-room, whistling a merry tune. WSC much disliked whistling, and interrupted his discussion to listen with distaste. Suddenly there was a scraping sound, followed by a wild Highland yell of distress as the unfortunate whist-ler lost his footing. Then a moment's silence, when presumably he was in mid-air. This ended with a stupendous thump, causing the wine in our glasses to ripple. I couldn't help bursting into unseemly and unfeeling laugh-ter, convinced that a drink or two (or three or four) usually takes the danger-ous edge off a fall. WSC was furious: 'It is most callous of you to laugh. You might at least go and pick him up.' I did as I was bidden; he was quite intact, but we never finished our discussion of the death penalty.

Within the same general theme of English law, the talk fell on sexual assaults on children. Here again, WSC was unequivocally, indeed vehem-ently, in favour of the strongest sanctions against offenders unless proven mentally ill. He quoted St Matthew: 'Whoso shall offend one of these little ones . . . , it were better for him that a millstone were hanged about his neck and that he were drowned in the depths of the sea.' I remembered that when at Number Ten WSC had followed closely the case of several well-born and well-off men who had been sentenced to prison for particularly unpleasant homosexual offences against young Boy Scouts. 'That they, with all their social and financial advantages, should have used their position to corrupt and abuse those children is unforgivable,' he had said. The conversation – at Chequers – had then followed on to the founder of the Boy Scout movement, Baden-Powell (who was not, of course, a homosexual). I noted WSC's remarks at the time, when someone referred to Baden-Powell in patronising terms: 'Of course he was a publicist. How could he not be, any more than the founder of the Salvation Army [Booth]? Have you ever read his first textbook for the boys? It was admirable. Read that bit about cleaning your teeth and being clean in word and deed. There's no harm in that, is there?' Ferociously: 'Is there? When the Nazis and the Soviets occupied Poland, they put down the Boy Scouts. They knew! They hated all decency!'

On the use of television for political publicity WSC had considerable reservations, and he viewed its increasing influence with misgivings. His view was conditioned by his own experiments while still Prime Minister. A test film had been made in which, among other things, he had recited a charming and politically instructive little poem about the ducks in St James's Park, and the envy they inspired among the disaffected for their secure lives (an error, in fact: they flew in and out of the Park and were subject to the perils of all wild birds). One line, quoting the angry Socialist leveller, ran: 'We're human beings, not feathered superfluities,' and WSC rendered it with exces-sive histrionic power. We watched the film at Chequers, and I sat next to

Nellie Romilly, CSC's sister. When it was over she spoke her mind: 'It's not for you, Winston. You appeared like Punchinello.' WSC was not particularly pleased by this frank criticism, but he agreed that it was not for him.

I'm not sure. With more coaching and practice, he could have been as devastating as he was in his live speeches recorded on the news-reels. True, he was at his best when stimulated by a live audience; but then, it was equally true that he rose to the highest peaks of oratory in his wartime radio speeches with only a very small number for company. I should here interject that the stories circulated to the effect that some of his greatest broadcasts were made by an actor simulating his voice are as absurd as they sound.

WSC sometimes inadvertently listened to the local Monaco radio and was astounded and not particularly amused by its commercial jingles. 'Do they really expect to sell their wares with that rubbish?' he asked. The answer, 'Yes indeed, or they wouldn't do it,' left him somewhat depressed, as did the flaunting billboards on the outskirts of Nice. Driving to the airport, WSC appeared to be deep in thought and I did not interrupt him. Suddenly he pointed to an advertisement for Perrier sparkling mineral water: a huge bottle, spouting bubbles, with the legend 'L'eau qui fait Pschitt!' 'I've never seen it spelled that way,' he said gloomily.

On arriving at Nice airport, a messenger handed over a letter addressed to me by Jean Cocteau, whom I had never met. It was a charming and elegantly expressed apology for an offence which was not defined, which I could not identify and which I was quite sure he had not committed. His signature was followed by a little drawing of a flower. I never did find out what it was about.

If all this sounds, and indeed was, rather dull, one must remember that peace and tranquillity were what WSC sought and what suited him best, as long as they were accompanied by sunlight and the chance to paint a little if he felt like it. He enjoyed the company and visits from agreeable and easy people whom he knew well. The contrast with his earlier life could hardly have been starker. Then, fulfilment of the alleged Chinese curse, 'May you live in interesting times,' was to WSC the most supreme of blessings; now, happiness consisted in having a number of small things to which to look forward. Nevertheless a leavening of 'adventures' was still welcome.

When staying at La Capponcina, WSC took advantage of the loan of a 180 ton motor yacht, *Aronia*, owned by Jack Bilmeir and berthed in Monte Carlo harbour. Jack was a most interesting and jolly figure. Starting from nothing he had built up a successful shipping line, with, among other things, adventurous blockade-running forays in the Spanish Civil War. He called it the Stanhope Line, and when I asked him why, replied it was because he had lived in Stanhope Lane. During the War he had courageously accompanied his ships on the Arctic convoys, the most perilous of all, taking war supplies to ungrateful and unresponsive Soviet Russia. I got to know him well and he became a good and almost embarrassingly generous host. This friendship was to have a most benevolent effect on my later fortunes, when they most needed it.

Jack had invited me to go on a four-day cruise to Corsica, to look at a lead mine he wanted to buy. The mine, 'not currently being exploited', lay in the mountains to the north of the island. We anchored in a beautifully remote bay, inaccessible from the land. We bought crayfish from the local fishermen and a haunch of wild boar from a local farmer, who had shot the poor pig from his bedroom window. The offshore wind brought that wonderful maquis smell of pine and herbs. It was idyllic. The next day we climbed a thousand feet or so up the mountain to the lead mine. 'Not currently being exploited', as the would-be vendor had expressed it, was perfectly true. It had been totally worked out in Roman days. Jack, who had pinned some hopes on it, sat down on a rock and laughed until the tears ran down his face.

Among my fellow guests was Kenneth Whitaker, a large and impressive figure from the City. We hit it off rather well and struck up a friendship that was to stand me in very good stead in 1967 after my resignation from the Diplomatic Service. I requited his kindness ill, and vainly regret it.

The shorter coastal trips on *Aronia* had revived WSC's memories of the many cruises he had undertaken, some of them as First Lord of the Admiralty on the official yacht *Enchantress*. The First Lord had explored *Enchantress* from deck to keel. In his investigations he had found a tank of turtles, to be turned into soup. He was much moved by their plight and ordered their immediate release. But turtles are normally tropical or subtropical creatures, and *Enchantress* was in the North Sea . . .

Aronia was a sturdy and fast boat, and had been used for running cargoes of ball-bearings from Sweden, under the Germans' noses, in the War. But she wasn't big enough for the sort of accommodation WSC would have needed for anything longer than day trips, fun though they were. One had taken us to Antibes, whence we had driven to Vence to see the Chapelle de la Rosaire, decorated by Matisse as a thank-you to the nuns who had tended him. WSC greatly admired the vivid contrasts of colour and black and white, quoting from his own 'Painting as a Pastime' on how he would discover many new and dazzling colours when he got to Heaven.

We had lunched at a sumptuous restaurant and at an adjoining table Picasso was entertaining a considerable number of guests. When his bill was presented, he took a menu card, scrawled a few charcoal lines across it and initialled them. The restaurateur was delighted and tore up the bill.

As *Aronia* re-entered Monte Carlo harbour, WSC's eye lit on the largest yacht in the harbour, a white vessel with rakish lines and a streamlined primrose-coloured funnel. 'Who does that belong to?' he enquired pensively. He was told that it was *Christina*, the property of Aristotle Socrates Onassis.

I was to meet Ari soon after at a party. (A number of people assumed that his name was Harry and mispronounced it accordingly.) His charm was enormous, when he chose to exercise it, and not connected in any identifiable way at that point with the power he exercised in Monte Carlo. Apart from his huge fleet, mainly consisting of tankers and called the Olympic Line, he had leased the Greek National airline, also 'Olympic', and had a controlling interest in the Société des Bains de Mer (styled by Christopher Soames the Société des Salles de Bain), the company which owned the Casino, the Sporting Clubs and the major hotels of Monaco.

I asked Ari why had had chosen Monte Carlo as his headquarters, and his reply gave one of the reasons. After the Turkish–Greek war of 1922, Ari, whose family lived in Smyrna, had been reduced to orphanage and destitution. After what remained of his family had gone to Athens, he was sent out to Argentina on an emigrant ship to seek his fortune. The ship had called at Genoa to pick up more emigrants, and had then paralleled the Riviera coast. Ari, in a mood of deepest melancholy, was looking towards the distant shoreline in the dark. He was leaving his country, the survivors of a much-loved family and all his friends to go to an unknown country where there was no-one to greet him. Lights appeared on the shore, a town 'glistening like diamonds', in his own words.

'What is that?', he asked.

'Monte Carlo.'

Ari determined that if he ever could achieve it, that was where he would establish himself.

Although I saw Ari on quite a number of occasions, I never suggested bringing him to meet WSC and the Reves at La Pausa, nor did Ari himself ever seek such an invitation. I made it a rule only to introduce people to WSC if he wanted it, or if it was necessary for a business or political reason. This caused hurt feelings, but I did not feel that it lay within my duties to arrange for people to gawk at a retired lion. It was therefore not until Randolph came in 1956 to see his father and stayed with Ari that a meeting took place. Randolph requested me to ask his father and Wendy and Emery if he could bring his host to dinner. They assented with interest.

WSC had met Onassis's brother-in-law and arch-rival, Stavros Niarchos, at La Capponcina. He had been brought to dinner by the beautiful, kind and altogether incomparable Odette Pol Roger, an old friend of the Churchills after whom WSC had named a racehorse. Her devotion and that of her family to WSC was long-lasting. When he died she put the champagne that bears her name into mourning, with a black band round the label. WSC had got on well enough with Niarchos and was quite interested to meet others of his kind.

The day before the dinner Ari telephoned me to ask me if I would lunch with him 'as a matter of urgency'. I was intrigued. Was he going to offer me the chairmanship of his companies? No. He wanted his card marked on what he should or should not say at dinner. I told him to say anything he liked – after all, he had a brilliant and original mind – but to keep off Cyprus. At that time Greece's demands for 'Enosis', the union of the island with Greece, were being disgracefully pressed by terrorism and the murder of British soldiers in the island. (It seems to be our lot to be murdered by those we save.) WSC was deeply incensed.

We dined at a long rectangular table, with Wendy's usual impeccable attention to decor, food, wine, flowers and comfort making a most attractive

cadre. Ari sat opposite WSC and for a while all went well. Then WSC said:
'Mr Onassis, what is your comment on your country's monstrous conduct on
the Cyprus issue?' or words to the same challenging effect.

Ari fumbled in his pocket and produced a letter with a Greek stamp on it,
depicting the island of Cyprus and an inscription in Greek.

'What has that got to do with it?'

'It quotes what you said when you were Under-Secretary for the Colonies,
Sir Winston.' (WSC's first ministerial position in 1905.)

'What did I say?'.

'You said that Cyprus should belong to Greece.'

Explosion. How could anyone drag up something that had been said more
than half a century ago in a totally different context, if indeed it had been said
at all? The dinner ended on a rather subdued note and Ari left muttering the
1950s equivalent of 'I've blown it.'

Not so. When I saw WSC to bed that night he said: 'That is a man of mark.
I would like to see him again.' And he wrote to CSC: 'Randolph brought
Onassis (the man with the big yacht) to dinner last night. He made a good
impression on me. He is a very able and masterful man and told me a lot about
whales.' (Actually, I'm not sure tht Randoph himself did come.)

Ari at that time had a whaling fleet. Now such an idea fills one with justified
horror and indignation, but only thirty-five years ago it was generally looked
on as rather adventurous and an understandable activity. Were we just ignorant? I do hope so.

Not unnaturally an invitation to *Christina* followed, for the whole La
Pausa party to go for a day trip along the coast. Ari took the restaurant band
from the Hotel de Paris, and I have a photograph of myself entering the
(freezing) swimming pool to the tune of the 'Entry of the Gladiators'. Further and more extensive invitations were to follow and WSC's retirement
entered on what one might call the Cruising Era, which was to bring him
diversion and interest in the most luxurious way possible, but was to cause an
unhappy breach in his relations with the Reves.

Chapter 23

MY ORIGINAL remit from the Foreign Office was to deal with WSC's transactions with foreign dignitaries, his general involvement with international affairs and his speeches thereon, if any. I was not to be concerned with his private affairs and finances and above all not with domestic politics. Those concerned must have realised that with the best will in the world this was unlikely to be feasible.

One of the first of the rules to be broken was that concerning finance. It is no secret that WSC's lifestyle presupposed a very large income and that this was not readily forthcoming. For one so wise and so far-sighted he was quite amazingly extravagant (though, to be fair, he once rebuked me for using a sheet of Number Ten headed writing paper to note something he wanted). It was well said of him: 'Winston, you are easy to satisfy. The best is always good enough for you.' (This, I think originally attributed to F.E. Smith, was quoted to WSC one night at dinner. With a winning smile, I observed that I assumed that this also applied to his choice of Private Secretaries? It earned me a distinctly chilly look.) He had made generous and careful provision for his family through the sale of his books, and various people attempted to invest his capital in the most profitable way. The results were very mixed indeed, as is usually the case.

There were only two ways of helping, either by making more money or by curbing expenditure. The latter would have been both sad and unseemly if it changed his style of life. Surely Winston Churchill had earned the right to his champagne and his cigars, his entertaining and his foreign travel? In any case, it would have been virtually impossible to achieve. Besides, I am quite certain that his children would have immediately assisted if it became necessary, and happily it never did.

Nevertheless, WSC's occasional flights of fancy were flamboyantly extravagant. Returning from leave, I was disconcerted to find that in CSC's absence WSC had caused a bridge to be built to a little island in one of the two Chartwell lakes. It was only a few yards long, but because of the muddy bottom it had cost £4,000, at the prices of the 1950s. About a year later I was even more taken aback to find that the bridge had been replaced by another. The original was hump-backed and the erector had decided that it was both unaesthetic and difficult to negotiate. The price of the second effort was proportionate to the first.

I was therefore compelled to turn to the second alternative, and cast about for ways to increase the cash-flow. The literary rights were already committed, and the reproduction rights of his pictures were a minor but useful addition to the budget through their use as Christmas cards by Hallmark, the giant greeting-card company, of which more later. Hopes had been entertained of the profitability of the Chartwell farm, and Christopher had laboured long and anxiously. A new breed of pig, the Landrace, was expected to be a money-spinner. 'I'll make the farm pay whatever it costs,' WSC is reported to have said. But it was in vain.

What was left? Film rights, television rights and sound-recording rights. In 1956 and before WSC had received offers for the film rights of some of his books, notably *My Early Life*. This is perhaps the most charming of all his many works, lively, humorous, sparkling with military adventure and concluding in 1908 with the words: 'And so I married and lived happily ever after.' WSC gave me a copy quite early in my time with him. At that particular moment he had apparently felt that he had ill-used me on some issue, and he had written an unusually long and entertaining inscription on the fly-leaf. Not long ago, I lent the book to an old neighbour, a doctor, who was dying of cancer and who had enjoyed an eventful youth. After his death, I waited a proper few months before asking for its return, but it was not to be found. I was told that later it had turned up in a Sale Room, but I could never trace it. 'Une bonne action est toujours punie.' It is a loss that I really regret.

When serious interest was expressed by a major Hollywood studio in making a film of *My Early Life* WSC was excited. Disappointment was to follow when he was informed that he had sold the rights to Warner Bros. in 1941, for £7,500. His former solicitors had lost the correspondence relating to the transaction and had informed WSC that he was still in possession. When the true position came to light, WSC was mortified, but told me that he intended to minimise his disappointment to CSC 'because she has always worried so much about money'. It was touching.

However, all was not lost. Warner Bros. generously relinquished their claim and MGM began lengthy negotiations, which seemed to be conditioned by the rise and fall of various magnates within the company and their consequent quarrels. During this time, in my absence, WSC was persuaded to recite in front of the camera a passage from one of his early books. It ran: 'The problems of Africa are the problems of the world . . .' This bite was then grafted on to a film called, I think, *Uhuru*. It was about the Mau-Mau rebellion in Kenya, and portrayed, in Sarah's words, 'noble Africans being brutalised by nasty British'. It was a travesty of the truth and I was outraged that WSC in his old age should have been so misled as to the film's theme and persuaded into agreeing to preface it. The film-makers ultimately agreed to remove the offensive passage.

The *Early Life* rights passed through a number of hands under the tutelage of a British theatrical agent, Hugh French. He brought Richard Burton to see me in my flat. I did not have the right to select an actor to portray WSC, but did have the right to veto the studio's choice. Burton wanted to have the part, and was smarmy. I think that he would have done it admirably, but studio politics and changes of ownership ruled otherwise.

Various somewhat bizarre figures came and went. One, perhaps better left anonymous, I remember vividly. At an American dinner party my neighbour said: 'I believe you know my husband, who is much interested in acquiring the rights of *My Early Life*? I assented cautiously. 'Did you know that he was a concert-class tenor?'

'No'.

'Well, I love hearing him sing. It's the only time that his mouth is open and he isn't telling lies.'

Not all the profferred treatments (outline scripts) were of a high quality. I quote from a letter I wrote commenting on one effort:

Dear Hugh,

In my considered opinion, this script is utterly useless. It is so full of impossibilities of taste, of fact and of dramatic construction that I can only regard it as a bad joke. If you wish, I will expand on this at length, but to read it makes me hover between nausea and hysterical laughter.

I fully understand that a film cannot follow exactly the text of a book, but this treatment only touches the book at rare intervals. Even if this were a plot for a film about entirely imaginary characters, I do not think that many audiences would be strong enough to sit through it. It reproduces every dramatic cliché that I, in my very limited experience of films, have ever seen in the worst of them. The writer shows absolutely no understanding of Sir Winston's character and still less of the way life was lived at the turn of the century. He obviously has no knowledge of history and little of the English language. The only interesting question arising from the treatment is 'Has the writer ever read the book?' And, on reflection, has he re-read his own work? It is full of inconsistencies even within its own surrealist framework.

Finally I had to go to New York for another reason: to remonstrate with Columbia Pictures, a subsidiary of which was selling gramophone records of WSC's wartime speeches without royalty or authorisation. As it turned out, they were probably not breaking any law, as the copyright position was complex. I met their Chairman in a glass wonder of an office eyrie over Fifth Avenue. His half-squash-court-sized desk was on a plinth, and my chair was placed below, looking up at him. I thought that this supplicatory posture was unsuitable, so perched myself on the window sill, at an acute angle, causing him to look up over his shoulder if he wished to see me. In spite of these somewhat childish antics, we reached a satisfactory conclusion and went on to talk of *My Early Life*. It was ultimately agreed that Columbia would distribute the picture and that Carl Foreman (American) would produce it.

Carl was a distinguished figure in the movie world. His greatest strength lay in script and screenplay writing, with such successes as *High Noon* and *Bridge on the River Kwai* to his credit. He had been a member of the Communist Party in his youth and had been driven to work abroad by Senator McCarthy's activities. Not unnaturally, when Carl was suggested, we undertook some fairly thorough investigations; we found no suspicion of his patriotism or integrity, though we might rightly criticise his political judgement. In 1960 I went to New York in the *Queen Mary*, an autumnal voyage in every sense of the word. The sea was rough, the weather cold; it was one of the old lady's last trips, and she creaked and groaned. The bottom of my bath was abrasive and the food nothing to write home about. The only memorable feature of the trip was the suitably maritime names of the ship's Master, Captain Diver (who, poor fellow, had a slipped disc) and my steward, Haddock. I was glad to get to New York.

Anthony Moir, WSC's admirable and devoted solicitor from the firm of Fladgate, had done all the spadework and it remained only to settle the price and sign the contract on WSC's behalf by power of attorney. I fought hard, unscrupulously hinting at rival bidders itching to jump in. There were none in sight, but the eventual terms were more than acceptable: £100,000 down (a very large sum in 1960) and, I think, 6 per cent of the gross takings. I had been seriously advised by a film-actor friend against having anything to do with net takings: they apparently have a way of melting into nothing.

The night before the televised signing, Carl, with whom I had made friends, telephoned me in some agitation. 'Anthony,' he said, 'you must dine with me alone tonight.' I had an agreeable dinner engagement, but sulkily cancelled it. We went to a prominent Jewish Club. Carl told me that until a few years ago he couldn't have taken a Gentile there. I was puzzled and pointed out that my London Club, founded in 1762, had never had any prohibition against Jews, but my host assuaged me by telling me that until fairly recently he couldn't have gone there either, because they did not accept Jews of Russian origin.

It was rather an uneasy meal until finally Carl blurted out: 'Anthony, we can't sign the contract tomorrow.'

'Why not?'

'To be exact, you won't sign it when I tell you that I was once a member of the Communist Party.'

I was exasperated. 'Carl, we did do our homework, you know.'

'Well, what did you think?'

Enough was enough. 'We just thought that you were a talented movie-maker, and a political illiterate.'

I am glad to say that Carl forgave my insult and he and his beautiful English wife Eve became long-lasting friends. I will never forget his last farewell. He telephoned me from California and told me in a matter-of-fact way that he had a brain tumour and was going to die in a very short time. He just wanted to say goodbye to a friend.

I returned to London by air, went directly to Hyde Park Gate and found WSC dining with Violet Bonham Carter. I produced the cheque for £100,000 with the pride of a retriever emerging from a turbulent river with a particularly fine duck. WSC sent for his chequebook and said that he was going to give me £25,000. My mouth watered but this was totally impossible. It would have been like stealing fuel from a very important locomotive who needed it to draw the train. Anyway, the Foreign Office would not have liked it.

When the film appeared it was all right. No more. This was what I expected. Whatever the talent of the film-maker, the account of WSC from birth to 1908 could not have been more than an adventure story. Drama must be parabolic. Everyone knew that WSC had triumphed, and that his youth was only a preamble to the truly great sequel. There was no apotheosis in that period of his life, and no devastating setbacks, such as the Dardanelles, either. The film respected truth and made WSC much-needed capital. That was enough. It was directed by Richard Attenborough, now mysteriously a peer. I recollect that he had one physical characteristic of Rufus the poodle.

The sale of gramophone record rights was less fraught but also, naturally enough, substantially less profitable, fetching £20,000. The purchaser was Decca, who behaved both scrupulously and generously. The records sold came from two sources: the wartime speeches recorded by the BBC, and the speeches delivered in the House of Commons and elsewhere. The latter were not sound-recorded; however, shortly after 1945, WSC had been given an elaborate state-of-the-art recording device which was installed in his bedroom at Chartwell. With this, from his bed, he redelivered many speeches and readings from his own works. The final edited content was of about twelve hours' duration and formed an incomparable record of WSC's finest oratory.

The quality was mixed. The BBC recordings were contemporary: here WSC's voice was stronger and more resonant and, above all, was stimulated by the drama of the wartime hour. Their power was matchless. The post-war recollections just did not stand up. How could they? They were full of rather jolly interjections, like flies in amber, subsequently of course edited out. Thus:

'Rufus [Poodle], you filthy beast, you've spilt my coffee.'

'Darling, I'm so sorry, I didn't mean to hurt your feelings, but it was rather clumsy'.

'No, I can't see him now. Tell him to come back later. Can't you see I'm trying to record this bloody speech? Now, as I was saying . . .'

The texts themselves remained superb, but compared with the contemporary recordings, they lacked fire. Nevertheless I defy anyone to listen to the records as a whole without a lump in the throat.

WSC's oratory has been examined from many angles, and indeed has been the subject of D.Phil. and D.Litt. theses. Outstanding, gripping, moving, poetical, tempestuous . . . why, certainly, yes. But was it such a key feature as a war-winner? I suggest that his demonic energy, his total determination, his experience of so many war-related roles over so many years and his piercing irrelevance-stripping intellect, both analytical and creative, were far more important in the whole five years of his first Prime Ministership. But in 1940 perhaps it was another matter, and without his eloquence would the country have slipped away from its duty? I do not think so.

The television and film rights to the six volumes of *The Second World War* were sold to Jack Le Vien. I met him and concluded the heads of agreement in 1959, when WSC visited Washington and New York, more of which in its place. I met Jack with some reservations: contact with the film and television world is not necessarily conducive to trust. My suspicions turned out to be entirely unjustified, for Jack behaved with total integrity throughout the making of both a twenty-six-episode television series, entitled *The Valiant Years*, and a large-screen version, *The Finest Hours*. He drew entirely on 'stock footage' (newsreel material) and interviews with major wartime figures, and the results were dignified, exciting and commercially successful, a difficult combination indeed.

Jack, whose father had been a regular cavalry officer in the American army, had himself served during the War, going on to be editor of Pathé News and then independently producing first-class and accurate documentaries of Hitler ('The Black Fox') and many other figures. At the height of his career he suffered a massive stroke, which left him intellectually unimpaired, with a considerable degree of mobility, but with his power of speech reduced to a few words. I cannot pay sufficient homage to the way in which he has accepted this devastating disability. To visit him is an enduring pleasure, for it is evident that he understands all that is said to him and he retains his sparkle and sense of humour, looked after with the utmost care and devotion by Josephine Catto. They are a true example of courage, endurance and fidelity.

Before leaving the cinema world, I must record a visit to WSC by Cecil B. de Mille, he of the epics and the armies of extras. He had given WSC a splendid curved cinema screen and accompanying projectors at Chartwell, and on a visit to London he had been brought to Hyde Park Gate by Toby O'Brien. De Mille told WSC that his super-colossal film *The Ten Commandments* had been inspired by the latter's essay on Moses. WSC reflected: 'In which of my books was that published, Anthony?'

I had not been paying much attention to the conversation and answered at random: 'In *Great Contemporaries*, I think.'

WSC exploded: 'Damn your skin, that's not at all funny.' De Mille and Toby looked stunned.

Toby is well worth recalling. He had done effective work for the Conservative Party under Lord Woolton, and WSC liked him. On a previous visit the talk had been of Lord Mountbatten. Toby had suddenly referred to the mistaken views of 'Vanessa Atalanta'. This foxed me, but not WSC, who was well up on his butterflies. 'Ah,' he smiled, 'You mean the Red Admiral.' I was asked to write a short obituary on Toby. I ended it thus: 'He never failed to sharpen a dull dog, nor to help a lame one over a style.' There was a press strike when Toby died, and it was never published.

History is history, and nothing portrayed or written of Winston Churchill can diminish his stature. Nevertheless, both in his lifetime and after it did sometimes become necessary to spike the guns of the mendacious, the malicious and the self-advertisers. Naturally political criticism or unfavourable historical judgement did not fall into these categories. There were however quite a number of libels, and in his very old age WSC would not have been able to take up arms himself.

In 1964 Richard Crossman, a Labour Member and Cabinet Minister, (rejoicing, or perhaps not, in the nickname of 'Double'), published his memoirs, originally serialised in *The Sunday Telegraph*. Part of them covered his activities as a propagandist in Algeria after the Anglo-American liberation of 1942. He stated that, following on a decision that there should be a ten-day pause in the bombing of Italy due to adverse weather forecasts, a broadcast was made to the Italians telling them that they would have a respite from bombing to give them an opportunity of renouncing Mussolini. He alleged that this broadcast caused much annoyance in London, and went on: 'What we all believed out there, but what we could never substantiate, was that the RAF raid on Milan which took place in bad weather and with heavy RAF casualties was Churchill's savage reaction to our propaganda coup.'

This was an exceedingly nasty allegation, in effect accusing WSC of killing his own men out of pique. From my own wartime flying I was reasonably sure that there was no such thing as a ten-day weather forecast, but I did some rapid research, consulting the Air Ministry and Bomber Harris, now retired and living at Marlow. They were both helpful and indignant at the slur. It emerged that there were no ten-day operational weather forecasts, that WSC had never interfered in RAF operations in Italy and indeed that the only Bomber Command attack on Italy in the period had incurred a loss of only two aircraft, due to collision.

So far so good. But *The Sunday Telegraph*, who had inadvertently let the libel slip through, was an old friend of WSC's. Lord Camrose in particular had been a close and valued ally and supporter, going back to a decade before the days when Chartwell was purchased by Churchill's friends and given to the National Trust for the family to live in for WSC's lifetime. WSC and CSC were very fond of him and enjoyed the friendship of his family.

How, then, to proceed? Crossman was a thick-skinned and arrogant individual and was unlikely to yield to an appeal for decency. I had my own views on the matter, but it was clearly family business, for WSC at this time was within months of his death and not capable of reaching a clear decision. I consulted with CSC and Randolph, who were, unusually, in complete agreement. Legal steps must be taken to force Crossman to withdraw, and the *Sunday Telegraph* would not be brought into any action.

After a good deal of legal toing-and-froing, Crossman agreed to withdraw. His first draft was on the lines of 'reminiscing many years later by my fireside, I may have got a few details wrong . . . ' This was too much. I redrafted the apology myself, and after a few agonised squawks it was published. It contained the phrases: '[the story] had been proven to be without foundation and was clearly indefensible,' and 'I failed to take the precaution of checking the facts.' Crossman was also required to pay £600 to the Royal Air Force charity, reduced from £700 on his plea of financial stress. Steps were taken to give the withdrawal wide publicity, as so often the accusation is remembered after it is withdrawn. A rather laborious way of saying mud sticks.

Herbert Morrison, the Labour Cabinet Minister who had been in the wartime Coalition Government, was another offender. In an interview on the BBC with, I think, Eamon Andrews, he said that Winston Churchill had broken his parole when he escaped from the Boer prisoner-of-war camp in Pretoria during the South African war. This was an old canard, and WSC had won a libel case denying it many years before, so I telephoned first Andrews, who was thrown into confusion, and then Morrison, who was bland. 'Of course, I'll issue a statement apologising,' he said. 'Please tell Winston how sorry I am.' I did so, and awaited the statement. None came in spite of two reminders. Nothing further was done, because the remark, although offensive, was not as gross as Crossman's libel. But the incident did confirm my view of Herbert Morrison.

The other libel that I can recall was on the whole aimed at me rather than WSC. It was in the then new magazine *Private Eye*. The Canadian Foreign Minister and later Prime Minister Lester Pearson had been visiting London and had suggested calling on WSC. The latter declined. He held Pearson in low regard in particular because of his joining the pack against Britain at the time of Suez, in vivid contrast with the stout-hearted Menzies of Australia and Holland of New Zealand. Word had got out, and at a cocktail party a serious journalist had asked me for an explanation, which I was quite prepared to give as off-the-record background. A lanky figure with a face like a badly bred lurcher was hanging about with his ears flapping but I did not suppose he was eavesdropping with such care. One does not expect it in a friend's house. He was identified as a founder-member of *Private Eye*.

A cute little paragraph appeared under the most erudite quotation from Nietzsche, 'When the God dies the Priest becomes immortal'. It went on to suggest that the views WSC expressed were not his own, that they were forced on him by me, and implied that I was probably obtaining his signature by subterfuge.

I was entertained and rather flattered. After all, it does not fall to many to be called Winston Churchill's Svengali. I trotted off to show him the article. To my consternation he was furious. 'Send for the lawyers,' he instructed. When they came the conversation went something like this:

WSC: 'Read that article.'
LAWYERS: 'Tut, tut, tut, tut!'
WSC: 'Is it or is it not libellous?'
LAWYERS: 'It is indeed libellous.'
WSC: 'If we sued, would we win?'
LAWYERS: 'We would undoubtedly win.'
WSC: 'We will sue.'
LAWYERS: 'But Sir Winston, you are not libelled, except in the implication that you are incapable of expressing your wishes. It is Anthony Montague Browne who is libelled.'
WSC: 'Anthony, you will sue.'
AMB: 'Absolutely not. First, I can't afford these gentlemen, and secondly, we should make fools of ourselves if we did.'

Long persuasive speech by WSC, who could charm a bird off a tree when he wanted to, resulting in my sulky agreement to sue.

LAWYERS: 'There is just one more point, Sir Winston. You will probably have to give evidence to the effect that AMB is not improperly influencing you, or forging your signature.'

WSC, with extreme vigour: 'What! Get up in the witness box in front of that gutter-muck! You will not sue!

Exeunt disappointed lawyers. No, to be fair, relieved lawyers, I think.

Chapter 24

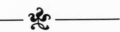

L ET US return to 1958 and the South of France. In September of that year WSC, and CSC, went on the first of a number of cruises on *Christina*, which were to enliven and entertain his declining years. The selection of fellow guests caused unhappiness. To Ari's initial request for suggestions, I replied, after consultation with WSC and CSC, that our host should choose whomever he thought appropriate. To our consternation the Duke and Duchess of Windsor were included in his list. WSC then said that in that case he would not go. It wasn't that he disliked the Windsors, but he was a formalist and envisaged constant jumping up and down to suit their whims. Moreover, since 1940 he had never felt the same about the Duke and thought that it would be wrong for him to associate with him so closely.

I telephoned Ari and conveyed the news. He had already invited the Windsors, but immediately put them off, adding in his telegram that he would thereafter lend them the yacht and that they could take it out and sink it if they felt so inclined.

Next came even worse embarrassment. CSC approached me in a somewhat agitated frame of mind. She loved the sea, she thought that the cruise would be a wonderful opportunity for her to be with WSC, but she did not want any association with the South of France background and would not come if those with this connection were invited. This included Wendy and Emery Reves. She knew that it was not my responsibility, but would I please, please see to it? And to prevent any further gaffes such as the Windsor invitation, would I telephone at once to Ari and if I could not get him, then telegraph him?

Here was sadness. WSC owed the Reves debts of hospitality and kindness, and indeed he had met Ari at their table. They might be bitterly hurt. The least that could be done was a letter of explanation, however delicate and difficult to frame, or even a telephone call. I prepared a draft letter and broached it over lunch alone with WSC and CSC. CSC was emphatic. No explanation was called for; Winston could go where he liked and with whom he liked, and he was under no obligation to give explanations. WSC was undecided but he desperately wanted his wife to accompany him and was rightly convinced that a cruise would benefit her nervous tension and exhaustion. It would be best, he said, to treat the cruise as just a different social engagement. I was making a mountain out of a molehill. His friendship for Emery and affection for Wendy would be undiminished and he would return to stay at La Pausa as before.

As I feared, much hurt was done. Ari, pressed by the Reves for an explanation of their omission from the guest list, told them of my telegram. It was couched in Foreign Office style, where the word 'not' is rendered as 'not repeat not' for clarity, and this did not help. I was cast in the role of the serpent responsible for the expulsion from the Garden of Eden, which distressed me for I shared King Lear's feelings on ingratitude. The full results were not evident until quite some time later, when WSC stayed in the penthouse of the Hotel de Paris in Monte Carlo instead of going to La Pausa, and the wound never fully healed, in spite of resumption of social relations after an interval.

The cruise itself was a great success. *Christina* had started life as a wartime escort frigate of some 1,850 tons, built in Canada. Ari had converted her, at a German shipyard, into a floating mini-palace, regardless of cost. She has often been described, usually with considerable inaccuracy, so I won't give a detailed inventory. Ari had retained the old steam reciprocating engines because they were so quiet, so in spite of her rakish lines *Christina* was not particularly fast, cruising at 12 knots and with a top speed of 18, thus making for long peaceful periods at sea. The longest occasion without sight of land was eight days, between Tenerife and Trinidad, and WSC enjoyed it most of all.

There were some eight guest cabins. They were most comfortably appointed, but *Christina*, having been a warship, was slim in the beam, and everything was a bit compressed: for instance, the clothes hangers could not be hung squarely in the narrow cupboards. These minor faults were completely eclipsed by the overall comfort and ease of such a large vessel. The swimming pool's floor was a mosaic in mock lapis lazuli of bulls and acrobats, taken from the fresco in Knossos in Crete. It could be raised hydraulically to form a small dance floor over the pool, and one of Ari's entertainments was to set it descending gently into the pool when dancing was proceeding, with brightly illuminated jets coming in from the sides. The pool water could be heated, and also chilled in the tropics.

There was a twin-engined Piaggio amphibian aircraft that could be lowered into the sea by a crane in sheltered waters, and was used to drop or pick up guests and to fetch mail and newspapers. I was allowed to fly it from time to time, and it was a jaunty little machine rather like a high-spirited pony. Many years later this aircraft was to be the source of the greatest tragedy of Ari's life. His son Alexander, at the time of the Churchill cruises a rather bad-mannered boy, was to change into a really delightful and interesting young man, with a passion for flying. Ari had taken on a new pilot and Alexander, by this time highly proficient, was checking him out on the Piaggio. The aircraft had just been overhauled, and the aileron control wires had inadvertently been reversed. Taking off from Athens airport, the Piaggio had become uncontrollable and crashed, killing Alexander and severely injuring the new pilot. I saw Ari soon after and feared for his reason. His grief was desperate and he never recovered from the loss. He could not be persuaded that the accident had not been the result of sabotage and he offered a huge reward for information, never collected.

Poor Alexander. The last time I saw him he reminded me of an incident on one of the cruises. He had been teasing his young sister Christina, and my even younger daughter Jane, until I put him in the swimming pool and withdrew the ladder so that he could not climb out. There was no danger, because the pool was shallow, the water very warm and we were in the tropics. Alexander had never said a word about his treatment because he said that he knew that his father would take my side and just punish him more severely.

Alexander's death was only one of a whole number of tragedies in Ari's family. His male relations had been decimated, or worse, in the Graeco-Turkish war of 1922, when the Turks had occupied Smyrna. His father had been a wealthy tobacco merchant, and Ari had found himself transformed in a matter of days from a comparatively rich young undergraduate, and a candidate for the Greek national water-polo team, to penury and the role of janitor in his own house, now occupied by a Turkish Divisional Commander. His grandmother, to whom he was devoted, died as she came down the gangway of the refugee ship in the Piraeus.

Later, when he had made his earlier fortunes in tobacco and shipping in the Argentine, worse was to follow. His much-loved sister Artemis had been severely burnt by an exploding paraffin lamp, and could never wear a swimsuit or a décolleté dress. She was pregnant at the time, and told me that while in the hospital she heard her husband, who thought her unconscious, telling the doctors that he did not care about his wife's survival as long as the baby was saved. Both in fact did survive, but the baby was born severely mentally handicapped. Artemis was later divorced and married happily a truly engaging and honourable orthopaedic surgeon, Théodore Garafalides (it means 'carnation' in Greek), who came on nearly all our cruises to watch over WSC.

Ari married Athina (Tina) Livanos, the younger of the two daughters of George Livanos, a well-established and respected ship-owner. After parting from Ari, Tina first married Sunny Blandford and then Stavros Niarchos who had previously been married to Eugénie, Tina's elder sister. Both Eugénie and Tina died from drug overdoses. Ari himself suffered a lingering end, from, I think, motor neurone disease. When I last heard from him, some months before his death, he was apparently keeping his eyelids open with sticking plaster. And finally, after all these tragedies, his only daughter Christina also died of a drug overdose. It was as though the Furies of Ari's classical fatherland were pursuing him and his line to extinction.

But in the late 1950s little of this was apparent on *Christina*. To continue to sketch her agreeable amenities, there were, besides the conventional lifeboats, two high-speed Chriscraft launches, a Dragon class sailing yacht, a two-seater hydrofoil with a Mercedes 300 engine in it, capable of 70 m.p.h. in calm water, and a glass-bottomed boat to observe reef-fish. The food and wine were superb, and one of my clearest memories is of Clément, a magician of a chef, bouncing from side to side of his galley in a heavy sea and swearing picturesquely as he burnt himself while preparing meals that would have done credit to a three-rosette restaurant on terra firma.

On Mont Agel, above Monte Carlo, 1960.

AMB with Prime Minster Harold Macmillan as he leaves Churchill's house at Hyde Park Gate, December 1960.

'Tito told a number of risqué stories, choking with laughter': Sir Winston and Lady Churchill, with AMB on left, entertained to high tea by Marshal Tito in his villa near Split, 1960.

Port of Spain, Trinidad, March 1961: Churchill with Eric Williams, Prime Minister of Trinidad, accompanied by Lady Hailes – wife of Patrick Hailes, Governor General of the West Indies Federation – and AMB.

Churchill with Toby the budgerigar on the cruise on *Christina* to the West Indies, March 1961. (Photograph courtesy of Jane Hoare-Temple)

At the American premiere of the film *The Finest Hours* at the Beekman Theatre, New York, November 1964; AMB and his first wife Nonie with the Duke of Windsor and the film's producer, Jack Le Vien.

Above AMB helps Churchill feed the deer in Richmond Park, March 1963.
Below Mourners following the gun carriage at Churchill's state funeral,
30 January 1965. From front to rear, far side: Randolph Churchill (son),
Christopher Soames (son-in-law), Nicholas Soames (grandson), Jeremy
Soames (grandson), Peregrine Churchill (nephew); near side: Winston
Churchill (grandson), Julian Sandys (grandson), Piers Dixon, Major John
Churchill (nephew), AMB.

Money grubbing: AMB at Peter de Savary's ranch in West Texas, 1985.

At risk of going on too long, there was a bar with a glass top, below which a procession of miniature vessels revolved, from fully rigged ships to triremes to Mississippi stern-wheelers, brought up by Moses in his reed basket, towed by Moby Dick. There has recently been press correspondence on the bar stools, covered in white leather, and with sperm whales' teeth to grip in bad weather. It is said that the leather came from sperm whales' genitals. I don't remember being told at the time, but it fills me with sadness. As I have said, our attitude to whaling thirty-five years ago was not the same as it is today. But it should have been – or better.

Naturally there was a fully equipped operating theatre, laundry and dry cleaners. The latter was put to full test in 1959. We had anchored off Glyfada, outside Athens, and our Ambassador to Greece, Roger Alan, had come to dine with his wife. He was dressed in an elegant white dinner jacket. WSC's eldest daughter, Diana Sandys, was fiddling with her wine glass, made of very thin Baccarat glass, slightly elastic. She squeezed it too hard and it exploded, showering her neighbour Roger with Château Cheval Blanc. Roger's dinner jacket was whisked away, to return pristine in about an hour, its owner meanwhile dressed against the air-conditioning in CSC's evening stole. 'Never known them do that before,' said the tactful Ari, squeezing his own glass until that too exploded. But his was filled with Evian water.

On the return voyage, we again anchored at Glyfada, and the Alans were once more bidden to dine. But this time a cable came, saying that Roger was on a mountain-climbing holiday. 'Why isn't the Ambassador coming?' enquired WSC, who liked Alan, somewhat querulously.

Nonie replied: 'I think that when he received the invitation he grabbed his white dinner jacket and ran for the hills.'

I should add that Ari, and indeed WSC and CSC, invariably invited Nonie and our then five-year-old daughter Jane to come on the cruises. Jane's school indulgently gave her leave both on this occasion and later, reasoning quite correctly that such journeys would be more educative than many terms of school – and definitely more memorable. Jane, and Ari's own two children, were looked after by the latters' governess and spent an idyllic time, eating in the officers' mess and enjoying the run of the ship with desultory lesson periods thrown in. I tried my hand at tutoring in geography, but it was a dismal failure, the answer to one question, 'What is the capital of Russia?' being answered 'Cuba?' Politically interesting, anyway.

The ship's officers were very high-grade, Ari hand-picking them and the crew from his fleet. On the first few cruises, the Captain was a German, later replaced by a Greek ex-naval officer. The German led to an absurd misunderstanding. I had been told that he was an former U-Boat commander, and in our chats referred to the terror which the claustrophobic conditions of his war service would inspire. He seemed puzzled, and more so when I said that to be hunted by destroyers, so much faster than his craft, must have been an abominable experience. He replied: 'They weren't faster. I could always fly away.' I thought that his reason was impaired until I learnt that, far from commanding a U-Boat, he had been a Messerschmitt pilot.

We left on this first cruise from Monte Carlo on 3 September, heading for the River Guadalquivir and Seville, via Majorca, the Spanish coast and Tangier. Among the guests were Lowell Guinness and his Mexican wife Gloria, Tito Arias (Margot Fonteyn's husband, who was Ari's international lawyer), Théodore Garafalides and his wife (Ari's sister) and Nonie. Peace reigned, the weather was superb, CSC was happy and relaxed. We lunched on deck and dined in the elegant dining room, air-conditioned to almost lethal chill, which didn't matter to the men as we wore dinner jackets. The murals, representing beautiful women at different seasons of the year, incorporated Tina and an unnamed beauty who mysteriously had been given two left feet.

On the outward journey there was an afternoon that I shall never forget. For once it rained and WSC suggested a game of poker. He, Ari, Lowell Guinness and Tito Arias sat down.

'Come on Anthony,' said WSC, 'come and join us. Five is the best number for poker.'

I politely declined and, on being pressed for an explanation, said that I would spoil their game as the stakes proposed were well over my head.

'It doesn't matter,' said Ari airily, 'we'll play for baby stakes.' So we sat down.

'We'll start with fifty pounds' worth of chips each,' said Ari. My heart sank. The smallest chip was one pound, and one could lose the lot in a couple of hands. I had learned poker in the RAF in a fairly rough school, but I felt that with these rich and skilled players the position was going to be embarrassing. So I played the most timid of games, backing only strong cards and mathematical likelihoods.

I soon began to realise that I was sitting with not only about the worst players I had ever encountered, but also the unluckiest. On top of this, I was consistently dealt remarkably good cards. As my pile of chips increased, I began to play a more expansive game, with ever-better results. My opponents became increasingly grumpy and morose, demanding new cards, and declaring that they were seated in unlucky chairs. Still my winnings built up. 'We'll have one more hand and then we must change for dinner,' Ari declared gloomily. It was a jackpot hand. (It would be boring to both cognoscenti and others to describe what this is.) It went up and down, with the stakes growing ever higher, and no-one holding adequate cards to open. Finally Ari did, declaring to the dealer with a flourish that he would stand pat on his hand – either a stupendous bluff or a sign of real strength. I held a pair of threes, asked for three cards, and to my amazement received two more threes. Then came the betting. Up Ari and I went, raising each other until finally he said: 'Anthony, I won't take away all your winnings, I'll see you,' and he flung down three aces and two kings, a Full House. A hand like that looks as if it would carry all before it, but it is beaten by four of a kind, even if they are only threes. There was an outraged splutter of Greek oaths from my host, and I departed to change, carrying in my sun-hat a minor diplomat's ransom of francs, pesetas, pounds, dollars and IOUs (all redeemed!). Fortunately the weather changed and there was no second session to test my luck.

At Tangier our Consul-General, Bryce Nairn, and his artist wife Margaret came on board to lunch. They were old friends of the Churchills' and esteemed by both WSC and CSC. Bryce's father had been an ophthalmic missionary in Marrakech, and had been assassinated by a fanatical anti-Christian. The fatal wound, inflicted in the bazaar, came from a stiletto so fine that he had not realised he was wounded until he got home, though it had punctured his heart.

At one point WSC had suggested to the Foreign Office with diffidence and tact that Nairn deserved a more senior appointment in an Arab country, as his knowledge, particularly of Morocco, understanding and linguistic abilities were unusual. It is worth noting that very few of WSC's suggestions or requests were accepted once he was out of office, and I cannot recollect one of his recommendations for an honour being successful – and he did not make very many.

After Tangier we went up the Guadalquivir river, with the great Spanish National Park to the north and fighting-bull breeding farms to the south. I longed to disembark to the north, and go into that wild country to see the wonderful bird life, and especially the eagles, but, as always on the cruises, we were hastening along on an unnecessarily tight schedule.

We tied up in Seville, and soon afterwards some local dignitaries came on board. Two of them informed WSC that they were planning a bull-fight in his honour, and they hoped that he would attend. WSC considered them and replied carefully: 'I shall do no such thing. It is not a bull-fight. It is a bull-torture,' and he turned away. I rejoiced, and so did Nonie, but I am sorry to say that not everyone followed suit.

Later that evening, before we went in to dinner, Tina came on deck wearing a scarlet silk dress that might have been painted on to her.

'Do you like my new dress, Anthony?' she asked.

'Wow! Yes indeed!'

Ari was nearby. He considered his wife with distaste, I think mainly on the grounds that she would shock the Spanish grandees. He spoke with a rolling accent: 'Well, I don't agree with you, Anthony. I think she looks like a little French tarrrt.' Tina said something deeply disobliging in Greek, and seized Ari by the throat. He remained totally calm. 'Little Tina, don't squeeze me there, or my false teeth will fly out and embarrass everybody.' The Spaniards exchanged amazed glances. Tina was not precisely discreet. In front of Ari, she said: 'Anthony, did you know that Ari seduced me in a Chriscraft on Long Island Sound when I was sixteen?'

The Duchess of Alba, herself absent, had thrown open her palace for WSC to visit. It did not impress him. I suppose under festive conditions it would look different. It was hard to tell what would and what wouldn't impress WSC. Brendan Bracken said that he would drive through many miles of beautiful country, smoking his cigar and glaring at the floor. I had only noticed this in the not over-impressive scenery of the habitual drives to Chartwell or Chequers, when in any case he was deep in thought, and generally speaking I had found him more ready to be impressed by God's work than by man's, by a mountain, a waterfall or a storm at sea rather than an architectural masterpiece. And with this outlook I deeply sympathised.

We left Seville abruptly to get through the Guadalquivir locks at the right tide. I had actually to pluck Nonie with dripping hair from her coiffeur's attachments, and we pier-jumped just in time. Typically, Ari had a motor-boat at standby in case of need. The dinner as we sailed down that memorable river passage was enlivened by caviar from a Guadalquivir sturgeon, and by CSC who was radiant and in the most punchy of form. When I bade him goodnight in his cabin WSC said that to see her thus rejuvenated him.

It must not be forgotten that CSC was at heart, and by Edwardian Liberal inclination, something of a bluestocking. WSC himself was deeply erudite, surprising those who did not know him with this wide and often esoteric knowledge, but the intense and burning pressures of his career had forced his concentration on essentials. The conversation at that dinner turned to English literature of the first thirty years of the century, and CSC held the floor. Alas, I can only remember two passages, both anecdotes of Henry James, whom CSC had known and not altogether liked. He was, she said, a snob, as so many emigrés are and perhaps have to be.

At a party a young man had bounced up to James and said: 'Mr James, we haven't met for five years,' to receive the somewhat dunching answer: 'A very suitable interval, I think.' And at a dinner, James, whose conversational style apparently tended to be as convoluted as his prose, began to describe an incident: 'It was the strangest, nay, the most bizarre, no, the most unaccustomed ...' when his vis-à-vis interrupted: 'Oh, come on, Mr James, pray don't trouble yourself. I am a person of no social importance: any old adjective will do for me.'

Lowell Guinness, who had been both a fighter pilot and a Member of Parliament, was good at encouraging WSC to reminisce on historical events, and I wish I had retained more than a superficial recollection of them all. Some did stick in my mind, or were noted. Questioned by Guinness on Nehru: 'Well, I did say that he might be the Light of Asia, and that he had overcome the twin demons of hate and fear, and I meant it. But I did some-times feel that he needed a good kick in the pants – not that he wore pants. He could depart so easily from commonsense, that rarest and most essential quality in a public servant of whatever rank.'

Guinness questioned WSC on Bomber Command, and received very much the same answer as I had several years before at Chequers: 'It is difficult to assess. In the full tilt of war, it was our only means of hitting back. I was of course ultimately responsible, as for most things in those days. But later I was not so sure of the effectiveness of that bludgeon. And the moral side can indeed strike a reproachful note.' I remembered that General Ira Eaker, Commander of the US Eighth Air Force, is reputed to have said of his bomber offensive that he felt like a man who did not know quite what he had bought, but did know that it was very expensive.

The cruise came to an end at Gibraltar, and we dined with the Governor at the Convent. The dinner concluded with the ancient ceremony of the Keys, impressive historically as evidence of the intense importance of securing the fortress against a hostile hinterland. Personally I found it sad. Like the Queen's Birthday Parade ('Trooping the Colour') and much other pageantry, it had survived when the substance of our military power, the days when our writ ran over a quarter of the Earth's surface and our long-lasting influence for good in the world had vanished in what WSC called 'a monstrous act of self-mutilation'. These surviving theatrical spectacles are little more than confetti on a heroic memorial.

The Governor was General Keightley, who had commanded our forces in the disastrous 1956 Suez episode. He had also, at the end of the War, commanded the Fifth Corps in Italy, which had been involved in the shameful forcible repatriation of the dissidents to torture and murder by the Communists. Where the burden of guilt should justly lie remains unclear – but it is indeed a most grievous burden.

The next day we flew back to London, WSC rejoicing that this experiment had been so successfully therapeutic for his wife.

In November of the same year (1958) WSC went to Paris to receive from General de Gaulle the Croix de la Libération. It was a moving occasion in the courtyard of the Hotel Matignon (the French Number Ten; de Gaulle was not yet President). The veterans on parade at the ceremony all held the Médaille Militaire and the Cross of the Companions of the Liberation. I have already touched on the lunchtime conversation, but it is perhaps worth adding a personal note. The General asked me: 'If you had been a Frenchman in 1940, what would you have done?' I replied that if I had been the age I was, seventeen, I would have made every endeavour to join the Free French forces overseas, and if this was impossible, I would somewhat reluctantly have joined the Resistance. However, if I had been in, say, my forties, with a family and employees as my responsibility, I would quite possibly have concluded that my duty lay to stay in France and make the best I could of developments under the Pétain government. After all, little was known at that time of the future horrors of the concentration camps, and Hitler's invitation to the New Order would have had attractions for a humiliatingly defeated nation. De Gaulle considered, and answered rather doubtfully: 'C'est une réponse.'

For a time I believed that Bonny Prince Charlie (Gérard André's name for de Gaulle) was genuinely fond of his creator (the British one), who had also saved him from the Americans and delivered his country from the enemy.

In February 1959 WSC, CSC, Walter and Biddy Monckton, the Colvilles and I flew in an Olympic Airways private aircraft to Marrakech. WSC had nostalgic wartime memories and the dry desert climate (Marrakech is in effect a very large oasis) suited him. He sat in the exotic and lush gardens of the Mamounia, which had been one of the world's great hotels, and painted the Atlas mountains with their dramatic changing shadows and snow crests. He seemed at peace and happy. He didn't mind being watched while he painted, and over his shoulder related his opposition to the 'Unconditional German Surrender' policy forced on him by the Americans at the Summit

meetings. He was convinced that it had prolonged the war and taken away the
support that the underground German opposition to Hitler might otherwise
have expected. He broke off, without looking up from his canvas, and said:
'Go and put on something warm. They say of the breeze off the Atlas that it is
too gentle to blow out a candle, but strong enough to snuff out the life of a
man.'

My own stay was full of misadventure. On our first night I was hurrying to
bathe and change for a rather grand dinner of welcome. While I was in my
bath, the lights went out. There was nothing to do except wait, running the
hot water. When the lights came on I was startled to see that the bath was
blood red. Was I bleeding to death? No, it was the water, but the stain was
difficult to remove and I got some distinctly odd looks at dinner.

The following day I was attacked by an abscess on a tooth and a kidney
stone. The latter was small and yielded to massive draughts of champagne,
but I don't recommend Marrakech dentistry. Worse was to follow. We lunched with the Governor, a delicious meal with chilled almond soup, pigeons
stuffed with dates and fragile honey-filled cakes. As we left, the Governor
asked if he could do anything for us. WSC said: 'No, thank you.' The King
had provided him with a magnificent American limousine and two detectives,
and he was very happy. I remember being amused when we got lost in the
mountain roads, and the detectives, Arabs from Rabat, could not manage to
get the local Berbers, who disliked them, to understand their enquiries,
whereas Sergeant Murray and I had no difficulties.

The Governor turned politely to me, and offered a horse, to see the countryside and the huge palm groves. I gratefully accepted, stipulating very
firmly that I wanted a kind, quiet old nag because I was a very poor horseman.
'Certainly, my friend,' said the smiling Governor. 'A horse will be brought to
the Mamounia at three o'clock tomorrow.' At the appointed time WSC
declared that he wanted to see the horse, and we took our coffee and brandy
through to the entrance courtyard. Dead on three o'clock there was a trampling of hoofs, and two grooms in scarlet livery arrived on geldings, holding
between them a pure-bred Arab stallion from a stud. He was covered in sweat
and was striking sparks with all four shoes. His ears were flat back and he was
showing his teeth. I made anxious enquiries, and learnt that his name was
Sauve-qui-peut and that he hadn't been ridden 'for a very long time'.

'I'm not going to ride that monster,' I declared resolutely.

'You must,' said WSC firmly. 'You asked for a horse and you've got a horse.
We shall lose face if you don't. Here, have some more brandy and you will feel
better.' I reflected that it was the threat to my entire body and not just to my
face that worried me, and meditated on suggesting to WSC that as he felt so
strongly he should ride the horse himself. The trouble was that he would
certainly have accepted, so I drank about a quarter of a pint of 'Héritiers de
Jean Frémicourt', saluted WSC with 'Moriturus te salutat', and waddled out
in my disreputable corduroy breeches.

I offered Sauve-qui-peut some sugar lumps and he tried to bite me. With
the help of the grooms I managed to get aboard. Sauve-qui-peut at once tore

himself loose and shot out into the main road. The grooms followed with dismayed cries of 'Attention, Monsieur, c'est très dangereux' dwindling in the distance. We must have resembled an early Western, acting the 'we'll head them off at the pass' scene.

As soon as we were out of sight of the hotel, I hung on to the pommel of my saddle, and begged Sauve-qui-peut most urgently to slow down. He responded by leaving the main road, fortunately relatively empty of traffic, and heading across country through a landscape of disused wells, barbed wire, rocks and cactuses. It was like a bad dream, but it all ended quietly enough. Sauve-qui-peut knew where he was going; to the old racecourse where he used to exercise. When he got there, we lapped the grooms several times, their shouted remonstrances achieving a strange Doppler-effect as we shot by them, until the stallion had had enough fun, and I was winded and speechless.

Was this a malicious joke on the part of the Governor? Certainly not: he just wanted to show that a request for the least of Moroccan horses produced something much grander. But I walked like a very old retired jockey for days afterwards, and I rather wondered what I would have got if I'd asked for one of the dancing girls for which Marrakech was famous.

On 18 February we drove to the port of Safi, some seventy miles away, and boarded *Christina*. Nonie had flown out to join us. In spite of the beauties of Morocco and the charm of many of its people, I wasn't sorry to leave. The cruelty to animals was abominable, and one sometimes saw on the tourist roads children dangling pathetic broken-limbed small squirrels and birds fluttering from strings, to be sold to the European passers-by who would buy them to put them out of their misery, to be replaced no doubt by others. It made me feel sick with anger and grief and I wrote letters imploring intervention to the most senior Moroccan authorities. The replies were polite, no doubt for WSC's sake, and gave assurances of action, but I saw little later evidence that it was carried out.

The cruise from Safi took us to the Canary Islands, and we were joined for a part of it by Margot Fonteyn and her husband. I do not know anyone who knew Margot and did not love her. Leaving aside her artistic abilities, her affectionate kindness, bubbling vivacity and sense of humour would have endeared her to the very grumpiest. I once asked how she managed to be so modest. She took the question seriously and said that when she had just started to make a great name for herself, she had once returned to her flat to find some dozen of her close friends waiting for her. She exclaimed: 'What fun! A surprise party!' but they disillusioned her. They had come, they said, to say that she was becoming so conceited and arrogant that they would soon sever their friendship. 'So', said Margot, 'I vowed to do my best not to be conceited and arrogant.' And she most certainly succeeded.

The Canary Islands visits were uneventful, and *Christina* sailed east to cruise up the Moroccan coast. At Agadir WSC reminisced of the aggressive adventurism of the Kaiser, whose sending of a warship, the *Panther*, to that port in 1911 had done much to consolidate the Anglo-French Entente Cordiale and thus to make our intervention against Germany in 1914 the more likely. His recall of much long-forgotten historical detail, down to the size and armament and even the band of the *Panther* amazed and fascinated Ari – and certainly me.

All the party except WSC and CSC disembarked at Agadir and drove north at breakneck speed up the coast to dine in a renowned fish restaurant at Mogador (now Essaouria), where we were to rejoin the ship. During the drive the weather deteriorated dramatically, and it became clear that *Christina* could not safely enter the small and rock-strewn harbour. The dinner was not very good but was rendered hilarious by Ari's attempts to get through to *Christina* on the restaurant's telephone. A connection from a small Moroccan town to a ship at sea was a challenging venture in 1959 and was made the more difficult by the operation of the flush of the lavatory, immediately adjacent to the telephone. Poor Théodore Garafalides was to blame: his frequent visits coincided with Ari's interrupted establishing of communication. The cistern sounded as though it was digesting a rusty chain and repeatedly drowned out Ari's bellowed instructions to the Captain to lie offshore and not to attempt the harbour entrance.

One of the great advantages of associating with a multi-millionaire is his ability to pull appropriate rabbits out of hats at short notice. When we finished dinner a tug was standing by to take us out to the brilliantly illuminated and plunging *Christina*. The tug wove through the harbour reefs, rolling dramatically while we, well alcoholically fortified, staggered to and fro in the small bridge enclosure. A sharp lurch caused Tina to seize a white porcelain handle: it was the vessel's main fuse and it came away in her hand, plunging everything into darkness and cutting off various essential mechanical functions. We drifted perilously while the Moroccan crew cursed us all and called on Allah until someone lit a match and the fuse was restored to its socket. We were happy to take acrobatic leaps into *Christina* and head away from the coast, to disembark and fly home from Tangier.

We returned to the yacht somewhat more calmly in July 1959, flying to Nice on the twenty-second to dine in Monte Carlo and embark that night for a cruise in the Greek islands. To his great pleasure, CSC accompanied her husband, and Nonie came too, as did the Morans, and Diana and Celia Sandys. There were a number of other guests, of whom the most notable was Maria Callas, accompanied by her husband, Giovanni Meneghini.

One of our first stops was at Capri, and we anchored off the Piccola Marina on the south of the island. Once again my abscessed tooth blew up, so while the rest of the party visited Anacapri, the Blue Grotto and the other tourist spots, I toiled uphill to the island's only dentist. My teeth do insist on being treated in the most exotic spots, I reflected, I do wish they wouldn't. I was right; the dentist had a pedal drill and I sat in a kitchen chair. He told me that he had treated Axel Munthe, the Swedish romantic autobiographer and doctor, which put his age up to an impressive but alarming figure. On returning to the yacht towards sunset, I felt in need of a strong drink and some relaxation, so, suitably fortified, I swam off in the warm and silk-smooth sea. The combined effect of the anaesthetic, alcohol and the sea was soothing, and

I drowsily watched the setting sun. 'Time to go home,' I said to myself. But *Christina* appeared to be an awful long way off, and receding further. The peaceful water concealed a strong southward current. The next stop appeared to be Sicily or North Africa. Fortunately, *Christina* had an almost naval watch system, and the officer on the bridge had been following me. Within ten minutes a launch picked me up. But it was sobering.

Gracie Fields and her amiable Yugoslav husband came on board that night, and she sang in that beautiful and very powerful North Country voice that had earned her fame and great affection. Sadly, WSC was less than delighted and asked me in what he thought was a low voice: 'God's teeth! How long is this going on for?'

We then sailed through the Straits of Messina and the Gulf of Corinth. At dinner WSC talked of the escape of the German battle-cruiser *Goeben*, which in 1914 evaded our ships in the Straits and sailed to Constantinople, reinforcing the wavering Turkish will to war against the Allies. I was astounded to hear him quote without hesitation from his own description of the incident in *The World Crisis*. '[The *Goeben*] . . . carrying with her for the peoples of the East and Middle East more slaughter, more misery and more ruin than has ever before been borne within the confines of a ship . . . ' Historical hyperbole perhaps, but what a memory!

The company on board was not as harmonious as it had been, and was again to be. Maria Callas was indeed a great actress and a greater singer, but she seemed almost to be trying to parody the stereotypical prima donna in her behaviour. Snatches of her conversation come back to me. 'I like travelling with Winston Churchill. It relieves me of some of the burden of my popularity.' Poor Meneghini was ordered to turn off the air conditioning in their cabin, whatever the outside heat: 'Sopranos hate air conditioning even more than they hate other sopranos,' was her rather engaging explanation. When we drove from the port of Naplion to the great Greek theatre of Epidaurus, the locals had erected a huge 'V' of flowers in the middle of the stage. Maria exclaimed: 'Flowers for me! How kind! But why is it a V, Anthony?' I replied that it was undoubtedly meant to be an M for Maria, but that they had not had time to finish it. Maria's reactive smile was rapidly replaced by the sort of glance she should have remembered when she sang 'Medea'. When we reached Lesbos, the island home of Tina's family, the Livanos, the church bells were rung for WSC, and Maria appropriated them as her own tribute. It did not in the least matter, and I don't think WSC was even aware of it.

Meneghini was not very attractive. He may have been the Svengali of a great artist but he was an absolute pill. He seemed to me to epitomise the very worst traits of a greedy and selfish Milanese bourgeois. The female guests vied with each other not to sit next to him at meals, one reason being that he wore pipe-clayed white shoes, and tended to leave their slacks or skirts covered in white powder as evidence of his attempts to establish a closer acquaintance. (He became known as Meningitis.) One really could not blame Maria for leaving him, but her dramatic sortie with Ari was then still some little time off.

Going through the Gulf of Corinth, we visited Delphi. There were very few people about, and the two resident eagles hung over the ruins, black crosses on a perfect sky. It was impressive. The cryptic oracle could well have spoken and even the exclamations of the Greeks, one of the noisiest races in the world, were subdued.

> The sonorous echoes of the voice
> Of ancient Delphi's arcane choice,
> With treble meanings overlaid
> Proclaim celestial debts are paid
> In coin that's common – and delayed
> Take what they offer and rejoice . . .

Off Athens, the Greek Prime Minister Karamanlis and his wife dined on board. The conversation was of no great moment, but WSC came up with most felicitous quotations from Byron, to this day revered in Greece. He could still do this and astound everyone, and the Greeks were thrilled. Afterwards Ari commented with some awe on this facility and went on to speak favourably of Madame Karamanlis's derrière, which was indeed most shapely.

From Athens we sailed to the island of Santorin, dramatically composed of the crescent-shaped remnants of the rim of a giant volcano. Some say that when it exploded and collapsed, à la Krakatoa, the resulting tidal wave had wiped out the ancient Cretan civilisation. Some say that this was Atlantis. And some say bunkum. At all events there is a very deep sheltered anchorage, too deep for most ships to anchor, and a very steep zig-zag track from the landing to the villages on the rim. It is also said that this is the only place in Greece where you will see the donkeys treated kindly (sadly, I didn't notice it), because the islanders believe that they are apt to be reincarnated as donkeys if they behave badly, and they don't want to think that they are beating their grandfathers. The other local superstition relates to vampires, said to flourish there. No-one will open their door to a single knock after dark. You have to give three knocks, which vampires may not do. (But why can't three vampires get together and each knock once?)

Returning to verifiable fact, on reaching the top of the climb and going into a tavern we were astounded to find our payment refused by the owner. It appeared that when Santorin had been devastated by an earthquake some years previously, Ari had been in Athens. He reasoned correctly that most of the wells on the island would have collapsed, and sailed at once, with *Christina*'s swimming pool filled with fresh water and with hoses and mobile pumps to deliver it, together with the ship's own output of thirty tons of water a day, to the inhabitants. Santorin in those days was very little visited and retained the ancient virtue of gratitude. Its other peculiarity was a steaming islet in the middle of the bay. You couldn't land on it, but swimming towards it the sea became progressively hotter. As I discovered too late, the sulphur also destroyed one's swimming trunks.

Thence to Rhodes. En route Nonie had courageously gone self-taught water-skiing with amazing results. She had been a superb horsewoman, challenging Pat Smythe at show jumping, so perhaps this had something to do with it. However, she had developed the most virulent sore throat as a result of her activities. Théodore Garafalides, orthopaedic surgeon, did his best, but when we reached Rhodes, his brother-in-law, formerly a nose and throat doctor but now a major hotelier, came on board with a menacing equipment of instruments of most ancient vintage. They debated over the patient in Greek. Théodore said something briskly and his relation almost physically assaulted him. What had he said? 'I only told him that he might be a good hotelier, but when it came to medicine he would do better to remain as silent as a sea-urchin,' Théodore explained amiably.

The tourist attractions of Rhodes are now well known and we saw them under the best of conditions – the valley of butterflies (actually moths), the Akropolis of Lindos. Two incidents linger in my memory, one of significance only to me and the other of debatable, but I believe profound, consequence to Ari.

The night *Christina* was to sail, after a jolly and very bibulous dinner, the Mayor of Rhodes insisted on taking me to see the many-kilometre-long fortifications of the old Knights. Soon his car stuck in the soft sand and we continued on foot through remote groves of oleander, with the battlement looming close or far. In the distance we heard *Christina*'s horn, indicating her departure. We looked at each other in consternation and raced back, slipping in the sand and sweating in our dinner jackets. Soon we were pursued by a large and hostile pack of feral stray dogs, like Disney characters in the moonlight. I love dogs, on the whole more than people, but these were not the sort with whom you could discuss friendship. At last a police jeep met us and I reached *Christina* just as she was casting off. The checking of passengers on board was not a strong point.

Ari's misadventure was very different. As we lay at anchor, he was amusing his children by doing trick dives into the shallow swimming pool. He misjudged a 'dead-man's dive', and hit the bottom with a thump that shook the boat, floating to the surface semi-conscious. Théodore, members of the crew and I jumped into the water and lifted him out, whereupon he lost consciousness for a few minutes. When he recovered he angrily refused suggestions of an X-ray, but allowed Théodore to examine his head and neck, which seemed, as far as he could tell, intact. Thereafter Ari's demeanour changed substantially. His equable temper became aggressive, though never to his guests. He drank more than before and fell into abstracted silences. Above all, he began to pay marked attention to Maria Callas, whom he had always treated courteously but with no particular concentration. Years later, in a late-night atmosphere that seemed to invite confidences, I asked him if he believed that it was his mental disturbance that launched him on this disorganised and damaging romance. He first brushed the idea aside, but as we parted, muttered rather haltingly: 'Anthony. What you said. Perhaps . . . yes.'

After Rhodes, *Christina* headed north to Lesbos, to Ari's birthplace Smyrna and then through the Dardanelles to Istanbul, where we anchored off the Golden Horn. We passed through the Dardanelles at night, occasionally lit up by a Turkish searchlight.

'Why did we not pass in daylight?' I asked.

Ari replied: 'It would have been very interesting, but it might have brought on very sad thoughts and memories for the Boss.'

At dinner WSC did speak of the Dardanelles, in a meditative historian's mood. I do not recollect what he said, or even the general theme, but I think he simply rehearsed the old strategic arguments. He did add: 'I was unpleasantly surprised at Ian Hamilton's pessimism. When his train drew out from Victoria on his way to take up the command of the operation, he apparently said to his ADC: "This will end in disaster. I kissed my wife through her veil when we parted!" The Scots are quite entitled to be superstitious, but this was no mood in which to embark on a campaign.'

At Istanbul the Archimandrite (Patriarch of Constantinople and Head of the Greek Orthodox Church) came on board for lunch and a brief cruise up to the Black Sea and back. I saw Ari in earnest conversation with the ship's Captain. 'I was saying to him: "All sailors believe a priest on board brings bad luck. This guy is one hundred priests' value. And there is an eight knot current running. So be very, very careful." '

After Istanbul we headed for the peninsula of Mount Athos. Once some 40,000 monks had lived in the monasteries that studded the slopes, but they had now declined to fewer than 1,500, including a number of anchorites who lived on ledges of the sea cliff like swallows in their nests, their food and drink reaching them by means of a lowered basket. No female creature was allowed on Mount Athos, not even bees. It struck me that one would have to be not only kinky and desperate but exceedingly ingenious to get into any mischief with a bee.

Théodore told me a shocking story of Mount Athos. When he was a newly qualified doctor he was in Macedonia, and had been summoned, as an orthopaedic specialist, to see a young monk who was sick. He diagnosed tuberculosis of the spine, and said that the boy must be moved to a hospital immediately. The senior monks refused to let him go: he was too beautiful for them to lose they said. (Théodore put this in a much earthier way.) He had to get a magistrate's order to have the boy removed.

Christina headed home for Monte Carlo via the Corinth Canal. Off Athens the movie magnate Spyros Skouras came on board. He was the son of a Corfiote shepherd family and had made a great name in Hollywood. It was said that no Greek could understand his Greek and no Englishman his English – not quite true, but he did have his idiosyncrasies. As we leant on the ship's rail looking at dolphins (which the Greeks call 'Basil'), Skouras said: 'I've a great idea for a movie. It will be about the Benzedrines.'

I pondered. 'You mean about the drug-taking generation?' I hazarded.

'I don't know if they took drugs or not. I mean the Benzedrines' Empire in Constantinople.'

Enlightenment dawned. 'Oh. You mean Byzantines?'

'Benzedrines, Byzantines, it would make a great movie.' The last time I heard of him was at a luncheon party in Monte Carlo, given by Lord (Esmond) Rothermere. The conversation was ordinary enough until Skouras suddenly announced:

'I am seventy-something years old, and make love every day.' There was a silence while the company digested this information. Then Rothermere asked thoughtfully:

'Doesn't it get rather boring?'

The end of the cruise saw the end of Ari's marriage to Tina. His courting of Maria had become more obvious and indeed obsessive, taking rather unusual courses, such as rendezvousing with her in the middle of the night in the ship's galley to eat Greek mezedes (hors d'oeuvre) that he called 'Saletés Grècques.' I was to see three of the four parties involved quite frequently, particularly Ari: there is no doubt that the liaison and the broken marriages brought deep unhappiness to them all.

Ari never brought Maria on subsequent cruises when WSC was present, thinking it inappropriate to have his mistress on board in the latter's company. One night at dinner in Monte Carlo, I found myself next to Maria. We had always been on reasonably good terms, and I was rather surprised to find myself subjected to a maximum freeze. 'What's wrong, Maria?' I asked, 'I thought we were friends?'

The reply was explicit: 'Superficially you are charming, but underneath you are hard and cold and ruthless, and I hate you.'

I was rather hurt. 'What have I done?' I asked plaintively.

'You know what you've done. Be careful. Not for nothing am I called the Tigress!'

I sought enlightenment from Ari. He looked shifty:

'Anthony, I had a little problem. Maria said to me: "Why don't you take me on the cruises with Winston Churchill? Am I not good enough for him?" And I said: "Little Maria, I would like to take you, but Anthony says I can't." '

'You shit!'

'Yes, I know. But you don't have to live with her.'

Marriage to Ari seemed to have become something of an obsession with Maria. Previous to our (lasting) rift, she had said to me across a small dinner-table, in the presence of Ari:

'Anthony, tell Ari he ought to marry me.'

It was half in jest, but Ari answered her seriously: 'Maria, I can't do that. This is a pay as you go arrangement.' Meneghini had in fact refused her a divorce, but no doubt that could have been circumvented: Meneghini was a Roman Catholic and Maria Greek Orthodox. In his book *My Wife Maria Callas* Meneghini claimed that at their parting he had put a curse on his wife and Ari. If so, it was quite an effective one.

Chapter 25

I N THE SPRING of 1959 WSC had two preoccupations: whether he should stand again for Parliament at the next General Election, which eventually took place on 9 October, and how and when he should make his long-premeditated visit to the US. Of the two, the latter was the major consideration. In spite of Eisenhower's rebuff to his bridge-building attempts in the immediate post-Suez era, WSC still saw him as the old and stalwart friend of wartime. He cared enormously for Anglo-American friendship and would not even contemplate that the 'Special Relationship' might be a thing of the past as far as the Americans were concerned, however much successive British Governments sought to dress its corpse in modern clothes. After a good deal of discussion with CSC, the Foreign Office, Number Ten and the Americans, a date in early May was fixed.

The Constituency question was soon settled. In spite of strong pleas by CSC, and gentler ones from other members of his family, WSC was determined to stand again, though he agreed that this should be the last time. In this particular discussion I remained strictly neutral. It was true that the Constituency was most infrequently visited by its Member, that he knew very few of those he represented and indeed even of the senior members of the Association. But the constituents' problems were dealt with highly efficiently, albeit indirectly, via his admirable and unrecognised Agent, Colonel Barlow-Wheeler, his very effective Constituency Secretary, Lettice Shillingford, and others, and Government Departments reacted smartly to his by-proxy enquiries. Moreover, his Constituency Chairman, Alderman Donald Forbes, assisted by the excellent organiser Major Healey, did a first-class and loyal job of public relations on his behalf, succeeded later by the no less devoted Mrs Moss. So in spite of mutters that the electorate of Wanstead and Woodford were disfranchised, I think the bulk of the voters were quite happy for him to continue and proud that this noble if aged beast should represent them. CSC visited the Constituency for balls and other special occasions, and I usually accompanied her.

This political involvement was questionable. As I was still a member of the Diplomatic Service unpleasant use could have been made of it, and in today's House of Commons no doubt would have been. I do find it a little disconcerting to see from the official biography how many of WSC's political speeches I did write, very mildly parodying his style and embodying his known and long-held political views. The vigilance of CSC and other members of the family was a potent safeguard of misuse by proxy of WSC's position. CSC was in any case a Liberal rather than a Conservative and was doubly watchful for any improper exploitation of her husband for Party ends. To be fair I cannot remember any being attempted. Would the same pertain in today's politics?

During his post-retirement years WSC was still expected to make speeches and send messages, and both tasks were becoming onerous. I found myself willy-nilly drafting one after the other. Most have long since faded into oblivion, forgotten not only by their recipients but by their author, and I am indebted, as for so much else, to Martin Gilbert for recording them so meticulously. Short and infrequent they may have been, but one had to be exceedingly careful as they received wide publicity and it would have been worse than an error to put words in which he did not fully believe into WSC's mouth. I did nevertheless encounter reproaches, and none more outspoken than from Violet Bonham Carter, when WSC had sent an anodyne message of support for the Conservative Party, and its nuclear policy, before the 1964 General Election. My back was broad enough to sustain these shafts, as I was absolutely certain of WSC's views. Still, it was not very agreeable to be called a forger, and CSC flew to my support like an avenging fury, fortified by a telephone call from WSC himself. Anyway, I was too fond of Violet Bonham Carter to be seriously wounded.

CSC's Liberal attachment was the cause of one of the most spectacular of her infrequent but famous firework displays of rage. At lunch alone with WSC and CSC at Marrakech, the conversation had fallen on Omdurman and the fate of Gordon of Khartoum. On hearing of Gordon's heroic death, when reinforcements had been denied him by the Liberal Government, Queen Victoria is said to have sent Gladstone, the Prime Minister, a telegram en clair (not cyphered) beginning 'You have murdered Gordon.' I quoted this with approval, and absent-mindedly and imprudently went on to ruminate aloud on the part the Liberals had played in our national and Imperial development. 'Why', I asked rhetorically, 'have the Liberals always been so anti-British?' Lightning flashed and thunder rolled. I listened, half appalled and half amused and admiring, while shafts of elegantly phrased but cutting invective were directed at my head. WSC said nothing, with a quizzical smile on his face. I also kept quiet. The following day CSC said to me reproachfully: 'Really Anthony, you were so rude to me yesterday that I was quite embarrassed.' Attack is indeed a good form of defence and I continued to say nothing. In any case I was very fond of her and admired her too.

Julian Amery, an old friend of the Churchills, and now of mine, did pull my leg about my position. At a time of stuttering uncertainty in our national affairs, he said: 'Anthony, if things go on like this, the nation may in its distress turn again to its old Leader. And then you will rule Britain. What would you do?' I replied that I would first shoot some six hundred of our very worst people. 'You would have plenty to choose from,' Julian reflected gloomily.

WSC held Julian in regard. He was the son of his old friend Leo Amery. When Amery was a big boy and WSC a little boy at Harrow, the latter had pushed the former into the swimming-pool, with the excuse that he couldn't be very senior as he was so small. Their friendship nonetheless grew over the years, and it was Amery who quoted Cromwell's words of dismissal to the Long Parliament – 'In God's name, go!' – when attacking Neville Chamberlain during the debate amid the 1940 disasters, which led, of course, to WSC's premiership. WSC also respected Julian's war activities, parachuted into that wasps' nest, Albania, and his subsequent political record. He should have gone further than he did, but if political promotion follows merit, it is usually a matter of coincidence.

Julian did not lightly abandon friends, either national or personal. In 1961 he came to see me to seek WSC's intervention to prevent the execution of Adnan Menderes, the former Prime Minister of Turkey, who had been deposed by a coup in 1960 and subsequently sentenced to death. WSC's perennial humane instincts were aroused, and he told me to go ahead. The telegram to our Ambassador in Turkey ran thus:

Following personal for Ambassador from Montague Browne.

Unless you judge that it would have an adverse effect on the fate of those concerned, Sir Winston Churchill would be grateful if you would deliver the following strictly personal message to General Gursel.

Begins

I have retired from public life and I do not wish to intervene in the affairs of Britain's friend and ally, Turkey. But I should like Your Excellency to realise the beneficial effect that it would have among all who wish you well and throughout the world if your Government were to show clemency in commuting the sentences of death recently promulgated. With high regard and respect
WINSTON S. CHURCHILL

Ends

It was given the highest priority, but there was no reply, and Menderes was hanged, macabrely clad in a white garment like a nightie.

After his adoption as the Wanstead and Woodford Parliamentary candidate, with his immediate domestic political future settled, WSC exclaimed as he left the meeting: 'Now for America.'

President Eisenhower was warmly welcoming and invited WSC to stay at the White House. The rest of the time in Washington would be spent at the British Embassy, then a few days in New York to see Bernie Baruch. The party was to be small: WSC, a secretary, Sergeant Murray, Sheppard (a trained nurse) and myself. Lord Moran addressed a long, persuasive letter to his Eminent – and by now almost only – Patient, explaining why he should accompany him. WSC was vexed: 'No, I don't want that bloody old man,' he said. Actually he was rather fond of Moran, but he would have been an encumbrance on this journey.

WSC prepared meticulously for his talks with the President. He had suffered a further, if minor, deterioration in his health, and his family and I feared both that the strain of the trip could have serious consequences and that he might leave a tragically diminished memory with his American friends. But as he was adamant to make this political effort for Anglo-American relations, which proved to be his last, I set out on a damage limitation exercise. WSC was persuaded not to make any major prepared speeches: he was bound to address the dinner or luncheon parties he attended, but this would be impromptu, or impromptu from a draft, and infrequent. I briefed the White House, the Embassy and Baruch appropriately and they all were wonderfully helpful, even the White House suppressing its endemic tendency to leak. Jim Hagerty, the Presidential spokesman, and Eisenhower's personal aide, the remarkable Ann Whitman, were both outstanding and understanding.

The journey was WSC's first in a jet, the De Havilland Comet. Given the steepness of climb immediately after take-off, now so well known to all passengers but contrasting dramatically with the shallow angle of ascent of propellor aircraft, I thought that WSC would be disconcerted. Not so; just annoyed at having to put his cigar out. We had headwinds and had to land in Iceland to refuel. I feared a rush of dignitaries to greet the transient VIP but managed to head them off by messages in advance. Otherwise all went smoothly. I noted only one fragment of dialogue: 'Anthony, what time is it?' I gave the local time. 'No, I mean tummy-time.' A very good way of referring to one's own built-in clock.

At New York, we transferred to the Presidential aircraft, the Constellation *Columbine*, waiting with a very welcoming number of officials. The occasion was slightly marred by a scruffy Customs man who pushed his way through the dignitaries, shouting that he must ask 'Mr Choichill poisonally what he'd got in his baggage.' Two very large and silent plain-clothes figures picked him up under the shoulders and removed him, his feet pedalling furiously.

CSC had warned me: 'You won't enjoy the White House. The food is bad and you get nothing to drink but iced-water.' She was totally out of date, her view no doubt reflecting Mrs Roosevelt's regime. Eisenhower had after all lived in France during his NATO command of SHAPE, and the food and wine were excellent. We lived very much en famille with the President and Mrs Eisenhower, and there were only two formal meals, at both of which WSC spoke briefly from a prepared draft. He restricted himself to pleas for Anglo-American unity, with which 'all would be possible'. There was no note of recrimination, and Suez was not mentioned. I believe that a bit of plain speaking would not have been out of place – after all, Britain was the injured party – and could have done good in indicating that we would not necessarily always be the compliant servant and suitor; but I obeyed my stringent instructions from WSC and the Foreign Office in my drafting.

Before one dinner I met the Vice-President, Richard Nixon, a brooding, intense and impressive figure, who seemed of very different mettle from the 'attender at State Funerals' role attributed to the Vice-President ('I had two brothers: one is a very successful shoe-salesman but the other became Vice-President and was never heard of again,' ran the old American joke.) At another meal I sat next to a Democrat, at least I suppose he must have been. He said: 'You know the President is very intelligent.'

'Yes indeed, indeed,' I agreed.

'I mean he can read.'

'??'

'Yes, I know he can read. I've seen his lips moving.'

Rather spiteful, but in those days American political invective was much more ad hominem than ours (alas, no longer true); another quip going the rounds was that the President could not walk and chew gum at the same time. Time has, I believe, caused Eisenhower's American critics to reassess him more favourably.

My most vivid impression remains of the trust and warmth the President showed at the more intimate family meals. The business of the most powerful man on Earth keeps no office hours. Eisenhower, as a wartime Commander-in-Chief, was well used to dealing with urgent matters without faltering in his stride, and in the presence of WSC and myself affairs of very considerable secrecy were brought up, briefly discussed, and decided. On our flight home WSC asked me if I had kept a record of his conversations with the President.

'Yes.'

'Will you send a copy to the Foreign Office?'

'Yes, certainly.'

'Will it include the matters of internal American secrecy we overheard?'

'No.'

'Good,' smiled WSC.

Halfway through the visit, I was sitting by WSC's bedside while he finished his breakfast. 'Look at this,' he said suddenly, holding out a finger. A small area at the tip was jet black. 'I burnt my finger the other day while I was lighting a cigar, and now it has gone numb.' The first doctor to see it looked concerned. After we had left the room he told me that it was gangrene. I asked if it would spread. It might, he replied; the patient's circulation was obviously bad. Here was a pickle. WSC was as brave as you could be, but he was something of a hypochondriac, and the word gangrene would conjure up terrible visions of the deadly First World War gas gangrene. Should he fly home at once, cutting short his programme? I communicated with Lord Moran in London, who was neutrally reassuring, but the matter was taken out of our hands by WSC himself: 'I don't care what's wrong with my bloody finger,' he said, 'I feel very well and I won't have my programme changed.' And that settled it.

We flew back to New York once again in the *Columbine* and the pilot took us on a rooftop-high tour of Manhattan Island in perfect weather. WSC settled in with Bernie Baruch and I stayed in the flat immediately below him with our Ambassador to the United Nations, Bob Dixon, an old friend. I think it was there that I first met his two dazzling daughters. I remember only one incident. After dinner, in the May heat, I took a stroll in the adjacent Central Park. It was late and the park was deserted. Behind me I heard footsteps. When I stopped they stopped. Oh Hell, I thought, muggers. Why didn't I listen to what I was warned about? Two large figures approached and one addressed me. 'Good evening, Mr Browne. We saw you set out for your walk, so we thought we'd better keep you company.' They were two of the protection squad the US Government had assigned to WSC, and I was delighted to see them.

Was WSC's last major political foray a success? Yes and no. From a personal point of view it was excellent. Eisenhower had treated him with touching warmth and sensitivity. The only sour note was his diatribe against Field Marshal Montgomery. 'Monty gives interviews saying that I was not a competent Commander in the field, only a professional good chap. In his writing he slates me again and again. And then he has the gall to suggest coming to stay with me!' We had flown with the President by helicopter to his Gettysburg farm, and after the visit had hovered over the battlefield with the curator of the museum. All had been astounded that WSC could pick out with the utmost accuracy the main features of that terrible engagement: Round Top Hill, Pickett's charge, with their distances and significance, were fluently and dramatically described. WSC had walked many of the Civil War battlefields and his descriptions are very close to the greatest of his prose. It was a triumph for a very old man.

Did the Americans reckon the visit worthwhile? Here I venture immodestly to reproduce two letters addressed to me, one by the President and the other by Ann Whitman, his exceptional and devoted personal aide, self-effacing, powerful and talented.

> I was delighted to inscribe a photograph for you this morning, which I hope will serve as a small memento of your visit here. Mrs Eisenhower and I truly enjoyed your stay at the White House and only wish you and Sir Winston could have been with us longer.
>
> Primarily I want to express my personal appreciation of your devotion and help to my old and dear friend. It gratifies me greatly to know that Sir Winston has such a capable and dedicated assistant.
>
> DWIGHT D. EISENHOWER

And from Ann Whitman:

> Of course I showed the President your letter to him, and your note to me too! No secrets, I.
>
> As for me, I shall never forget May of 1959 either. As I tried haltingly to say, I have truly revered Sir Winston all of my adult life. I find my sentiment fully shared by all my friends and, as I am sure you know by reading our press, by all Americans. I doubt if he will ever quite realize what his coming here, under all the difficulties the trip presented for him, did to rekindle the deep affection of the man in the street for the people of your country. And the President felt a deep sense of gratification and compliment from the visit, as well of personal enjoyment in seeing the great and good friend he so much admires and loves.
>
> Incidentally, *you* made a tremendous hit, too – just in case you failed to realize it.
>
> I am enclosing a couple of photographs and one of our weekly magazines that contained a particularly touching story of the visit.
>
> Yesterday we spent a sixteen hour day on a trip to New York, a trip so fraught with minor disasters as to be unbelievable. But these things the public fortuna-

tely will never know. And tomorrow the President goes to Colorado for a whirlwind weekend trip to the new Air Academy and a visit to his mother-in-law. At this moment I am literally praying to be left behind, a very uncommon state for me.

Again, it was wonderful to meet you. Please come over again soon or arrange a Summit meeting in London, or something. I leave it all to you.

ANN WHITMAN

But did what WSC say influence American policy towards Britain, even in such relatively mundane matters as the mitigating of discrimination against our bids for US contracts? Not one jot. I think we had long since been filed as 'past business'.

On a purely materialistic level I find it hard to blame them. Sentimentally and morally, it is another matter. How often has the thought occurred to me that my feelings towards the United States are the obverse of General de Gaulle's towards his own country. He is said to have loved France and disliked the French. I love the Americans, but I do not always love America, though I admire and respect much that she has done.

The General Election of 9 October 1959 was the last WSC was to contest. His majority was 14,000: down it may have been on his previous score, but not at all a bad tally for a virtually inactive candidate. What he said in his few election speeches was perfectly straightforward, acceptable and based on his long-held views, but the votes went to the afterglow of his past.

Thereafter he went to Cambridge to plant an oak tree to inaugurate Churchill College. The various big-wigs standing about had not reckoned with the vigour of his spading, and they had to skip nimbly out of the way to escape their shoes being filled with earth. Churchill College was the fruit of the Prof.'s repeated and sadly justified jeremiads on Britain's rapid recession from the front ranks of research and technology. It was Jock Colville who had carried the idea forward, though the Prof. himself would have preferred to see the College at Oxford, and it is very much to Jock's credit that it was built. Please God that it will live up to its founders' purposes; it certainly got off to a good start with Sir John Cockcroft of atomic energy fame as its devoted and effective Master, and Sir William Hawthorn an equally dedicated successor.

WSC attitude to the universities was ambivalent. He once said: 'I am not an educated man,' which was nonsense, but it was meant seriously and referred to his not attending a university. I venture to quote from *My Early Life* a passage that encapsulates a good deal of WSC's philosophy, which did not seem to have changed much over the next half-century:

It was not until this winter of 1896, when I had almost completed my twenty-second year, that the desire for learning came upon me. I began to feel myself wanting in even the vaguest knowledge about many large spheres of thought. I had picked up a wide vocabulary and had a liking for words and for the feel of words fitting and falling into their places like pennies in the slot. I caught myself using a good many words the meaning of which I could not define precisely. I admired these words, but was afraid to use them for fear of being absurd...

I know of course that the youths at the universities were stuffed with all this patter at nineteen and twenty, and could pose you entrapping questions or give baffling answers. We never set much store by them or their affected superiority, remembering that they were only at their books, while we were commanding men and guarding the Empire. Nevertheless I had sometimes resented the apt and copious information which some of them seemed to possess, and I now wished I could find a competent teacher whom I could listen to and cross-examine for an hour or so every day.

So I resolved to read history, philosophy, economics, and things like that; and I wrote to my mother asking for such books as I had heard of on these topics. She responded with alacrity, and every month the mail brought me a substantial package of what I thought were standard works . . .

From November to May I read for four or five hours every day history and philosophy . . . It was a curious education. First because I approached it with an empty, hungry mind, and with fairly strong jaws; and what I got I bit; secondly because I had no one to tell me: 'This is discredited.' 'You should read the answer to that by so and so; the two together will give you the gist of the argument.' 'There is a much better book on the subject,' and so forth. I now began for the first time to envy those young cubs at the university who had fine scholars to tell them what was what; professors who had devoted their lives to mastering and focussing ideas in every branch of learning; who were eager to distribute the treasures they had gathered before they were overtaken by the night. But now I pity undergraduates, when I see what frivolous lives many of them lead in the midst of precious fleeting opportunity. After all, a man's life must be nailed to a cross of either Thought or Action. Without work there is no play.

Thus it was not altogether surprising that WSC should entertain a low opinion of dons (academic teachers at universities: now I suppose inevitably styled 'professors'). 'Scientists should be on tap, not on top' was followed by 'Dons usually make a muck of it'; but such sweeping judgements were invariably mitigated by his knowledge of individuals, of which the Prof. (Cherwell: a genuine professor, by the way) is the prime example.

WSC had become Chancellor of Bristol University, and in his more vigorous days took a considerable interest in its activities. Later, inevitably, this lapsed, but he still maintained a proper correspondence with Sir Philip Morris, the Vice-Chancellor, and this led to misunderstandings, as Morris assumed that he was more vigorous, and would be able to undertake more on the university's behalf, than was the case. When Bristol was raising funds, WSC was asked to lead the appeal and to contribute to it. He couldn't do the former, and he was not affluent enough to take more than a token part in the latter, which I rather embarrassingly had to explain to the Vice-Chancellor. He took it well and to his credit never suggested that WSC should resign in favour of a more active man.

At this time WSC was in good health and good spirits and there was a resumption of something of the old sparkle at the dinner table. I fed Boswellian questions to stimulate the trend, and noted some of the responses. In what circumstances, other than personal, should a diplomat,

Civil Servant or senior military figure resign, I asked? I reflected that both Moley Sargent and Ivone Kirkpatrick had at one moment or another contemplated resignation when holding the office of Permanent Under-Secretary of State, the Head of the Diplomatic Service. Possibly others had as well, but these were the only two of that rank who seemed to me to command full respect. Most of the others had an element of time-serving, or at least excessive pliability, which of course tended to endear them to their political masters. WSC replied: 'There is sometimes the strongest case for resignation, but you must never be a professional resigner. That gun backfires more often than not. My father got it wrong. But to stay on in the hope of mitigating disastrous policies is rarely successful. It's like accompanying a drunkard on his round of bars, and saying to him: "Well old boy, I'll buy you a small whisky instead of a large one." You are only putting off his downfall.'

This train of thought led WSC to recount the evidence against him by a hostile witness in a libel case. 'He said that he'd watched me coming out of Boodles drunker than any man he'd ever seen. But I never went into Boodles. In those days they wouldn't have me.' Quite what the relevance of this evidence was to the matter in question I couldn't discern, but it prompted CSC to talk of the criminal libel case against Lord Alfred Douglas, of Oscar Wilde fame, during the First World War. She said that after the Battle of Jutland in 1916, the greatest naval engagement of the War, the first British communiqué gave only a bald and rather brief statement of the losses on either side. The Germans had sunk far more of our ships than we had of theirs, and to this day the battle is considered in Germany to have been a great victory. But the fact was that the German High Seas Fleet never left harbour in strength again, and thus we could reasonably claim a strategic long-term success. To correct the first impression of disaster, WSC had been brought in, though no longer First Lord of the Admiralty, to draft a longer and more illuminating communiqué. Lord Alfred Douglas had published an article claiming that the two communiqués were part of a financial swindle, the first being designed to depress British Government stocks to an attractive level for a purchaser, and the second to send them rebounding to his profit.

Criminal libel is of course a Crown prosecution, not an individual one. CSC had attended the case at the Old Bailey and during a recess had lunched at a small café near the Court. On leaving she had come face to face with Alfred Douglas. 'And do you know,' she said, 'he looked so evil that I crossed myself.' I thought that this was the punch-line of the story; but no.

'Well dear,' she went on, 'in 1940 when Winston was Prime Minister, Lord Alfred Douglas, who was living in Brighton, sent him an elegant and highly complimentary sonnet he had written. And it was a good poem too.'

I was present at an interesting dinner-table discussion between WSC and Violet Bonham Carter on the Navy. Nothing in the wide-ranging capacity of Violet Bonham Carter's intellect astonished me, and her contributions on the subject were informed and thoughtful. She and WSC debated why it had been, and perhaps still was, that young naval officers were so frequently outstanding in initiative, professional competence and even innovation, and yet that after a certain rank, probably Captain, it all fizzled out, and they often became narrow, hidebound, irascible and hostile to anything new. Various long-forgotten names were adduced on both sides of the question. WSC finally summed up by supposing that the isolation of those holding higher naval command, with their word unquestioned by their subordinates, led to 'impervious ossification'.

Violet Bonham Carter added: 'Yes, Winston. And pink gin.' She went on to criticise Admiral Dudley-Pound, the Chief of Naval Staff in the earlier part of the Second World War.

WSC would have none of this. 'Well, it's true that he used to sit at meetings like an old parrot on its perch, with his eyes closing, but the moment the Navy was mentioned he bounded up. I remember watching him at the wheel of his own car coming up the drive to Chequers so fast that he almost overturned.'

I was not sure whether WSC meant this as a compliment or a criticism. He rounded off his thoughts with comments on recent First Lords. The appointment of a distinctly wet and petulant individual as successor to the First Lord of the Admiralty had been bruited. 'It wouldn't do,' he reflected. 'It would be a bit hard on the Navy to have two First Ladies in succession.' I reminded him of his reply to an Admiral who had objected to a course of action as being 'contrary to the traditions of the British Navy'. The reply ran: 'Rum, lice, sodomy, the lash! Those are the traditions of the British Navy.' He listened with amusement and said: 'Well, it is rather a good rebuke, but that's the first time I ever heard it.' He attracted the attribution of witty obiter dicta as a magnet to iron filings, in addition to his own authentic and prodigal output.

A sad incident marred those quiet days at 28 Hyde Park Gate. While the Churchills were at Chartwell the house was burgled, in spite of a policeman on duty outside. The major historical victim was a small gold snuff-box, inscribed: 'This snuff-box, taken from Nelson's dead body, we now confide to you. The Other Club 1940.' Those are the words I remember: the real ones may have been slightly different, but I don't suppose there is anyone left who knows. I asked the police Inspector how he imagined the thieves could dispose of such a relic. 'Scrunched up and sold for gold scrap,' he replied briefly.

I had on my desk a so-called Cabinet Box. It was a rectangular, steel-lined and leather-covered affair, similar to the one the Chancellor of the Exchequer likes to brandish as he leaves for his Budget speech. On it were inscribed the Royal Cypher and my initials in gold, and it was shut by a Bramah lock. I was very proud it, because it was given to Private Secretaries at Number Ten, and the more so because when I left the Treasury had tried to wrest it back from me for my successor as an economy. I had successfully resisted. The thieves had jemmied it open and stolen a small sum of French money and some war medals. But they had left behind in the middle of my desk a large, unlicensed, fully loaded .455 revolver. My father had carried it in the South African and First World Wars and I, briefly, in the Second World War. (I had substituted a Smith & Wesson .38, because I was told that the Japanese cut off the hands of anyone taken prisoner with a forty-five, on the grounds that the calibre was barbarous.) It was there because I thought one would feel more than usually foolish if an assassin got into the house and all I had, if the armed Sergeant Murray was absent, was a paper-knife. The police, with remarkable tact, studiously avoided seeing it.

Chapter 26

M Y T A L E is desultory, but so was WSC's life in retirement; and so were his recollections, nearly all of them voiced at dinner or luncheon (far too good to be styled merely 'lunch'). I asked him how he had regarded a stormy and hostile House of Commons in his earlier days. 'Well,' he replied, 'I always thought it was most entertaining to see a lot of old gentlemen in a rage about nothing at all.' I sometimes wonder how he would have reacted to the present collection of yobs, and how indeed any statesman would or could react? For something of a courteous contrast, take WSC's words in the House of Commons on 10 April 1951, when he was still Leader of the Opposition, and commenting on the Labour Chancellor Hugh Gaitskell's first budget:

'I think', he said, 'I shall be expressing the opinion of the whole House if I pay our compliments to the Chancellor of the Exchequer upon the lucid, comprehensive statement which he has made to us this afternoon, and upon the evident lack of hatred or malice which I felt was apparent while he was unfolding his proposals.'

When WSC spoke of Great Figures, be they Royal, or neo-Tsars such as Stalin, or Presidents, there was always respect, even a degree of reverence, in his approach. To our own Royal Family he was passionately loyal. The fact that the Duke of Windsor, whom he had strongly supported at the Abdication, had, in WSC's words, 'fallen below the level of events' made no difference at all to his automatic assumption that the Sovereign could do no wrong.

I often wondered if this instinctive loyalty, not just in the case of our own Royal Family, and WSC's romanticism and regard for the great, sprang from his degree of rejection by his father. Amateur psychology (and professional too) tends to be not only misleading but boring, but here I think there really was something in the psychological explanation, and it had dangerous implications in his relations with powerful and charismatic foreign political leaders.

In this context there are a good many candidates for the most successful exploitation of WSC's trust. General de Gaulle was certainly one of them. His manoeuvring to prevent our joining the Common Market has now been exposed in detail by the publication of some of the official archives under the thirty-year rule. At the time I remarked that de Gaulle was most successfully seeking to prove the much-quoted adage that no country can afford to show gratitude. WSC replied: 'It would indeed be sad if so melancholy and so historically disprovable a maxim should be the epitaph on so great a man.'

Following the deterioration of Anglo-French relations on the Common Market issue, WSC resolved on a private pro-French gesture that would indicate his continuing sentimental regard for their country. He first considered asking Geoffroy de Courcel, the admirable French Ambassador and incidentally a personal friend of mine, to dinner. For once being a suitably dutiful Civil Servant, I consulted Philip de Zulueta, who had succeeded me from the Foreign Office at Number Ten, and was Macmillan's trusted and able Private Secretary. Back came the reply that the Prime Minister begged WSC not to issue the invitation. It could, he said, be interpreted as a breach between the Government and WSC on the issue. I got blasted for my sneaking intervention, but, as always, WSC reluctantly kept to his determination not to embarrass his successors, who were well aware of the devastating effect that his disapproval could have if made public.

As an alternative I suggested that I should ask the Minister at the French Embassy, Gérard André, to lunch to meet WSC and CSC. Gérard was a close friend and a stalwart Anglophile, and the lunch, which took place at Hyde Park Gate, was a great success, with WSC on top form and leaving Gérard in no doubt of either his undying affection for France or his anger and disappointment at her present stance. He ended by drinking Gérard's health: 'To a good Frenchman.' Gérard was well regarded by de Gaulle and the conversation was faithfully reported, though to what effect I know not. I don't think de Gaulle was capable of remorse, let alone self-doubt.

Gérard was a real asset to diplomatic society. I was extremely fond of him, though he had out-finessed me over the site of the NATO Southern Command HQ. He had saved my bacon one night in 1949 when I was a Resident Clerk and he was on duty at the Embassy. Aroused from a deep sleep, I was about to make a blunder in reacting to a 'Most Immediate' telegram, which involved the French. 'Anthony,' Gérard had said firmly, 'before you do what you propose you should put your head under a cold tap and have another think.'

His parties were always fun, with appropriately excellent wine and cuisine. I can only remember one, where I met Maurice Chevalier, who was as charming as on stage, in spite of the most tombstone-white and prominent false teeth I have ever encountered. He talked of his celebrated romance with Mistinguett. He and she, as young dancers, were in an act at the Folies Bergères. It involved them being rolled up together in a long carpet, and when it was unrolled, emerging together to dance or sing. They were sometimes, through faulty timing, left rolled up for a considerable period and they were both scantily clad. 'The consequences were inevitable,' said Chevalier happily.

But back to the Common Market. WSC had had mixed feelings in his time in office. Now, in his retirement and deliberate withdrawal from current issues, it would have been totally inappropriate to seek his support on one side or the other. But this of course is what those on both sides of the argument did. The fact was that WSC was undecided, and this was out of character with his record and his personality. It would have been grossly improper to seek to polarise his view, and indeed to seek clarification of his sybilline speeches of the late 1940s. A pious hope for the rapprochement between humiliated France and devastated Germany did not amount to a policy for a United Europe, even on the day of the pronouncement when WSC was in full vigour. A fortiori, in his old age, how reprehensible to seek his endorsement on either side.

In the summer of 1957 WSC was invited to address a United Europe meeting in London. After a discussion with the Foreign Office, I drafted something pretty watery; this was such an undecided issue for Britain that here really was a case for WSC not to go further than his previous pronouncements, which were very general as far as Great Britain was concerned. However, he added his own words to the draft: 'My message to Europe today is still the same as it was ten years ago [his Zurich speech] – unite; Europe's security and prosperity lie in unity.'

Unite, yes. But how? In what degree? With what abdication of individual national sovereignty? My conviction was that WSC had never devoted detailed thought to these questions, but that in his Zurich speech he had not contemplated Britain being an integral part of a United Europe and that this view had not changed over the years.

In November 1949, in a speech in London, WSC had been more explicit:

> The French Foreign Minister, M. Schuman, declared in the French Parliament this week that 'Without Britain there can be no Europe.' This is entirely true. But our friends on the Continent need have no misgivings. Britain is an integral part of Europe, and we mean to play our part in the revival of her prosperity and greatness.
>
> But Britain cannot be thought of as a single State in isolation. She is the founder and centre of a world-wide Empire and Commonwealth. We shall never do anything to weaken the ties of blood, of sentiment and tradition and common interest which unite us with the other members of the British family of nations.
>
> But nobody is asking us to make such a desertion. For Britain to enter a European Union from which the Empire and Commonwealth would be excluded would not only be impossible but would, in the eyes of Europe, enormously reduce the value of our participation.

It may well be argued that the emphasis on the Commonwealth had even in WSC's lifetime lost relevance, although it had not become the meaningless fiction that it is today. But perhaps the clearest statement of WSC's hopes for Britain's future is expressed in his old age in the very last paragraph of the fourth volume of *A History of the English-Speaking Peoples*, published in 1958. I was present when he wrote it and it was neither ghosted nor suggested to him.

> Here is set out a long story of the English-Speaking Peoples. They are now to become Allies in terrible but victorious wars. And that is not the end. Another phase looms before us, in which alliance will once more be tested and in which its formidable virtues may be to preserve Peace and Freedom. The future is

unknowable, but the past should give us hope. Nor should we now seek to define precisely the exact terms of ultimate union.

His Zurich speech of 1946 did indeed call for a 'kind of United States of Europe', with the now somewhat perversely fulfilled demand that there 'must be a partnership between France and Germany'. But he concluded that while France and Germany should take the lead in this urgent task, 'Britain and the British Commonwealth as well as mighty America, and I trust Soviet Russia – for then indeed all would be well – must be the friends and sponsors of the new Europe.' In other words, Britain and the Soviet Union who, with America and the Dominions, had won the war would be the partners of, rather than the participants in the new European unity.

It is quite possible to pick an isolated quote to support a particular point of view of WSC's true convictions on Europe. One might start with his offer of union with France, or a form of union at least, in 1940. But this was dictated by the desperate need of the hour (for both countries) and was the brainchild of Jean Monnet via René Pleven. And the offer was of course rejected by France. I doubt if such a shotgun marriage could long have survived, even under the necessities of war.

Later came the Zurich speech of 1946, the Hague, Strasbourg and quite a number of other reasonably specific pronouncements by WSC. It should, however, be noted that all of these were before his resumption of office after the 1951 General Election. As I have said previously, in his last administration he was too heavily engaged and perhaps too old to undertake a crusade of such major proportions as United Europe, with his Foreign Secretary and heir apparent opposed to him. And perhaps his heart was not wholly in such a huge undertaking in any case.

General de Gaulle, later so gleefully responsible for the rejection of the British application to join the EEC, had not always been a committed European. He saw French leadership of the EEC as the great counter-balance to the withdrawal from Algeria. And so it indeed proved. Harold Macmillan later referred in almost visible capital letters to his own 'Grand Design', which envisaged Britain emulating France by giving up her colonial responsibilities and playing a leading part in a United Europe. De Gaulle took pleasure in relating Macmillan's dismay at the French rebuff to our approach. He is said to have quoted with a chuckle the chorus of an old French song: 'Ne pleurez pas, Milor'.'

To be fair, de Gaulle had been a strong proponent of the union of 1940; but later, as France's strength returned, everything he said was hedged. As far back as 1946, WSC's son-in-law, Duncan Sandys, had visited de Gaulle at Colombey-les-deux-Églises and had found the General in favour of a European Federation, but with a whole shopping list of conditions including such extraneous points as a common Anglo-French policy towards the Arab states and a recognition of France's position in Syria, as well as more apposite demands relating to the occupation of conquered Germany.

Later de Gaulle's position seemed to crystallise to support for 'l'Europe des patries' ('a Europe of national States') and this was not too far from what I construed as WSC's view. Different days produced different words, however, and it would have been easy to construct several different cases. In January 1963 WSC began a letter to Paul Henri Spaak, the Belgian statesman, which was not despatched. I quote below the opening lines, but they do not provide any conclusive evidence of WSC's later views:

> My Dear Spaak,
> I was moved by your eloquent remarks. It is to me further proof, if this were needed, of your statesmanship and far-sighted approach to the problems that confront us. The future of Europe if Britain were to be excluded is black indeed.

But the whole question had been put to public test in 1962. WSC had broken his hip in Monte Carlo and, against the vehement protests of the local French doctors, had, as I shall relate, flown home to England in an RAF Comet. Among his visitors in the Middlesex Hospital was Field Marshal Montgomery, who emerged to tell the waiting press, quite truthfully, that the patient was in excellent form. Unfortunately he went on to declare that WSC was totally and fundamentally opposed to Britain joining the EEC. This was not an invention, but a serious misinterpretation of an old and sick man's views by a totally black-or-white-and-no-middle-ground interpreter. I heard it on my car's radio as I drove home from the Middlesex, where I had left Monty. Consulting nobody, I immediately released to the press a statement of WSC's views on the subject that he had embodied in a private and unpublished letter to his Constituency Chairman, Mrs Moss, in August 1961. It ran thus:

> The problem of British and Commonwealth relations with the European Economic Community occupies a position of major importance and interest. I feel that it may be useful to you if I send you my general thoughts on the matter.
> For many years, I have believed that measures to promote European unity were ultimately essential to the well-being of the West. In a speech at Zurich in 1946, I urged the creation of the European Family, and I am sometimes given credit for stimulating the ideals of European unity which led to the formation of the economic and the other two communities. In the aftermath of the second world war, the key to these endeavours lay in partnership between France and Germany. At that time this happy outcome seemed a fantasy, but it is now accomplished, and France and West Germany are more intimately linked than they have ever been before in their history. They, together with Italy, Belgium, Holland and Luxembourg, are welding themselves into an organic whole, stronger and more dynamic than the sum of its parts.
> We might well play a great part in these developments to the profit not only of ourselves, but of our European friends also. But we have another role which we cannot abdicate: that of leader of the British Commonwealth. In my conception of a unified Europe, I never contemplated the diminution of the Commonwealth. It is most important to consider correctly the initiative taken by the Government in applying formally for accession to the Treaty of Rome, the statute that set up the European Economic Community. This application for membership is the sole way in which, so to speak, a reconnaissance can be

carried out to find out for certain whether terms for British membership of the Community could be agreed which would meet our special needs as well as those of the Commonwealth and of our partners in the European Free Trade Association.

In the negotiations that we expect will take place in the coming months, the Six Countries should recognise that the Commonwealth is one of the most valuable assets that we could bring, for them as well as for ourselves, and should be ready to work out arrangements to prevent any damage to Commonwealth interests.

There are other considerations. We have obligations to the other European countries who are members of the European Free Trade Association. The Government have emphasised that satisfactory arrangements for them are a pre-condition for our entry into the Economic Community, or Common Market as it is called. The position of our farmers is also of major significance.

To sum up my views, I would say this: I think that the Government are right to apply to join the European Economic Community, not because I am yet convinced that we shall be able to join, but because there appears to be no other way by which we can find out exactly whether the conditions of membership are acceptable.

It will be seen that this was a fence-sitting letter. In the conflicting circumstances of WSC's age, the public need for an expression of his views, the Prime Minister's dignified, perfectly proper, but urgent request for his support and WSC's family's (and my own) determination that improper use should not be made of him, such a position was inevitable. It might have been better to keep total silence, but this would have implied a negative stance, particularly in view of Monty's indiscreet intervention. So, after agonising, I had cobbled together as best I could what I, feeling that I knew WSC's thoughts better than any one else at that time, considered could do the least harm.

However, when Monty gave his account of WSC's views, I received a telephone call from Philip de Zulueta at Number Ten. 'The Prime Minister has asked me to find out "What the hell that boy Browne is doing,"' he said mildly. I bristled and suggested that he wait and see what WSC's formal views were when the Constituency letter was published that evening. This was not good enough, and a messenger arrived from Number Ten for a copy. The milk-and-water contents did not get anyone anywhere, but it took the heat off and pacified both Macmillan and the Euro-antis. Now the whole scenario is so out of date as to render the letter irrelevant, which on the whole is the least of several evils.

I had been questioned quite frequently to find out what was WSC's 'real attitude to European involvement', and even if I had extrapolated from his pronouncements of more vigorous days, which would in any case have been wrong, the conclusion would not have been enlightening: 'with but not of' is perhaps the best one could do.

Piecing together various conversations with WSC and others over the twelve years of my service with him I think that it is fair to summarise thus.

The offer of union to France in 1940 was a desperate attempt to stave off her defeat. If it had been accepted, the resulting arrangement would have crumbled once the extreme pressures of the time had relaxed.

WSC believed more in the 'Special Relationship' with the US than in Europe, but he did not think that one excluded the other. Moreover the Commonwealth, or at least the old Commonwealth, was not then the charade it has now become. Stalwarts such as Bob Menzies of Australia, Jan Smuts of South Africa and Sid Holland of New Zealand were still very much visible, and it might even have been possible to cement much closer relations with Pakistan if we had not been so frightened of alienating the already fundamentally hostile Nehru.

If Britain had taken the initiative before the Treaty of Rome in 1957 things might have been different. WSC had reproached the Labour Government for their indecision at that time. If he had been able with all his old fire and eloquence to lead Britain into Europe, the country might have been persuaded that our interests really did lie in that direction. But we would have to have been the founders and the leaders, not the aspirant candidate of later years, hoping that we would not be blackballed. Then our pole position just might have caught the public imagination. But I don't think WSC would have wanted to do it.

France was in a totally different position, and it was not too difficult for the French to realise that the Green Pool, the Coal and Steel Pool and similar steps were designed to form a crutch to raise France to a position that her own efforts could not justify, to appease her then very large agricultural community and later to enable her to turn her back on the loss of her Empire and North African territories and look to renewed glories as the leader of Europe.

Our powers of persuasion with successive French Governments progressively diminished. Immediately post-1945, they were considerable, and we were astonishingly popular as well. The menace of Russian aggression and the weakness of the political system, with Prime Minister after Prime Minister rising and falling, maintained our position quite reasonably, and for a long time the French also looked to us to support them in case of a resurgently aggressive Germany. Now, of course, all these positive elements have gone. WSC did not live to see their evaporation and his calculations always took for granted a reasonable France, grateful for her liberation and aware of the value of British friendship.

I quote below an extract from a letter addressed to me by Bernard Baruch in January 1962. He was a wise man, and something of a prophet:

> When I last saw Winston and everybody had left the room, he turned to me and asked me what I thought of the common market. I haven't sent him anything and I am wondering whether it would be wise to send anything because I do not believe in something about which a lot of people are deluding themselves.
>
> France agreed with you and us on nuclear energy and then she ran out. She took a position on NATO which she never implemented to any degree. I wonder if she can take the lead in formulating a common market in Europe with that record.
>
> I might add for your information that if you have a common market you must have a common defense, which, you may recall, I suggested should be added to

the Marshall Plan and that is what brought about NATO. Herewith is a copy of a cartoon which appeared in *Punch*, which is apropos. Also, if you have a common market, you must have a common currency. Maybe this will come some day but I hardly think it can come under the leadership of France, at least not now.

In the recently published Cabinet Papers a letter I wrote in 1961 to the Prime Minister's Private Secretary, Philip de Zulueta, is quoted:

> Dear Philip,
>
> I feel that I should send you a copy of a letter which is typical of many being addressed to Sir Winston. I am in something of a quandary in answering, because I do not think that Sir Winston himself has any very decided view on the Common Market question.
>
> Have you any formula that is a) reasonably non-committal, b) helpful but not too vacant?
>
> Yours ever Anthony

The missive to which it refers was a staunch and well-worded appeal to WSC to preserve the Commonwealth and stay out of Europe. Not unnaturally Philip was unable to meet the two conditions for a formula.

WSC deplored indecision. He might vacillate and ruminate for days or weeks, but this was only while his internal jury was debating the evidence. When the process was complete, the verdict was clear. I think that if I had known for certain what his views on Europe were, I would have said so publicly, even at that late stage in his life, and would no doubt have been much abused by one side or the other. But on the European issue, for every point to be made from WSC's speeches and writings, there is usually a countervailing argument to be found elsewhere. 'Europe Unite' is balanced by WSC's tirade to de Gaulle during the war. As far as I am aware there is only an oral tradition of the words, but they ran something like this: 'If we have to choose between you and America, it will always be America. If we have to choose between the Continent and the open sea, it will always be the open sea.' But this was when we had an Empire and a Navy. Nevertheless, I think that in some almost incoherent but deeply felt way, WSC's last thoughts returned nostalgically to our great days, and his own Anglo-American origins.

How can one tell what his conclusion would have been in the present vastly changed circumstances? His approach to a new challenge was invariably courageous and constructive, but would the new European picture and Britain's disastrously diminished role in the world have caused WSC to veer from his American attachment?

Chapter 27

I N T H E spring of 1960 Onassis suggested a more ambitious cruise, to the West Indies. Both WSC and CSC liked the idea. Nonie and my seven-year-old daughter Jane were also bidden, and I managed to persuade her school to release her, on the grounds that a West Indies cruise with WSC would help her history as well as her geography. Lord and Lady Moran came too. Our departure was not auspicious. We were supposed to embark at Gibraltar, but the weather had deteriorated rapidly and a storm was blowing. On our first approach the aircraft was tossed about so violently in the eddies from the Rock that luggage was thrown from the racks and poor Toby the budgerigar was precipitated, squawking indignantly in his cage, into his owner's lap. The pilot desisted after a second even bumpier attempt and we flew to Tangier. Fortunately the Consul-General was still the friendly and energetic Bryce Nairn and in the space of less than an hour he had alerted the authorities, commandeered transport and accommodation at the Rif Hotel, the newest and largest in Tangier, and deserted his own guests, who included T.S. Eliot, to come and smooth our path. I was left with Sergeant Murray at the airport to deal with the immigration authorities, who were dilatory and sulky at our unprotocolaire arrival. I finally had to request to use their telephone and when asked to whom I wished to speak, replied that it must be the Governor of Tangier or the King's Chamberlain in Rabat. Things then improved without the call going through.

In the hotel the chef was determined to show his paces and what he produced was distinctly unusual. Unfortunately it took an unconscionable time, and WSC's patience broke. As I have already said, his manner to servants was never good, however much he was willing to help them in misfortune, and now he erupted in petulant anger at being kept waiting. CSC tried in vain to quell him and finally said: 'Winston, you are embarrassing me so much that I will go to my room without dinner,' which was effective, and the repentant WSC subsequently sent for the chef to make amende honorable, which he did with grace and charm.

The next day Ari met us on *Christina*, which had battled through the extremely rough Straits. As we boarded her, I noticed that the sea was breaking over the pier in Tangier harbour, and when we sailed, after a sybaritic lunch, we ran into a mature storm. Ari said that he was aware that it would be uncomfortable, but he did not want to stay near Gibraltar: 'Anthony, that Rock looked like an evil witch yesterday. Let's get away from her to the open sea.' *Christina* was a very large yacht, and as an ex-frigate was a good sea-boat, but it was not much of a size against a full Atlantic storm and before we reached gentler weather at the Canaries, we were thrown all over the place. Jane had a jolly little cabin to herself, where she determinedly unpacked in spite of seasickness. A particularly violent lurch threw her into her suitcase, which then closed on her, so she retired crestfallen to our cabin to sleep with her mother while I found an enormous silk-cushioned sofa in the drawing room and did very well. That night the only diners were WSC, Ari and myself. The movement was too violent for WSC to get up, so he ate in bed, supported by about twenty pillows, while Ari and I sat cross-legged on the floor. (Easier for him than me, he said, because at the Turkish school he had attended in Smyrna, all the little boys had to sit thus on the floor.) We dined off caviar and a mixed grill, and we each clutched a bottle of Pol Roger between our legs.

The following day the weather improved and we progressed smoothly along what Ari called the Pullman Route, via the Canaries to the West Indies with the north-east trade winds behind us and gentle seas. It was the most lotus-eating of existences, with eight days out of sight of land after Grand Canary.

Early one morning the Captain woke Nonie and me: 'Come on deck at once and you will see something you will probably never see again.' It was a grey morning, and a choppy sea. All that we could see was a small dark islet, with the waves breaking over it. I had no idea that there were any islands so far west. Volcanic, perhaps? But as we watched the islet spouted, and with a brief flourish of a huge horizontal tail, vanished. It was a Blue Whale, the greatest creature that has ever been on Earth, and now a rarity, particularly in those latitudes. The disgusting activities of the whalers had seen to that.

Years afterwards I was to win a bet with Adrian Conan Doyle, son of Arthur Conan Doyle, with the knowledge that the whale encounter encouraged me to acquire. I met him on a train going to Switzerland and after a rather boozy dinner we disputed the title of the greatest creature 'ever on Earth'. Conan Doyle voted for one of the giant dinosaurs and I for the Blue Whale. The Natural History Museum was to be the arbiter and the stake was a dinner for four of the winner's choice at the loser's expense. I won, and Adrian told me to send him the menu together with a list of the best wines that I could imagine. We would dine at his château near Vevey and he would send tickets to attend. 'I am', he announced, 'inflately rich on the royalties of my father's books.' Alas, I never collected, for Adrian died before we could meet.

On board we lunched daily on the after-deck. *Christina* had preserved some of her original warship lines, and we were very close to the water. On one occasion a following glassy swell rose above us as it slowly overtook. There was no risk of it breaking, and in it, keeping pace, was a dolphin rolling a piggy eye at us. He appeared to be suspended in blue aspic jelly and WSC was entranced. 'I do wish I could communicate with you,' he muttered.

We invariably changed for dinner, which seemed a little outré on a yacht in mid-ocean, but in any case the chill of the air conditioning made a collar and tie agreeable, and the atmosphere of the elegant dining room, the white-coated stewards, the remarkable food and outstanding wines and above all the formidable presence of WSC made formality totally appropriate. Halfway through dinner one night there was a flash of silver and a thump on one of the windows. The butler (probably the wrong nautical term) went out to investigate and returned with a beautiful flying-fish, lying on a Sèvres dish. The poor fellow had taken off from a higher wave and, attracted by the light, had with over-vaulting ambition broken his neck on the dining-room window of Winston Churchill and Aristotle Onassis. The former, anthropomorphic and in high philosophical vein, animadverted on the strange chances of marine life. I wish I could remember what he said. It was good stuff, but I did not note it.

Ari was an insomniac and a noctambulist (though not a sleepwalker). At Monte Carlo I had sometimes walked with him for four or five kilometres late at night. He liked company but he was perfectly prepared to walk by himself. Did he make his plans during these solitary midnight sorties, I asked? He said no: on the whole he thought of the past, and his thoughts were melancholy. He made the mistake of taking walks in New York and in due course the inevitable mugging took place on Fifth Avenue.

'Did it upset you?'

'No. I just said "Take it easy and be rrreasonable. You want my money. We neither of us want trouble." And I turned my pockets out.'

'How much did you lose?'

'I don't know, but it was worth it.'

On *Christina* the night walking was replaced by sitting cross-legged on the raised poop-deck, a few feet above the water, drinking whisky and soda, looking at the phosphorescent wake and the stars and talking to anyone who would sit with him. He was lonely and we took it in turns to stay up. We were once almost struck by disaster. I was the night duty companion – though it was a privilege and no burden – and was absorbed by Ari's conversation, and lulled by the excellence of the dinner and the post-prandial brandy. The sea had got up with astonishing speed and with no great increase in wind. Suddenly waves started to break over the deck between the raised poop and the entrance to the ship's interior. We waited for it to subside, but each successive sea came foaming higher. 'Anthony, we must go right now,' Ari advised. We waited for a lull and bolted across the open deck and tugged desperately at the door of the after-saloon. It was locked. We gazed unbelievingly at each other and particularly at our tropical dinner jackets (white wild silk for him, Huntsman's best black alpaca for me) while the ocean gathered its strength and struck. We were submerged waist-deep, but there was no great force in the wave and we emerged spluttering to scamper up the steps to the next deck. Ari said soberly: 'We must not do that again. If we had gone overboard no-one would have seen us. We are in the middle – Arctic there, Antarctic there, America in front and Africa behind.'

Rather earlier in the voyage the engines had been stopped to deal with an overheated bearing. We were some hundred miles west of Tenerife, where the 12,000-foot peak of Mount Taide was still faintly visible. The sea was smooth

as satin, with a gentle swell, and I had asked the Captain to put down a gangway for me to have a swim in the deep Ocean. It was an unusual sensation. The
sea was calm and warm, the ship theoretically would drift at the same rate as
the swimmer, and I was observed by friendly eyes from the bridge. But the
swells, so small from the ship, at water level appeared vast, great smooth hills
that obscured the ship and the horizon. I felt lonely, and from the top of a
wave realised that I was a half-mile from *Christina*. There was no danger. The
yacht gave a brief spasm of engine and drifted down on me. After I had
clambered up, Ari confronted me: 'My frrriend, I ask you never to do that
again. The Ocean is not known to man.' I obeyed him.

WSC made an unusual suggestion. 'Let us all grow moustaches,' he said. It
was one of the most quirkish initiatives I had ever heard him take, but he
always had been capable of startling one. So we did. I abandoned mine after
about ten days; it was a strange colour, looked unpleasant, and interfered with
my enjoyment of wine and cigars. But WSC was indignant, and pursued his
own rather longer. It did not become him.

The conversation at dinner rambled agreeably. In a silence, I, who looked
on myself to some social conversational extent as WSC's straight-man, tried
this:

'If you were to be reincarnated, and you were not allowed to be a human
being, what would you choose?'

WSC reflected only briefly: 'A lovely tiger,' he said.

'And you, Ari?'

'A Toby' (the budgerigar).

'Why?'

'Because everyone would love you, and look after you, and they would
think that they were fooling you. But you would be fooling them.' A reflective
pause, while we digested this philosophy. I thought that Ari in some ways
looked rather like Toby, but that did not seem an adequate explanation.
Finally WSC said:

'What about you, Anthony?'

I had not been prepared for the question, and finally said, Coleridge in
mind: 'An albatross.'

WSC puffed his cigar: 'That is a most foolish choice.'

I bridled; I liked the idea of that remote, lonely and wandering bird. 'Why?'

A vague sweeping gesture of the arm: 'All that bloody sea.'

Our first landfall in the West Indies was Barbados. The visit there and in
subsequent islands followed a regular pattern. The Governor or Administrator would dine or lunch on board and we would receive hospitality from him
on shore. WSC and CSC would drive through the capital and the surrounding countryside with the Governor in an open car, the rest of us tailing behind
in assorted vehicles of descending grandeur and ascending antiquity. The
greeting WSC received was invariably noisy and enthusiastic, far beyond
expectation in the twilight of colonial rule. Crowds waved flags, presented
cameras and ran alongside the lead car. It was touching and WSC, who had
his fair share of decent and understandable vanity, enjoyed it visibly.

I was rather cut out of some of the other and more enjoyable informal sorties and bathing parties, for WSC would usually not go ashore again, and wanted to sit under an awning on the stern observing and being observed, or else playing bezique. The latter was a task that I could not in decency delegate, quite apart from the fact that only CSC and I knew the game. Moreover there was forwarded mail and some cable correspondence to be dealt with and the odd cypher message via the Colonial Office. So I missed a lot of fun.

Trinidad and Tobago followed Barbados, and then St Lucia. Lord and Lady Oxford dined on board. He was the Administrator of the island. They were both strict Roman Catholics. It was Holy Week. So they both fasted totally and drank water, which not only must have been very painful to them, but upset Clément, the chef, as well. (It is always said that the English love a Lord, but in my experience foreigners love one even more, and Clément had excelled himself.) Nevertheless the Oxfords gave us an excellent lunch the next day in their hilltop Residence. WSC was on top form and delighted to chat with his old Chief's (Herbert Asquith's) grandson. He sought enlightenment on the routine and problems of administration in the dying days of the Empire. After all, his first ministerial job had been as Under-Secretary for the Colonies in 1905.

Oxford told us of an unusual problem. He had wished to have an area of dense bush cleared for, I think, increased banana production, but the locals were loath to carry out the operation on the grounds that the bush was infested by Fer-de-lance snakes, aggressive and deadly. Oxford had a wide-ranging fund of esoteric knowledge, and he understood that a certain Brazilian snake, itself non-venomous, was extremely partial to Fer-de-lance in its diet. So he wrote to the Colonial Office requesting permission to import some. No reply was forthcoming so, growing impatient, he obtained and released a suitable number of the reptiles on his own responsibility. No sooner had the Brazilians slithered off into the bush than a cable arrived from London. It read: 'Brazilian snakes. Do nothing so rash.' Puzzled, Oxford awaited developments. When they came they were disagreeable. It transpired that while the aliens liked eating Fer-de-lances, their true caviar was chickens. The locals, eggless and chickenless, had kicked up an understandable shindy, and viewed their Administrator's further thoroughly benevolent activities with serious suspicion. But to us, it was a most entertaining visit.

A call at Antigua also brought a minor problem. WSC, greatly to everyone's surprise, had expressed a wish to hear a steel band. After dinner, the First Officer was despatched to find one. There were then two on the island, the Red Army and the Brute Force. Neither could be found: one was at a wedding, and one at their own party. Brimming with post-prandial confidence, I told Ari that I would find one. Luck was with me and I located the Brute Force. (Or was it the Red Army?) They took a lot of convincing that they were being invited to play for Winston Churchill and Aristotle Onassis, but this accomplished they fairly scampered. Unfortunately, as we arrived over the rail on the port side of *Christina*, the First Officer, who had returned to the charge, appeared over the starboard side, accompanied by the Red

Army. (Or was it the Brute Force?) I don't think the bands loved each other very much, certainly not at that point. Ari took in the situation.

'When you've got two steel bands, then you've got prrroblems,' he announced. 'Sir Winston, what would you do?'

The Statesman meditated. 'There is always the Chevalerie de Saint Georges,'* he suggested. Ari's brow cleared. Largesse was discreetly distributed and that, to me, dismal and monotonous clatter continued into the early hours, long after WSC had had his fill.

The following day, the Antiguan Administrator, a New Zealand All Black rugger player named Turbott, had arranged an imaginative programme. We spent the day at Clarence House, overlooking English Harbour. The house was named for the future William IV, who had been stationed on the island. It was perched on an airy hill, overlooking the anchorage, which had been chosen both for the concealment that its entrance offered to the Fleet and because Nelson had said that the towing of the ships by rowing boats through the entrance when winds were contrary was good exercise for the sailors. Nelson had commanded the frigate *Boreas* and been married in Antigua. Clarence House was something of a museum to British naval power in the days of sail. One of the exhibits was a touching little note written by Nelson to a twelve-year-old midshipman on *Boreas* who was very naturally frightened of climbing the towering rigging of the ship. It ran something like this: 'Captain Horatio Nelson presents his compliments to Mr Midshipman Blank, and as the weather is clement, suggests that he join him at the foretop [or whatever the summit was called] at 3 p.m. today, where the view should be particularly fine.'

In the evening, we went down to Nelson's Dockyard, admirably restored by an organisation with which CSC had been associated, and in the dusk the Antigua Regiment colourfully beat 'Retreat'. All was sadly lost on WSC. Sunk in apathetic gloom, his only comment was: 'Britain has got rather good at beating retreat.'

Heading for Martinique, we anchored at dawn in a bay of the remote and then mainly unvisited island of Marie Galante, also French-controlled. I was surprised to see in the early light a rowing boat put out from the shore. The sole occupant (black) wore shorts and an official looking képi. He stopped just below me, looked up and shouted: 'Monsieur Browne?' Incredulously, I acknowledged my identity. No-one knew of our destination. Ari had decided on impulse to stop there the previous day. 'I have an official telegram for you,' went on the rower (in French). 'Will you please sign for it?' Easier said than done, but in due course the postman, for it was he, came on board, got his signature and a suitable acknowledgement of his services, and departed. The telegram was from the Prefect of Martinique. Would I please inform WSC of the Prefect's welcome to his territories and assure him of his services whenever he wished? Actually there was no mystery; knowing that our

---

* The old French term for British subvention to her anti-French allies: the gold sovereigns had St George and the Dragon on one face.

destination was Martinique, the Prefect had sent identical telegrams to all the outlying islands.

When we sought to depart, there was a literal technical hitch. Our anchor had become entangled, and when it eventually was brought to the surface, with it came an iron-bound wooden anchor of great antiquity, and half the crustacean population of the bay. WSC was fascinated, and identified it, with what degree of accuracy I know not, as the hook of an eighteenth-century man-of-war. The site of the Anglo-French naval Battle of the Saints in 1782, a rocky island group, was within view, and CSC had seen the skeletons of the French vessels on the rocks there some thirty years previously, so WSC may well have been right. It stimulated him to a fascinating albeit interrupted discourse, quite in his old style, on British naval power, complete with quotations from Mahan and Jacky Fisher.* He told us that in the old Navy, when a gunner was firing a salute of several guns, in order to get the intervals between each shot identical, he would chant: 'Twenty years a gunner and never been called a son-of-a-bitch before.' Ari was much taken with the idea, and for quite a number of subsequent meetings he would use this interesting phrase to indicate surprise or indignation.

From Martinique we sailed to the Virgin Islands, thence to the US Naval Base at Puerto Rico where we were received with suitable pzazz. In the evening we climbed on to an Olympic Airways DC6. My heart sank. This old piston-engined aircraft promised an interminable and uncomfortable flight. I reckoned without our host: the dinner was superb, and each and every one of our party had a bed. In the early morning we landed at the Azores, and breakfasted in the sun, looking at that white and sapphire sea.

WSC's association with Ari was not without critics, and I myself was not immune. It was suggested by kind friends that Ari had offered me employ-ment beyond the dreams of an impecunious diplomat. After WSC's death he did indeed ask me to join him. 'Come with me, Anthony. You'll make a lot of money and we'll have a lot of fun.' For a whole number of reasons I declined. I knew nothing about running two million tons of shipping, nothing about running Olympic Airways or about the Monte Carlo casinos and hotels, both of which Ari designated his 'hobby enterprises'. However friendly the Greeks, they would not have tolerated a foreign and uninitiated interloper. When I said a polite 'no', Ari asked me what I intended to do. I said that just for the moment, I would return to the Foreign Office. Ari reflected: 'In that case, Anthony, we'll have to buy you a little Embassy.' At that particular moment Ari was wearing a mustard-yellow tropical suit. He caught my faintly disapproving eye: 'You think that in this suit I look like a crooked little dago, Anthony? You are quite rrright.'

But both from the point of view of WSC's reputation, and from that of my own infinitely less important one, my mind was easy. CSC, Mary, Sarah,

---

* Admiral Lord Fisher, First Sea Lord up to 1910 and again during part of the First World War. Father of the Dreadnought battleships. Once WSC's close friend and later his fiercest enemy. His letters in the first phase used to end: 'Yours to the Pearly Gates', 'Yours till charcoal sprouts' and 'Yours till Hell freezes over.' WSC commented wryly: 'Hell did freeze over.'

Randolph and Christopher were fiercely protective of WSC. They would have intervened with vigour if they saw any risk. And they all knew Ari personally. Jock Colville, in his book *The Churchillians* (which I used to give as a Christmas present because it said friendly things about me), gave a very fair description of WSC's rationale towards lavish entertainment.

> Onassis found time, without the least appearance of being preoccupied, to sit with Churchill for hours on end, to talk to him and to conspire how best to make him feel an honoured and much wanted guest. When Churchill's faculties weakened, as his ninetieth birthday approached, Onassis was as ready as in more lucid days to devote time and ingenuity to his self-imposed task. There was something in Churchill that stirred the emotional chords in his nature and those who saw them together were not deluded by the commonly held belief that collecting illustrious scalps was the sole motive of his attentions.
>
> Clementine Churchill thought that her husband's least admirable characteristic was a yearning for luxury so pronounced that he would accept hospitality from anybody able to offer the surroundings and amenities he enjoyed.
>
> Churchill, whose nature it was to notice merits rather than defects, at least as far as social relationships were concerned, did not in fact stay with people he disliked. The Dukes of Westminster and Marlborough, as well as Lord Beaverbrook, were intimate friends. Lavish entertainment was a strong attraction, but it was not for that alone he found pleasure in the company of Maxine Elliot, Emery Reves and Aristotle Onassis. He drank their flowing champagne, and basked in the beautiful surroundings of their villas and yachts, without asking himself if he was accepting what they supplied for the wrong reasons.
>
> He was sorry his wife was so seldom willing to accompany him on these visits, but whether or not he fully understood her scruples, he felt no obligation to be bound by them. He himself was always pleased to gratify those he liked with all he could afford and every pleasure he could supply. He assumed that others felt as he did. His predilection for luxury was in any case but a small item to enter on the debit side of a long favourable balance sheet.

Ari had not publicised his association with WSC, but once the cruises had started it was impossible and unnecessary to conceal them from the Press. Ari's adviser, Nigel Neilson, a man of total integrity whom Ari liked and trusted and who controlled his public relations, told me that he had never had any instructions to publicise or vary any news story involving Churchill. Above all, had not Winston Churchill earned the right to happy and peaceful voyages in the sun, with the care and luxury that he undoubtedly enjoyed? I wouldn't have stopped it if I could.

WSC made Ari a member of the Other Club. He only came to it twice, both when WSC commanded his company. The late Lord Brabazon, next to whom I sat at one dinner, blamed me bitterly for the presence of a Greek. 'A Greek at the Other Club! Maintenant j'ai tout vu!' I was glad to be able to point out to him that the Portuguese Ambassador, the Marques de Soveral, known as the Blue Monkey, had been a founder-member of the Club in 1911. To digress – just for once – CSC told me that when Sarah was born, WSC was at the battle for Antwerp. Soveral had called on her, and, hearing that WSC was absent, had insisted on sleeping on a sofa, as he said that a man should be in the house at a birth. In recently published archives Soveral also emerges as a close and trusted friend of both King Edward VII and Queen Alexandra – no mean feat.

It is not too hard to explain the attraction between WSC and his Greek host. Ari was in genuine awe of major historical figures and WSC in particular. He had also a strong degree of the Greek quality of respect for the old. Did he exploit his friendship? I don't think so; certainly not in any business sense. He did not once ask WSC for an introduction to anyone. When we went ashore to meet local dignitaries, Ari put himself in the background unless WSC specifically asked him to drive with him, which he frequently did. Some social advantages undoubtedly did brush off on him, but I don't think that he felt that he particularly needed them. In any case it would have been impossible to keep WSC's presence on the *Christina* a secret, and we were greeted at every stop by photographers and journalists.

The other side of the coin was simple. If a British owner of a yacht of comparable size had offered WSC the sunny cruising he so enjoyed, he might well have accepted – if, and it is a big if, his host had been the sort of person whose company he would also enjoy. But British owners of very large yachts did not on the whole seem to fall into this category, and our tax structure had made them an almost extinct species in any case. It was, I think, Ari's devoted attention to his entertainment and comfort that so appealed to WSC, coupled with his unfeigned and intelligent interest in history. For if WSC was anything, he was a consummate historian.

A rather strange quirk of Ari's was to respect philosophy, to revel in history, but to dislike and despise poetry. 'Poets are seducers,' he used to say.

'Physically or intellectually?' I once enquired.

'Both,' said Ari bitterly. I don't know what unfortunate experience had engendered this view, but I managed to dredge up from the rag-bag of memory a quotation from Aristotle and presented it to his modern homonym at dinner. It ran approximately: 'Poetry is a much deeper and more significant matter than either philosophy or history.' (I write poetry myself, and use it as a warning signal: if I hear myself quoting my own verse I know that I have had too much to drink. But poetaster or not, I don't agree with Aristotle.) The quote provoked indignant incredulity. Cables were despatched to Athens University and great was the consternation when the quotation was verified. I think Ari even nourished suspicions that I had nobbled the authorities.

CSC's relations with her host were initially excellent, but as the early pleasures of being afloat which she so much enjoyed became more routine, so her criticisms became more acute. And indeed Ari was open to criticism. The real trouble was that he had many of the attributes of an Oriental as far as women were concerned. His courtesy towards her was impeccable, but it was quite plain that he did not look on engaging in a conversation with her as at all the same as listening to WSC, even though the latter was, in his old age, spasmodic in his responses and rare in his initiatives. This was a great pity, because CSC was a gifted and entertaining conversationalist, and was used to taking her part in exchanges, even if she had got used to being overwhelmed by her husband's glittering prodigality.

Incidentally, I was astounded recently to read that Asquith, when Prime Minister, had written that 'Clemmie is au fond a bore.' Perhaps the explanation is that with her rigid moral principles she had put him down, which indeed she was capable of doing, and that he had resented it? Or had she pursued her advocacy of WSC's political interests too vigorously?

At all events she became somewhat disenchanted with the cruises and with her host, even though he encouraged her to bring fellow guests of her own inclination. Perhaps Tina's absence as hostess was responsible for CSC's withdrawal.

In March 1961 WSC again sailed to the West Indies. We flew to Gibraltar and WSC, though walking with difficulty, inspected a guard of honour on the airfield. He used to say that when doing this you must not hurry, and must look each individual straight in the eye, so that he felt that you would know him. (It only once fell to me to inspect a guard of honour, at Edmonton in Canada, and I was so overwhelmed at my inappropriate stature for such an occasion that I forgot this advice.)

For me the Gibraltar arrival was marred by Théodore Garafalides, Ari's delightful and exuberant doctor brother-in-law. He greeted me Greek fashion, by sweeping me into his arms, and planting a smacking kiss on each cheek. He was six foot two; he had a fierce bristling moustache; it was in front of the Guard of Honour and the Governor; it was also in front of many cameras.

We refuelled in Grand Canary and WSC and Ari, hearing that my parents were in Tenerife, diverted the ship so that they could dine with us. Staying with them was Marshal of the RAF Sir John Salmond, a former Chief of Air Staff who had been a brother-officer of my father's before he joined the RFC in the First World War. He was also an old friend of WSC and a member of the Other Club, so it was a jolly party, enjoyed by everybody except the ship's Captain, as Tenerife harbour was thick with sludgy oil and it took many a weary day to wash it off the gleaming white hull.

We landed in Trinidad where Lord Hailes was Governor-General of the briefly enduring Federation of the West Indies. As Patrick Buchan Hepburn he had been Chief Whip during WSC's second prime ministership, and he made us very welcome. WSC did not have a total admiration for the Party Whips, though they had served him – or the Party? – loyally. At Number Ten he had asked for an opinion on a young Member, Paul Williams. Paul was an independently minded man and exactly the sort of character who, by Burke's definition, should be 'a representative, not a delegate' in Parliament. He was later a founder of the Monday Club, and was a bulwark against scuttle. However, the Whips' patronising and smug reply to the question ran: 'The boy was a good boy, but now he puts down saucy and unhelpful Questions.' WSC noted below: 'So did I.'

Somewhat unfortunately, our Trinidad visit coincided with that of the Prime Minister, Harold Macmillan, which made life a bit difficult for

Patrick. WSC had driven through the streets of Port of Spain in an open car, and received a riotous welcome, whereas Macmillan's had apparently been a good deal less enthusiastic. It may be uncharitable to ascribe it to this, but he seemed distinctly miffed at WSC's presence, though the latter lived on board the yacht, and kept out of his way.

Sadly, such pettiness was not entirely one-sided. On hearing that Macmillan would also be driving through Port of Spain, WSC had said that he would cancel his own tour. This could have been a courteous wish not to upstage the Prime Minister, but it wasn't. It was difficult to speak to WSC alone, at that moment, as he was surrounded by luncheon guests, and I have the note I hastily scribbled to him:

> WSC I do trust that you will reconsider your cancellation of this afternoon's drive round Port of Spain. It has been publicly announced, the Governor-General is to accompany you and the streets are lined with people. Cancellation would lead to rumours of a breach with the Prime Minister, or of your own ill-health and would cause endless trouble.
> I don't often urge things on you, but this is important. *Please!*
> A M B
> March 1961

(He went.)

When the present and former Prime Ministers did meet at the Governor-General's Residence, Patrick suggested that they might have a short conversation à deux. The great Actor-Manager replied: 'Must I? He hasn't anything to say.' Given his fulsome public eulogies of his former Chief, I thought he might have done rather better.

Macmillan at that time had just returned from a brief visit to President Kennedy and he told, not for the last time, of the President informing him that he had to have a woman every day or else he developed appalling headaches. 'A very strange confidence to make to a man of my age,' he commented thoughtfully.

From Trinidad we sailed northwards, stopping hither and yon as the fancy took Ari, who endeavoured to show WSC something beautiful and different in the islands. We lay for a morning off the flat island of Cariacou, alleged to be the factory and power-house for Voodoo artifacts and spells, and a malevolent something must certainly have been wandering about. The sea was extremely shallow, and to land one had to wade for some hundreds of yards from the launch. We had been warned that stone-fish abounded, particularly dangerous small creatures with a virulently poisonous spine on their backs. As I was about to reboard the launch, I stepped on a sharp something. Both the two Greek sailors manning the launch and I concluded that it was a stone-fish. They told me, with much urgent pantomime, that the only successful early treatment was to urinate on the wound. Now it is not easy to do this to the sole of your foot, and the absurd gymnastics necessary did not appeal to me any more than the sailors' kindly offers of assistance. So I sat tight until we reached *Christina*, where Théodore examined the wound anxiously and then relaxed with a roar of laughter. 'Stone-fish', he exclaimed, 'don't have square spines. Anyway, you'd have been paralysed by now.'

Anthony Eden (now Lord Avon) had a cottage on the island of Becquia close to Mustique, Princess Margaret's Caribbean resort. WSC resolved to call on him. He knew how deeply depressed and lonely he must be, in spite of his happy marriage to WSC's niece, Clarissa. Eden greeted the suggestion with enthusiasm. The younger British members of our party went to the Edens' cottage to bathe, and returned with them to lunch on the yacht. Eden took me swimming in the gentle rollers. I knew that he had looked on me as an irritant, possibly even as hostile, in his Foreign Secretary days, but you would not have realised it from his easy and agreeable manner. I had resolved to guard my too-ready tongue and in no circumstances to mention Suez, but as soon as we were afloat he took up the sad tale. For some twenty minutes he talked of that disaster, now from the trough of a wave, now from the peak. It was obsessive, but also eloquent and touching, and I wondered at those like Evelyn Shuckburgh (his Principal Private Secretary at the Foreign Office) who had first encouraged him down the dismal road of compromise and surrender, and then, when he tried so ineptly to retrieve the situation, had turned on him so viciously.

On 7 April we put into Palm Beach and anchored off the Sailfish Club. As I went onshore at the Club, an official greeted me. 'If you are Anthony Montague Browne,' he said, 'there is a telephone call for you.' Shades of Marie Galante – how could anyone know that I was at the Sailfish Club, when putting into Palm Beach had been a last-minute decision? The caller was Jack Le Vien, the television producer, in New York. Through friends in the Coast Guard he had monitored our progress and knew that the only likely anchorage at Palm Beach was off the Club. Simple enough, but impressive.

WSC had decided that he would like to visit New York, and this suited Ari, so instead of flying home from Florida we once more set sail and headed north. Then we ran into the worst weather I have ever encountered in such a small vessel. The wind rose to Force 10, gusting Force 11. The yacht plunged wildly, lying-to just off the wind. Priceless furniture was broken, bits of the deck torn up and crockery, bottles and glass flew out of their supposedly secure cupboards. Most were confined to their cabins, but after a month at sea no-one was sick. To my consternation, when attempts to play bezique on his bed-cover proved abortive, WSC announced his intention of getting up to view the storm. No-one could dissuade him. Ari provided him with a close bodyguard of four strong sailors, who accompanied him staggeringly to the after-saloon, styled the Games Room. It had never witnessed games such as these. WSC insisted on being hoisted on to the grand piano, the better to view the wild scene. It took his faithful four all their strength to keep him there and we were all on tenterhooks for the most disastrous of Humpty-Dumpty falls.

I hoped that WSC was not going to seek to take charge of events, with unforeseeable consequences. In his younger days he would have been quite capable of it. Sarah told me that in the 1930s the whole Churchill family were returning to Monte Carlo from Antibes by motor launch when the sea got up unexpectedly and the launch started to ship some water. WSC insisted on all on board cutting off their trousers, or in the women's case their expensive model beach pyjamas, at the knee to facilitate swimming, to the astonishment of the two-man crew, who recognised no danger and thought the amputations must be a bizarre British sea-ritual.

Jane, then nearly eight, put up stoically with being thrown about, only remarking faintly after a double catapulting from one bulkhead to another: 'Twice, Papa.' I thought it would cheer her up to go up to the bridge, which could be reached without going on deck. The Captain, who like most sailors in my experience was charmingly good with children, put her in his bridge chair. At that point *Christina* put her nose down into a monster wave and the bridge went dark with the depth of water passing over it. Jane stated calmly: 'I don't think I like this very much, Captain.' The sea-dog made a great effort. After all, he was a distinguished former member of the Royal Greek Navy. 'But this is what a cruise is for, Jane,' he forced out, rolling his eyes at me. 'It is great fun.'

After some seventeen hours of these fandangos, Ari took charge. 'It's no good lying-to,' he said, 'We are simply being moved along with the storm. Turn north and steam as hard as you can without running her under.' He was quite right, and in six hours we were in tolerable seas.

When we reached New York the storm had got there before us. There were nine-foot waves in the Hudson, where we anchored off 75th Street. The ferries had stopped running and there was no way we could land. Nevertheless the greeting the City gave WSC was great, with fire-boats escorting *Christina* with their hoses playing vertically, and helicopters overhead. The following night, braving the elements, some of WSC's friends came on board from police boats: Bernie Baruch, bolt upright and aquiline as ever, and Marietta Tree accompanied by Adlai Stevenson. Marietta was an enchanting American, the wife of Ronnie Tree, an heir to the Marshall Field fortune and a former British MP. They had entertained us lavishly in their white coral house in Barbados the previous year. Marietta was US Ambassador to the Human Rights Commission at UNO. She described it as 'a sort of human RSPCA, but not nearly so effective or respected'. Adlai Stevenson was a sensitive, honourable and highly intelligent man. It was easy to see why he was defeated in the US Presidential contest.

The dinner was a success, but as it progressed WSC began to show more and more clearly the accumulated damage of his years, and there were painful gaps in his memory. Towards the end of dinner I was called to take an urgent message on the telephone. The message was cryptic: 'Call Operator 17 in Washington.' This I did, and to my no small surprise found myself addressing President Kennedy. He was markedly friendly. Either he had the famous Royal memory for small-fry or else he had been exceedingly well briefed, for he spoke of our meeting in Monte Carlo. He then asked if WSC would come and spend a day or two in Washington with him. He would send the Presidential aircraft to New York to pick him up and would alter his own schedule to accommodate him.

Here was a dilemma. I had to decide at once, and I knew that if I asked WSC, he would accept immediately. It was just possible that WSC could achieve one of his tours de force and summon up the energy to carry off the occasion. But it was highly unlikely, and he had not kept sufficiently up-to-date with world events to sustain a serious high-level conversation. The thought of America, and indeed the world, seeing him at his worst was not endurable. So I took it on myself to decline the invitation without further reference. I explained the reasons briefly to the President. His charm was legendary and it was very evident in what he said. 'I understand your reasons, and I feared that this would be the case. Please give him my warmest and most admiring good wishes. And I think your decision does you credit.' I was moved. I only told WSC of the good wishes at that time, but later, with great trepidation, I gave him the gist of the whole conversation. To my surprise he took it totally calmly, and sent a cable to the President thanking him for his thought.

At the end of dinner, Adlai Stevenson proposed WSC's health with the words: 'To the man who was the world's conscience and the saviour of our freedom.'

During our enforced weather-bound stay, Bernie Baruch had arranged for Nonie and Jane to be taken on a tour of the city in a police-car, with the siren going, and then to go up the Empire State Building, while I spent some hours wrestling with WSC's unwillingness to make a decision on departure. We were first booked on an Australian Qantas flight, but then WSC decided that it left too early and we transferred to a later Pan-American aircraft. This earned me a shrill letter of rebuke from Qantas when we reached home. It had never occurred to me that airline flights could be thus politicised, particularly as WSC was half-American in any case.

Chapter 28

I T W O U L D be wearisome to recount all the eight cruises, though to the participants they were both enjoyable and memorable. For WSC there was something of the law of diminishing returns. The cruises were as well organised, as luxurious and as colourful and varied as ever, but his own capacity for enjoyment was lessening. He, who had seemed for so long to defy age and ill-health, first fully and then spasmodically, was now suffering longer and longer periods of apathy, withdrawal, boredom and dwindling physical and mental activity. But he still looked forward to the yacht and was capable of writing letters saying that he was going abroad 'for some sun and fun'.

This took us in July 1960 to Venice. *Christina* was moored at the old Customs House, at the mouth of the Grand Canal and looking straight on to St Mark's Square. While most of the party went gondoliering, CSC asked me to accompany her to tea with Prince Clary, an old Austro-Hungarian Empire friend. He and his wife lived in a quiet palazzo about a half a mile up the Canale Della Giudecca, and the walk up the deserted quayside was Venice at its best, the area attracting no tourists.

On the front door was an enormous bronze knocker: dolphins, cherubs, suns and I know not what. I was fascinated. Our host, tall, slim, charming, looking exactly as he ancestrally should, explained that it was a Cellini or something of equal merit.

'How could you leave it on your front door?' I asked. 'Are the Venetians so very honest?'

'Far from it,' he smiled, 'but it weighs an awful lot and the oak of the door is as hard as iron. It would take a great deal of noise and tools to get it off, and my neighbours are very kind. Anyway it would be unmarketable, and most people think it is a fake.' A good philosophy, but would it stand up nowadays? At tea our hosts and CSC exchanged reminiscences. 'Do tell Anthony about your dance-floor misadventure,' she said. Prince Clary told us that in his youth he had been an excellent waltzer, which it was easy to believe. At a ball at the pre-1914 Imperial Court in Vienna, he had been allowed to dance with a young and beautiful kinswoman of the Emperor. Revolving round and round in his magnificent uniform, he had lost his footing on the slippery dance floor and had brought his partner down with a crash. Still spinning, they had scythed their way through the dancers to end up at the Emperor's feet. He was deeply affronted, and Clary was only saved from some terrible Viennese fate, such as being banned from Court, by the intervention of his numerous *hochgeboren* family.

Among our fellow guests for the cruise were Margot Fonteyn and her husband Tito. WSC fell for Margot; indeed it was impossible not to do so. She and Tito led lives that separated them for long periods, but there is no doubt that they loved each other and when he suffered the appalling gunshot wounds that crippled him and severed his vocal cords, she looked after him with devotion.

WSC had been invited to call on Marshal Tito of Yugoslavia during the cruise, and to avoid confusion Ari had dubbed the Panamanian Tito Arias 'Tito Tropicalis'. As I passed their cabin, Tito (Trop.) threw open the door, and lying on the bed was the lissom and totally nude Margot. Neither was disconcerted. Margot giggled and Tito said: 'Anthony, don't you think that our girl sometimes looks like wet sea-weed?' No, I didn't.

Tito Arias's friendship did have certain disadvantages. His politics were favourable to Fidel Castro, of whom WSC disapproved vehemently, not out of sympathy with the regime he had displaced, but because of the cruelty of his purges of his own people, and because of the potential incendiary possibilities of his influence on Soviet–American relations. Back in London Tito presented him with a huge cabinet of the finest Havana cigars, a gift from Castro. WSC sent them back without hesitation, but he did rather mourn over the loss. 'Some of them were nine, and even twelve years old,' he said sadly. I asked him the difference between these and younger cigars. 'They are, er, more majestic,' he concluded.

Tito (Arias) got into severe trouble by his association with left-wing, even revolutionary politics, and a disagreeable body known as the 'Caribbean Legion'. He was rounded up absurdly when a shrimp-boat carrying arms ran aground, and all concerned were captured. Ari reflected: 'Anthony, Tito is a fool. If his cause was just, which it wasn't but he thought it was, he could have had advice from the Boss [WSC], the greatest statesman on Earth, from me on finance, and perhaps from you, who are quite smart.' Tito's downfall in Panama was swift. At one point he took refuge in the Brazilian Embassy. During dinner there was a violent outcry outside. The Ambassador requested his butler to find out what the mob wanted. He returned to say:

'Excellency, they want Dr Arias's head.'

Tito replied: 'Please tell them they can't have it. It is engaged eating.'

The mob's rejoinder before dispersing was the message: 'Please tell Dr Arias that he is cynical.' These pleasantries did not, however, stop his opponents from shooting and maiming him. It would perhaps have been better if he had been killed outright.

To return to the Adriatic: cruising silently down the moonlit coast of Yugoslavia, Ari pronounced himself bored. He gazed at the dark hilly coast. Suddenly his eyes lit up: 'Look at that!' Up on the mountainside, a row of fairy lights showed, and music could be faintly heard. 'A night-club,' said Ari joyfully, 'we will visit it.' I reflected that a Greek is a man who uses a night-club as a Club, and reluctantly followed him, first on a launch to a rocky, but fortunately calm shore, then up a woodland path to what was indeed a jolly little night-club. Their astonishment at the invaders from the sea was picturesque but they soon recovered and slivovitz (plum brandy) flowed. Margot said:

'Dance with me, Anthony.'

'Margot, you know I can't dance with anybody, let alone you.'

'Anyone can dance with me.' So, feeling as foolish as I looked, I took the floor. After two circuits Margot said sadly: 'Well, I was wrong.'

After an exchange of messages via our Embassy in Belgrade, Marshal Tito invited WSC to call on him in his sea-coast villa near Split. Timing was tricky for nautical and Presidential engagement reasons, and we couldn't make lunch. Ari did not propose to join the landing party, but WSC insisted, quite rightly assuming that Tito would be interested to meet a fellow yachtsman, as he put it (Tito had a converted Liberty ship of some 10,000 tons). So our party consisted of WSC, CSC, Ari, Nonie and self. We were entertained to a most extraordinary high tea, with caviar, wild boar pies, sweet cakes, slivovitz and cigars.

It was a howling success. Tito's English was unexpectedly fluent and he was in the jolliest of moods. The conversation was mainly reminiscent of our wartime support of the Yugoslav resistance, but suddenly WSC, just as we were leaving, performed one of his astonishing feats of revival, and spoke solemnly of Tito's audacious breakaway from the Soviet bloc. Tito listened intently and replied in no less serious terms of the balancing act he was seeking to perform and the internal opposition he was encountering. Nothing was said of the horrors of 1945, now publicised and deriving from our shameful forcible repatriation of the dissidents.

Tito told a number of risqué stories, choking with laughter, and, as always brashly conversationally competitive, I reciprocated. As we returned to the launch, *Christina* lying about a mile offshore, Tito took me to see his swimming place, a beautiful and deep cove with the underwater lights of the Blue Grotto of Capri. There was a steel mesh net across the entrance. 'Sharks?' I enquired. 'Albanian sharks,' Tito replied. ·

That evening Tito, his wife and six 'Generals', actually his bodyguard, came out to the yacht for a buffet supper. Clément excelled himself, and lobsters, foie gras, chaud-froids, cold truffled scrambled eggs, bisque, brandy-snaps and much else covered the tables. The wines were of the same standard. Once out of their large naval launch, the 'Generals' advanced in what I think is called a flying-wedge, covering Tito from hostile fire. Madame walked behind. She was a striking figure, deeply tanned, raven hair, dazzling teeth, flashing eyes – and rippling muscles. One of the Generals had knocked back about six normal men's ration of drink, but was still vertical and coherent.

'What do you think of our Madame Presidente?' he hiccuped.

'Magnificent,' I replied with total sincerity.

'And would you feel, um, err, comfortable with her?'

Incautiously I spoke the truth. 'Well, she's the sort of girl who if she told me to get out and the door was locked, then I would leave through the window.'

Peals of Serbo-Croat laughter. 'I will tell our Madame Presidente what you say.'

'For God's sake don't do that,' I gasped. 'Don't spoil a jolly party.' In vain. My friend lurched over to the sofa, where the Marshal and Madame sat, and addressed them in inaudible Slobodian. To my great relief there was much merriment. Tito beckoned to me and said: 'You are right. I sometimes feel like that myself.'

When I got back to England, I received an autographed photograph of the occasion. When my wife and I went to Yugoslavia for a holiday, I took the photograph because I thought that in a dictatorship it would ensure an amiable reception. I couldn't have been more mistaken. When we stayed at the St Michael's Mount-style peninsula of Sveti Stefan, I put the photograph on my dressing-table, expecting superb service. Unfortunately Tito was deeply unpopular in that area, and the locals practically spat in my soup.

Christina threaded her way through the Corinth Canal to Athens, Crete, Rhodes, Lesbos, Skiathos, Hydra and Khalkis, where the philosopher is said to have drowned himself because he couldn't work out the reason for the ten-knot current, and Athens again, whence we flew home by Comet.

In April 1962 we were again at sea, sailing from Monte Carlo to Libya, via Sicily. In Tripoli, I received a message from our Embassy. King Idris of the Senussi, in the pre-Gaddafi days the benevolent but ineffectual ruler of the country, wanted to see Winston Churchill to express his thanks to him personally for the liberation of Libya from the Italians. The King was at his palace in the desert south of Tobruk, and he proposed to come to Benghazi if *Christina* would put in there. WSC decided that it would be far more correct for him to go to the King. The Embassy despatched Derek Riches, an able and imperturbable figure and a first-class Arabist, to meet us at Tobruk and interpret at the meeting.

Sailing between Tripoli and Tobruk I had my one and only row with Ari. He told me that he proposed to alter course for Crete, infinitely cooler and more beautiful than Tobruk, which should be avoided. I said that it was out of the question so to snub King Idris, not to speak of Derek Riches who was hurtling uncomfortably across the desert to assist us. Ari persisted, saying irritably: 'Anthony, you have no imagination. Crete will be much more fun for the Boss. And that is what the cruise is for.' The argument risked becoming acrimonious, so I finally told my host, of whom I was genuinely fond, that I would have formally to advise WSC to leave the ship at the next port if he was prevented from carrying out a useful duty in a politically sensitive area. Ari capitulated with grace and charm, and I did not mention the incident to WSC, but it did cause me to reflect on the capriciousness that seems to affect all tycoons, and indeed would-be tycoons: their belief that they are entitled to change their minds without regard for the inconvenience, or in this case worse, of others.

At dinner that night WSC asked the rather pensive Ari what he looked on as the greatest advantage that massive wealth could bestow on the individual personally. Ari replied without hesitation: 'Being able to go wherever you wish without consultation and above all without packing. I have five or six sets of all my clothes and things, and they are located in Monte Carlo, Athens, Paris, London, New York, Rome or wherever. I can just climb into an aircraft and go.' Yes, especially if you control Olympic Airways.

Arrived at the admittedly dreary port of Tobruk, WSC, Riches, Ari and I set forth in Royal limousines across the desert, formally and climatically unsuitably clad. We ran late. There had been a brief but heavy rainfall, and the desert had indeed blossomed like a rose, with a bewitching patchwork of wild flowers. WSC insisted on stopping to examine them. The palace, a former Italian military hospital, I believe, was surrounded by clucking hens and guarded by a barefooted sentry with a rusty Lee Enfield. The interior was rather like what I supposed a Russian grand bourgeois' house would have looked like in pre-Revolution days, with plush gilt chairs, knick-knacks galore and even a giant samovar. But the King himself had the dignity and charm traditionally ascribed to the desert aristocrat. The poor chap had had mumps very severely in his early youth, and in consequence his voice was high-pitched and he was incapable of begetting children, a very serious handicap in the Arab world particularly. His wife was Algerian, not veiled and speaking excellent French, and they had adopted two pretty little Algerian orphan girls.

The heat was intense, the conversation stilted and we were given a thick and not very cold mango concoction to drink. Definitely not WSC's scene; but he rose nobly to the occasion and the King did come across as simple and genuinely grateful to Britain. WSC was presented with a very flashy Order. I was informed that the King had proposed that I should have a lesser one, but our Embassy, totally correctly, had said that I would not be allowed to accept it. The tradition of the British Diplomatic Service of generally not accepting foreign decorations goes back to Queen Elizabeth I. She had sent two Ambassadors to Spain, and when they returned they were wearing the impressive heavy gold Order of the Golden Fleece. Probably coveting the gold as much as for any other motive, the Queen exclaimed: 'My dogs shall wear no collars but mine!' and took the necklaces from the crestfallen pair.

As we drove back to Tobruk, Sergeant Murray, who invariably accompanied WSC, showed considerable initiative. He produced glasses, whisky, ice and soda water, and there was a most grateful pause.

Leaving Tobruk we did indeed go to Crete, and the following night drove up the mountain on abominable roads to dine al fresco with Venizelos, son of the former Prime Minister. He had laid on a carefully thought-out evening in a mountain village, with local dancers and singing. The food was simple and very good, the wine local, rough but suitable and the attitude of the Cretans to WSC admirable. Sadly he did not enjoy either the temperature, the dancing, the wine or the food. It was a shame. They had tried so hard. The rest of us did our best, but WSC was sunken and only wanted to return to the yacht. I realised regretfully that it was more and more a mistake to try, or let others try, to arrange entertainment for him. He preferred just to sit in the sun, to play cards and be among easy friends. Among them on this cruise were the historian Bill Deakin and his Roumanian wife Pussy. Bill had helped WSC with his books before the War and had been a gallant wartime SOE officer, preceding Fitzroy Maclean in a mission to Yugoslavia. He had parachuted in with the task of deciding whether our assistance should be directed to Mihailovic or Tito, a hideously difficult assignment which he had carried out with integrity and credit. It was a situation in which no decision could be totally right. WSC held Bill and Pussy in high regard and affection.

Heading for Beirut, there was a happy incident that cheered up WSC. A cruel north wind was blowing, and heading into it were hundreds of migrant birds, mostly wagtails and golden orioles. The pathetic travellers were exhausted, flying at wave-top height, and countless numbers must have fallen. The yacht slowed down to give them a much needed staging point, and soon the decks were alive with the small creatures, so exhausted that one could pick them up in one's hand. Bread-crumbs, suet, and seed from the former ship's parrot's store were produced, and many saucers of water. The birds' first act was to bathe in the saucers, before they even drank, presumably to get the salt off their wings. WSC was enchanted by them and they sat all round his chair or the deck, as though he were St Francis. We altered course to pass close to Cyprus, and the following day the birds took off as soon as land was sighted. If they escaped the vile practice of the islanders of catching small birds with bird-lime, they would have had an easy passage to Turkey, only forty miles of sea from Cyprus.

The idyllic scene was marred by a hawk. He, also a migrant, had sat on the masthead until, hungry, he had most naturally swooped down and eaten a wagtail. The Greeks are generally very far from behaving acceptably to animals, but the sailors were outraged. They captured the miscreant and confined him, feeding him on chicken, until the little birds had a head start, when he too left the ship.

Beirut was not much more of a success than Crete. Our Ambassador, my one-time chief in the Western Department of the Foreign Office, was Sir Moore Crosthwaite, still a bachelor and now somewhat prim and dried up. He had arranged an elaborate picnic at Baalbek among the ruins of Nero's stupendous temple of Jupiter. We all enjoyed it – except the Principal Guest.

In the evening Moore Crosthwaite and various Lebanese dignitaries came to dine. Moore arrived first. It was a hot evening and he naturally wanted a drink. I was drinking a concoction of Ari's barman called a 'Flier'. It consisted of a very large Daiquiri cocktail in a silver tankard, topped up with champagne. It tasted delicious, and gentle too, but that it was most certainly not. Moore opted for one, and then for another. I thought that I knew him well enough to warn him, but he was affronted: 'My dear Anthony, please let me assure you that at my age and with my somewhat ascetic habits I know enough not to get drunk.' Well, undoubtedly the dessicated albeit charming Ambassador was right, but he hadn't experienced a pint of Fliers on a hot evening. I watched with anxious sympathy his efforts to subdue events, and to my immense admiration by halfway through dinner he was back in the conversation and making total sense. But he had had to forgo some really memorable wines.

On our way home to London, I reflected that this must be the last cruise. WSC could surely not want another. There was another reason too. I wondered if Ari was getting a little weary of the long absences that entertaining WSC involved. He had on occasion left *Christina* for varying periods, leaving his host's duties to Théodore Garafalides, but admirable and dutiful man that Théodore was, neither his English nor his background of interests made him an adequate substitute, and WSC missed Ari's vital presence. Indeed, Ari had once said of his brother-in-law: 'Consider Théodore. I love him. Anyone who knows him likes him and trusts him and his patients adore him. But medicine and shooting apart he is a child.' His absences were indeed necessary for business reasons, but he also told me that the long periods without female company were very trying 'for a Greek' and he could not be accompanied by a mistress. He actually said quite a lot about his compatriots, not by any means always flattering.

'Anthony, do you know why there are so few Jews in Greece?'

'No.'

'For the same reason that you don't find sharks in crocodile water.'

A long cruise exhausts friendships faster than anything. I don't mean shipboard quarrels; apart from the eighth and last cruise there were none of these. But close and enforced propinquity sucks intellectual and social intercourse dry.

> *Dinner on board*
>
> Suspended on the tinkling glass,
> The conversational bubble floats.
> The empty tropic seas that pass
> Drown empty intellectual boats
> And fill the ever empty day
> And we have nothing left to say.
>
> And though the changing ocean rolls
> In splendour to the changing sky,
> Unmagnetised our listless Poles
> Of aging flesh and avid eye
> So chart our commonplace decay.
> And we have nothing left to say.
>
> Consigned by smoking lanes of spray
> To ossuaries of turbid dark,
> And sank in bubbling disarray
> Our over-burdened, empty ark,
> Condemned to aqueous silence we
> Shall neither say, nor think, nor be.

Yes, I know that it is not very good, but it does represent the way I ungratefully felt.

My own relations with Ari were usually good, and remained so long after WSC's death. I had known him before his meeting with the Boss and enjoyed his company. He had not sought access to my master through me. I sought nothing from him, and I think that vastly rich men do appreciate that. But tycoons move on. Even the company of WSC became a norm, conducted with affectionate courtesy, but no longer with the fascination, amounting almost to reverence, of the great living monument.

Rather to my surprise, CSC was not disturbed by the changing atmosphere. She did not always want to accompany her husband, and she enjoyed the rest that the cruises gave her, knowing that he was well looked after, in the company of friends and cocooned in the luxuries he still enjoyed. Her own vitality ebbed more than it flowed. One morning I had found her gazing into a mirror with an expression of great sadness. I was concerned, and asked her why this all-too-visible melancholy. She said: 'Anthony dear, it is so sad to see Winston's boredom and progressive decline. And, as for myself, I am so tired. In old age you make more and more efforts to look and behave appropriately, with less and less result.' She then gave a chuckle: 'It reminds me of an incident I was told recently.'

Randolph had apparently gone to see Diana Cooper (widow of Duff Cooper and one of the great beauties of her age). He found her sitting in front of her dressing table, weeping bitterly. Randolph was genuinely fond of her:

'Diana, darling, whatever is the matter?' he asked.

'Randolph, I'm getting so old,' sobbed Diana.

'Well, it's not going to get any better,' was Randolph's practical but not altogether comforting reply.

I was surprised when in 1963 WSC accepted Ari's invitation and left on 8 June on the last and the least fortunate cruise. The guest list was partly ours and partly our host's. I had suggested Jock and Meg Colville, both because WSC enjoyed their company and because Jock had long hoped to be invited. Young Winston came, and finally, after a tussle, WSC was persuaded to include Randolph. The latter had after all introduced Ari to WSC and had maintained a dignified silence over the successive failures to take him. On his side Ari had invited Prince and Princess Radziwill. 'Stash' Radziwill was rather a jolly, stout Polish exile, and his wife Lee was Jacqueline Kennedy's sister. She had a striking, high-cheek-boned, almost Red Indian face, but didn't have much to say. Stash later did some rather successful property deals, with Ari's support.

At first all went well, and I was amused by an example of Ari's cavalier way of doing business. We were three days out of Monte Carlo when I asked Ari, who was in the pool, for some writing paper. 'In that drawer,' he said. On top of it was an unopened letter marked 'By messenger. Most Immediate. Urgent.' I showed it to Ari: 'Be kind and read it to me,' he said, 'I'm all wet.' It was from Lord Douglas, the Chairman of British European Airways, with whom Ari's Olympic Airways had a consortium. It ran approximately:

'Dear Ari, I hope that we shall always be friends, but your unbusiness-like methods are making it impossible for our consortium to continue. Unless you reply by immediate telex or telephone etc., etc.' It was dated six days previously.

Ari was not particularly disconcerted: 'Oh dear, we shall have to send him a little cable. Anthony, you're a diplomat. You help me write it.'

Later things started to slide. We stopped briefly off Elba, where Nonie and I had passed holidays, and dropped the Colvilles off in Sardinia. Jock and Meg had got on well with their host, and given pleasure to WSC. Thence we proceeded to Stromboli in the Volcano Islands. Its own volcano is in perpetual minor eruption, with incandescent rocks popping up and down out of its crater like ping-pong balls at a shooting gallery. It was spectacular, especially at dusk, but as we reached it silence fell and the volcano was dark and dull. 'Come on, Volcano, show your paces!' Ari shouted indignantly, giving a tug on *Christina*'s siren control. There was a piercing wail, clouds of soot rained down on us from the funnel and dead on cue Stromboli, refreshed by its rest, erupted with a roar and a dazzling pyrotechnic display. Ari fell back, muttering in Greek. 'I don't like that omen,' he explained.

After we passed the Straits of Messina, heading up the Adriatic, the cruise really came apart. Randolph had hitherto behaved well, treating his father with respect and affection, and I was congratulating myself on having pushed for his inclusion. Alas, it was premature. 'Mai sans nuages, et Juin – poignardé.' Suddenly at dinner he erupted like Stromboli. For no apparent reason his rage was directed at his father, but then he began to particularise with violent reproaches relating to his wartime marriage. What he said was unseemly in any circumstances, but in front of comparative strangers it was ghastly. Nonie intervened with great courage, but Randolph, who was fond of her and normally treated her with regard, swept her aside as 'a gabby doll' – the mildest of his remarks that evening. I was equally unsuccessful in trying to divert his abuse from his father. Short of hitting him on the head with a bottle, nothing could have stopped him. Ari did his best, but was ignored. It was one of the most painful scenes I have ever witnessed. I had previously discounted the tales I had heard of Randolph. Now I believed them all.

WSC made no reply at all, but stared at his son with an expression of brooding rage. Then he went to his cabin. I followed him and found him shaking all over. I feared that he would suffer another stroke, and sat drinking whisky and soda with him until he was calmer. I will not record what he said, but it was plain that means must be found to remove Randolph from the ship.

I sought out Ari, who was quite extraordinarily upset. 'But how could we have prevented it?' he said repeatedly. He had already reached the same conclusion as me, and was a jump ahead. Randolph was writing for, I think, the *News of the World*. Ari telephoned the King of Greece's Royal Chamberlain and arranged for either the King or Queen Frederika, who was a controversial figure in Britain at the time, to give Randolph an exclusive interview at their palace on the eastern Greek mainland. The next morning a cable of invitation was received. Randolph was pleased and flattered, but how was he to get there in time? Ari said that we would put into Corfu that evening and an Olympic Airways aircraft would fly Randolph to Athens. After a harmonious but rather silent dinner Randolph departed, humming 'Get me to the

Church on time'. I accompanied him in the launch to the harbour. After a while he fell silent, and I saw that he was weeping.

'Anthony,' he said, 'you didn't think that I was taken in by that plan of Ari's and yours, do you? I do so very much love that man [WSC], but something always goes wrong between us.' I could only hope that there would be enough time left for Randolph to demonstrate his love, and WSC his.

Our next stops were the islands of Skorpios and Ithaca, both in the Aeolian Sea. The former was Ari's private property, wild and beautiful with only a little chapel on it. He was planning to build a villa there, which he ultimately did, and indeed married Jacqueline Kennedy on the island. Both he and his son Alexander now lie buried there.

Not all private islands could have been so agreeable. I once met a Greek ship-owner who invited me to stay on his island. 'It is a very happy island,' he claimed, 'all the peasants smile. If I see one who does not smile, I say to him "Go! You go today."' I reflected what a terrible place it must be, with everyone going about with compulsory strychnine grins on their faces. Another private island had been stocked with game by the owner. The birds and beasts apparently didn't like the place, or possibly the owner, and they all took off, flying or swimming, for the nearby mainland. A stag had caused a panic by turning up in a small village by moonlight. The villagers had never seen such an animal and concluded that it must be the Devil.

Ithaca, Odysseus' home, was where Ari recruited the men for his fleet. He told me that it was common practice to take as many men as you could from one island, first because they would know each other and be less lonely, and secondly so that the wives could keep an eye on each other while their husbands were away.

That afternoon we drove up to the windy peak of the island, crowned with a miniature monastery. Its sole inhabitants were an old white-bearded monk and his wife. Ari had given the monastery a diesel generator and obviously liked the old monk, with whom he exchanged a store of apparently ribald jokes. One of them went wrong. The patriarch was taking me up some steep steps to the monastery roof, where the view was spectacular. Ari called out something in Greek, at which the venerable figure uttered an expletive, raced down the steps like a lamplighter and attacked him. Ari was laughing so much that he could hardly defend himself.

'What was all that about?' I asked.

Gasping, Ari said: 'I shouted to you in Greek to watch out if you went up the stairs in front of that dirty old man.'

Passing through the Corinth Canal, we went on to the island of Milos, home of the Louvre Venus, the reason for our detour being that Théodore claimed that the best yogurt in the world came from that island, and eaten with the equally outstanding Milos honey, it did wonders that rhino horn could not rival. (Poor old rhinos! The mischief that absurd legend has caused. And why should the Chinese want aphrodisiacs? There are enough of them anyway.) Whatever the properties of the yogurt, it was absolutely delicious, with a faint flavour of coconut and lemon. It was brought on board as a gift, in little fig-leaf boxes. The bearer told us that *Christina* was lying at just about the place where the unfortunate Venus of Milo had met with her amputation: a caique was bringing her out to the steamer that was to take her to France when a sling slipped and she crashed into the caique, her arms breaking off and disappearing into the vast submarine volcanic crater that forms the anchorage. I have not been able to verify the story.

The cruise ended at Glyfada, just outside Athens. There was a lunch party near the great temple of Neptune at Sunion, and I was saddened but not particularly surprised to find that Byron had vandalistically carved his name on one of the pillars. Byron, with all his genius, was a howling cad.

That evening we all went to dine at a waterside restaurant. At a very large table were officers from a British Naval squadron, including an aircraft carrier, there on a 'showing the flag' visit. An officer came over and asked me to have a drink with them. It occurred to me that both from the showing-the-flag-aspect and as what might be considered an appropriate courtesy to a twice First Lord of the Admiralty and twice Prime Minister, the carrier might give a fly-past. I raised the point with my table neighbour, who was enthusiastic, so, having acquitted the correct protocol, I suggested it to the Admiral. His lip curled: 'Oh, all right,' he said, 'we'll give the poor old man a fly-past if that's what he wants.' I withdrew both the suggestion and myself from the table. I can only assume that WSC had stepped on the Great Man's toes at some point in his career.

And on this rather melancholy note ended not only the cruise, but all the cruises. I have dwelt on them at perhaps excessive length, but they were a substantial part of WSC's post-retirement life and brought him sun and happiness, and a rest for CSC – just as the stays at La Pausa had done. Moreover, though most parts of Churchill's life have been raked over and discussed both accurately and fancifully, I do not think that the cruises have ever been described in any detail.

It had been WSC's hope to take up Ari's offer of a cruise starting in the Pool of London, visiting the northern fjords of Norway and the midnight sun in the month of June, and then sailing to Leningrad via the Swedish inland waterway if *Christina*'s draught allowed it. Tentative soundings had been taken of the Russians, who were warmly welcoming. But in May 1960 the shooting-down of an American U2 high-altitude reconnaissance aircraft by the Russians had caused the break-up of the Summit meeting in Paris, and it was then clearly impossible to pursue the plan. A member of the Soviet Embassy expressed his Government's private regrets, and hoped that there would be another opportunity, but it was not to be, and I think on the whole that it was better that way.

Chapter 29

———— ❧ ————

DURING THE ten years of WSC's retirement events in his life worthy of historical record inevitably became fewer. Suez and its aftermath, the collapse of Anthony Eden, WSC's attempts to restore Anglo-American relations, his seeking for a rapprochement with Russia, and his increasingly rare speeches and messages on national matters were the exceptions. The reasons for this diminuendo are straightforward. His own health, though erratically resurgent, often to his doctor's surprise, was gradually deteriorating, and he was sadly aware that he had neither the mental muscle, the memory nor the energy to take up any sustained theme. But beside these decisive difficulties lay also his own profound melancholy at Britain's decline and the stormy and forbidding international outlook. This was not the 'Black Dog' of which many of WSC's biographers have written, which in thirteen years I never heard him mention and which allegedly was a subjective mood of deep depression, having little to do with outside events. It was an objective, detached and sadly logical reaction.

Prescience had always been one of his outstanding gifts. Violet Bonham Carter said: 'Demons seem to whisper things to him.' And as he himself has said: 'I have not always been wrong.' I often pondered on the reasons for this remarkable trait, which had served him, and our country so well. It certainly arose from decades of experience of public affairs, from an extraordinarily powerful knowledge and understanding of history and from an equally extraordinary flair for divining national reactions to events. But there was more than this and what it was I have never been able to define.

Be that as it may, this gift was of no comfort to him in his old age, and he saw with dismaying clarity the future course of the breakdown of our will to rule and its consequences. After a very silent dinner alone with him, I tried to rally his spirits. How could he be so melancholy when he considered his extraordinary career, the devotion that he inspired in his fellow countrymen (and of course in his family and friends), and his unchallengeable place in history? And on top of this he was revered in so many countries other than our own. Why, even in Germany only eleven years after the end of the War, he had been cheered in the streets of Bonn. And then there was the Nobel Prize for Literature, his painting and so much else. I did my best, and it was not difficult to be passably eloquent, because it was all true.

True, but in vain. WSC reflected and answered heavily: 'What you say is historically correct. I have worked very hard all my life, and I have achieved a great deal – in the end to achieve NOTHING,' the last word falling with sombre emphasis. And since his greatest aspirations were for a powerful British Empire and Commonwealth in a peaceful world, what he said was, by his own definition, also historically correct. I felt that I could not leave it there. Would not the world be a much worse place if we had not won the War? Without his Iron Curtain speech and the part he and like-minded men had played in building the dykes against the Communist flood, would not large parts of the globe be in an even worse state? And so on. WSC paused for quite a long time, shrugged his shoulders and replied only, 'Perhaps.'

In spite of this accidie, or at least against its general background, WSC's calendar was rarely blank, and his comments on affairs were still capable of deep insight and trenchant wit. Visitors still flocked to see him, some with genuine motives of reverence and personal friendship.

Early in WSC's retirement, the Foreign Office rang to say that Harold Macmillan, then Foreign Secretary, attached great importance to WSC receiving the Burmese Prime Minister, U Nu, who had expressed a wish to visit him. WSC was recalcitrant, and it was one of my few attempts to persuade him to do something he did not want to do. The meeting took place, first at the House of Commons and then at Hyde Park Gate. As we were leaving the House, a battery of photographers requested – yes, in those days they did request – a pose. As WSC and the Burmese stood, a figure appeared from inside the House and stood behind them. It was Desmond Donnelly, a Labour Member. As we got into the car, he took me by the shoulder: 'I know you didn't like what I did,' he said engagingly, 'but my constituents do like to see their Member with the Great.' At Hyde Park Gate little of consequence was said. WSC was not very warmly disposed to his guest, who had been imprisoned by us for subversion in 1940, but was intrigued by his confiding that he had been an alcoholic at the age of six. 'A very serious reflection on his parents' views on upbringing,' said WSC later, ' but he had a face like a celestial baby's bottom.'

To jump ahead, Desmond Donnelly became a true friend. He was that rare animal (even rarer on the Labour benches), a patriot, and he had undertaken at some personal danger, career-danger if not physical, a number of useful tasks while on his parliamentary travels abroad. He became more and more disillusioned with the Labour Party, and in 1970 he stood as an Independent in his former constituency of Tenby, in Wales. Here he made a mistake. He should have crossed the floor and joined the Conservatives, and they in turn made a bigger mistake by running a Conservative candidate instead of sup-porting Desmond, whose views embodied those of a sensible middle-of-the-road Conservative, and who would have won Tenby, for he was locally popular.

At his request I went down to speak for him. I was heckled in Welsh, which rather surprised me, for Pembrokeshire is known for its pure English. After a while it also irritated me, and I addressed the heckler: 'Sir, if you would mind addressing me in some known human language . . .' A look of pain crossed Desmond's face, but he took it stoically in spite of losing the seat, and wrote to me:

I am writing to thank you most warmly for your telegram – and I do want you to know how very grateful I am to you for your courage in coming here and standing on my platform. The warmth of your friendship means very much to me.

The truth is that without the television in this day it is practically impossible, and I felt the election slide away in the last week.

Thereafter I received an insolent rebuke from the Conservative Central Office for my intervention. I replied suitably, adding that if they managed to move away from gutless and foolish policies I would speak for them too (and probably lose them seats?). Desmond's end was tragic. Things went badly for him, financially, politically and personally, and one day he checked into an airport hotel and took his life. We none of us knew of his desperation: his dignity did not allow of his showing it.

A most agreeable visitor was Ayub Khan, President of Pakistan. He telephoned personally to say that he wanted to pay his respects during the Commonwealth Prime Ministers' meeting of 1958, and when WSC had replied that it was more fitting for him, as a retired Prime Minister, to call on the President, he had brushed protocol aside and insisted on coming to Hyde Park Gate. Nevertheless WSC was late for the appointment on his return from his afternoon visit to the House of Commons, and it was left to me to greet the President. He was the most unpompous Head of State one could imagine. He arrived alone, and when I offered him some fresh orange juice on that warm afternoon, he replied thus: 'As the Head of a Moslem State that is what I should drink. But as a former British officer I would like a whisky and soda.' This he got.

Our conversation ran something like this:

> AK: 'Have you ever met Nehru?'
> AMB: 'Yes, several times.'
> AK: 'The trouble with that fellow is that he's never been shot over.'

If one had closed one's eyes, one might have been in an old-fashioned (British) Indian Army Mess. The President added thoughtfully: 'People believe that Nehru is thinking deeply. He isn't. He's in a trance.' At this point WSC arrived and the conversation proceeded with greater formality. When the President had left, WSC said: 'I do like that man. He's just the sort of figure they need. We've always got on best with the martial races. What a sad waste...'

In 1961 the Prime Minister of Israel, David Ben-Gurion, called on WSC. It was a visit of more significance than most at that time, as Ben-Gurion took the opportunity to give his succinct views on the Middle Eastern situation, obviously intending them to be passed on to the Prime Minister. Egypt, he said, was preparing for war and had more and better (Russian-supplied) aircraft than Israel as well as Russian instructors. The future of Jordan depended on the survival of one brave man: the King. And Iraq 'would probably be able to deal with any internal disruption by the Communists'. All this I duly reported to the Foreign Office.

WSC replied by describing his grief and anger at the murderous activities of the Irgun and Stern Gang directed against the British forces and civilians, 'the Jewish people's saviours'. But, he said, nothing would alter his own abiding faith in the Jewish people. And the conversation left politics and became more animated. Ben-Gurion referred to WSC's essay on Moses. It is curious how that rather undistinguished example of his literary work kept bobbing up. This time I avoided my previous lapse with Cecil B. de Mille and in due course sent Ben-Gurion a copy of the book with a deprecatory note from the author. 'Why', he said to me, 'will people keep referring to that bloody pot-boiler?'

One incident jarred the harmony. The visit was to have been quiet and private, only WSC, Ben-Gurion, the amiable Israeli Ambassador and myself being present. But with the security guards who accompanied Ben-Gurion a couple of hangers-on had come to the house, to be segregated in another room with suitable refreshment. One of them produced an outsize camera and attempted to force his way into the room where the meeting took place. I pushed the door shut on him, and unfortunately trapped his fingers (with excessively dirty nails). There was an agonised outcry; judging by Ben-Gurion's expression, I felt sorry for the would-be photographer when he got home.

I don't know whether it was as a result of this meeting, but not long afterwards Sir Isaac Wolfson invited me to join a party he was flying out to Israel in the new Britannia prop-jet aircraft 'to see the new Israel.' WSC encouraged me to go; I wanted to go; but the Foreign Office did not approve on the grounds that the acceptance of such hospitality might be considered prejudicial to impartial views.

Some of the Chartwell visitors were distinctly odd. A venerable German brewer from Tübingen, who also was the generous patron of the city's university, wrote a polite and diffident letter asking for ten minutes with WSC. He said that WSC and Monty, in that order, had obtained a supply of penicillin for his city when an epidemic was threatening its children in 1945. He wanted to express his gratitude. WSC, in an expansive mood, gave him rendezvous at Chartwell. When he arrived, he was accompanied by two young Americans, whom he had picked up en route. They were missionaries of the Church of Jesus Christ of Latter-Day Saints, i.e. Mormons, and were somewhat dazed to be swept into WSC's presence in the garden. He rose nobly to the occasion, and showed them round, finally suggesting a whisky and soda. The brewer accepted with alacrity but the Mormons said no.

'May I have water, Sir Winston?' one asked. 'Lions drink it.'

'Asses drink it too,' replied his host, sotto voce.

'Strong drink rageth and stingeth like a serpent,' said the other, austerely.

'I have long been looking for a drink like that,' WSC muttered.

After they had left, I congratulated WSC on his side of this cross-talk. 'None of it was original. They just fed me a music-hall chance,' he replied with a grin.

Apart from these exotics, there was a steady stream of lunch and dinner guests, both in London and at Chartwell. WSC and CSC relied more and more on old stalwarts, such as Field Marshal Montgomery, who was invariably stimulating and unselfconsciously cock-a-hoop. I found him immensely endearing. Monty took to consulting me on his speeches in the House of Lords and elsewhere. I was flattered, and I have ventured to quote extracts from our correspondence in Appendix A.

On 1 October 1962 the Prime Minister (Harold Macmillan) and Mountbatten came to lunch at Hyde Park Gate, and as Monty had very recently been at Chartwell I had the opportunity of comparing the styles of the three Ms, all great showmen. The differences were vivid. Monty rested his case on solid achievement and unshakeable simplistic opinions, themselves resting on equally unshakeable self-confidence. Macmillan's world-weary elder statesman style was switched on and off according to the audience. Mountbatten seemed, to my perhaps over-critical eye, to be seeking to make up by flash and self-advertisement for the lack of any very solid achievement. In the words of a biographer, his naval commands, though gallant, had 'left skid marks all over the sea'; his Supreme Command in South-East Asia had been undistinguished, and his tenure as the last Viceroy of India had been horribly marred by the huge massacres at Partition, which can be blamed, at least in part, on the haste with which British withdrawal of control took place.

At that lunch, on hearing from WSC that I had served under him in the Arakan, Mountbatten gave a quite brilliant little dissertation on the campaign, and on the good fortune of those who had served under him. WSC's attention seemed to wander, Macmillan preserved a Buddha-like inscrutability, and I reflected that the description did not exactly tally with what I thought had in fact taken place. I was reminded of one of the few Latin tags I retained, Cicero's crashing epigram: 'O fortunatam Romam me Consule natam' ('Oh lucky Rome to be born while I am Consul').

I had intended to keep a note of the luncheon conversation for WSC: as we were only four I thought something of significance might emerge, but it didn't. WSC's only contribution of note was that although he regularly attended the 'Songs' ceremony at Harrow, he had not enjoyed a single day there or at any other school. And when Mountbatten asked what the Crimean coast at Yalta was like, he replied briefly: 'The Riviera of Hell'.

Shortly afterwards Violet Bonham Carter lunched, and launched an eloquent and stinging attack on Harold Macmillan and all his policies. WSC reacted with vigour, and in quite his old form knocked her off her perch. She was visibly hurt by some of her old friend's robust reflections on the contemporary Liberal Party, and when she was leaving I attempted to unruffle her feathers. I suggested that having known WSC for so many years, she must realise that criticism of a friend invariably produced a counter-attack: if WSC was anything, he was loyal. She reflected, and said: 'Yes. Lip-loyal.' It was the only time I ever heard her speak bitterly of WSC, and I don't think there was a great deal of truth in it.

On private occasions, WSC himself was quite willing to criticise Macmillan, and criticise him severely. He thought very little of Macmillan's 'wind of change' speech in South Africa (characterised memorably by Lord Lambton: 'For the sake of a phrase he has confounded a Continent'). WSC considered that the pendulum on colonialism had swung too far and too fast. He was convinced from personal experience, personal predilection and his extraordinary depth and width of historical knowledge that benevolent colonial rule was infinitely preferable for those ruled than the corruption, anarchy and tyranny that seemed inevitably to succeed it. To replace British-style colonial rule with tribal nationalism, 'the disease of childhood', was to do no kindness. On the African independent states' rapacious demands for Western aid, much of it destined for personal enrichment and Swiss bank accounts, and even more for armaments, his comment was scathing. 'And all the time their unfortunate peoples are increasing, to live in squalor and under oppression. Their demand to us is: "We breed: You feed." '

'Discrimination' was not a major issue in WSC's active lifetime, though it was beginning to become so, and he was well aware of the arguments. His summing-up was: 'Prejudice should go. Choice should remain.' (And you can read that any way you choose).

WSC could show a surprising degree of acerbity on questions that should not normally have worried him. When the Hilton Hotel at Hyde Park Corner was being built, Charles Clore, the large-scale businessman and property developer, wrote to WSC. He was involved in the building of the hotel – one of the first central London architectural blots, or, if you are particularly kind, anachronisms – and he was proud of it. He wanted to call the hotel the Churchill Hilton. WSC knew something of Clore's reputation, though from what source I know not, and didn't like what he knew. He instructed me to sent the curtest negative by telegram. I thought this was unnecessarily wounding: Clore was no worse than a great many entrepreneurs, though as a personality he was not very attractive. WSC was adamant, and the hotel did not bear his name. Others were not so meticulous and two night-clubs sprang up, called respectively 'Winston's' and 'Churchill's.' Legally it would have been difficult to prevent it, and at worst the sort of ridiculous case that had been successfully avoided over the *Private Eye* libel could have wound its extravagant course through the Courts, leaving a string of exceedingly fat lawyers in its wake, so I kept very quiet about the cheeky annexation.

But these brief flashes of strength of feeling were becoming sadly rarer. At a time when WSC was in one of his most severe and lengthy dips, both of health and of morale, he received a request from the American Air Force academy at Denver, Colorado, for his views on a suitable motto for the institution. This should encapsulate its guiding principles as a new establishment to rank with West Point and Annapolis. WSC was unwilling, indeed unable to rise to the challenge and I put it aside for a better moment. But time passed, and the reminders became pressing. So I took it on myself to choose from the vast treasury of his works and speeches the words he had used as the 'theme of the work' of his history of the Second World War:

In War: Resolution.
In Defeat: Defiance.
In Victory: Magnanimity.
In Peace: Goodwill.

The quotation was quite old. Eddie Marsh, WSC's Private Secretary and close friend for many years from 1905 until after the First World War, remembered him formulating it as he walked, his tone of voice varying from 'a roll of musketry' at the first lines to 'pure benediction' at the last.

Eddie Marsh was an original if ever there was one, and CSC told many tales of him. He had got so lost in the maquis while holidaying in Corsica that he had eventually emerged torn and bleeding and with the balance of his mind disturbed. He had been overheard giving advice to a young friend to 'try anything once. Except of course incest and country dancing.' He used to correct WSC's punctuation with the severity of a headmaster. Sadly I never met him, but I believe that I follow him as the longest-serving of all WSC's Private Secretaries.

I obtained the author's sadly listless assent to the selection and sent it off. Whether the Air Force used the words I don't know, but I have always felt they expressed succinctly the true outlook of Winston Churchill.

As time passed the inevitability of the end of WSC's life made clear practical measures necessary. In 1963 the Prime Minister had set up a committee to make plans for the State Funeral. It was chaired and indeed most actively managed by the Earl Marshal, the Duke of Norfolk, and those who worked on the Committee were both wonderfully efficient and touchingly devoted. I have a copy of the intricate plans, involving the movement of large numbers of troops, of distinguished foreign guests, of crowds and of clergy, of trains and much else, and I thought I saw in it something of the genius of our Nation when individuals from among its best really set their minds to a task. The Committee sat in Northumberland Avenue, and I used to sneak off to the meetings. When WSC asked me where I was going, I replied, truthfully, that I was going to the Foreign Office to read my telegram distribution, but he was not, I think, taken in.

The earlier days of the planning of the operation, given the code name of 'Hope Not' by Bernard Norfolk, were complicated by WSC announcing that he wanted to be buried at Chartwell, on the croquet lawn, looking south over Kent to the distant coast. Personally I could not think of any reason why he shouldn't have his way, but it caused a flutter, Harold Macmillan being quite strangely agitated. The suggestion, he said, would cause all sorts of problems: the croquet lawn would have to be consecrated, for instance. (Why shouldn't it be?) The only material problems that I could see were that it would be difficult for those who wished to visit the grave, and there are many thousands every year. Also, it might be thought irreverent to play croquet there. But perhaps, like the dying Australian stockman in the poem, he would have liked to hear 'the sturdy station children playing overhead'? At all events, CSC was pressed into service and Winston Churchill concluded that he would be buried in the little churchyard of Bladon, just outside the

Blenheim estate walls, where his father, mother and brother, and now CSC and three of children lie. He had visited Bladon with the Duke of Marlborough and the Vicar before reaching his final decision.

During the long period of preparation, the Hope Not Committee meetings continued, and I came more and more to like and admire the Duke of Norfolk. Bernard Norfolk was the least pompous of people, and jolly and entertaining company. On the occasions I lunched with him at the Turf Club, he invariably ate nothing but hors d'oeuvre. An interesting quirk.

Sorties, other than the cruises and stays on the Riviera, became rarer and rarer, and much of my time was devoted to explaining to usually devoted but sometimes self-important people why WSC could not open this or attend that or write a foreword to the other. Much was I cursed for my negative and unfeeling attitude to worthies who, they were quite sure, deserved more consideration. Unfortunately they were also quite frequently distinguished figures, both British and foreign, and to have acceded to their requests could have done good. But the dangers of failure, and above all WSC's ever-increasing withdrawal and reluctance, had to prevail. For these reasons I had, I hope politely, turned down a request from Kurt Hahn, the educationalist, founder of Salem and Gordonstoun, for a discussion with WSC on modern education. I was entertained to receive a furious telephone call from Hahn, whose excellent English deserted him. He required me to give the sternest rebuke to 'that secretary man Montague Browne', whose stupid reply 'I' had obviously not seen. I said I would do that, but sadly I could not alter the decision.

WSC continued to take a real interest in his horses, most effectively managed by Christopher, and he still went to watch them run. Very rarely did I accompany him. For one thing, racing bored me, and I was a fish out of water with the racing fraternity. (Why do so many of them style themselves 'Captain', I continue to wonder? They are not retired naval officers, and I have always been led to believe that it was improper to use your rank in retirement unless you had been a field officer or above. And then I do not like their hats – those snappy little brown hats, worn at a jaunty angle, which in the 1930s were known as 'The Shah's in town'.)

I did however accompany WSC on one racing venture, to Düsseldorf in the summer of 1956, to see his horse Le Prétendant run. The horse finished one from last, but the warmth of WSC's reception was memorable. The German Jockey Club gave us a spectacularly good lunch. I suppose it is a reflection of my character that I tend to remember menus more accurately than important conversations. We drank champagne out of huge bell glasses, with a peeled peach floating in each one. I was seated between a pleasant, rather silent young German and a vivacious and dramatically attractive Valkyrie. Naturally enough, I talked to her and we got on splendidly. Halfway through lunch my male neighbour addressed me:

'There are two interesting things about me,' he said.

'Which are those?' I enquired politely.

'In the first place, I am the only German you will meet who is not a "Herr

Doktor", and in the second, I am the husband of the girl with whom you are getting on so well.' But it was said with a charming smile. On the way back, in a small private aircraft, we were bumped about vigorously, and WSC grumbled that the going had been too soft for Le Prétendant and that the peaches ruined the champagne. But his welcome had been a great success, and reinforced his benevolence towards post-Hitler Germany.

About a year later he had a horse running on the West Coast of the United States. The racing arrangements were nothing to do with me, but I was astounded to hear that WSC's trainer was unwilling to accompany the horse, on the grounds that we were very unpopular in the USA post-Suez, and 'he might be booed on the course.' Christopher was furious, and the excellent vet, Carey-Foster, volunteered to go. We kept it from WSC, who would in all probability have gone himself.

A more sombre venue, on which I cannot put a precise date (it was kept secret at the time), was the Atomic Weapons Research Establishment at Aldermaston. In about 1958, WSC was invited by the Director to visit and see the progress made in building up the independent nuclear deterrent, of which Britain had been a principal progenitor, and by which WSC set so much store as a peacekeeper. We drove down early, and were shown the various processes of making the toys. After lunch, films were shown of the tests at Montebello and Christmas Island. They were without sound-track and rough-cut, but the effect was numbing. On the way back to London WSC was silent. Finally he said: 'What did you think of that?' I made a banal response, and returned the question. WSC said: 'If I were God Almighty, and humanity blew itself to bits, as it most certainly could, I don't think that I'd start again in case they got me too next time.' This was not quite what I expected. He went on: 'I always feared that mass pressure in the United States might force them to use their H bombs while the Russians still had not got any. It's always been a tendency of the masses to drop their Hs.'

This and other incidents were the increasingly rare sparks in a fire that had already burnt grey. However, WSC could and did take a searching interest in some political issues. As late as 1962–3, Anthony Wedgwood Benn, who had succeeded to his father's title as Lord Stansgate, successfully sought WSC's support for legislation to allow a peer to renounce his peerage. I drafted the replies to Benn's letters, which were succinct and convincing, and somewhat to my surprise WSC clearly and firmly believed that Benn was right. I don't think his support had any marked effect on getting the legislation passed, but he did let people know of his views and it did Benn's cause no harm, particularly, according to what WSC told me, as he had on more than one occasion brought the matter up in the Smoking Room at the House of Commons.

I will not go through the pressures and persuasion that finally caused WSC to announce in 1963 that he could not stand for Parliament again. Martin Gilbert has covered the ground fully and fairly. My own part had been, at CSC's urging, to dissuade him from continuing. I needed no urging: his retirement was long overdue and it did neither the House nor WSC much good for him to be assisted to his habitual place on the Front Bench immediately below the gangway to listen, all too obviously uncomprehendingly, to Questions or a debate. The incomprehension was primarily due to his deafness, but the result was painful to see, and I hated to think that he might be remembered thus in the House of Commons, his second home for so many years and the scene of so many of his triumphs. That was the case for his withdrawal, even without taking into account the feelings of his Constituency, loyal and publicly silent, but privately increasingly uneasy. But it was obviously painful to participate in any steps to deprive him of one of the few real pleasures remaining to him; the decision marked a clear downward step in his interests in what remained of his life, and the physical effect was all too visible.

Jock Colville had followed up suggestions that WSC should be made an honorary Life Member of the House, but in vain. This unprecedented honour would have been a happy solution, and WSC would have gone to Westminster less and less frequently, without suffering the sad withdrawal symptoms he did. Jock had written to me telling of the failure of the idea, turned down by the Conservative leadership of the time. It is possible that the Labour Party would have been more receptive. Any any rate, I see from the official biography that I greeted the negative news thus:

> It is perhaps appropriate that those responsible for our own very rapidly closing twilight should not wish to honour the setting sun. So I suppose we must await a Socialist Government who may treat him more honourably than his 'friends'. It would not be the first time ... At the French Embassy last night Anthony Wedgwood-Benn spoke to me of a Bill which would allow Sir Winston to sit in the House. Whether this is the same as Life Membership, I do not know. In any case we can now only wait on events.

WSC's final departure from the House of Commons, on 27 July 1964, was marked by a joint Resolution of Thanks from the Government and Opposition. It was agreeable enough, but CSC had had to suggest quite firmly that the original somewhat lukewarm draft should be pepped up.

Chapter 30

——— 🐾 ———

T H I S I S a story of decline. WSC's own slow descent was not a steady path, but a series of recoveries and relapses, each of which took him further than the last. There is no doubt that the breaking of his hip in June 1962 did damage that went beyond the immediate trauma. He had gone to Monte Carlo, staying in the penthouse suite in the Hotel de Paris that Onassis had put at his disposal. On the second day of his stay, Howells, his male nurse, woke me in the early morning and told me that WSC had had a fall and was apparently seriously injured; he had already summoned Dr Roberts. I found WSC lying silently on the floor, propped up on pillows. He was conscious and dignified, but obviously in pain. The rather trite analogy of a wounded stag crossed my mind. He was rapidly transferred to the new Monaco hospital, and when he had recovered from the application of a huge plaster cast, I went to see him. I thought he was dozing, but after a minute he greeted me with a smile. I sat in silence and after a further interval he asked, quite courteously, that the others present should leave the room. He told me in an almost inaudible voice to make sure that they had gone, then said in a strong tone: 'Remember, I want to die in England. Promise me that you will see to it.' I gave the required promise unhesitatingly, but privately wondered if I would be able to carry it out, for he seemed mortally stricken. I rang Number Ten, and within a very short time Harold Macmillan had ordered an RAF Comet ambulance to stand by to fly to Nice to bring WSC home.

Loud was the fury of the local doctors, with the notable exception of Dr Roberts. Did I realise that the move might kill WSC, a man of eighty-seven who had suffered many strokes? Yes, I realised only too clearly; but I also knew that it was the only course to take, and CSC concurred on the telephone without hesitation.

On the journey home WSC, who had been sedated, made only one remark. 'I don't think I'll go back to that place,' he muttered, 'it's unlucky. First Toby and then this.' I had thought that he had forgotten Toby, the budgerigar, who had been his constant companion and a most engaging little nuisance. In the Hotel de Paris penthouse in 1960, WSC and I had been playing bezique with Toby strutting about the table, picking up cards and chattering his only phrase: 'Toby, Toby, my name is Toby.' Something alarmed him, and he flew through the door into a room with an open window and out into Monte Carlo. We located him in a tree, but before anything could be done he had taken off and was never seen again. Large rewards were offered by WSC and Ari, but there came no news. Great was the sadness, and I shared it.

When the Comet reached Heathrow, a crowd had gathered to see WSC carried off on a stretcher, bound for the Middlesex Hospital. He rallied his strength, and with an obvious effort gave the V sign.

I was much relieved when Professor Sir Herbert Seddon took him in charge. He was considered to be the greatest authority on broken hips, and was additionally a sympathetic and wise man. Determined too. He told me that his colleague Philip Yeoman was to carry out the operation.

'Why not you?' I demanded rather brusquely.

'Because Yeoman will do it twice as well as I can,' replied Seddon. 'Now please stop fussing and leave us with our patient.' Which I did, and all was well; but the accident marked yet a further step down the slope, and a considerable one.

In spite of family consultation it had become increasingly difficult to strike a balance between putting off nearly all the many would-be visitors and thereby giving the impression that WSC was senile, and opening the gates too wide to people who might bore and tire him and who still expected dazzling flashes of insight and Olympian judgements on events. WSC was not senile: he was not incontinent; he could feed himself; he could enjoy some books and a limited number of games of bezique; and he liked the company of a few, and of course of the close members of his family. But the many strokes had taken a heavy toll, and deafness and melancholy and a failing concentration and memory made it impossible for him to play a part in any general conversation, thus giving the impression of a far worse state of mind than actually was the case.

In 1962 the young King of Morocco, via his Ambassador, sought a meeting. I warned the latter that it really would not be productive, but he had his orders and WSC wearily acquiesced. The King devoted much of his visit to questions on the British trade unions, on which he appeared to be unexpectedly well informed, and a dissertation on the damage they had done and would continue to do to their country. Quite right too, but not really the kind of conversation in which WSC could be expected to play a great part.

That particular afternoon was redeemed by the arrival of Ari Onassis. WSC's face lit up, and after a couple of whisky and sodas he achieved the sort of startling rekindling which took everyone by surprise, though alas becoming less and less frequent. 'Tell me about your interview with the American Senatorial Committee,' he said. This was not new to me, but I hadn't realised that WSC was interested. The story went back to the Korean War, when Ari had done vastly well from his tankers. Laid-up post-1945 American tankers were unmothballed, but could only be leased by American entities. So Ari formed an American company with distinguished American figures on the Board, and controlling the majority of the shares. In due course the Senate took exception to these arrangements, which had touched even such sans-reproches as General Bedell Smith, and summoned many witnesses to give evidence to their Committee. Ari was among them, and though he was under no legal obligation to obey, he duly turned up and was given a scorching and contemptuous dressing-down by the Committee. Seething with rage, he had finally broken away from the lawyers hanging on to his coat-tails and began his reply at the top of his notably loud voice: 'Gentlemen! You sons of beetches!' I have only Ari's word for the scene, but he re-enacted it with superb histrionics and low comedy for WSC's benefit, who hovered between mirth and consternation at such reckless disrespect for a body of representative government.

During another visit WSC summoned Ari to chide him for not attending the dinners of the Other Club, of which WSC had made him a member (to the displeasure of some, as I have mentioned). Ari evaded the point and told me later that he would never go unless with 'the Boss': he realised that his membership would cause annoyance and had only accepted because of WSC urging it. He was right about the last point; WSC looked on membership as almost as high an accolade as the gift of a picture.

The Other Club has been described often enough, and a rather bad book has been written about its history. This is a brief résumé. In 1911 WSC, Lloyd George and F.E. Smith (later Lord Birkenhead) were invited to join 'the Club', the old dining club illuminated by Samuel Johnson and many others. 'The Club' told them that they would like to have some young and sparky politicians. Pleasantly complimented, the three agreed, only to be blackballed when their names came up for election. As WSC put it: 'It was rather like asking a man to dinner and kicking him down the steps before he entered your house.' Vexed by this unsought affront, they founded 'The Other Club', to meet once a month in the Pinafore Room at the Savoy when Parliament is sitting. There is no *placement* and you sit where you will, with the result that the more modest members often find themselves rather out of things at the wings of the long table.

The food and wine are remarkable, both for quality and (very reasonable) price, and have maintained their standard year in and year out. The same cannot be said for all the members, as a sort of progressive Gresham's Law has set in with the present system of universal suffrage on candidates.

The rules are relatively few and distinctly succinct, and it is not too hard to deduce that F.E. and WSC were responsible for them. To quote just a few – and, no, I am not breaking discretion, they have been reproduced in extenso on several occasions:

> *Rule 2:* The object of 'The Other Club' is to dine.
> *Rule 3:* The Club shall consist of no more than fifty Members; and not more than twenty-four Members of the House of Commons (now disregarded).
> *Rule 8:* The Executive Committee shall settle all outstanding questions with plenary powers.
> *Rule 9:* There shall be no appeal from the decision of the Executive Committee.
> *Rule 10:* The names of the Executive Committee shall be wrapped in impenetrable mystery.
> *Rule 12:* Nothing in the Rules or intercourse of the Club shall interfere with the rancour or asperity of party politics.

The Executive Committee, by the time I was appointed (not elected!) to the Club in 1958 had been reduced to one survivor: WSC. One day he had said as an aside as I bade him goodnight: 'By the way, you are now a member of the Other Club. You must accompany me on Thursday.' I was grateful and flattered, but unfortunately he had forgotten to inform anybody, including the two Hon. Secretaries. The Club in those days was a socially well-mannered place, and I was greeted warmly, except by one member, who shouted: 'Anthony, what the hell are you doing here?' It did not go down very well with his peers, who guessed correctly at the circumstances, but it was rather disconcerting.

The affable social atmosphere did not prevent Rule 12 being scrupulously observed and exchanges ricocheted round the room, some of them entertaining. Before my time Duff Cooper (Lord Norwich), holding forth on military strategy, was attacked with: 'Oh do shut up, Duff. You were the worst Secretary of State for War in living memory.' Duff Cooper's face purpled and the veins in his forehead swelled. Then he subsided and said sweetly: 'How can you say that with Jack Seeley sitting there?' And he was right.

Lord Goddard, the Lord Chief Justice, was a favourite of WSC's (referred to as 'Old Goddamn'). He made the mistake of informing the dinner that he was about to retire from the Bench, because he was getting old and silly and wanted to go before people noticed it. 'Too late!' was the kind-hearted chorus. Goddard was anathema to the left and the Liberal wets because of his severity. But Walter Monckton, who certainly didn't share his views, said of him: 'If I was guilty I'd hate to come up before Goddard. But if I was innocent, I wouldn't mind at all: he wouldn't tolerate unfairness.' We could do with some Judges like him today.

Gerald Templer (Field Marshal) was a sporadic diner at the Other Club, but he stopped coming. I admired him almost without reservation, and asked him why he was deserting us. 'Because politicians are such shits,' he replied. 'I've had enough of them.' Stories of Gerald's fierceness and outspokenness are legion, including his inflicting Grievous Bodily Harm on a young and vigorous burglar when he himself was in his seventies; his pulling the Minister of Defence (Duncan Sandys) out of his chair by his lapels at a defence meeting; his remark to Lord Mountbatten: 'Dickie, if you ate nails, you'd shit corkscrews'; but he was a wonderfully warm-hearted friend and a student of wildlife, who persuaded a number of people, including me, not to shoot woodcock, on the grounds of their beauty, their little-understood migratory pattern and their courage in defence of their chicks. I have long ago given up all shooting on moral (or sentimental) grounds, but I would be out with two guns if a flight of IRA would pass over my head.

Though the Other Club was his plaything and his joy, WSC was not really a Club man. He was an honorary member of a great many Clubs without visiting them. In 1952 I was put up for Pratt's, which belongs to the Duke of Devonshire. It is a jolly place, where one eats a sort of breakfast from seven in the evening until very late. You all sit round one table and are placed by George (all the waiters are called George) or by Georgina, who is the presiding and most admirable Queen Bee. I love going there, for the conversation is nearly always interesting and good, and your neighbour at the table could vary from Harold Macmillan, a frequent attender, to Paddy Leigh Fermor of literary and guerrilla warfare fame, or Peter Kemp, who wore a Spanish Foreign Legion tie and had as many wounds as General Bernard Freyberg, known to WSC as 'the salamander', because he had been so many times through the fire without succumbing.

When WSC heard that my proposer, Tom Martin, was looking for support, because I did not know many members at that time, he seconded me, and the Proprietor (the present Duke's father) added his name, which clinched the matter.

WSC never went to Pratt's in my day, but when in Opposition from 1945 to 1951 he frequented it quite often. He sometimes cooked his own chop on the open coal fire (which gives credence to his claim that he knew how to boil an egg), and once succeeded in putting it out, to the annoyance of the members. Did he enjoy the atmosphere there, I asked him?

'Oh yes,' he said, 'very much. But I did once get such an unexpected buffet from a young gentleman. I think he was a Guards Officer and someone's guest. He had been hitting the bottle, and I think it had been hitting him back, but he was behaving perfectly quietly, and listening to what I had to say. He got up to leave, and stopped by my chair. I thought he had come to say goodnight. But no. He said: "I don't know who you are, but never in my life have I heard anyone talk such nonsense!" With that he lurched through the door and was gone.'

'What did you say?' I enquired.

'I had nothing left to say. I didn't know who he was either.'

In these years (1960–3) I saw a good deal of Randolph. A subject inevitably under discussion was the authorship of WSC's official biography. He had always half-intended that Randolph should be entrusted with the task, but the question had been deferred time after time, mainly because of WSC's increasing difficulty in reaching a decision, but also because of incidents, either personally experienced or reported to him, of Randolph's intemperate outbursts. Randolph had more than once asked me if I knew his father's intentions in the matter, but had never requested me to intervene on his behalf. However, I had long been convinced that he was the right man for the job. He would have been bitterly and permanently hurt if he had not been chosen, and it seemed imperative that the lives of father and son should be brought closer while there was still time. But quite apart from this, when Randolph devoted himself to writing it was excellently executed, and there was every reason to hope that the literary ability which had illuminated WSC's biography of his own father would find its counterpart in Randolph. So I did not hesitate to lobby when opportunity offered. It was however Randolph's own efforts which ultimately won the day. His biography of Lord Derby was critically well received, and in particular Harold Macmillan had spoken well of it to WSC.

In May 1960 Randolph himself popped the question, and a little later at Chartwell WSC said: 'He can do it.' We had not been speaking of the biography and I had some difficulty in sorting out who could do what? I had already got a draft letter set by for the eventuality, but I was tactful enough not to produce it immediately. Randolph's happiness was great and he expressed it in an eloquent and affectionate letter to his father.

Over the years I had acquired some ability in interpreting WSC's random thoughts. When in office he had had a disconcerting habit of assuming that one had been present, when in fact it was another member of the Private Office. Thus he would suddenly ask: 'What did he say to him?' and be considerably displeased by a request for elucidation. 'Why don't you all pool your luck?' he would grumble. This elliptical approach persisted in his retirement. Thus, earlier in the afternoon when he had decided on the authorship, he had suddenly demanded: 'Where are the little people?' I looked around but could see no sign of fairies or other apparitions. I was about to reply that I supposed they must still be in Ireland, when Alan Hodge and his wife appeared. Alan was WSC's able literary assistant, as well as joint Editor of *History Today*, and both he and his wife were of limited stature. WSC was fond of Alan, and admired his knowledge and industry, though not particularly his literary style. He also was pleased that the Hodge cat was called 'Johnson', as a reply to Dr Johnson, who called his cat 'Hodge'.

In his withdrawn state of the 1960s, accentuated by his increasing immobility after his broken hip in 1962, WSC could still surprise even those close to him by a shaft of wit, or a lapidary and illuminated comment on affairs.

Luncheon talk was on France, and the efforts made by her Prime Minister Pierre Mendès-France in WSC's last years as Prime Minister to restore his country to economic order.

'I was disappointed,' said WSC, 'I thought he could really do it.'

'Do what?', we asked.

'Mend his France,' he grinned with some satisfaction.

And on China: 'I am entirely in favour of unwaggable tails.' This foxed WSC's audience completely. It turned out that one of the Chinese hierarchy, years before, had rebuked those who sought to influence his country's policy. 'China's tail will not be wagged,' he is reported as saying, but with what authority of translation, I know not.

WSC used to reflect on what he believed, or hoped, was China's essentially peaceful nature. 'Think of it,' he used to say, 'they invented gunpowder hundreds of years before the West, and they only used it for fireworks.' And during the Korean War, he resisted a somewhat half-baked suggestion that China should be invaded with the words: 'That would be the greatest folly. It would be like flies invading fly-paper.'

When CSC was gently persuading a particularly silent and apathetic WSC to make an effort and concentrate on a question, she received the following: 'I eats well, and I drinks well and I sleeps well, but when I sees a job of work, I comes all over a tremble.'

WSC's letters in this period, though progressively fewer and further between, could still show the whimsical touch of old. I have only a small number – after all, I saw him nearly every day; but when suffering from flu, I received the following by hand:

My dear Anthony,

I am so sorry at the persistence of your affliction. There is nothing I am afraid that I can do, but I am sure you know how much I feel for you.

Always Your friend

W

And following a visit to the Worthing Conservatives I received this:

AMB Private

This seems to me to be a monstrous charge. I was particularly struck by a large dish of caviar which stood upon the buffet and was never offered to anyone.

I will however be worthy of Worthing.

W S C

Actually he was wrong in two respects. It wasn't caviar, and he wasn't being charged for it, but with age he became more and more worried about his finances, while paradoxically still indulging in spasms of extravagance. Thus, on a letter drafted by his accountants, increasing by £200 per annum a payment of rent paid personally to his Trustees, he angrily scrawled 'a dirty swindle!', and it took some efforts to prevent him despatching it.

As I have said, it was no part of my remit to deal with WSC's finances, but I got increasingly sucked into them, and though I did not initiate investment advice, I did sometimes comment on it. Martin Gilbert generously writes: 'Montague Browne was a wise, conscientious and thoughtful friend and adviser, not only with such correspondence as remained, a fitful fragment of former days, but with financial guidance.'

Not all my duties were of a Private Secretarial nature. One summer's afternoon at Chartwell, I received an urgent summons from WSC, who was sitting on the terrace. Two of his black swans had got out of their appointed anti-fox protected area and were cruising at large on the lake. Could I swim? I dubiously agreed, and was then pressed into submerging myself in the muddy, weedy and waterlily-strewn waters to herd the birds back. They didn't like it, and expressed their views in strong Western Australian voices. Seen from water-level, they loomed like ships of the line under full sail, and I fled, calling forth from WSC both exhortations and cries of contempt. I was reminded that he had always rebuked lack of intestinal fortitude. During a wartime air raid, he was heard addressing his cat Nelson, who had gone to ground under a chest of drawers in his bedroom: 'Come out, Nelson! Shame on you, bearing a name such as yours, to skulk there while the enemy is overhead!' But Nelson paid no heed to these reproaches, and no more did I. Swans are alarming creatures when angry.

Into this increasingly circumscribed life came occasional shafts of light. Their power to interest and cheer WSC was sadly diminishing month by month, though a fan letter from the United States, addressed merely to 'The greatest man in the World, England,' did indeed raise his spirits when it was delivered without delay to No. 28 Hyde Park Gate, and for a day or two WSC showed it with almost childish and most engaging delight to his visitors and family. I always wonder who the enlightened postman who made the decision could have been?

Then in early 1963 the two Houses of Congress passed a resolution by a large majority to confer Honorary Citizenship of the United States on WSC. There has been some debate on the number of precedents for this honour, but I believe the pundits settled for only two: Lafayette and Pulaski, both of whom had earned their distinction fighting against England in the War of Independence. WSC's reaction was muted. Only a few years earlier he would have been thrilled and would have used the occasion for at least a resounding pronouncement on Anglo-American relations. As it was he asked me to draft a suitable and brief statement of thanks, which Randolph would read out when he accepted the award on his father's behalf. I felt that this was too low-key, so after consultation with WSC and CSC I drafted something a bit more robust.

Dean Acheson, the former American Secretary of State under President Truman, had recently said that 'Britain had lost an Empire and had not found a role in the world.' Quite true too, but he might have added that he had played an enthusiastic role in the first part of this scenario. I therefore suggested, and WSC and CSC accepted, a warm and indeed sincere expression of thanks on behalf of WSC and his descendants, and a very brief historical survey of the rarity of such an honour 'between two great sovereign powers. I say "sovereign powers" with design and emphasis, for I reject the view that Britain should now be relegated to a tame and minor role in the World.' Randolph read it with the expressive vigour of which he was so capable, and it was well received, even by Acheson who remarked that it was the only time that a newly elected citizen had, with his first utterance, 'busted an ex-Secretary of State in the snoot'.

President Kennedy's own address at the presentation reflected great credit on his eloquence, or that of his speech-writers. Inter alia, he said that Winston Churchill had 'mobilised the English language and sent it into battle'. There was curiosity about the origin of this phrase, and it was eventually run to earth as the wartime creation of Beverley Nichols, of all strange people.

Joyce Hall, the founder of the vast Hallmark enterprise, was so taken with the exchange that he had it published in a small booklet and circulated through his many shops and emporia. I have already described Joyce's contribution to WSC's income over the years by buying the reproduction rights to several of his pictures annually, to publish as Christmas cards. He was the only major tycoon I have met of whom no-one spoke anything but good.

Joyce's story is too long to tell here. Briefly, he was one of three sons of an itinerant Middle West preacher who deserted his children and their mother. By extraordinary effort and imagination the boys built up a greetings card business, which became the biggest in the world, besides dealing in property, furniture, jewellery and many other things. Joyce's two latter-day heroes were Winston Chuchill and Eisenhower. A staunch Republican, he initially despised Truman but later came to admire him. I stayed with Joyce on a number of occasions in Kansas City and grew very fond of him. One had to be careful not to admire an object because it would promptly be given to you. At a breakfast meeting, when I commented on his rather vivid Mexican dressing gown, he took it off and insisted I wear it then and there. Staying alone in the large flat over his headquarters in Kansas City, I thought that the tropical ducks in the large indoor pool looked a bit wan, in spite of the correct steamy atmosphere and plant life. I told him, and within days they were flown home to their own habitat and released.

I must not drag on, but Joyce really was remarkable. He invited me to lunch with Walt Disney at the 1968 World's Fair. Disney was enchanting, though engaged in dismantling a life-size dummy of Abraham Lincoln, whose delivery of the Gettysburg Address in the Illinois Pavilion was out of sync. Finally, I am indebted to Joyce for a chance of seeing a tornado at close quarters. As we drove out to lunch in Missouri in a tepid and windy rainstorm, the radio announced the approach of a tornado at State Line.

'Where is that?' I asked the driver.

'Right here,' he replied briefly. And so it was, a sort of huge elephant's trunk swinging about, and laced with blue lightning in the gloom. Every now and then its extremity would touch the ground, with an explosion of dust and debris. It passed some three hundred yards from us, and the car shook violently. When we reached the farm, Joyce took an innocently proprietorial pride in the phenomenon, which had killed nobody.

WSC liked Hall very much, but the latter was too awed in his presence to do himself justice. I do miss him. His last, somewhat misguided act of kindness was to persuade the *New Yorker* (to which WSC referred as the 'New Porker') to publish a profile of me, complete with sketch. I did the interview extremely badly and came out smug, arrogant and self-opinionated. Undoubtedly true, but not the impression that I was seeking to give.

It was later in the same year, 1963, that I had the melancholy task of drafting a message from WSC to the Americans following Kennedy's assassination. I had thought that by now, with WSC's eighty-ninth birthday approaching, it was not only permissible but right that he should no longer originate messages, though he was still bound to respond to them. But on the day of Kennedy's death I received such a volume of requests for his reactions that it was obvious that something had to be said. The original was addressed to the President's widow, and although delivered by our Embassy, somehow got lost and was never acknowledged, but I released the text to the press, so it achieved its purpose. Anyway, the Americans liked it and *Time* magazine commented on the eloquence of the 'old lion's sibilant wrath'. Parody may be necessary, but it is a dangerous game, and Private Secretaries should eschew it unless driven into a corner, which I frequently was.

Among the few notes I kept at the time, I found one, in the shape of a letter to my parents, in which I commented on WSC's increasing consideration as his age advanced and his vigour declined: with most old people it is the other way round. But 'put your finger on the bell and make it ring like bloody hell' still persisted. I, and indeed my family, had always received the greatest kindness, but I don't think that it could have been said of the working WSC that he spared his staff, however warm-hearted and generous he was to them. Jo Sturdee (later Countess of Onslow) had been one of his principal 'young ladies' when he was in Opposition. At a picnic in the Atlas mountains she had slipped and broken her ankle. WSC, who was anxious to pursue his dictation, greeted her with: 'Can you still take down?'

I have painted a picture of WSC's withdrawal from active interest in events and this is true enough. But it was not a straight line on the graph of his later life and there were surprising blips, both of reaction and recollection.

When we were both reading the morning papers, a reference to Harold Watkinson, a former Minister of Transport, caught his eye. 'Did you know that when opening a new road with a flare from a Verey pistol he succeeded in setting the assembled journalists on fire?' I didn't know, and I didn't think that WSC was even conscious of Harold Watkinson. 'Yes, indeed he did,' WSC continued, 'look it up. It was his claim to distinction.' I pondered long on how and why this particular incident had found a place in that vastly capacious, but now capricious, memory.

That afternoon in the garden at Chartwell, there followed a brief disquisition on fishing. 'I once caught a big pike. Someone said that I had shot it basking on the surface, and that this was unsporting.' He went on to relate that before 1914, on arriving to stay at a Highland estate in pouring rain, he had met Sir Edward Grey, the Foreign Secretary, returning from the river.

'Had a good day in this weather?' he had enquired.

'Superb, marvellous,' replied Grey.

'What did you catch?'

'Oh, I didn't catch anything,' said Grey.

I pointed out that there was nothing very surprising in this. Grey was a passionate naturalist, who when congratulated on becoming Foreign Secretary had replied: 'Yes, it will be very jolly watching the wildfowl in St James's Park,' and it was quite possible that he had seen otters and all sorts of interesting creatures.

WSC looked at me doubtfully: 'You know, my dear, you have a great deal of "l'esprit de contradiction".'

'But didn't you yourself?'

'No, I didn't!' Well . . .

Finding him in such a chatty mood, and the annual dinner at Trinity House (the ancient organisation responsible for lighthouses, lightships and other marine markers) being close, I asked him a favour. He was an Elder Brother of Trinity House: could he arrange for me to spend a day or two on an isolated lighthouse to observe the birds in the migrating season? I received a dunching reply: 'No. They would not have room for an idler.'

CSC overhead the exchange and rose to my defence thus: 'Winston does not like you going away, Anthony. He misses you.' A kind attempt that received no corroboration from WSC; but he did send for his Elder Brother's uniform to show me, and to explain its genesis. CSC thereupon related that immediately after 1918 Clemenceau had met WSC at a reception preceding the Trinity House dinner and had asked him why he was attired as a semi-naval officer?

'Je suis un Frère Aîné de la Trinité,' explained Churchill.

'Ah,' said Clemenceau, visibly impressed, 'Quelle belle situation!'

WSC thought that his wife was making fun of him and sulked briefly. Then: 'Well, it may well be true, but I said it on purpose.' And at this he returned to his book.

I had often noted his almost loving attitude to books, treating them delicately, and carefully folding back a half-page, never a corner, to remember his place 'because book markers fall out'. He had slender, beautiful hands, and the triple-banded signet ring that young Winston now wears once slipped off and vanished down the loo. WSC had apparently found the amount of work necessary for its successful recovery embarrassing and had apologised profusely to those concerned, which he didn't often do.

Leaving him, CSC took me off for a walk to a spot where in pre-1939 days a genuine gypsy had been given leave to park his genuine caravan. His name was Donkey Jack. He was a very different character from the modern 'traveller'. WSC, always romantic, had discussed with him the Romany origins and had been surprised by his erudition. In due course Donkey Jack died, leaving Mrs Donkey Jack to live alone in the caravan. 'One day,' CSC went on, 'we found Mrs Donkey Jack dead on a pile of autumn leaves. She looked so natural and appropriate, like a dead bird in her proper home in the woods.' This was rather an unusual speech for CSC. I was touched, and noted her words verbatim. Mary later told me that after Donkey Jack's death the Council had tried to move his widow from the common land. WSC had fiercely espoused her cause and she stayed.

That evening I reflected ruefully that I had indeed become an idler, though WSC had not meant it unkindly, and quite possibly CSC's explanation was correct. But what, or who, had made me an idler? My actual work hardly extended to two hours a day, and the two secretaries, Miss Pugh and Miss Snelling, could have handled nearly all of it. Here I was, nearly forty, and I had been with WSC for eleven years. A lot of people thought that it was a most glamorous job, with all the travel, the high living, the entertaining and the famous figures whom one met. They were wrong. My working years were fast slipping away. There may have been plenty of icing, but where was the cake?

In that case, why hadn't I called an end? I had wanted to enter politics, being in some ways a pre-Thatcher Thatcherite on a good many issues, and when Anthony Nutting, Anthony Eden's friend and Minister of State at the Foreign Office, resigned over Suez in 1956, I had hoped to approach his Constituency at Melton Mowbray to be considered as a successor candidate, breathing fire, increased independence from the United States who had led the pack against us, a modified imperialism and reform of the unions (see Chapter 13). WSC had written to the Melton Mowbray Chairman in supportive terms, but had then asked me not to pursue my aim and to 'hold on with me. It won't be long.' Difficult to refuse, but in any case Melton Mowbray had already chosen their candidate.

In spite of WSC's – and CSC's – friendship I had felt it best to preserve a degree of formality in my relations with them, for my own sake as well as theirs. In 1961, after rather a jolly dinner, WSC had said: 'I think we have known each other long enough for you to call me Winston.' I expressed my – genuine – appreciation, but I did not take up the flattering invitation. It just would not have sounded right. In answer to modern enquiries as to what I did call him, the answer is: 'Prime Minister' when he was in Office, 'Sir Winston' afterwards, and, subsequent to his invitation, nothing at all. About six months later he suggested that he should place a photograph of me with others on the crowded desk in his study at Chartwell. Here again, I was both touched and pleased, but did nothing about it. My relations with the Churchill family were good and easy, and I did not want there to be any hint that I was taking advantage of my somewhat lonely position, and of WSC and CSC's age. The time had passed when I had anyone to whom to refer in any kind of formal way. I had kept Number Ten and the Foreign Office informed of anything of interest to them, but there was less and less of this nature. The last Foreign Office request for a report on my activities had been from Harold (later Lord) Caccia, the Head of the Diplomatic Service, in 1961. I reproduce WSC's reply – which I did not draft!

> My dear Caccia,
>   Thank you for your letter. I am glad to give you a report on Anthony Montague Browne.
>   As you know, he was one of my Private secretaries when I was Prime Minister, and has been responsible for my affairs since I gave up office. I do not know what I should have done without him during these years. His knowledge of the world, and of international affairs in particular, has been of high value. He has always been diligent in his duties and willing to undertake any task required of him. I have a high regard for his command of the English language. I have also been deeply impressed by his skill in negotiating complicated affairs on my behalf, and by the excellent relationships which he establishes with people of all kinds and all nationalities.
>   I set great store on his invaluable services to me, made available with the encouragement and approval, first of Lord Avon and subsequently of Harold Macmillan. And I trust that they will not stand in the way of promotion in the Foreign Service which his gifts and qualities most certainly merit.

The 'hope' in the last paragraph was not fulfilled. I had at one time been one of the youngest Counsellors in the Service, and when WSC died I was one of the oldest.

Chapter 31

────────── ❧ ──────────

WITH 1964 came an ever-deepening melancholy. There are few
events to recall, and the days passed in idle depression. One happiness was the marriage of WSC's grandson, Winston, to Minnie
d'Erlanger, which did illuminate WSC's life for a time. He was extremely
fond of the courageous and outspoken Winston, and I wish he could
have lived to see what a remarkable girl was to bear the great-grandchildren
of his name. This apart, there was little of good cheer. Max Beaverbrook
died, and, as I have already described, even in WSC's now withdrawn climate, the loss was a deep grief to him. His departure from Parliament,
inevitable and overdue, underlined to him his already well recognised
decline.

Faithful friends such as Monty, Ted Heath, Norman Brook and the Colvilles continued to come and see him, and his family remained loving and as
attentive as possible. We all did our best, and some things still gave WSC
pleasure, but his increasing physical enfeeblement, his ever-deteriorating
hearing, and now a perceptible dimming of his mind made each day a visible
burden. No longer able to manage the stairs, and it being impossible to install
a full-scale lift, he moved his bedroom to what had been my ground-floor
office, looking over the garden of No. 27 Hyde Park Gate, the annexe to No.
28. He seemed contented in a withdrawn way, and came to meals in the
dining room, where a short lift had been successfully installed, descending in
a sort of gilded bird-cage, in CSC's words, 'looking like a very important
owl'.

His last birthday, his ninetieth, on 30 November 1964, produced a flood of
presents, messages and letters. (The official biography states that there were
over 70,000.) I cannot match Mary's description:

> Clementine's present to him was a small golden-heart enclosing the engraved
> figures '90'. It was to hang on his watch-chain, and joined the golden heart with
> its central ruby 'drop of blood' which had been her engagement present to him
> fifty-seven years before. During the afternoon the Prime Minister called to
> bring Winston good wishes from the Cabinet.
>
> That evening there was the usual hallowed family dinner party: Randolph,
> Sarah, myself and Christopher, Winston and Minnie, and Arabella, Julian
> Sandys, Edwina and Piers Dixon, Celia Kennedy (Sandys); and Cousin Sylvia.
> The only guests not members of the family were Jock and Meg Colville, and
> Anthony and Nonie Montague Browne. Monty had been invited but was him-
> self ill in hospital.

The house glowed with candlelight and flowers, and we were united yet one more time in drinking first Winston's health and then Clementine's. But this birthday evening had for us all a poignant quality – he was so fragile now, and often so remote. And although he beamed at us as we all gathered round him, and one felt he was glad to have us there – in our hearts we knew the end could not be far off.

On 10 December WSC managed to attend the Other Club for the last time. A member later wrote: 'It had become increasingly difficult to awake the spark, formerly so vital; and all that could be said was that he knew where he was and was happy to be there. With that his colleagues had to be, and were, content.'

On 6 January 1965, WSC gave me his 1964 Christmas present. It was four beautifully bound volumes of his speeches, edited by Randolph. To my surprise, with touching effort, he had managed to sign them, his signature diminishing from 'Winston S Churchill' to an exhausted 'W' on the last volume. They were the last documents he ever signed.

Several versions exist of WSC's last words. No-one knows what they actually were. During the night of 9–10 January 1965, he suffered a massive stroke and never regained consciousness. He had been in reasonable health in the preceding days, and one must assume that his last words on the night of 9 January were of a banal nature.

Certainly he had repeatedly reflected on his end. Christopher Soames related that his father-in-law had said: 'I'm so bored with it all,' not long before the fatal stroke. I myself had more than once been greeted with: 'How much longer do you think I have to go?', or 'How much longer do you think I must wait?', and it was no good delivering a placebo with that forthright personality. I could only reply that it lay in God's hands, and that meanwhile WSC enjoyed the admiration, gratitude and affection of a vast number of the peoples of this Earth, in addition to the undying devotion of his family and friends. Sadly, it did not do much to comfort him.

The only contribution I can make on his last words relates to some months previously, when we were playing bezique, or attempting to play, because WSC's previous skill had weakened and withered. We finished the game. He sat back in his chair. Then his head fell forward. I took his hand to feel his pulse and rang for the nurse. His eyes opened and he gripped my hand with a surprisingly powerful clasp. He looked steadily at me, with something of his old penetrating blue gaze, and said very clearly and in a strong voice: 'No more!' Then he lost consciousness again. I think that at that moment he believed that his life had ended.

When it came to the morning of 10 January he was deeply unconscious, and even a layman did not need the confirmation of Lord Moran and Sir Russell Brain that this was the end of the road. The family were informed by CSC and I told the Queen's Private Secretary and the Prime Minister. Pressed on how soon death was likely to take place, I could only say that I thought it would be later than one might expect, given WSC's extraordinary vitality, but even I did not guess that he would defy the darkness for another fourteen days.

The Duke of Norfolk, the Earl Marshal, was in Scotland, and as pre-arranged, I sent him a telegram: ' "Hope Not" imminent.' His wife, Lavinia, later told me that he had been out all day and in the evening, when he asked if there had been any communication, she replied: 'Only a nonsense telegram.' Later he saw it and leapt into action, and all his superb organisation was brought to complete readiness for the State Funeral. (Randolph related that when he asked Norfolk what exactly a State Funeral was, he received the crisp reply: 'One for which the State pays.')

The next fourteen days have been described by many pens, best of all by Mary Soames. To me they remain a blur. I was so preoccupied with messages, telephone calls, final meetings of the Hope Not Committee, dealing with the press and so on. At intervals I went into WSC's bedroom, formerly my office. There was no visible change, and he lay as though asleep, with a nurse sitting beside him and occasionally moistening his lips. I sat with him briefly, and held his hand. His hands were beautiful. Aristocratic is a silly word to describe physical attributes; aristocrats come in all shapes and sizes, but there was something aesthetically appealing about those hands, and the word did seem suitable.

Early in the morning of 24 January one of the nurses telephoned to say that finality was very close. I went to Hyde Park Gate where the family was assembling. In his bedroom we stood, and as his breathing slowed, some of us knelt. Shortly after eight o'clock, with a little sigh, his breathing stopped. It was the same hour and the same day of the month of January that his father had died.

Later that day I went to Kensington Town Hall to register the death. Registrars in my experience are agreeable people, congratulatory on births and marriages and sympathetic on deaths. The Kensington Registrar was no exception, but he fired an unexpected question. 'What should I put down as Sir Winston's occupation?' he enquired gently.

I hadn't thought of that. 'Retired' didn't seem right. So I said: 'Statesman.'

For some time before the coffin was closed, family and closest friends came to look on him for the last time. Violet Bonham Carter stood for ten minutes by him. She finally said: 'Goodbye, Winston' and left silently. Jock, the yellow cat, of whom WSC was engagingly fond, came into the bedroom, jumped into the coffin, peered into the still face, and went away, never to re-enter that room again.

The Lying-in-State in Westminster Hall was deeply impressive, as indeed was everything Norfolk touched. It has been stated that WSC himself played a substantial part in the organising of his funeral. This is untrue. The only injunction he had given me was: 'Remember, I want lots of military bands at my funeral.' He got nine. My only direct contribution was to suggest two pieces of music that I knew he liked, the Dead March from Saul and the slow movement of Beethoven's Eroica symphony.

I visited the Lying-in-State twice, both times late at night with CSC. Here again, the mournful dignity and the silent, endless procession of those coming to pay their last respects have been ably described and photo-graphed, and I have nothing worthwhile to add. Meanwhile I was fully occupied with the final details of the funeral and the requests, mostly reason-able, for seats in St Paul's Cathedral. The lists had been drawn up long ago, but there were inevitable alterations and changes of priority. The press behaved with extraordinary forbearance and kindness during the whole time, and their telephoned enquiries were mostly fielded by the Earl Mar-shal's office.

The Earl Marshal himself, in any case an old friend of the Churchills', was omnipresent and apparently omnipotent. When I told him of CSC's fears that the burial at Bladon would be over-run by photographers, he said: 'Tell Clemmie not to worry. If necessary I'll surround the whole village with a barbed-wire entanglement.' He meant it, too, but it did not turn out to be needed.

One aspect of the Funeral did cause a certain amount of difficulty. Who should walk behind the coffin in the procession from Westminster Hall to St Paul's and from St Paul's to Tower Pier, where the coffin would be embarked on a Port of London launch to go to Waterloo Station for the train to Bladon? CSC took the matter firmly into her own hands. The closer male members of the family, if of sufficient age, should walk behind the coffin. I should also do so, as the sole representative of all those who had worked for him.

On 30 January the funeral took place in full and impressive State cere-mony. For me the scene was blurred. I had feared marring things by weep-ing, as I share my late Master's facility for tears. I had slipped a disc not long before and the lesion was not healed. The discomfort of the long, slow march was a helpful distraction, but the black melancholy thoughts of the decline and decay of so much of what WSC had striven for kept obtruding. Well might the Nation mourn him.

The Service in St Paul's was without modern parallel. The Queen, accompanied by Prince Philip, General de Gaulle and Eisenhower were among the six Sovereigns and fifteen Heads of State present. After the Ser-vice, the procession re-formed and headed for Tower Pier, where the coffin was placed on the Port of London Authority launch, and those who were going on to Bladon for the burial followed in another. The Earl Marshal then departed from the strict programme. At the end of the Pier, he stood at the salute, a lonely and windswept figure, until the launches were out of sight in the sleet and mist. I thought of 'Morte d'Arthur', which WSC had much admired, but could only remember odd lines:

> ... And over them the sea wind sang,
> Shrill, chill with flakes of foam ...
> And on the mere the wailing died away.

Then came a sudden shattering blast of sound as four Lightning fighters of the Royal Air Force flew low over Tower Bridge in tight diamond formation and climbed away into the overcast. The quayside cranes dipped in salute as the launches passed, for London was still (just) a major port. We went below and were handed half-pint mugs of hot rum and water – the old grog of the old Navy.

At Waterloo the coffin was put on the train for Bladon, and with the curious and temporary degree of relief that accompanies the lifting of emotional tension, we lunched and drank champagne – and I have not the slightest doubt that WSC would have approved. The Earl Marshal had hurried to Waterloo by land, and I found him in his compartment. He had taken off his Earl Marshal's greatcoat and cocked hat, and was wearing an open-necked shirt and a green tweed jacket underneath. Very sensible too.

The procession to the graveyard at Bladon was brief, and we were few in number. As we filed passed the grave for the last time before it was closed, I was astonished to see a small and not particularly distinguished row of medals lying on the coffin. I could only suppose that it had fallen from the chest of one of the military coffin-bearers, and I wondered if it would remain there to perplex archaeologists of many centuries hence. We took our departure for London in the freezing dusk.

Lord Moran, at the top of his stylistic form, later wrote:

> And in a country churchyard, in the stillness of a winter evening, in the presence of his family and a few friends, Winston Churchill was committed to the English earth, which in his finest hour he had held inviolate.

At the back of my own mind there was the old quotation from WSC himself, of the death of Richard Coeur de Lion:

> worthy, by the consent of all men, to sit with King Arthur and Roland and other heroes of martial romance at some eternal Round Table, which we trust the Creator of the Universe in His comprehension will not have forgotten to provide.

On the way home, my mind was a blank. I tried to say some silent prayers for that brave and generous soul, but they were choked and confused, and came to nothing. I could not mourn for him: he had so clearly and for so long wanted to leave the World. But I was submerged in a wave of aching grief for Britain's precipitous decline, against which he had stood in vain.   -

When I reached our flat in Eaton Place it had been burgled.

BOOK FIVE

———— ❧ ————

Money Grubbing
1967–1989

Chapter 32

T H E N E X T few days brought letters of quite extraordinary kindness, and if letters of sympathy are intended to give happiness, these most certainly were successful. If I quote a few of them, it is not entirely out of vanity, but to indicate the warm hearts and eloquence of the writers. (See Appendix B.)

There also came by hand a parcel. In it was a bound Order of Service for the St Paul's ceremony. Those in the funeral procession had been given them at the Cathedral, but we could not carry them as we marched behind the coffin to Tower Pier. With the packet came a short note from Brigadier Sir Randle (Gerry) Feilden, the Earl Marshal's right-hand man. 'I was horrified to see some choristers and others at St Paul's descend like vultures to pick up the bound Orders of Service. You, of all people, should have one and I should be honoured if you would accept mine.'

I worked at Hyde Park Gate for some weeks after the funeral, helping CSC as best I could, but not very much was in fact needed, for she grasped the situation with determination and fortitude. When I said something admiring to this effect, she replied: 'Anthony dear, I have been thinking of it and preparing myself for it for so long.' She was of course surrounded by a united, loving and helpful family and by the best professional background of advisers, prominent among whom were WSC's solicitor, Anthony Moir of Fladgates, and his accountants Wood, Willey & Co., and there were in any case few or no controversial issues.

My health had been rather faltering for some time, and I had intended to take long leave abroad. This was not due to any particular strain, and I most emphatically did not require 'counselling', now apparently such an essential accompaniment to the everyday stresses and sadnesses that are an inevitable part of the lives of us all, but I seemed to be living up to the old engineering definition of the perfect machine: one in which every part wears out simultaneously. So I took off to the Middle East, India and South Africa, initially in one of Ari's tankers, the *Olympic Dale*.

On return, some two months later, I found a letter from Sir Michael Adeane, the Queen's Private Secretary, asking me to call on him. I was still in Crown employment as a Counsellor in the Diplomatic Service, and the Foreign Office had indicated that they wanted to discuss my future, to be a several-year posting abroad with a hint that it would be as Head of Chancery (the political section) of the Washington Embassy, after a period of re-indoctrination in London.

Michael Adeane was as usual straightforward and brisk. The Queen's Private Office then consisted of three Private Secretaries: Michael, and his two assistants, Martin Charteris and Edward Ford. Edward Ford, Michael said, wished to retire before long. The Palace was looking for a successor. Both he and Martin Charteris were of much the same age and if a new third party was a success, he could look forward to the position of Principal Private Secretary before very many years. He suggested that I should remain a member of the Diplomatic Service and be paid as before, but should be seconded to the Palace for a period of about a year while, in his words: 'we look at you and you look at us.' Meanwhile my functions would be something of a roving commission, but I would principally be concerned with supervising the making of a film or films on the Queen's pictures, palaces and works of art.

I was both surprised and flattered by the suggestion. The Queen's Private Secretary holds an Office of State, being responsible for the Sovereign's relations with both the Government of the UK and the Commonwealth Governments, besides many more functions, both ex officio and formal and personal. It is the hell of a job. Incidentally, it brings with it a Privy Counsellorship, various ascending degrees of the Victorian Order and a peerage on retirement. That apart, there are agreeable dwellings in one of the London Palaces and at Balmoral, etc. But the real attraction is that at certain moments, for instance in a constitutional crisis, the Private Secretary can be, and frequently has been, in a position of major importance and of the highest responsibility, where his advice can be of lasting national significance.

On the other side of the coin, there would have been the endless ceremonial and formal occasions. It is perhaps my Ulster blood, but I dislike and distrust tinsel, because it obscures dangerously the reality of advance or decline. Moreover I was haunted by the fact that I was poor and likely to continue to be so. The then Palace salary was adequate in the light of those days, some £5,000 a year as I remember it, plus numerous easements and perquisites, and, as Michael Adeane said, 'You don't have time to spend it anyway.' But I had grown very thin (not physically, alas) on thirteen years of service on London pay, with none of the allowances that gave a diplomat a chance to fatten while he was abroad, and I had had to keep up a suitable household, dress the part for many occasions and educate Jane, by then aged twelve. I owed my family a duty and I did not like the idea of having to exist after retirement solely on a pension of those times, my inheritance expectations being small and my hopes that my parents would live for many years being fervent.

These negative considerations did no more than flit through my mind. I was conscious of the honour done me by the suggestion and the historical background. I was a monarchist, and it did not take me long gratefully to accept the proposal and the probationary period.

Shortly afterwards I was installed in an office in St James's Palace. It was the room in which King Charles I had spent his last night on earth, before walking to Whitehall for his execution, wearing two shirts against the cold lest people should think that he was trembling from fear. (And the brutal order was given at the scaffold for the drums to roll, so that the King's last speech could not be heard.) My secretary sat in the little tower that overlooks Marlborough Gate. It was an agreeable and civilised milieu in which to work.

St James's Palace housed the Lord Chamberlain's Office. He was Lord (Kim) Cobbold, ex-Governor of the Bank of England, and with him were Eric Penn and Johnny Johnston, both former Guards officers with distinguished war records. They were ultra-efficient, kind, humorous and excellent company: the very best sort of courtiers and totally devoted to the Queen. One of Eric's first gambits was to show me round St James's Palace, originally an asylum for women lepers in the eleventh century, lying in a marsh, and subsequently built as a palace for Henry VIII. The cobblestones in the courtyards are sometimes carved with a crude little cross, to mark the graves of the poor original inmates.

In July 1965 I was summoned to meet the Queen. She was at Holyrood House, the Royal Palace at Edinburgh for her annual visit. I flew up, unsuitably clad for the flight in a morning coat for the Holyrood garden party, and lunched in a small gathering, seated on the Queen's right. Prince Philip looked at me with surprise and asked, but in an agreeably friendly way, 'Hello, what are you doing here?', to which I thought it best to return a vague answer.

The Queen herself was unexpectedly informal. Light-footed, her conversation covered a whole variety of topics, varying from the future of France to the personality of the Astronomer Royal. That H.M. was well-informed came as no surprise, but her succinct and sharply delineated comments did. When in the presence of the Great one tends either to be tongue-tied or to talk too much. I consciously, if excessively, opted for the second: after all, I was in effect being interviewed. When I left I concluded that if indeed I received the appointment, the personal side would be truly agreeable.

The making of the films was fascinating, even to one who has only a limited acquaintance with the arts. The Queen's pictures are of course an extraordinary treasure-house of the centuries, the peaks being reached by the great Royal collectors, among whom George IV is rather surprisingly prominent. The experience was perhaps wasted on me, even though there would never be another chance to see so prized a collection at such easy and close quarters. As I recollect, there were more than 800 Leonardo da Vinci drawings at Windsor and more than thirty Canalettos, just to start with. And the palaces themselves were a panorama of British history. The film-makers, one team for television and one for the broad screen, were dazzled and delighted, and pleasant and easy to deal with.

A press enquiry to the Palace Press Office, who were not aware of my raison d'être at the Palace, elicited the reply that I was there to ensure that the film makers did not trip over cables and cause problems, which in a way was quite true.

Meanwhile my association with the Churchill family continued agreeably, and in particular I saw a good deal of CSC. When Winston Churchill's Will was published, I found that he had generously left me £10,000. CSC followed this up with a gift of a pair of his cuff-links, heavy gold and given to him on his eightieth birthday by King Peter of Yugoslavia. They had allegedly been worn by Peter's father, King Alexander, at the time of his assassination at Marseilles in the 1930s. CSC also added a second of WSC's pictures to the one he had already given me.

Another gift, albeit not a particularly welcome one, came in the Honours List. It was a CBE (Companion of the Order of the British Empire). I am not companionable and there is no British Empire. Moreover Civil Servants, and I include Diplomats, tend to look on Honours in the same way as a waiter looks on tips and have a similarly precise, albeit unspoken scale of values. My pourboire on this reckoning was seven and a half per cent. WSC had attempted to give me the same award in 1955 in his retirement list, but, according to Jock Colville, 'the suggestion had raised such a Whitehall squawk that it had deafened the ducks in the Park,' because of my (then) junior rank in the Service. So he had given me an OBE (one down), known in Britain as 'Other buggers' efforts', and to the French as 'Ordre Britannique embusqué'.

I have reflected before on the deficiency of our Honours system, and it is wrong to mock the Order of the British Empire, if – and only if – it is awarded for proper reasons. The sheer debauchery of our present arrangements has taken away a most potent incentive to public service. Peerages and knighthoods should be rare animals, and never, never given when the recipient has merely achieved prominence to the advantage of his own occupational advancement or enrichment. Thus an industrialist should not be allowed to 'buy' an award by contributions to Party funds, often with money not his own; a celebrated actor should not be knighted just because he is successful; and above all politicians should not have the inalienable – in their own eyes – right to a peerage. As a newspaper once expressively put it: 'This is spitting in the face of the House of Lords.' To be Utopian, the stage should get one knighthood in a decade and one peerage in thirty years. The press ditto. Industry much the same, with sufficient flexibility to make exceptions if true national – not Party or personal – advantage could be shown. Diplomats should not have the pre-emptive right to a KCMG at a certain level; the military should not be automatically knighted at the rank or equivalent of Lieutenant-General. In the war Lieutenant-Generals were truly significant figures, commanding many thousands of men. Now, alas, they are often only the top layer of bureaucrats in what is perilously close to an inverted pyramid.

Is this sour grapes? No. I held these views, and expressed them, all my working life, so perhaps I was rewarded according to my own formula.

To pass on to more constructive matters, steps were being taken to raise funds for a national memorial to Winston Churchill. Field Marshal Alexander headed the appeal and was ably assisted by a group of advisers. The objects of the appeal were much debated. Alexander and his supporters rested their case on the visit to WSC in his last years by Mr Edward Houghton of the English Speaking Union of the United States, who first suggested a memorial foundation of an educational nature. WSC had instructed me to draft a reply giving the idea general support, and expressing the hope that British technological advancement could be a principal feature.

Others suggested a monument of a more physical nature. One of the most commendable proposals was that the fund raised should be used to buy for the National Trust areas of coastline as they came on the market.

Randolph's idea of a suitable monument was for a column of the same height as Nelson's in Trafalgar Square, to be erected at Covent Garden, surmounted by a statue of WSC. 'Nelson and he would be looking at each other,' he said. Actually, they couldn't: Nelson is looking south towards the coast and France, but this apart it was an imaginative picture.

In addition to the statue in Parliament Square, Winston Churchill now has two national memorials: Churchill College at Cambridge and the Winston Churchill Memorial Trust. But to say this is to neglect his books, his pictures, his recorded oratory and above all these his immeasurable contribution to his country and to the survival of democratic freedom. 'Si monumentum requiris, circumspice',* is written of Sir Christopher Wren in St Paul's Cathedral. Yes, and on a world-wide scale for Sir Winston Churchill.

In 1965 CSC had taken counsel of Norman Brook, the former Secretary of the Cabinet, a staunch friend and a much-respected servant of the country and WSC in particular, and of whom the latter was wont to say: 'He has a remarkable mental muscle.' Bill de L'Isle (Viscount de L'Isle and Dudley VC, an old family friend) was also co-opted and so was I. In the event CSC did not need very much advice. The memorial should be a foundation to give travelling scholarships (later styled Fellowships) in different disciplines, for those awarded them to travel abroad and acquire knowledge not available in Britain, and to bring it back and disseminate it for the benefit of the country. Norman Brook was to set up the Board of Trustees, Bill was to set up the Council who would administer the scheme, and I was to be a member of both Trustees and Council, to represent the family and Sir Winston's general views. The fund, raised by subscription and augmented by a generous Government donation at the instigation of the Prime Minister, Harold Wilson, was then adequate for these purposes. Although the English Speaking Union had been to some extent the mother agency of the Memorial, CSC wished it to be entirely independent.

This is not the place for an extended history of the Trust, but to summarise, we have now had some 80,000 candidates or would-be candidates through our (the Council's) hands, and the Trust's capital has grown to over £16 million. The Council, whose members usually serve for between five and ten years, has included a wide variety of highly distinguished figures, such as Sir Peter Scott of environmental fame; Lord Penney, the physicist; Sir Colin Cowdrey, the cricketer; Sir George Pinker, the Queen's gynaecologist; Sir Trevor Holdsworth, Chairman of the Confederation of British Industry; eminent trade unionists; the Curator of the Victoria and Albert

* 'If you seek a memorial, look about you.'

Museum; and many others. For nepotistic and pietistic reasons I am allowed to chair the Council, succeeding such swells as de L'Isle and Terence O'Neill, former Prime Minister of Northern Ireland. It is the greatest fun and enlivens my retirement no end, for the Council is a true working body, unremunerated and unsung.

We have managed to send some 2,700 Fellows abroad under the two themes, WSC's 'With opportunity comes responsibility' and our own 'The chance of a lifetime'. Their 'disciplines' have varied from care of the mentally handicapped to motorway maintenance, drug control, disposal of farm effluents, the cause and treatment of cleft palates (this one a success story, via research into alligators, of all things), ballet dancing, plumbing, dry-cleaning and ship-building to name only a few.

The Trustees, chaired by Mary Soames, preside over the finances and the observance of the purposes of the Trust. The Council selects the annual categories for Fellowships and chooses the Fellows from written applications and interviews.

It had seemed to me difficult for Britain to slide much further in the international field, but I was wrong. Betrayal succeeded betrayal. To take only one manifestation of many, the decent, long-established and often elderly servants of Britain in Aden were casually thrown to the wolves in the shape of the bitterly hostile and fanatically cruel opponents of our regime, themselves supplied and supported by the Russians, the East Germans and the Nasserites of the Arab world. It hardly caused a ripple, though some of those who had sought to avert the worst vainly attempted to rally courage and fair play in Parliament. I viewed these events with growing horror. It made me wonder if the legend of the wounded hyena tearing its own guts out had come to life nationally in Britain, and it was in this light that I saw the unfolding of the Rhodesian tragedy.

Britain, now so pusillanimous towards our enemies, made up for it by intransigent severity towards our friends. Two incidents, one trivial, the other serious, focused my feelings of shame and anger. A cartoon of Ian Smith, the Prime Minister of Rhodesia, appeared in the British press. It distorted and maliciously emphasised his injured face; the injury had occurred when Smith had crashed in his Hurricane fighter while operating in North Africa in the War. The cartoonist was not British. No-one seemed to be particularly disturbed. Shortly after I was bidden to dinner in St James's Palace by the hospitable Lord Cobbold, the Lord Chamberlain. George Brown, the Foreign Secretary, was present and he was unwontedly sober. As we walked into dinner he said to me: 'What would your old boss have said about Rhodesia?'

I thought that I could guess what he might have said, but I replied: 'I don't know. He's dead.'

Brown persisted: 'Well, I know. He'd have said "I'll crush those rebels,"' pronounced with a grotesque imitation of WSC's voice.

This was too much. I waited until we were seated, and then, finding George Brown one seat away from me, addressed him thus: 'I wish you wouldn't seek to quote Winston Churchill on such an issue, and still less imitate him. He is dead. And I don't think that he would have shared your foolish and cowardly opinions.'

That tore it. A look of agony crossed Cobbold's face. George Brown set off on a tirade which included such shafts of wit as: 'You're a fascist.' This particular attack has long been a feature of the left-wing armoury when they have nothing more significant to say, and I had long ago prepared an answer, just in case it came my way.

'I am not a fascist,' I proclaimed indignantly; 'fascists are Italian Socialists: I'm not Italian and I'm certainly not a Socialist.' The poor girl sitting between us was caught in a no-man's-land of invective, but gallantly interjected something diverting and the Foreign Secretary and I simmered into silence. What I will say for him is that he didn't pull rank. He could have: after all he was the Foreign Secretary and I was only a Counsellor verging on superannuation.

I had studied Rhodesian history: Rhodesia had been offered Dominion, i.e. independent status, in 1941, and had declined it, saying in effect: 'Let's win the war first.' They had contributed to our victory, both by active participation in the fighting and by the training of many RAF pilots under the Empire Flying Training Scheme. The white regime was not viciously repressive – indeed, compared with the situation in many newly self-governing African countries it was positively idyllic – and Ian Smith's slogan 'Equal rights for all civilised men' was an encouraging start. Duncan Sandys had said to Roy Welensky, the then Prime Minister of Rhodesia: 'We have lost the will to rule,' which received the reply: 'But we haven't.' And both were speaking the truth. I held no particular brief for the average white settler personally. Rude people had said that Kenya was the Officers' Mess of a bad regiment, and Rhodesia the Sergeants' Mess of ditto. Still one might ask, but Britain didn't: 'If you were African, in which country would you rather live, Rhodesia under Ian Smith or Uganda under Idi Amin?' (or, indeed, Rwanda, Zaire, Angola, Somalia, with etceteras going off the page).

The almost uncontrollable and involuntary violence of my reaction to Brown led me to think seriously about my suitability as a Private Secretary to the Queen. Neutrality, balance, silence, lack of prejudice must be central to the role, whatever one's private thoughts might be. I realised clearly that I was probably not suitable as a Royal Private Secretary in the existing climate, and that I would risk doing more harm than good in that role. Moreover, if one disapproved of one's country's course of action, then as a democrat one should seek election to Parliament to make a contrary voice heard.

So, with a heavy heart and without consulting anyone, I addressed the following letter to Micheal Adeane:

4th January, 1966

My dear Michael,

We had agreed that the question of my future should be left in abeyance until now. I think that I should let you know without delay that I have reached a conclusion – a conclusion that you may well have reached on your side.

I feel that I am not the right man for the job. There are a number of reasons for this decision, which I will gladly give you orally, though perhaps Disraeli's advice 'Never explain' is best. What I would like you to believe is that I am truly and deeply honoured by the fact that you should have considered me, that I cannot conceive of more charming and stimulating colleagues for and with whom to work, and that it is after a great deal of heart-searching that I send you this letter.

I am sending a copy of this letter to The Lord Chamberlain with a covering note.

Yours ever,

ANTHONY

Lt.-Colonel The Rt. Hon. Sir Michael Adeane, GCVO, KCB,
St James's Palace

Michael's reply was heartwarming. He said that neither the Queen nor her servants shared my conclusion that I was not the right man for the job and were therefore disappointed. However, it had indeed been agreed that there was no commitment on either side until the end of 1965 and there was thus no reason why I should not reach my negative decision. I was asked to carry the supervision of the film-making to a conclusion, which in fact took most of 1966.

I viewed, and continue to view this episode with great sadness. My forebears had served the Crown over a span of more than four hundred years, mainly as soldiers but in Tudor days at Court, and at distinguished levels. Was I wrong in my decision? I fear not.

In due course I was summoned to take leave of the Queen. I wondered if I would be asked why I had reached my decision, and determined on a truthful, if incomplete reply, thus: 'Because, Ma'am, your Private Secretary must be silent and impartial, and I am partial and noisy.' In the event Her Majesty did not ask the question, but gave me a framed photograph signed by herself and Prince Philip and a friendly farewell.

On the anniversary dinner given by the Duke of Norfolk for those principally concerned in Winston Churchill's State Funeral, my doubts as to my abilities to contain my feelings in matters on which I felt deeply were confirmed. I was sitting on Bernard Norfolk's right, and the officer who had commanded the bearers of the coffin on his left. The officer spoke of Rhodesia and 'colonialism' in terms that seemed to me both ignorant and foolish, and I could not restrain myself from a violent riposte, which spoiled the dinner.

It now remained to resign from the Diplomatic Service. I could not in good conscience return to the Foreign Office. I had been too long away; and I contemplated with horror and deep foreboding our policies in many parts of the world. Perhaps if I had taken part in planning them each successive little cowardice, every betrayal of a minor friend, each new concession or unctuous apology to our enemies could have seemed justifiable. 'I tell the tale that I've heard told / Mithridates he died old.' As it was, I was beginning to doubt the honour and indeed the sanity of my colleagues, though I never doubted their personal ambition. They were a very different lot from twenty years before.

I wrote this in 1966, and if it seems exaggerated, I would ask the reader to cast his mind back to those days.

So in due course I called on the Chief Clerk, Sir Colin Crowe, who was an old friend. What, I enquired, would my pension be after approximately twenty years' service?

Colin pointed his thumb earthwards. 'Nil,' he said.

'??'

'The Rules say that if you resign when the Service wishes you to remain and is prepared to employ you, then no pension is payable.'

'Supposing I was dismissed because of bad conduct or idleness or incompetence?' I enquired.

'Well, then you'd get a pension,' admitted Colin.

It seemed to me that my course was obvious: all I would have to do was to turn up when it suited me and tell everyone who would listen my opinion of our foreign policy (if any). I suggested this to Colin.

'I don't think you'd do that,' he smiled. He was right, and I returned, outraged. What private employer could get away with that?

I concluded that if the Service was to be pettily bureaucratic, I would play them at their own game. I read the Rules with a barrack-room lawyer's care. Aha! There was a rule that said that if a member of the Service was unable to serve in any particular part of the world because of his health, then he might be allowed or required to retire. I had been told that kidney stones made it undesirable to spend long periods in a tropical climate and I had indeed most painfully suffered from them. (Ari's medical brother-in-law, Théodore, had offered his helpful advice on one occasion: 'Anthony, c'est une douleur atroce.'*)

The Chief Clerk was dismissive. 'It won't work, chum,' he said cheerfully, 'but you can see the Treasury Medical Adviser if you wish.' I did and struck gold, or at any rate a sensible and sympathetic outlook in the Adviser, Doctor Medvei. The interview was brief. He looked at my X-rays and said that if I really wanted to resign, he thought that I had every right to do so after twenty years, of which nearly thirteen had been with Winston Churchill. 'The medical evidence sustains this view,' he concluded, 'and I will recommend your retirement on medical grounds.'

I was slightly dunched to find that the pension was a munificent £800 a year. (I have noted that when I leave a job, the salary attached to it almost immediately rises astronomically, as though it were a balloon shedding ballast. Diplomatic Service pay is now a very great deal larger, even taking account of inflation.) Meeting Colin at a Palace reception shortly afterwards, I could not refrain from muttering: 'It won't work, chum.'

My attempts to enter Parliament are soon told. The Conservative Central Office, with what degree of sincerity I cannot tell, welcomed me on to the

---

* 'Anthony, it's an atrocious pain.'

Candidates List and I put my name forward to various safe (or at least acceptably fightable) constituencies as they came on the by-election market. At forty-four, I was too old to go through the mill of the young political aspirant, and I thought that my twenty years of public affairs and the experience of working for WSC for thirteen of them would let me off. Anyway, out of either pietas or optimism, I was almost invariably short-listed, usually to three or four and in the case of Chislehurst to two out of eighty applicants. But there is only one winner in such a contest, and whatever the Central Office might or might not have said of me, the local Selection Committees do love their little hour of power, and Association Chairmen are usually keenly sensitive to the whiff of an OBE if the Party line is dutifully toed. And in those days the Party line was implacably wet.

I took some comfort from the words of WSC in his wilderness days. 'What is the use', he asked, 'of sending members to Parliament to say popular things of the moment and saying things merely to give satisfaction to the Government Whips and by cheering loudly every Ministerial platitude?' And: 'What is the value of our parliamentary institutions and how can our parliamentary doctrines survive if constituencies try to return only tame, docile and subservient members who try to stamp out every form of independent judgement?'

His daughter Sarah wrote: 'What price politics, since they won't listen to you?'

I was a Thatcherite on many, but I trust not all political themes long before I had even heard of Mrs Thatcher. Moreover, I was sometimes thunderingly tactless when provoked by parochialism. Later on, when I was being interviewed at Ruislip as a potential European Parliament candidate, a splendid lady looked at me indignantly and said: 'But what do you know of Ruislip?' Ruislip, admirable community though it no doubt is, was not exactly the whole of a Euro-constituency, but with Kipling in mind I could not refrain from declaiming rhetorically: 'What do they know of Ruislip, that only Ruislip knows?' Like the unfortunate Sir John Harrington, the seventeenth-century inventor of the water closet, I have seldom been able to refrain from a 'scurvy jeste' at the wrong moment.

My final effort, in a Home Counties constituency, seemed to be going rather well. My wife and I were on the platform in the last stages of selection when I was asked to speak on national defence. This was my favourite topic, and I warmed to it. The Young Conservative defence expert obviously thought I overdid it. (He, poor fellow, had bottle-bottom spectacles and wouldn't have known a boomerang from a howitzer – rather like a subsequent Conservative Minister of Defence, who was unfortunate enough to be photographed attempting to insert a mortar-bomb into the barrel the wrong end first.)

'Mr Montague Browne,' he said, creative diphthongs flying all over the place, 'you seem to me to be rather militaristic.'

I did my best. 'Well, Sir,' I replied, 'I do hope I'm not. Few people who have fought in a war want to do it again. That is why . . . [si vis pacem, and all that]. Within the twenty-three nations of the Atlantic Treaty and the Warsaw Pact, only four have no national service: Iceland, Luxembourg, Canada and Britain. Surely even people like you can see . . . ?'

My wife hissed in my ear: 'You've blown it.' And she was quite right.

Our military decline, to continue so sadly, and as far as those responsible were concerned so smugly, had not passed unnoticed abroad. The Soviet bloc's reaction was almost incredulous glee, and the Middle East countries were either dismayed or delighted, according to political preference. Admiral Brown, the former Commander of the formidable US Sixth Fleet in the Mediterranean and later Chairman of the American Chiefs of Staff, was reported to have spoken approximately thus at a dinner table.

'I love the Brits, and they were our best and probably our only reliable ally. And their wartime conduct spoke for itself. But now all they've got is Generals and Admirals and Air Marshals – and bands.'

Can we wonder that our world influence has diminished to a governessy lecturing, and even that is often pointed in the wrong direction?

I suppose that even if I had achieved a seat no-one would have paid any attention to my jeremiads ('What price politics since they won't listen to you?'); so I tried no further.

Chapter 33

———— ❧ ————

WHICH BRINGS me to my part-title of 'Money Grubbing'. I had separated from Nonie in 1969 and was divorced in 1970. The fault was entirely mine: she had been a loyal and admirable wife and a devoted mother and in the divorce proceedings was as undemanding as it is possible to be. I am happy to say that after my marriage to Shelagh Macklin, and after Nonie's own two subsequent marriages, she remains a wonderful friend. But this book is not about my private life.

After leaving the Service in 1967, I naturally enough had been faced with the necessity of making a living. Some of my friends were kindly helpful. Alan Lennox-Boyd (Lord Boyd, the former Cabinet Minister, whom I much admired) was especially diligent in my interest. He was Managing Director of Guinness, and an impressive and much-respected figure in business and finance. I found myself asked on a variety of occasions to lunch at Park Royal, the London headquarters of Guinness, without knowing why. After a while the invitations ceased, though I continued to see Alan. One day he told me that he had intended me to succeed him, after having taken an individually tailored course at the Harvard Business School. However, his colleagues and the Guinness family did not find the idea acceptable. I was hardly surprised. Vain though I am, such an appointment of a man with no business experience would be almost impossible. But what fun it might have been!

Ronnie Grierson (Sir Ronald Grierson) had also been helpful. A successful banker and all-round financier, he had changed his name from Rolf Hans Griessman, for the most respectable of reasons. He had fought in the War and had been wounded, and it would certainly not have been agreeable to be captured with his original name pointing to his German birth. He had asked me to dine alone with him and the Aga Khan, for the discussion of unspecified employment after WSC's death. It was a kind thought, but whatever the job might have been I would not have been appropriate for it. Max Beaverbrook had heard of the incident through his own mysterious and omnipresent if not omniscient network, and expressed the same thoughts in rather more robust terms.

Some time earlier Beaverbrook had invited me to dine to meet his son Max Aitken, known as 'Little Max' but in no pejorative sense as he had been a most gallant and distinguished fighter pilot and had a genial and forceful personality. He was also very attractive to women, and did not neglect the fact. Beaverbrook's letter of invitation had been brief and somewhat quaint. Thus:

Dear Anthony,

I would like you to dine with me at Arlington House next Wednesday, to meet my son. He is a sturdy middle-aged man and I think you would get on with him. Yours ever

MAX

I duly dined and did get on with him.

After WSC's death, Max (Aitken) asked me to lunch in the Express building in Fleet Street. A number of possibilities of employment were discussed, some definitely appealing – or at least apparently so to one who did not know the newspaper world. I learned later that the most agreeable of the proposals had been made simultaneously to someone else. On my way home I met a friend.

'Where have you been?' he asked.

'Lunching with Max Aitken,' I replied. 'I do like him him. He is good-natured and fun. And apart from that he is deceptively intelligent.'

A few years before my friend had been unwise enough to let his beautiful wife go on a cruise on Max's yacht *Drumbeat*. The inevitable had happened, and she and her husband had parted. This I had forgotten, but my friend hadn't: 'Deceptively intelligent?' he said bitterly. 'Oh no, a man can't be that clever at both ends.'

At a further lunch I met John Junor, whose column in the Sunday press causes grief to many who usually deserve it. I liked him for a few reasons: for a brief but charming paragraph of unwontedly lyrical prose about the happiness of two wild geese flying together in a Northern sky; for arranging enough *Express* coverage to scupper a man who was peddling shooting expeditions to Spain to massacre migratory thrushes ('Real hot-gun stuff' ran his brochure); and for attacking political wets and scuttlers. On the other hand, I remembered Beaverbrook saying: 'Junor's a black Scot. I can control him, but not many people can. He's got a lot of the Devil in him.' Indeed, his charm was not legendary.

Junor took a dislike to me – easy enough for anyone to do, but in this case I think it was linked to my apparent assumption of ease of ability to take on a senior position without going through the mill, and perhaps a substantial chip on his own shoulder. At any rate, a not unfriendly column about me by Robin Douglas Home in the *Sunday Express* had been edited to a point where I appeared not only unemployed, which I was, but unemployable too. It was accompanied by a photograph taken some years previously when I was suffering from a serious hangover. Douglas Home apologised and told me of the editing, which was none of his doing. My instincts not to work in Fleet Street were much strengthened, and when an offer was made to me, which included writing my memoirs, I declined.

To the rescue came Kenneth Whitaker, the Chairman of the Discount House Gerrard and Reid, subsequently Gerrard and National after taking over the National Discount Company which, in that picturesque American term, was about to go belly up. (The National had numbered among its Directors Enoch Powell and David Money-Coutts, later Chairman of Coutts

Bank.) I had been befriended by Kenneth on board Jack Bilmeir's yacht *Aronia* on the way to look at a lead mine in Corsica, as I have described earlier. Kenneth now offered me a non-executive Directorship, at which I jumped. There is not space here, nor would it be of great interest, to describe fully the activities of a Discount House. In effect it was a bank of a wholesale nature, banking for other banks in their surplus sterling funds and deploying them in Treasury Bills, Government Bonds, Bills of Exchange, Certificates of Deposit, etc., and underwriting the Bank of England's weekly Treasury Bill issue. Discount Houses had the right to borrow from the Bank of England as the 'lender of last resort', a rather cataclysmic term for a facility exercised quite frequently for very short periods.

Columbia Pictures, to my surprise, offered me a seat on the Board of their British production company. I asked their Chairman why. He replied that he had once negotiated with me and that I was such a son-of-a-bitch that he would rather have me on his side of the table. Also Sidney Cohn, his legal adviser, a Supreme Court lawyer of distinction and a friend of mine, had recommended me.

So far so good, but non-executive Directorships in those days and a pension of £800 a year were not enough to keep up on. At this stage Toby O'Brien, by then one of the doyens of the public relations industry, intervened with the best of intentions and the most complicated and potentially dangerous effects. He introduced me to Dick Hammerman, an agreeable, energetic and honest life insurance man from California with a good reputation. Hammerman had started a small but innovative and vigorously growing British life company called International Life (ILI). It was a pioneer of the equity-linked life assurance policy, selling a ten-year endowment plan, and Hammerman had attracted a sound and talented young team. The equity investment was undertaken by a number of London merchant banks, who were allocated funds in accordance with their relative success – an interesting but faulty system. Over what term, for instance, was performance to be judged, and was there not a risk of an investment manager gambling if he saw his performance slipping and he knew that he was going to be judged on a monthly basis?

But these snags were dwarfed by two much greater considerations. First, the majority shareholder of International Life was the Geneva-based Investors Overseas Services (IOS), which ran a large number of mutual funds (Unit Trusts) mostly in US dollars, of which the largest was the Fund of Funds. Their leading light was Mr Bernard Cornfeld, and they employed some 13,000 people throughout the world, most of them 'self-employed' direct salesmen, who were remunerated on a pyramiding commission scale. Secondly, the International Life direct sales force was a wholly-owned subsidiary of IOS. Salesmen are much the same the world over, but they vary in quality and honesty; they are enthusiasts and they need watching. The sale of investments door-to-door was and is, of course, prohibited by law, but the sale of life insurance policies was not; and here lay a risk, for the essence of International Life's policies was the success of equity investment and the day-to-day activities of the sales force were out of our control, which should never have been the case.

At the time, however, things appeared rosy. IOS itself was looked on by some perceptive heads with misgivings, but a larger number of people, who would now probably deny it, admired and envied its placing power, its scale and its success, with subsidiary companies sprouting all over the world, and a bank flourishing in Luxembourg, Munich and Geneva. Prestigious names had been attracted to its main Board.

In England, the ILI Board included a partner in Guinness Mahon, the merchant bank, Lord Lonsdale (member of a North of England regional NEDDY), Sir Harmar Nicholls MP (a former Government Minister) and Sir Eric Wyndham White (formerly Director of GATT). I was offered a part-time executive Directorship, to work on the international expansion of ILI, and the salary was well above the average English scale, because most of the higher management was American. I was tempted, but took the precaution of consulting a jury of friends. The ones I can recall were Lord Cromer (the former Governor of the Bank of England), Bill de L'Isle (Chairman of the Phoenix Insurance Group), Freshfields (solicitors to the Bank of England and also to Gerrard and National, International Life and IOS), Jock Colville, who had joined the merchant bank Hill Samuel, Kenneth Whitaker, and Sir Brian Mountain, via a friend. (Mountain was a major figure in the insurance industry.) There were also a well-known economist and two or three others whose names I do not recollect. I thought that I had really covered the field.

Of these distinguished people, only two spoke out against my association: Sir Brian Mountain and Kenneth Whitaker. Of the remainder, opinions varied from cautious approval to enthusiasm. Bill de L'Isle wrote: 'There may be some raised eyebrows, but pay no attention. It is a golden opportunity.' So in I plunged.

At first all went well. My colleagues were about fifty–fifty British and American and for the most part young, optimistic and hard-working. The American work ethic is undoubtedly more potent than ours, though in my experience it does tend to adopt a new shibboleth too easily and to lose itself in a maze of meetings. I have always preferred to work in relative solitude, and I do not share the illusion that taking your jacket off is necessarily a sign of effective endeavour, though it does have the advantage of encouraging you to wear a clean shirt. My office was well appointed, and I had no fewer than two secretaries, one of whom, Margaret Lewis, was a gem who ultimately followed me when I became a Managing Director of Gerrard and National. On top of this the work was interesting and I did not find it too difficult to hack through the pseudo-technical terms of equity-based life assurance, or at least to acquire sufficient knowledge of capital movements to enable me to carry out my overseas tasks.

Other aspects were not quite so reassuring. I sent myself to the brief course that taught the IOS salesmen to market their wares. I was not impressed; surely there must be more than this to teaching someone of little experience to sell life policies? It seemed not. What was more disquieting was that the fast-talking 'instructors' seemed to resent my presence in the back row of their pupils. Directors were not expected to attend trainees' lectures, it seemed. Dick Hammerman, the Chairman of International Life, supported me robustly and told me privately of his intentions to take control of the sales force under the company's wing sooner rather than later. So far so good; particularly as the underlying product was sound, and the investment side was not in IOS hands. The sacrosanct Life Fund both looked and was secure.

IOS, as the majority shareholder, were insistent on frequent visits to their headquarters in Geneva for 'strategic planning' sessions and to impress their visitors with the size and efficiency of the organisation, of which in their view life assurance was only a dull and minor part. Size did impress: efficiency appalled. Riddled with confused and overlapping areas of authority, pullulating with unnecessary and dodgy advisers and permeated with almost wilful extravagance, it was like a fifteenth-century landscape of anarchy, where sales barons fought savagely for higher places in the hierarchy and above all for ever larger commissions in even juicier areas of exploitation. Their dress was flamboyant, their communications polyglot, their education tenuous and their greed unlimited. Surely people like this could not have built up such an international financial octopus? But they had. Could they sustain it, even increase it? Now that was a very different matter.

Presiding over this bizarre crew was Mr Bernard Cornfeld. His approach to me was condescendingly friendly. At one of our earlier meetings, a day-long discussion of 'corporate identity', I ventured to ask how the Group wished to be identified by the European business community? Before a suitably ponderous answer could be given, a little voice replied: 'As a Jewish conspiracy.' And indeed unkind people in the US had dubbed IOS 'Kosher Nostra'.

After one or two visits Cornfeld expansively suggested that I might soon join his main Board. I was increasingly uneasy at what I could see in Geneva, though the London operation seemed sane, rational and businesslike, so I asked if I might wait until I knew a good deal more about IOS and its activities. Cornfeld was nettled: 'That's an offer I only make once,' he said brusquely. I cursed myself for my pusillanimity: I had missed a chance of a quantum leap in my finances. But at least twice in my life timidity has paid off (the second time was when I declined to become a Name at Lloyd's) and thank God the invitation was not renewed!

A history of the rise and collapse of IOS has been written with a considerable degree of entertainment value not entirely matched by accuracy, and I don't intend to pursue at length the fall of that Tower of Babel, from which International Life emerged with a substantial degree of immunity, though in the interim various raids on it were attempted. Fortunately, British insurance companies are protected or disciplined by quite effective laws, and I found the Board of Trade well disposed, albeit originally cautiously neutral, as were the Bank of England once they were assured of the determination of the British Board to protect their policyholders.

In Geneva the internecine snarling and tearing continued merrily, every now and then spitting out choice snippets of scandal. One main Board director had left a Board meeting to sell all his shares when the bad news became apparent – though only to the Directors. An American business consultant who had come to advise on the mess said that he was obliged to carry a gun owing to the threats of the robber barons of the IOS sales force. Finally Sir Eric Wyndham White managed to oust Cornfeld, by a complex series of manoeuvres in which he contrived to vote Cornfeld's own shares against him. (Cornfeld commented rather winningly: 'It wasn't very knightly of him.')

We were relieved, for we knew Wyndham White to be an honest and well-intentioned man; but the respite did not last long. He had neither the means nor the power to sort out the situation: IOS was well and truly bust. Control was ultimately taken by Robert Vesco, a man described as a 'Chicago pool-room smoothie' and who is still on the run from United States justice as I write (1994). In London we knew little about him and felt quite reasonably safe with International Life's Life Fund, the heart of the company, securely invested and held in reputable British banks. However, the sniff of some £80 million of cash and easily realisable securities was too much for Vesco, who turned up, asking quite civilly and properly if he might, as the majority shareholder, look into the Company's affairs. He was accompanied by two rather unsavoury henchmen, one of whom had been a Rhodes Scholar, which gave an entirely erroneous impression of respectability. Vesco's first gambit was to suggest, then demand, that all the Life Fund's liquid assets should be transferred to the Overseas Development Bank, owned by IOS.

By this time I had reluctantly found myself elected executive Deputy Chairman of International Life. The Chairman, Dick Hammerman, had suffered what came close to a nervous breakdown, and the British Directors had been in effect ordered by the Board of Trade to grasp the situation and isolate our policyholders from the IOS cauldron. Easier said than done: the bad news from Geneva was frightening policyholders into cashing in their policies, although they were actually perfectly safe.

The pressure from Vesco became rapidly more insistent and our relations deteriorated from formality to hostility. The climax came when he ordered the Treasurer of ILI to make the transfers of the liquidity to the IOS bank. The Treasurer, Tom Orts, stout-hearted and totally honest, came to me for confirmation and I told him to disregard the order which was both ultra vires and illegal. The next day I received a polite invitation to lunch with Vesco alone in his hotel. Over an enormous, tough and tasteless steak sandwich he first requested, then wheedled with extravagant promises as a dressing, and finally threatened. I told him that I wouldn't and indeed couldn't cooperate with him. As I rose to depart there was the following exchange.

VESCO: 'Do you know that I come from Trieste?'
AMB: 'Oh?'
VESCO: 'Yes, and in Trieste we have ways of dealing with people who are as awkward as you.'

I sought elucidation from a friendly but venal figure in Geneva who had accepted Vesco's terms. 'What did he mean?' I asked.

'Don't be dumb,' was the reply, 'He's threatening to rub you out.'

I reflected that this was the first time my life had been threatened since the War (and even then the Japanese didn't threaten: they just had a go), and that it was exceedingly unlikely that any such steps would be taken. But it would be difficult to take counter-measures as it was only my word against his, so I redoubled my efforts to find a British purchaser of IOS's share in ILI. Ultimately I was successful and the shares were sold to a London entity which, though by no means ideal, was a good deal better than IOS and satisfied the Department of Trade and Industry. I had said that I would resign as soon as this was accomplished, and I wasted no time. Before going I arranged the appointment of a British Managing Director, Richard Ellis. This was a most fortunate choice. Richard was a highly qualified actuary with a lifetime of insurance experience. Moreover, he had a most unusual intellectual capacity, coupled with total integrity. The company was in good hands – operationally at least.

Tail between legs, I lunched with Kenneth Whitaker and sought his advice. After a certain amount of hesitation and consultation he telephoned me and spoke thus:

'Anthony, stop messing about and come and work for Gerrard. We are going into the Eurodollar market next year and you can run that side.'

'But Kenneth, I wouldn't know a Eurodollar if it got up and bit me,' I protested.

'Nor do we,' Kenneth rejoined briskly, 'but you can learn and we'll hire two young professionals as dealers.' And so it proved, and I was both grateful and relieved.

The City was very different from most of my previous experiences. Hindsight is of course twenty–twenty, but the symptoms that were to lead to, for example, the collapse of the tertiary banks and later of several of the Lloyd's syndicates were perceptible in the individuals involved quite a long time before the roof fell in. City gents, and the diminutive is certainly not always justified, come in all shapes and sizes, but they did seem to live by a very different standard from say, the old Diplomatic Service. No doubt they had to, and would not have been good at their jobs if they haddn't, but they were sometimes not the sort of people with whom one would wish to go tiger shooting. It was not that they would run away, so much that on turning to do so oneself, one might well find every convenient tree already occupied – but this is not a good analogy, for in the first place I wouldn't go tiger shooting and in the second tigers are quite good at climbing trees, and in the third I am not referring to physical courage anyway. But when I considered some of my contemporaries, or more probably men about ten years younger, I was struck by their sheer lack of intellectual horse-power or any general historical or political knowledge. I am referring inter alia to what I saw of Lloyd's and its satellites, and it was this, added to my natural timidity, that saved me from becoming a Name. I should add that at Gerrard we came in early, had our first Directors' meeting at 8.45 a.m. and worked hard until about 4.30 p.m. And now, I believe, the directors keep considerably longer hours than that.

These melancholy reflections on the quality of our present leaders and their accolytes, greater and lesser, are not, of course, directed solely at the City of London: industry and above all politics deserve acid censure of which only a Swift or a Pope would be properly capable. 'Debauched by ease/No King can govern and no God can please.' My own observations are flawed. Number Ten and Winston Churchill gave one a wonderful point de mire if nothing else, and later life was bound to seem rather mundane. I also had inherited from that time an unfortunate tendency to meddle, to pick up a letter from someone's desk and say: 'This is how you must deal with this.' Undoubtedly an irritating habit, which I sought vainly to eliminate.

A generalisation on these generalisations. It would be very wrong to conclude that they applied to the majority, but it would be too laborious to qualify each disobliging reference with 'but of course X, Y and Z were notable exceptions.' Just as a chart shows rocks and shoals and does not refer much to the greater areas of deep and safe water, so the new observer's eye lights more on what is bad than what is effective and good. But at the end of the road, I so much wish that those of whom I speak could have reflected on President Kennedy's Inaugural Speech: 'Ask not what your country can do for you: ask what you can do for your country.'

Gerrard were tolerant of my ignorance and my failings. Up to a point. The working Directors had a duty to their shareholders – and to themselves. But I was lucky in the 'two young professionals' recruited by my amiable colleague Peter Miles, subsequently Keeper of the Privy Purse at the Palace. These two, David Brayshaw and David Somerset were not only effective but saved me from many a pitfall which one at least of my senior colleagues would have not found displeasing.

The Chairman, Kenneth Whitaker, remained a good friend, but alas his earlier verve, which had taken Gerrard to first place in the discount market, was deserting him. His style was autocractic and probably more suitable to a smaller firm than Gerrard had become. And for an autocrat to preside, he must get it right, whereas wrong decisions taken by a Board are obliterated by common guilt. Sadly, Kenneth didn't get it right. The crunch came when the Board considered Gerrard's corporate finance holdings, which Kenneth had purchased with minimal consultation. Gerrard found itself owning Kenyon's, the undertakers; a genealogical research company; cottages in Aberdeen; and finally, and most damagingly, a vast slice of Roll-Royce shares. Not all of these were necessarily bad investments, but they hardly lived up to a Discount House's requirement of rapid liquidity. (Ever tried selling an undertakers at short notice?)

Kenneth's explanation of Kenyon's was airy and charming: 'Very steady stuff, the horizontal business,' he said, 'and it gives us an outlet for our old top hats.' But the atmosphere was bad and it became increasingly apparent that there must be a change. It came when I was in New York in 1975. I was awoken at 6.30 a.m. by a call from a fellow Director in London, a young, sprightly and agreeable man. 'The Board have decided that it is time for Kenneth to step down,' he began without preamble. 'Do you agree?'

I said 'Yes,' and have regretted ever since that I did not qualify my assent. Kenneth could have been made non-executive Chairman, or the stepping-down could have been a gradual process involving full consultation with his successor, the latter holding the Board's veto if necessary. Whether Kenneth would have accepted any of these is uncertain, but he was not given the opportunity and the two non-executive Directors told him bluntly: 'They want you to go.' I suppose it had to be the non-executive Directors, but neither of them seemed to me to have the necessary temperament for the task. In any case Kenneth was bitterly and permanently hurt. He was a proud and generous man, and he had shown me great kindness. Perhaps if I hadn't been woken out of a deep sleep, I would have done better? But that is not much of an excuse, and I continue to reproach myself – and to wonder which of my colleagues had instigated the execution.

Under the new regime the company's first duty was to sell off our unsuitable corporate holdings. Meeting succeeded meeting while we pondered the problem. Finally Richard Lascelles, the able and likeable Assistant to the Directors, produced the solution, in the shape of a schoolfriend of his, Peter de Savary. Now Peter was – is – a remarkable man with practical ingenuity and great energy coupled with a truly imaginative mind. He took on the task of disengagement and with unexpected rapidity produced a solution which obtained for Gerrard more cash than we had expected, satisfied the companies being sold – and earned for himself a highly satisfactory percentage fee. For me there was an additional bonus of making friends with this unusual, sometimes maddening but always entertaining figure.

Meanwhile the international side of the business prospered quite reasonably. My two 'young professionals' were rapidly gaining a first-class reputation in the Eurodollar markets, and I myself was greatly assisted by the friendly counsel of Ernst Brutsche, the (German) Treasurer of Citibank in London, and later boss Treasurer in New York. A good egg. Moreover, competition in London in the area in which I was mainly concerned, the Eurodollar Negotiable Certificate of Deposit market, was not then enormous, before the New York heavyweights moved in.

My original remit from Kenneth Whitaker had given me responsibility for an ambassadorial role to foreign banks, and I travelled extensively in Europe, the Middle East, South America and particularly the United States. We had opened a small – and not very successful – office in Wall Street, and gone into partnership with a small – and unsuccessful – company in Chicago, and I had to visit them at frequent intervals. Bankers the world over are hospitable people and Americans particularly so. I lunched and dined with most of the major operators and was admiring of their weight, their energy and their determination, this last not always admirably exercised. What shook and suprised me in the 1970s was the apparent acceptance of over-lending as a virility symbol. I was introduced to young Vice-Presidents who had lent billions to distinctly rocky countries. They were the heroes of the hour, and when I once said: 'But what makes you think you'll get your money back?' it was as though I'd spat on the floor.

To digress a little, British banks should certainly not throw stones. The folly, indeed the immorality, of forcing loans on people who should never have been borrowing reaped its own disastrous reward. Remember 'Your flexible friend' (the credit card) and 'Take the waiting out of wanting'? And 'My Bank manager lent me × thousand pounds for the holiday of a lifetime, and he'd never even met me'? Or something very similar. Those so irresponsibly responsible should have been dismissed. But of course they weren't, and the commercial banks, the clearing banks, the worst offenders, sought to recoup their losses by remorseless and ill-informed pressure on their small customers, and by putting up their charges for an increasingly sketchy and inefficient service.

Back to New York. It is such a lively place, and so much goes on, that one is bound to fall flat sooner or later. My personal debacle (professional errors apart) was ludicrous but harmless. I had appeared on an early morning television chat-show called 'New York A.M.'. In spite of my protests, the studio had insisted on making me up lavishly. At the end of the show, I realised that I was running late for a meeting with a major bank at the other end of Manhattan. Snatching a look at myself in the studio mirror, I thought that I could get away without waiting for my make-up to be removed: I merely looked unusually healthy. But this was a mirror with studio lights . . . On reaching my meeting, four clean-cut young American bankers awaited me. They greeted me with looks of incredulity and distaste. What had I done to them, I wondered? Then I caught a glimpse of my face in an ordinary mirror. Shock, horror! I looked like the Whore of Babylon. Transfixed, I blurted out: 'Oh, my God! I didn't have time to take off my make-up.' The looks of distaste turned to loathing. Then enlightenment dawned on one face.

'Gee,' he said, 'You shouldn't tell it like that: I saw you on "New York A.M."' Relief, but ruined hankies and suspicious looks in the 'Men's Rest-Room' (has anyone ever seen anyone resting there?) while I effected repairs.

Gerrard's dollar business took me to many parts of the United States. Only a few stick in my memory. Nashville, Tennessee, does, because someone spilled a huge chocolate malted milkshake over me on the aircraft, and because one could not get a moment's sleep at the hotel as everyone, staff and guests, appeared to own at least two geetars and played them night and day.

In Miami I was invited to dinner by some very odd characters, and went out of curiosity. My host was a beautifully mannered Chinaman and his boss was a young man of mixed race who was popping curious pills as though they were peanuts, the while pacing up and down cracking his fingers, narrating his alleged seduction of the stewardess on his flight down from New York, and occasionally bursting into song. His suggestion was that Gerrard should lend him a rather modest sum of dollars to refurbish three DC6 aircrafts. I was astounded: DC6s were virtually museum pieces. What did he want them for? 'They'd only have to do about three trips each,' he told me . . . His other proposal was on a totally different scale: a large loan to buy gold bullion at a knock-down price . . . I had made it very plain that Gerrard was not that kind of bank, without adding my conclusions about the quality of such deals, whether legal, practical, prudential or ethical, but I thought it wise to say that I would consider them, and give my answer in forty-eight hours, which I did, on the telephone, from the Bahamas, my next port of call.

After a time, I was additionally made responsible for the banking side of Gerrard. This was not nearly such a grand job as it sounds. It is true that we had our own cheque-books, but in my day there were only some five hundred accounts. However, it was illuminating to be sitting on the other side of the desk to a loan-seeker or an overdrawn account-holder, rather than to be, as one would normally have been, in his chair.

I don't think a longer tale of my on the whole happy passage at Gerrard would be of much value. When you've seen one interest rate you've seen the lot, and we ate, drank and breathed the creatures. Roger Gibbs succeeded Kenneth Whitaker. He had a City family background and had been a stockbroker. His regime was successful: he avoided Kenneth's mistakes and our shareholders were satisfied; but he did not have Kenneth's personal boldness and was perhaps inclined to be overborn by determined people, which could be disadvantageous. I have in mind, for instance, the time when Gerrard assumed control of the money-brokers Astley and Pearce, when the latter became over-extended. We subsequently sold the company to its own management for what I regarded as an inadequate figure. I was glad to see them go: in their troubles they reminded me of the American Navy anti-motto: 'When in danger, fear or doubt/Run in circles, scream and shout.' But their management did achieve rather too good a deal with us.

If the above appears a bit chilly, it is only an attempt to be impartial. I was and remain fond of many of my ex-colleagues, and I am grateful to them for many kindnesses. Moreover, the lifestyle was not arduous and the cuisine was excellent. But all in all I was not particularly sorry to approach Gerrard's mandatory retirement age.

My departure had the usual ballast-loss effect on salaries. Since then I have watched the increase of top City pay, not just outstripping the rate of inflation but leaving it behind like the star-ship *Enterprise* vacating a hostile galaxy, with a mixture of distaste and apprehension (and of course envy). It would be an interesting economic exercise to plot its cause and effects. Of course on the scale of the national economy it is not particularly significant, but socially I believe it to be dangerous indeed. One of the roots was the arrival of the heavyweight American houses in the City. Anyone who has read Michael Lewis's remarkable memoir of Salomon Brothers *Liar's Poker* will see the connection: dealers ('traders' in America) demanded and received vast salaries and bonuses, because they were at the cutting edge of the operations (in foreign exchange and securities of many types and quality) and because it was claimed that the work was so intense and stressful that the dealers burned out early. And then of course the managers, directors or whoever was one up on the scale felt that they must be paid more than the people working for them. Neighbouring businessmen – and I include the press and broadcasting – didn't see why they should be paid less than mere brokers or salesmen, and on and up goes the spiral. Civil Servants (and the armed forces, though not to the same extent) caught the infection, ignoring their advantages of security of tenure and the Honours escalator.

Will it stop? I doubt it. The Remuneration Committees of companies are often composed of non-executive Directors. And whom do they depend on for their positions? Why, the very people whose salaries they are deciding, and whose level of pay is reflected in their own. The people who might be expected to blow the whistle, the shareholders, are dwarfed in their power by the major shareholding institutions – pension funds, Unit Trusts, insurance companies and so forth. And their executives expect to see their salaries on an approximate par with their opposite numbers in the companies in which they invest. Amateur socio-economic babble? Perhaps; but also common logic. In all truth, and with the added twilight sadness of old age, it is a dismal fact that greed is the motivation, however genteelly wrapped. And it was not always so.

Some months before my retirement Peter de Savary approached me. He had been a steady customer of Gerrard in dollar trade bills of exchange, thus financing his oil trading on which he had founded his very considerable fortune, and we had got to know each other well. His gambit was surprisingly like that of Ari Onassis some seventeen years before. 'Anthony, you don't want to retire. Come and join me and we'll have a lot of fun and you'll make some money.'

Peter was a neighbour in the country and we had seen quite a lot of him and his beautiful and talented sculptress wife Marcia. Moreover, as I have indicated earlier, he was great fun, so I did not hesitate to accept his offer; and, for most of the time at any rate, I did not regret it. Richard Lascelles had already joined Peter, and I both liked him and trusted his judgement. He and Peter had been at school together at Charterhouse, and while Richard's career had been a perfectly normal one, Peter's had not. According to his own account he had left Charterhouse because of a rather too close an acquaintance with his housemaster's au pair girl. He added that the only 'O' level he had got was in Scripture.

His stories, mainly told against himself, were sometimes startling, but always entertaining and I think usually true. While working in a glue factory in Canada he had dropped an important nut into the vat and had been forced by his fellow-workers to jump in (the glue was only lukewarm) to retrieve it. When he emerged he held the nut aloft in triumph, only to solidify in that position like the Statue of Liberty. When in Nigeria, during the night before an important meeting he had been bitten on the lip by a mosquito in his sleep. The bite had swelled up until his lip resembled the ladies of that African tribe who take such pride in tea-saucer-sized mouths. Not only had his conversation been reduced to an incomprehensible quacking, he had concluded that he had been stricken by some horrible tropical disease.

Peter's business talents were remarkable: extraordinary energy, a very rapid appreciation of deals and events, an outstanding albeit somewhat one-

sided memory and a salesman's ability that could have sold snowballs to an
Eskimo in a blizzard. At the time he was emerging from his cocoon of private
company business into the larger but inevitably more controlled world of the
public company, and it was here that he saw one aspect of my functions,
primarily on the banking side and as a Chairman or Deputy Chairman who
could run Board meetings. The other aspect was to be as an intermediary in
exploring new activities. At least, this was the theory.

The eighties were a time of confident expansion and Peter's affairs prospered. I found myself on the Board of a Savile Row firm of tailors and cloth
merchants, a public company with a Stock Exchange quotation, but it did not
prove suitable for expansion into the property field, and we withdrew, my
only memento being two not very well cut suits at a discount of 10 per cent on
the price charged to Americans and Arabs. After that came a suitable little
'quoted' property company, Alfred Walker, which rapidly expanded,
changed its name to Landleisure PLC and acquired assets that went literally
from Land's End to Scotland – industrial property, hotels, a chain of sixteen
travel agencies, nursing homes and finally the Aspinall Curzon Casino, for
which we paid £80 million.

I don't like casini. High gambling seems to me downright immoral, and
those who indulge in it are usually fairly sleazy characters. But I am forced to
admit that John Aspinall had shown the most remarkable good taste in his
enterprises, of which the Curzon was the flagship. The furniture, the flowers
and the atmosphere gave an impression of discreet luxury. The food was as
good as the very best London restaurants and the service was quiet and well-
mannered. When Landleisure took over, I had become its Chairman, albeit
only partly executive – the least important part, actually. During our negotiations I found to my surprise that the casino's cellars held superb vintages
valued at about £1.2 million. This seemed an awful waste. I don't think most
habitual gamblers would know if they were drinking red ink, and this wine, at
the interest rates of those days, was costing well over £100,000 per annum
just sitting there. So as soon as the deal was completed we sold the major part
at auction, replacing it with perfectly sound wine at about a tenth of the price.

Through friends of Peter's I also became a director of a rather jolly little
bank in Nassau, Bahamas. By Bahamian standards it was quite old (1951) and
had a distinctly good name, being one of the very few banks not required to
give evidence in the Royal Commission on drug trafficking. I understand that
one is legally prohibited from disclosing the names of casino players and sums
won and lost, and certainly the Bahamian law of banking confidentiality is
strictly enforced, so I can't say much about those aspects, though they were
not in the least reprehensible. Actually there is very little to say: trust banking
is a quiet business, even in a tax haven.

Only one incident in Nassau made me smile. A character straight out of a
gangster movie had staggered into our bank carrying a heavy suitcase. It was
full of dollar notes and he wanted to open an account. The manager, a dour
and experienced Scot, told him he couldn't. He demanded to see a Director,
and as I was available at the time, he was referred to me for a definitive refusal.
To the consternation of my colleagues, I said: 'But of course you can open an

account,' and added after a pause: 'All we need is a reference from a first-class international bank who have known you for five years.'

Our sweating would-be customer muttered faintly: 'You've got to be joking,' and limped off with his suitcase to find a bank that would accept his money. As I remember it, there were registered offices running into three figures of banks of all shapes and sizes, so I expect that he did not have far to go.

The work in which I was engaged involved a good deal of travel, apart from Board meetings in Nassau. Shelagh sometimes came with me and we had several highly enjoyable cruises on Peter's yachts, which succeeded each other with bewildering rapidity. Peter was deeply into yachting and was a first-class power-yacht skipper, as well as no mean helmsman in sail. His great ambition was to win the America's Cup, and he came very near to doing so at Newport, Rhode Island, in 1983.

Peter's restlessness was legendary. To take just one example, when Shelagh and I were staying with him and his second wife Lana, a honey from South Carolina with an appropriate voice, he decided that the wet spell of weather was intolerable. Early in the morning we were bundled into his private jet to fly to his ranch in West Texas where the sun shone, stopping only en route to buy a birchbark canoe. We were usually accompanied on these journeys by a splendid Doberman with the equally splendid Southern name of Beauregard.

Beauregard is worth recalling. An amiable, if temperamental fellow, his favourite game at Nassau was retrieving coconuts which had fallen from the trees into the swimming pool. A senior Bahamian politician came to lunch and had a swim. Beauregard, who must have been somewhat short-sighted, mistook his head for a coconut and sought to retrieve it . . . The swimmer took it awfully well.

Flying on a hot and stormy night from Houston, where Peter had oil interests, to Nassau, we had been airborne for about an hour when there was a thump and one of the jet's engines cut. Peter was nervous of flying (and later had good reason to be after his light aircraft crashed into the sea in the Caribbean; the unfortunate pilot was killed and one of Peter's daughters very nearly drowned), and immediately told the pilot to land at the nearest airfield, wherever it might be.

'Mr de Savary,' replied the pilot patiently, 'we're over the ocean.'

'What's the weather like down there?'

A pause, then: 'Force seven and a twelve foot swell.'

Silence fell and we all drank our whisky and sodas. Beauregard, who had been asleep on the floor, woke up and initiated a gas-attack that would have shamed the First World War German chemists, shooting us embarrassed glances the while. The ventilation system carried the air forward into the cockpit, causing the two pilots to shoot us reproachful looks, which plainly said: 'Cowards!' Peter suddenly started to giggle:

'Have you seen the life raft in this aircraft?' he asked.

'No.'

'Well, it's a sort of American doughnut shape, and its sides zip up like a tent. And we're all going to be in there with Beauregard!' But all was well.

When I last enquired about Beauregard, I learnt that the poor fellow had become so difficult and so hyperactive that the vet had recommended castration. 'Beauregard is now a consultant,' Peter told me sadly.

The eighties property boom brought de Savary success on a large scale. He acquired another quoted company, Highland Participants PLC, originally engaged in oil search and development. Into the company went two ship repair dockyards on the Tyne, a bunkering port at Falmouth, Hall Russell, the Aberdeen shipbuilders who built the new *St Helena* vessel for that eponymous and romantic run, and light naval vessels in an indoor shipyard. Finally, Southampton Airport was brought to me by a friend and Highland bought it. I became Deputy Chairman of the company, which, with its emphasis on physical and practical effort rather than sheer property values, attracted me.

Landleisure, by then worth over £160 million, was sold in an agreed takeover, the terms being to the satisfaction of the shareholders. I was glad to see the last of the casino. One of the more remarkable proposals made by those running it was that I should fly to the Far East to woo back a massively rich and massively high-playing potentate. As a sweetener I was to take him a gold machine gun – and this was a serious suggestion. I would not of course have undertaken such an outlandish mission, but the picture of the greetings I would have received from the various Customs authorities haunted me.

Fond though I was of Peter, fun though the work was, better than average as the remuneration was, it became apparent to me that I was temperamentally in the wrong game. Peter began to remind me of a story of Johnnie Kimberley's,* who told me that when staying in Monte Carlo he had gambled all the evening without putting a foot wrong. On his way home to his hotel with his friends, clad in a new tropical dinner jacket, he had stepped on to the surface of the swimming pool, confident that he would not sink.

Peter did like being a one-man band and he was good at most of the instruments in it. Especially the trumpet. So far so-quite-good, but he alienated too many able people who had originally been only too anxious to work with him, and he supplanted their responsibilities with minimal tact, which was surprising as he was fundamentally a kind and sympathetic person. I don't include myself among the above: I had too thick a skin and had seen too much to have any personal ambitions, but I did realise that public companies were not his métier, and indeed he was tracking back to private ownership.

My retirement in 1989 was fortunately timed. Cracks were beginning to appear in the market and the tide had definitely turned against property. Peter remains a friend of whom I think fondly and gratefully in many ways. He was a pirate, but a rather decent pirate with a sparkling mind and a kind heart. Life with him was never dull. Perhaps it would have been better if it had been.

---

* Fourth Earl of Kimberley: a jolly fellow. His forebear cannot perhaps have been quite so bonhomous. CSC told me that when Asquith was Prime Minister he had written to the then Lord Kimberley asking if he could stay with him 'Friday to Monday', as he was electioneering in the area. He received a somewhat chilling telegram in reply. It read: 'I beg you will do no such thing. Kimberley.'

Chapter 34

THE DEATH of WSC did not end my connection with what I can best describe as Churchilliana – nor, happily, did it diminish my friendship with CSC, with Mary and with Winston and Minnie Churchill. The main new 'duty' – not in fact a duty at all but a fascinating and absorbing task – was the Memorial Trust. Moreover, world interest in Winston Churchill did not notably diminish. On two occasions I was invited to give the Commencement Address at Westminster College, Fulton, Missouri, founded in 1851 and the site of WSC's great Iron Curtain speech. It was fun; I enjoyed my newly acquired freedom from the Diplomatic Service's discipline of discretion, and I was delighted to read in the local Missouri newspaper the headline 'Raises liberal heckles'. I couldn't have annoyed the College too much, for they gave me a repeat visit and an honorary degree of Doctor of Laws together with a beautiful purple robe.

On my first visit the ceremony and speeches had been preceded by a buffet lunch, where we drank iced tea. Not a bad drink at all, but not wholly conducive to a nervous amateur's speech before a large audience. ('You can't make a speech on iced water. It is a bleak beverage.' WSC.) Thus, on my second visit, I secreted a flask of vodka in my hip pocket and, strolling away from the buffet into the garden, dumped half my pint glass of iced tea and replaced it with vodka. 'Oh, your tea does look weak,' exclaimed my kind hostess, 'let me get you another glass.'

'No, thank you,' I replied hastily, 'Weak it is not.'

So far so good, but when we went to robe, the charming and kind President addressed me: 'I know that Sir Winston would not have expected you to speak without a drink,' and he produced a huge mahogany-coloured glass of Bourbon whisky and water. They say you can't have too much of a good thing, but my subsequent performance did demand a substantial degree of self-control.

On the way to Fulton I stayed with an American friend in St Louis and at his request addressed a men's luncheon. I thought that my right-wing views would go rather well with this Middle Western Republican audience, and I was puzzled by interruptions that seemed positively hostile. My puzzlement grew when it became apparent that the hecklers looked on me as a wet, a pinko, even a crypto-Communist, and reproached me with WSC's co-operation with war-time Soviet Russia. The question of China was raised, which gave me the opportunity to point out that at Yalta the Americans had proposed discussing the future of Hong Kong with the Russians – and without the presence of the British. (Nobody believed me, but it was perfectly true and well recorded.) I could see my host chuckling quietly, and when we withdrew I asked him for an explanation. 'I suppose I should have told you,' he said without notable remorse; 'some of those men were members of the John Birch Society.'*

Interest in great historical figures is generally supposed to lapse, or at any rate go into a trough, after their deaths, possibly to re-emerge after a period of years. In WSC's case this does not seem to be the case, and books, articles and radio and television programmes have followed one another without much pause. It is perhaps because Winston Churchill is recognised not just as the last internationally great Prime Minister of Britain, but also as the last Prime Minister of Britain's great days. Moreover his personality, his literary and artistic abilities and his wit make him a favourite and almost inevitable subject for study.

Not all posthumous views on WSC were friendly, and indeed there is no reason why they should have been: he certainly did not feel that historians owed him any duty of reverence. Sometimes, however, critics had to be answered, and if no-one else undertook it, I butted in. The serious writers took it in good part if they were corrected factually, but some others were obviously out only for publicity and had no pretensions to historical value.

In November 1974 the actor Richard Burton published a lengthy article in the *New York Times* headed: 'To play Churchill is to hate him'. It was a masterpiece of self-advertisement, spiteful idiocy and lies, in which Burton claimed close acquaintance with WSC and cited various non-existent dinners and luncheon meetings. (In fact, if he had ever met WSC at all, it must have been very briefly after a theatre performance.) The *New York Times* asked me to write a reply, which I agreed to do on condition that it was printed unaltered or not at all. In the event my criticism of the paper for publishing such rubbish was excised, and my accusations of mendacity and requests for dates and places of alleged meetings gained no response from Burton.

In 1983 the posthumous memoirs of Meneghini, *My Wife Maria Callas*, were serialised in the *Sunday Times*. His account of the 1959 cruise in *Christina* was remarkably imaginative. 'Churchill had brought his little dog Toby.' Well, yes, he had brought Toby; but Toby was a budgerigar. 'Gianni Agnelli with his wife Marella were on board': they were not. And as a climax, Meneghini said that the yacht had been 'a pigpen' of wife-swapping and other unseemly activities. I was abroad and missed the serialisation until my friends started making jokes about it. I read the article and concluded that both Meneghini and the Editor of the *Sunday Times* had gone mad. Orgies, with Winston and Clementine Churchill, the very old Morans and other highly respectable near-contemporaries? I was inclined simply to laugh at it, but Mary Soames pointed out that if such a sleazy story went unquestioned and Meneghini's book was published, future generations might believe it. I

---

* An ultra-far-out, somewhat dotty, right-wing group.

am not quite sure why I did not sue for libel: I was intimidated by the massive costs and the possibility, as a barrister friend pointed out to me, that the jury would think the tale too absurd to be credited and award minimum damages. (And anyway I am an unlitigious person.) So I wrote a brief and somewhat contemptuous letter to the Editor which, after a certain amount of whingeing and attempts to edit it, was published prominently but, typically, without any apology. I had always looked on the Editor as a rather pretentious little fellow, but it would never have occurred to me that he could be sufficiently foolish as to publish such ludicrous lies. Thereafter I wrote to him suggesting that as he had been let off very lightly and as I hadn't sought any damages, he might give a donation to a struggling little charity with which I was involved. His rejection of this mild suggestion was shrill and instantaneous. I have never met Mr Rupert Murdoch, but the Editor in his autobiography gives an account of detecting Murdoch taking imaginary pot-shots at his (the Editor's) back. I felt a distinct warmth of approval for the would-be marksman.

Later that year, I was surprised to find the book printed in hardback and repeating the libel. This time I did take action and extracted a public apology from the publishers; and the book was withdrawn. Again I rather foolishly did not sue for damages; the legal costs daunted me.

Echoes of Winston Churchill from other quarters were both more truthful and more agreeable. The Other Club was an excellent source, for many of WSC's friends, ministers and military Commanders were still alive and often spoke of him. At Pratt's, too, one used to hear reminiscences that were entertaining and, I think, only mildly embroidered. In his widowerhood Harold Macmillan was a frequent diner, and invariably friendly and entertaining. He told me that when WSC was Minister of Munitions in the First World War he was asked to use his influence on a wounded young officer whom he had known socially, who had a good record in France and was at present on convalescent leave in England. He was stumping the country preaching that the war must be brought to an end at any price. The man in question was also an accredited poet and writer. (Macmillan did not give his name but he sounded like Siegfried Sassoon.) WSC asked him to call, and explained that the war had acquired a landslide momentum and could only be ended by defeat or victory. He deployed all his eloquence to persuade the young man that his efforts were in fact counter-productive to his purpose. All in vain. Finally WSC dismissed him thus: 'I will do violence to no man's conscience. But apart from any other argument that I have sought to advance, I would suggest to you that sadly, regrettably, reprehensibly, war is common to man. War and gardening. Good day to you.'

Macmillan's little touches of malice were not infrequent. Speaking of figures of the time, he said: 'Now who is that rather pushy young politician? Peter, Peter ... Peter Slater!' (Peter Walker had been the Walker of Slater, Walker, the merchant bank led by Jim Slater that came to grief, but long after Walker had left it.)

The last time I saw Macmillan was again in Pratt's. I had taken an American banker, Chairman of the Boston Federal Reserve, for a drink there after

dinner and Macmillan was at his friendliest. As we were leaving he called to
me: 'Anthony, would you mind giving me a hand up the stairs? My legs aren't
any good.' (He wasn't in the least drunk – just old and infirm.) My American
friend and I had the devil of a job getting him up the stairs, for he was a big
man. It then became apparent that he could not possibly walk to the Carlton
Club, where he was staying, although it was only a few yards down the road.
So while the Federal Reserve Chairman propped him up, I sought a taxi, who
at first unwilling to believe that we wanted to go such a short distance,
assented with alacrity when he saw the identity of his passenger and helped
us convey him to his night's lodging.

My American friend was astounded: 'Back home,' he said in wonder, 'an
ex-President would have a personal staff, transport and guards, all provided
by the State. Are you so ungrateful to all those who have served you?'

I said that on the whole yes, we were.

It was in Pratt's, too, that I last remember Bill de L'Isle. I had seen a lot of
him over the passing years and admired him much. A Victoria Cross is quite
something, but when it is allied to descent from two major poets, one a great
hero (Philip Sidney and Shelley) and a by-blow from William IV, the whole
is a cause for interest and even a certain awe. I had stayed with him at his great
family house of Penshurst. The wind howled, the fire crackled, we drank
rather a lot of port and it suddenly occurred to me that we hadn't seen anyone
since dinner.

'How many people are there in this vast house tonight?' I asked.

'Two,' said Bill. 'You and me.'

It was a strange and pleasant feeling. On this last meeting, before his fatal
stroke, he spoke of another forebear, Algernon Sidney, who had been sacrificed by Charles II to be impeached by the Parliamentary wolves, and
beheaded. The King had apparently felt a pang of regret, and sent a messenger to see Sidney in prison and tell him that as a special favour the King had
said that his family might receive his body (and presumably his head) to be
buried, rather than it being placed in a felon's grave. Sidney was not deeply
impressed by this concession. 'Tell the King', he instructed the messenger,
'that he may have my arse for a snuff-box if he list.' I thought that 'My arse
for a snuff-box' would make rather a good, if puzzling, title for a book.

Shortly before Ari Onassis' death I was able to take up his offer of assistance of 'wherever, whatever'. We were on the island of Paxos and my small
daughter and smaller step-daughter had adopted two starving kittens. When
we left we couldn't just say to them: 'Well boys, go back to starving,' and
BEA would not take them although they were quite legitimately going into
quarantine. A telephone call to the somewhat perplexed Ari produced
instant results on Olympic Airlines and we all travelled in style. And then Ari
died – as have so many of my friends.

As I have said, this book is not about my personal life. I live happily with a
remarkable and beautiful wife; I have a united and happy family and four
dogs and a cat. Most of us travel extensively when we can afford it. But it is

doleful to contemplate the world scene, and Britain's pathetic part in it, a million miles from Winston Churchill's hopes and intentions.

The British Empire's sun has sunk for ever, and Winston Churchill's bright star has long set. With intervals of intervention in the War and at the Foreign Office and Number Ten, my own life has been that of a spectator, albeit in a privileged seat.

> For want of me the world's course will not fail;
> When all its work is done the lie shall rot.
> The truth is great and shall prevail
> When none cares whether it prevail or not.

Appendix A

——— ✤ ———

Correspondence with Field Marshal Montgomery

23.3.63

My dear Anthony,
   Thank you so very much for the article in the D.T. about my speech. I had missed it. I look forward to hearing from you soon about the other matter – the role of the fighting Services particularly in the matter of sustaining British foreign policy.
                                                           Yrs ever
                                                MONTGOMERY OF ALAMEIN

31.3.63

I have begun to think out my speech at the Royal Academy Dinner about the role of the Fighting Services. Can you let me have the notes you promised? I like to get down to these things well ahead, particularly where they are to be broadcast live. Will Winston go to the Dinner?

The note I wrote in answer ran as follows, in an attempt to render something of the Field Marshal's staccato style:

The old phrase 'The White Man's Burden', now much derided, meant simply that the most advanced countries owed a duty to the others. This duty is still being carried out in the form of technical and financial aid and advice. But the other duty – that of ensuring that the social system in backward countries is advanced, that justice and freedom reign and that nationalism, the disease of childhood, does not cause them to attack their neighbours – is now neglected.
   Why is this? It is because of a change in moral climate in the West, which may be good or bad, and also because, even without such a change, we no longer are in a position to enforce our wishes, however benevolent.
   Domitian's motto was said to be 'Oderint dum metuant' ('Let them hate as long as they fear'). This is rather practical.
   Stalin is said to have remarked, 'The Pope? How many divisions has he?'
   Theodore Roosevelt said, 'Speak softly and carry a big stick. You will go far.'
   Lord Halifax (the 18th Century one) said 'Foreign affairs are a hard business and good nature is a bungler at them,' or words to that effect.
   The moral view that a pistol is intrinsically evil is not necessarily correct. It depends on who holds the pistol and what he is going to use it for.

It is no good being good and wise if no-one listens to your opinions and if you cannot enforce them. Even the most enlightened societies need a police force.

We are fortunate in this country in that the armed forces like the Civil Service, do not aspire to a political role. We are entirely safe from the military coups that are an everyday feature of life in the Middle East, in Latin America and every now and then in Western Europe. The action of the Services in support of our foreign policy reflects and will reflect simply the wishes of the Government of the day. There is no role for them independently of foreign policy, for which Ministers are responsible to the country through Parliament.

For the armed forces effectively to carry out their role they must be like policemen, visible on the beat. It is not helpful to have a large force locked up in Germany: the insurance of our foreign policy towards the Russians does not lie in that path, but in the West's possession of nuclear weapons. On the other hand a highly trained mobile force based in the United Kingdom, in Aden or in Singapore can clearly indicate that we are not 'paper tigers'.

Our armed forces are no longer on a scale to influence events directly. We have chosen to divide our national cake so that we have admirable social services and on the whole a very agreeable existence in our tightly packed country. There is not enough left over for defence, even with an £1,800,000,000 (?) expenditure, to enable us to say to another Power, 'Do as we say or you will regret it'. Quite apart from these considerations, no-one in the Nuclear Age is well advised to say anything of the kind to any country.

But for our foreign policy to be effective we must show our friendship is worth having. We must be prepared to intervene on a smaller scale in world affairs, to protect our client states, to ensure that our friends are allowed to develop their affairs in the way they wish (e.g. the Federation of Malaya and Borneo), and finally to come unhesitatingly to the rescue of our brothers and relations in whatever part of the world they may be. I have said nothing of the role of our armed forces in support of our foreign policy vis-à-vis the United States. It is of course obvious that without armed forces our great Ally will pay scant attention to what we say, knowing that we are incapable of fulfilling an independent role even in minor circumstances.

A.M.B.

Monty replied:

3.4.63

Thank you so very much for the notes. They are excellent and exactly what I needed. It is most kind of you to have taken so much trouble.

15.7.63

Before leaving Chartwell this morning, everybody seemed to be having a 'lie in' – except Clemmie. So I visited her and asked her to say good-bye to you. I am so sorry to have not bid farewell personally.

I always enjoy meeting you and find your conversation and ideas most stimulating.

My love to you both.

Later he wrote:

23.11.63

Thank you for your further thoughts on Africa. I am delighted to have anything from you on the subject and find myself in complete agreement with your thinking.

I hope you approved of what I said in the House of Lords on Tuesday 19th November. The Labour Opposition moved a censure motion on the Government defence record, so I examined A. V. Alexander's defence record, which he didn't like, I then went on to examine the general Labour defence policy today. And I finished up by saying we cannot deploy sufficient strength east of Suez (where the threat now is) and also keep 55,000 soldiers in Germany, without some form of national service.

I am studying Bezique!

8.4.64

Thank you for the notes on my speech to be made on April 20. They are – as always – excellent and I have worked them all in to the speech, which is greatly improved thereby.

6.7.64

What is the right answer to the enclosed letter? I would value your advice – as always.

Appendix B

———— ❧ ————

LETTERS RECEIVED ON WINSTON CHURCHILL'S DEATH

Letter from Mary Soames:

30th January, 1965

My dear Anthony,

This day has been the longest, saddest, but certainly the proudest day in my life, but before I go to bed I want to write to try to tell you how deeply, deeply, grateful I am to you for all you have done for my beloved Father. When you first came I think the job must have had an interest and some glamour – and there were many hands and heads to assist you and take their turns – But I am thinking chiefly of the twilight years – the slow declining, physical and mental, which was known to really, only a comparatively small circle of relations and friends until the last year or so – And even then, I used to realise that so many people hadn't the faintest idea that time had slowly and inexorably taken its toll. Your loyalty and steadfastness in these years is something all of us who loved him dearly can never truly repay. I realise there must have been times when you thought you couldn't bear – let's face it – the tedium, and the frustrations, the exhausting tensions which seem to build up in our family and the slow, and ever slower pace of each day. And yet you stuck it right out – right through to this bitterly cold afternoon at Bladon, when I know your heart grieved as much as any of ours.

You have helped and guided in a thousand ways – over important things, and over maddening trifles. God knows how Mama would have got through these years without your sensitive understanding and help. But what I feel most deeply indebted to you for is for your vigilance and determination in guarding my Father's fame and honour, when he could no longer fight his own battles.

And to the larger debt of gratitude, I must add one more item – my true thanks for your personal kindness to me – always – but particularly in these last three weeks. I am fully aware of the burdens you have carried of work and worry – and in addition you've had to cope with us as a family in all our full force and variety of temperaments! – I know you felt with us, and shared the anguishes and doubts and hopes.

Thank you dear Anthony, for your unfailing forbearance to me; I have found these last weeks so full of unexpected turns of the screw, and if I've weathered it at all, it is largely because of your patience and understanding, and sometimes very necessary, firmness.

I do thank you from my heart, but I also recognise that individually and collectively our debt to you is unrepayable.

With love to you and dear Nonie, and I hope you will be able to go on a holiday, which now you must need more than ever.

Yours ever affectionately and so very gratefully
MARY

Letter from Lord Avon (Anthony Eden):

2nd February, 1965

Dear Anthony,

I do want to send you just these few lines, which I hope you will not regard as an intrusion, to say how much, as an outside observer, I have admired all that you have done for Sir Winston in these last months and years.

These things are difficult to put into words, but your intelligent devotion and unfailing patience, not least towards his friends, are something which can never be forgotten by

Yours ever
ANTHONY AVON

Letter from Sir Edward Heath:

6th February, 1965 1

Dear Anthony,

I felt I wanted to send you a short note simply to say how much many of us here admired and respected the devoted way in which you cared for Sir Winston during the many years you were his private secretary and how grateful we are for the incomparable services you rendered him.

From time to time you have shown me many kindnesses and I would like you to know how greatly they were appreciated.

You will feel his loss almost more than any one outside his family but you have the satisfaction of knowing that the task with which you were entrusted has been thoroughly accomplished.

Yrs ever
TED HEATH

Letter from Bernard, Duke of Norfolk:

February 1st, 1965

Dear Anthony,

Thank you so much. You will never know what a help you were. From all I am told and the letters I have had it seems to have been a success. The reception through the country has thrilled me as I always hoped it would be great but never felt it could or would quite come off. I believe it did.

I am so upset about your own loss. It is quite unthinkable that such people exist. Have a good voyage and all my thanks.

Yrs ever
BERNARD

Letter from Monsieur Gérard André, Minister at the French Embassy:

24th February, 1965

My dear Anthony,

Now that the sad vigil has ended, I hope that in the inevitable and natural sorrow of the final parting, you will be comforted by the unique experience of having lived with him and served him.

You served him so well and you and Nonie were so good to him that he loved you as his own children. This must indeed be a wonderful memory.

Still, today is sad and I who was, thanks to you, privileged to see him not very long ago, share your feeling of loss and grief.

Love to Nonie and you

GÉRARD

Please do not answer this. I shall hope to see you as soon as you have a moment.

Letter from Sir William Dickson, Former Chief of the Air Staff, Marshal of the RAF:

31st January, 1965

Dear Montague-Browne,

It was all very moving and splendid in St. Paul's yesterday, and all of us who served the Great Man closely at one time or another, felt very proud. A glimpse of yourself amongst the Chief Mourners made me think how proud you yourself must have felt and moves one to write and offer you my congratulations on your long and devoted service to him and on the successful completion of no ordinary mission.

The dignity of Winston's years since retirement and the fact that his greatness grew in everyone's esteem during these last years, reaching the height of world appreciation witnessed since Jan. 24th is in no small measure due to the faithful and careful service you gave to him.

All those who know will always be grateful to you.

My kindest regards to you both and to Jane.

Yours sincerely

W.F. DICKSON

P.S. So sorry about the burglary.

P.P.S. Do not trouble to acknowledge this while you are so busy.

Letter from Sir Anthony Wagner, Royal College of Arms:

1 Feb. 1965

Dear Anthony,

I felt I must write a brief line (needing no answer) to say how absolutely disgusted I was to read of the burglary at your flat on that day of all days – one of the meanest actions ever perpetrated.

I must just add what a privilege we at the College have felt it to be concerned in this very great occasion and how much we have appreciated the way in which you yourself have helped us on all possible points.

I hope you may soon now be able to take your long planned holiday and that after that we may be able to see something of you both in a way which past circumstances have made difficult.

Yours sincerely,

ANTHONY WAGNER

Letter from Lord Hailes (Patrick Buchan Hepburn), Chief Whip under WSC:

1 February 1965

Dear Anthony,

I have written a few lines to Lady Churchill to say how touched and grateful we were to have been put in such a special place in St. Pauls, and would like to say this to you too. It made all the difference.

The service was faultless and just what Winston would have liked! And the TV programme beautifully done and most moving. If you had a part in all this, as I expect, you should be well content.

I expect your plans have been changed and so if you both have the time and inclination do come and dine again?

We were furious to see about the burglar, because that was a really mean thing. I do hope something will be recovered.

No reply please.

Yours ever,
PATRICK (HAILES)

Letter from Bernard M. Baruch:

February 16, 1965

My dear Anthony,

Memories of our beloved friend always include you for you gave him competent loyalty and affection, especially in the last darkening days. This challenged my greatest admiration and affection for you. I thank you for it.

What can I do for Lady Churchill or you, or any of the family. Tell me what your plans will be.

I was sorry I was absolutely physically unable to come to the funeral. Knowing my condition I am sure you understand.

Devotedly
BERNARD M. BARUCH

Letter from Robert Tuckman, News Editor, The Associated Press:

January 25, 1965

Dear Mr Montague Browne,

Although we spoke by telephone yesterday, I should like to put in writing, on behalf of The Associated Press, my sincere thanks and appreciation to you and your associates for the fine assistance during the past sorrowful days.

The medical bulletins were telephoned to us promptly on every occasion and our inquiries were received with unfailing courtesy and patience during what was most certainly a very trying time.

I would be very grateful if you convey to Sir Winston's secretary, Sergeant Murray and all others involved, our warmest thanks.

Sincerely,
ROBERT TUCKMAN
NEWS EDITOR

Letter from Mr Rose, WSC's former butler:

Feb. 3rd 1965

Dear Sir,

Thank you so much for kind letter but how sad for you and Mrs Browne being burgled I'm dreadfully sorry and I trust they's be caught and punished. We all thought Lady Churchill and you all wonderful and I went to Winchester Cathedral on Sunday to full up.

You looked so young Sir on the television and it gave me much pleasure to see you alltho it was all so sad to think we have all lost so great a Friend and Leader.

Thanking you for your kindness and I cannot tell you how very sorry I feel for you all and how you all will miss Sir Winston.

Yours respectfully,
FRANK ROSE

Letter from Lord Normanbrook (Secretary to the Cabinet):

24th January, 1965

Dear Anthony,

It was good of you to telephone me this morning. I appreciated it very much.

I am intensely sad and miserable. I haven't been able to do anything, or think about anything, all day. But this is selfish, I know. For him I cannot grieve, and I'm glad his ordeal is over. It's just that I find the loss so hard to bear.

I ought to have written earlier to thank you for letting me know about the funeral arrangements. I am very proud to be allowed to follow him to the end – and I have said so in a brief note which I sent to Lady Churchill today.

I should like so much to have a talk with you before you go away, and I will get in touch to fix a day and time.

I have admired so much the way in which you have helped him and the family over these years. And though it is not for me to thank you, I should like to say how very grateful his close friends are to you for all you have done.

Yours ever,
NORMAN

Letter from Sir Alan Lascelles, Private Secretary to King George VI and Queen Elizabeth II:

Dear Montague Browne,

Being probably the oldest extant private secretary, I should like to congratulate you, professionally, on the way you have handled all those things a p.s. has to handle in these last sad days.

I have helped to bury two Kings, so I know something of the strain that is put upon one.

But, personally, let me say also how grateful I am – for I greatly revered and loved him – for all you have done for him throughout the past years.

Yrs sincerely
A. LASCELLES

Index